The category of the person

The category of the person

Anthropology, philosophy, history

Edited by
Michael Carrithers
Steven Collins
Steven Lukes

The right of the University of Cambridge to print and sell all manner of books was granted by Henry VIII in 1534. The University has printed and published continuously since 1584.

Cambridge University Press

Cambridge
London New York New Rochelle
Melbourne Sydney

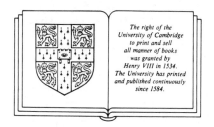

This volume is dedicated to the memory of Marcel Mauss, in whose words:

A comprehensive knowledge of the facts is only possible through the collaboration of numerous specialists. Sociology, though lacking the resources of the laboratory, does not lack empirical control, on the condition that one can truly compare all the social facts of history as understood by the specialists of each branch of history. This is impossible for a single person. Only mutual supervision and pitiless criticism, thanks to the facts being set in opposition, can yield firm results.

Published by the Press Syndicate of the University of Cambridge
The Pitt Building, Trumpington Street, Cambridge CB2 1RP
32 East 57th Street, New York, NY 10022, USA
10 Stamford Road, Oakleigh, Melbourne 3166, Australia

First published 1985

Printed in the United States of America

Library of Congress Cataloging in Publication Data

Main entry under title:

The Category of the person.

Bibliography: p.

Includes index.

1. Self – Addresses, essays, lectures.
2. Self – Cross-cultural studies – Addresses, essays, lectures. 3. Individualism – Addresses, essays, lectures.
4. Individualism – Cross-cultural studies – Addresses, essays, lectures. 5. Mauss, Marcel, 1872–1950 – Addresses, essays, lectures. I. Carrithers, Michael. II. Collins, Steven, 1951– . III. Lukes, Steven.
BF697.C288 1985 302.5′4 84–23288
ISBN 0 521 25909 6 hard covers
ISBN 0 521 27757 4 paperback

Contents

Preface

'A comprehensive knowledge of the facts is only possible through the collaboration of numerous specialists. . . . Only mutual supervision and pitiless criticism can yield firm results.' Behind these dry words lies the passionate communal spirit with which Marcel Mauss and his colleagues of the *Année sociologique* school sought to forge a new understanding of human life. Of all their creations one of the most remarkable was Mauss's last essay, published in 1938, on the notion of self or person. The basic lines of argument had already been sketched by Durkheim forty years earlier.

Mauss proposes that our seemingly natural and self-evident conceptions of our selves, our persons, are in truth artefacts of a long and varied social history stretching back, at least in principle, to the earliest human communities. Other societies have held very different notions of the self, and each society's notion is intimately connected with its form of social organization. The notion least like ours, that of the 'character' or 'role' *(personnage)*, Mauss finds in ethnographic materials from North America and Australia. In such societies each role was in daily life the locus of different rights, duties, titles and kinship names within the clan, and was on ceremonial occasions vividly exemplified by different masks or body paint. No general rules applied to 'roles' as such apart from the clan, nor were they thought to bear an inner conscience.

A revolution then occurred in ancient Rome, when the 'role' – the 'mask' or *persona* – was made the locus of general rights and duties as a legal 'person' and a citizen of the state. To this more abstract 'person' was later added the notion of an inner conscience and inner life, chiefly through Christianity. And this notion of person, now bearing both a conscience and a civic identity, became the foundation of modern political, social and legal institutions.

This sketch does little justice to Mauss's rich argument, but will arm the reader to face its complexity. Perhaps because of this complexity subsequent scholars have conducted little 'mutual supervision' of it. We have attempted in this volume to re-create, albeit under very different circumstances, Mauss's communal enterprise. Each of the authors was asked to address himself to Mauss's essay, which is translated here. Most of them, whether implicitly or explicitly, have addressed each other as well. And almost all of them attended and gave a first version of their paper at a series of seminars held in May and June 1980, in Wolfson College, Oxford, to whose Fellows we are deeply grateful for hospitality and financial assistance at that time.

Mauss's essay was given in French as the Huxley Memorial Lecture for 1938, and appeared under the title 'Une Catégorie de l'Esprit Humain: La Notion de Personne, Celle de "Moi" ' in the *Journal of the Royal Anthropological Institute* 68 (1938). (It was reprinted in Mauss's *Sociologie et anthropologie* [Paris, 1950] – with some printing errors.) A translation by Ben Brewster was published in Marcel Mauss: *Sociology and Psychology* (London, 1979). The translation by W.D. Halls was commissioned for this volume with the permission of Routledge and Kegan Paul PLC. In all important passages French terms are given in parentheses in the text. The following are usual equivalents:

moi – (the) self
soi – (one's) self
personne – person
personnalité – personality
personnage – role, character.

The quotation from Mauss that prefaces this volume is taken from the autobiographical sketch presented as part of his application for membership of the Collège de France in 1930. It appeared in *Revue Française de sociologie* 20 (1): 1979. G. Lienhardt's paper originally appeared in the *Journal of the Anthropological Society of Oxford,* 1980. L. Dumont's paper appeared in *Religion* 12: 1982, 1–27, and is reproduced here with the consent of the author, the editor of *Religion,* and the publishers, © Academic Press, Inc. (London) Ltd.

Contributors

N.J. Allen is Lecturer in the Social Anthropology of South Asia at Oxford University.

Michael Carrithers is Lecturer in Social Anthropology at Durham University.

Steven Collins is Lecturer in the Study of Religions at Bristol University.

Louis Dumont is Directeur d'Etudes at the Ecole des Hautes Etudes en Sciences Sociales, Paris.

Mark Elvin is Lecturer in Chinese History at Oxford University.

Martin Hollis is Professor of Philosophy at the University of East Anglia.

J.S. La Fontaine is Professor of Social Anthropology at the London School of Economics.

Godfrey Lienhardt is Reader in Social Anthropology at Oxford University.

Steven Lukes is Fellow and Tutor in Politics and Sociology at Balliol College, Oxford University.

A. Momigliano is Alexander White Professor in the Humanities at Chicago University, Professor Emeritus of Ancient History at London University.

Alexis Sanderson is Lecturer in Sanskrit at Oxford University.

Charles Taylor is Professor of Political Science at McGill University.

1

A category of the human mind: the notion of person; the notion of self

Marcel Mauss
(translated by W. D. Halls)

I: The subject[1]: the 'person' ***(personne)***

My audience and readers will have to show great indulgence, for my subject is really enormous, and in these fifty-five minutes I shall be able only to give you some idea of how to treat it. It deals with nothing less than how to explain to you the way in which one of the categories of the human mind – one of those ideas we believe to be innate – originated and slowly developed over many centuries and through numerous vicissitudes, so that even today it is still imprecise, delicate and fragile, one requiring further elaboration. This is the idea of 'person' *(personne)*, the idea of 'self' *(moi)*. Each one of us finds it natural, clearly determined in the depths of his consciousness, completely furnished with the fundaments of the morality which flows from it. For this simplistic view of its history and present value we must substitute a more precise view.

A note on the principle underlying these kinds of research

In so doing you will see an example – one that is perhaps not up to what you expected – of the work of the French school of sociology. We have concentrated most especially on the social history of the categories of the human mind. We attempt to explain them one by one, using very simply, and as a temporary expedient, the list of Aristotelian categories[2] as our point of departure. We describe particular forms of them in certain civilisations and, by means of this comparison, try to discover in what consists their unstable nature, and their reasons for being as they are. It was in this way that, by developing the notion of *mana*, Hubert and I believed we had found not only the archaic basis for magic, but also the very general, and probably very primitive, form of the notion of cause. It was in this way that Hubert described certain features of the notion of time. Likewise our much regretted colleague, friend and pupil, Czarnowki, began – but, alas, never finished – his theory of the 'parcelling out of extension', in other words, of one of the features and certain aspects of the notion of space. Likewise also, my uncle and teacher, Durkheim, has dealt with the notion of the *whole,* after we had examined together the notion of *genus.* I have been preparing for many years studies on the notion of substance. Of these I have published only a very recondite extract which is not worth reading in its present form. I will mention to you also the numerous times that Lucien Lévy-Bruhl has touched upon these questions in those works of his which deal with the primitive mentality, especially, as regards our subject, what he has termed 'the primitive mind' *(l 'âme primitive).* He, however, does not concentrate on the study of each special category, not even on the one we are going to study. But rather, in reviewing all of them, including the category of 'self', does he seek particularly to ascertain what element of the 'pre-logical' is contained in this study of the mentality of peoples, in relation to anthropology and ethnology rather than history.

If you will permit me, let us proceed more methodically and restrict ourselves to the study of one single category, that of the 'self' *(moi).* This will be amply sufficient. In the present short space of time, I shall conduct you, with some daring and at inordinate speed, across the world and through time, guiding you from Australia to our European societies, from extremely ancient history to that of our own times. More extensive research studies could be undertaken, each one of which could be gone into much more deeply, but I can only claim to show you how such research might be organised. What I intend to do is to provide you with a summary catalogue of the forms that the notion has assumed at various times and in various places, and to show you how it has ended up by taking on flesh and blood, substance and form, an anatomical structure, right up to modern times, when at last it has become clear and precise in our civilisations (in our European ones, almost in our lifetime), but not yet in all of them. I can only rough out the beginnings of the sketch or the clay model. I am still far from having finished the whole block or carved the finished portrait.

Thus I shall not discuss the linguistic problem which, for the sake of completeness, should indeed be tackled. In no way do I maintain that there has ever been a tribe, a language, in which the term 'I', 'me' *(je, moi)* (you will note that we still decline it with two words) has never existed, or that it has not expressed something clearly represented. This is far from the case: as well as possessing the pronoun, a very large number of languages are conspicuous for their use of many 'positional' suffixes, which deal for the most part with the relationships existing in time and space between the speaker (the subject) and the object about which he is speaking. Here the 'self' *(moi)* is everywhere present, but is not expressed by 'me' *(moi)* or 'I' *(je)*. However, in this vast domain of languages my scholarship is only mediocre. My investigation will concern solely law and morality.

Nor shall I speak to you of psychology, any more than I shall of linguistics. I shall leave aside everything which relates to the 'self' *(moi)*, the conscious personality as such. Let me merely say that it is plain, particularly to us, that there has never existed a human being who has not been aware, not only of his body, but also at the same time of his individuality, both spiritual and physical. The psychology of this awareness has made immense strides over the last century, for almost a hundred years. All neurologists, French, English and German, among them my teacher Ribot, our esteemed colleague Head, and others, have amassed a great deal of knowledge about this subject and the way this particular awareness is formed, functions, deteriorates, deviates and dissolves, and about the considerable part it plays.

My subject is entirely different, and independent of this. It is one relating to social history. Over the centuries, in numerous societies, how has it slowly evolved – not the sense of 'self' *(moi)* – but the notion or concept that men in different ages have formed of it? What I wish to show you is the succession of forms that this concept has taken on in the life of men in different societies, according to their systems of law, religion, customs, social structures and mentality.

One thing may alert you to the drift of my exposition: I shall show you how recent is the word 'self' *(moi)*, used philosophically; how recent "the category of 'self' " *(moi)*, "the cult of the 'self' " *(moi)* (its aberration); and how recent even "the respect of 'self' " *(moi)*, in particular the respect of others (its normal state).

Let us therefore draw up a classification. Making no claim to reconstitute a general history from pre-historical times to the present day, let us first study some of the forms assumed by the notion of 'self' *(moi)*. We shall then launch into historical times with the Greeks and work out from there some definite linkages. Beforehand, with no other concern save that of logic, we will make an excursion into that kind of museum of facts (I dislike the word 'survivals', when it is used for institutions still active and proliferating) which ethnography affords us.

II: The 'role' *(personnage)*, and the place of the 'person' *(personne)*

The Pueblos

Let us start with the fact that has been the point of departure for all this research. I borrow it from the Pueblo Indians, the Zuñi – or more accurately from those of the Pueblo of Zuñi, so admirably studied by Frank Hamilton Cushing (who was fully initiated into the Pueblo), and by Mathilda Cox Stevenson and her husband for a great number of years. Their work has been criticised, but I believe it to be reliable and, in any case, unique. It is true that there is nothing 'very primitive' about things. The 'Cities of Cibola' were once converted to Christianity and have preserved their baptismal registers. Yet, at the same time they have practised their ancient laws and religions – almost in the 'aboriginal state', if one may say so: this was roughly that of their predecessors, the cliff dwellers and the inhabitants of the 'mesa' as far as Mexico. In their material civilisation and social constitution they were, and have remained, very comparable to the Mexicans and to the most civilised Indians of the two Americas. 'Mexico, that Pueblo', writes admirably the great L. H. Morgan, who was so unfairly treated, and yet the founder of our disciplines.[3]

The document below is by Frank Hamilton Cushing,[4] an author much criticised, even by his colleagues at the Bureau of American Ethnology. Yet, knowing his published work and having considered very carefully what has appeared on the Zuñi and the Pueblo in general, strengthened also by what I believe I know about a large number of American societies, I persist in considering him one of the best portrayers of societies of all time.

If you will allow me, I will pass over everything concerning the orientation and distribution of the characters *(personnages)* in the ritual, although this has very great importance, to which we have already drawn attention elsewhere. But I cannot omit two points:

The existence of a limited number of forenames in each clan; and the definition of the exact rôle played by each one in the 'cast-list' of the clan, and expressed by that name.

> In each clan is to be found a set of names called the names of childhood. These names are more of titles than of cognomens. They are determined

upon by sociologic and divinistic modes, and are bestowed in childhood as the 'verity names' or titles of the children to whom given. But this body of names relating to any one totem – for instance, to one of the beast totems – will not be the name of the totem beast itself, but will be names both of the totem in its various conditions and of various parts of the totem, or of its functions, or of its attributes, actual or mythical. Now these parts of functions, or attributes of the parts or functions, are subdivided also in a six-fold manner, so that the name relating to one member of the totem – for example, like the right arm or leg of the animal thereof – would correspond to the north, and would be the first in honor in a clan (not itself of the northern group); then the name relating to another member – say to the left leg or arm and its powers, etc. – would pertain to the west and would be second in honor; and another member – say the right foot – to the south and would be third in honor; and of another member – say the left foot – to the east and would be fourth in honor; to another – say the head – to the upper regions and would be fifth in honor; and another – say the tail – to the lower region and would be sixth in honor; while the heart or the navel and center of the being would be first as well as last in honor. The studies of Major Powell among the Maskoki and other tribes have made it very clear that kinship terms, so called, among other Indian tribes (and the rule will apply no less or perhaps even more strictly to the Zuñis) are rather devices for determining relative rank or authority as signified by relative age, as elder or younger, of the person addressed or spoken of by the term of relationship. So that it is quite impossible for a Zuñi speaking to another to say simply brother; it is always necessary to say elder brother or younger brother, by which the speaker himself affirms his relative age or rank; also it is customary for one clansman to address another clansman by the same kinship name of brother-elder or brother-younger, uncle or nephew, etc.; but according as the clan of the one addressed ranks higher or lower than the clan of the one using the term of address, the word-symbol for elder or younger relationship must be used.

With such a system of arrangement as all this may be seen to be, with such a facile device for symbolizing the arrangement (not only according to number of the regions and their subdivisions in their relative succession and the succession of their elements and seasons, but also in colours attributed to them, etc.) and, finally, with such an arrangement of names correspondingly classified and of terms of relationship significant of rank rather than of consanguinal connection, mistake in the order of a ceremonial, a procession or a council is simply impossible, and the people employing such devices may be said to have written and to be writing their statutes and laws in all their daily relationships and utterances.

Thus, on the one hand, the clan is conceived of as being made up of a *certain number of persons*, in reality of 'characters' *(personnages)*. On the other hand, the role of all of them is really to act out, each insofar as it concerns him, the prefigured totality of the life of the clan.

So much for persons and the clan. The 'fraternities' are even more complicated. Among the Pueblo of Zuñi, and clearly among the others too – the Pueblos of Sia and Tusayan, in the Hopi tribe, those of Walpi and Mishongnovi – the names do not merely correspond to the organisation of the clan, its processions and ceremonies, whether private or public. They correspond principally to ranks in the fraternities, in what the original terminology of Powell and the Bureau of American Ethnology designated 'Fraternities', viz., 'Secret Societies', which we might very exactly compare to the Colleges of the Roman Religion. There were preparations in secret, and numerous solemn rituals reserved for the Society of the Men (Kaka or Koko, Koyemshi, etc.), but also public demonstrations – almost theatrical performances – and, especially at Zuñi, and above all among the Hopi, mask dances, particularly those of the Katchina. These were visits of spirits, represented by their delegates upon earth, who bore their titles. All this, which has now become a spectacle for tourists, was still very much alive less than fifty years ago, and is so even today.

Miss B. Freire Marecco (now Mrs Aitken) and Mrs E. Clew Parsons continue to add to our knowledge and to corroborate it.

Moreover, let us add that these lives of individuals, the driving force of clans and of the societies superimposed upon them, not only sustain the life of things and of the gods, but the 'propriety' of things. They not only sustain the life of men, both here and in the after-life, but also the rebirth of individuals (men), sole heirs of those that bear their forenames (the reincarnation of women is a completely different matter). Thus, in short, you will understand that with the Pueblo we already see a notion of the 'person' *(personne)* or individual, absorbed in his clan, but already detached from it in the ceremonial by the mask, his title, his rank, his role, his survival and his reappearance on earth in one of his descendants endowed with the same status, forenames, titles, rights and functions.

The American North-West

If I had time, another group of American tribes would well deserve in this study a detailed analysis of the same facts. These are the tribes of the American North-West – and it is to the great credit of your Royal Anthropological Institute and the British Association to have instigated a complete analysis of their institutions. This was begun by Dawson, the great geologist, and so magnificently continued, if not completed, by the great works of Boas and his Indian assistants, Hunt and Tate, and by those of Sapir, Swanton and Barbeau, etc.

Here also is posed, in different terms but ones identical in nature and function, the same problem – that of the name, the social position and the legal and religious 'birthright' of every free man, and even more so, of every noble and prince.

I shall take as a starting-point the best known of these important societies, the Kwakiutl, and confine myself only to some broad facts.

One word of caution: just as with the Pueblos, so also with the Indians of the North-West, we must not think of anything in any way primitive. Firstly, one section of these Indians, in fact those in the North, the Tlingit and Haida, speak languages which according to Sapir are tonal languages related to those derived from a root which it has been agreed to call proto-Sino-Tibetan-Burman. And even, if I may tell you of one of my impressions as an ethnographer – if not an 'armchair' one, at least a 'museum' one – I have a very strong recollection of a display exhibit concerning the Kwakiutl, the work of the esteemed Putnam, one of the founders of the ethnological section of the American Museum of Natural History. It was a very large ceremonial boat, with figures life-size, with all their religious and legal paraphernalia, which represented the Hamatse, the cannibal princes, arriving from the sea to carry out a ritual – doubtless a marriage. With their very rich robes, their crowns of red cedar bark, their crewmen less sumptuously attired but nonetheless magnificent, they gave me an exact impression of what, for example, Northern China in the very remote past might have looked like. I believe that this boat, with its somewhat romanticised representations, is no longer exhibited; it is no longer the fashion in our ethnographic museums. No matter, for at least this one had had its effect upon me. Even the Indian faces vividly recalled to me the faces of the 'Paleo-Asiatics' (so called because we do not know under what to classify their languages). And, from this point in civilisation and of settlement, we have still to reckon with many long and varied developments, revolutions and new formations that our esteemed colleague, Franz Boas, perhaps with undue haste, is attempting to trace back.

The fact remains that all these Indians, and in particular the Kwakiutl, installed in their settlements a whole social and religious system where, in a vast exchange of rights, goods and services, property, dances, ceremonies, privileges and ranks, persons as well as groups give satisfaction to one another. We see very clearly how, from classes and clans, 'human persons' adjust to one another and how, from these, the gestures of the actors in a drama fit together. Here *all* the actors are theoretically the sum total of *all* free men. But this time the drama is more than an aesthetic performance. It is religious, and at the same time it is cosmic, mythological, social and personal.

Firstly, as with the Zuñi, every individual in each clan has a name, even two names, for each season, one profane (summer) (WiXsa), and one sacred (winter) (LaXsa). These names are distributed between the various families, the 'Secret Societies' and the clans cooperating in the rituals, occasions when chiefs and families confront each other in innumerable and interminable *potlatch*,[5] about which I have attempted elsewhere to give some idea. Each clan has two complete sets of its proper names, or rather its forenames, the one commonly known, the other secret, but which itself is not simple. This is because the forename, actually of the noble, changes with his age and the functions he fulfils as a consequence of that age.[6] As is said in an oration, made, it is true, about the clan of the Eagles, i.e. about a kind of privileged group among privileged clans:

> For that they do not change their names starts from (the time) when long ago // Ōᵋ maxt!ālaLēᵋ, the ancestor of the numaym G īg îlgam of the / Q!ōmoyâᵋyē, made the seats of the Eagles; and those went down to the / numayms. And the name-keeper Wīltsēᵋstala says, / 'Now our chiefs have been given everything, and I will go right down (according to the order of rank).' / Thus he says, when he gives out the property; for I will just name the names // of one of the head chiefs of the numayms of the / Kwakiutl tribes. They never change their names from the beginning, / when the first human beings existed in the world; for names can not go out / of the family of the head chiefs of the numayms, only to the eldest one / of the children of the head chief. //[7]

What is at stake in all this is thus more than the prestige and the authority of the chief and the clan. It is the very existence of both of these and of the ancestors reincarnated in their rightful successors, who live again in the bodies of those who bear their names, whose perpetuation is assured by the ritual in each of its phases. The perpetuation of things and spirits is only guaranteed by the perpetuating of the names of individuals, of persons. These last only act in their titular capacity and, conversely, are responsible for their whole clan, their families and their tribes. For instance, from conquest in war are acquired: a rank, a power, a religious and aesthetic function, dancing and demoniacal possession, *paraphernalia*, and copper objects in the form of buckler shields – real *crown* shapes in copper, important currency for present and future *potlatch:* it suffices to kill the one possessing them, or to seize from him one of the trappings of ritual, robes or masks, so as to inherit his names, his goods, his obligations, his ancestors, his 'person' *(personne)*, in the fullest sense of the word.[8] In this way ranks, goods, personal rights, and things, as well as their particular spirit, are acquired.

This huge masquerade in its entirety, this whole drama, this complicated ballet of ecstatic states, concerns as much the past as the future, becomes a test for its performer, and proof of the presence within him of the *naualaku*, an element of an impersonal force, or of the ancestor, or of the personal god, in any case of the superhuman power, spiritual and ultimate. The *potlatch* of victory, of the copper won by conquest, correspond to the impeccable dance, to a successful state of possession.

There is no time left to develop all these subjects. Almost from an anecdotal viewpoint, I would like to draw your attention to an institution, an object commonly found from the Nootka right up to the Tlingit of North Alaska. This is the use of those remarkable shutter masks, which are double and even triple, which open up to reveal the two or three creatures (totems placed one upon the other) personified by the wearer of the mask.[9] You can see some very fine examples of them in the British Museum. And all those celebrated totem poles, those soapstone pipes, etc., all those objects which have become rubbishy goods designed for the tourists brought there by train or on cruises – all these may be analysed in the same way. A pipe I believe to be Haida in origin, one to which I have hardly given any attention, in point of fact represents a young initiate in his pointed headdress, presented by his spirit father, likewise behatted, bearing the grampus. Beneath the one initiated, to whom they are subordinate in descending order: a frog – doubtless his mother – and a crow, doubtless his maternal grandfather.

We shall not deal with the very important case of change of name during a lifetime – particularly that of a noble. It would entail expounding a whole succession of curious facts regarding substitution: the son, a minor, is temporarily represented by his father, who assumes provisionally the spirit of the deceased grandfather. Here also we would need to set out a complete proof of the presence among the Kwakiutl of dual uterine and male descent, and of the system of alternate and displaced generations.

Moreover, it is very remarkable that among the Kwakiutl (and their nearest kin, the Heiltsuk, the Bellacoola, etc.) every stage of life is named, personified by a fresh name, a fresh title, whether as a child, an adolescent or an adult, both male and female. Thus one may possess a name as a warrior (naturally this does not apply to women), as a prince or princess, as a chief or a female chieftain. There is a name for the feast that men and women give, and for the particular ceremonial that belongs to them, for their age of retirement, their name in the society of seals (those retired: no states of ecstacy or possession, no responsibilities, no gains, save those arising from past memories). Finally is named *their* 'secret society', in which they are protagonists (a bear – frequent among women, who are represented in it by their menfolk or their sons – wolves, Hamatse [cannibals], etc.). Names are also given to: the chief's house, with its roofs, posts, doors, ornamentation, beams, openings, double-headed and double-faced snake, the ceremonial boat, the dogs. To the lists set out in the *Ethnology of the Kwakiutl*[10] it must be added that the dishes, the forks, the copper objects, everything is emblazoned, endowed with life, forming part of the *persona* of the owner and of the *familia,* of the *res* of his clan.

We have singled out the Kwakiutl, and in general the peoples of the North-West, because they really do represent the extremes, an excessiveness which allows us better to perceive the facts than in those places where, although no less essential, they still remain small-scale and involuted. Yet we must understand that a large part of the Americans of the prairies, in particular the Sioux, possess institutions of this kind. Thus the Winnebago, who have been studied by our colleague Radin, have in point of fact these successions of forenames, which are determined by clans and families, who distribute them according to a certain order, but always following precisely a kind of logical distribution of attributes or powers and natures,[11] founded upon the myth of the origin of the clan, and legitimating the right of some person or another to assume the role.

Below is an example of this origin of the names of individuals which Radin gives in detail in his model autobiography of *Crashing Thunder:*

> Now in our clan whenever a child was to be named it was my father who did it. That right he now transmitted to my brother.
>
> Earthmaker, in the beginning, sent four men from above and when they came to this earth everything that happened to them was utilized in making proper names. This is what our father told us. As they had come from above so from that fact has originated a name Comes-from-above; and since they came like spirits we have a name Spirit-man. When they came, there was a drizzling rain and hence the names Walking-in-mist, Comes-in-mist, Drizzling-rain. It is said that when they came to Within-lake they alighted upon a small shrub and hence the name Bends-the-shrub; and since they alighted on an oak tree, the name Oak-tree. Since our ancestors came with the thunderbirds we have a name Thunderbird and since these are the animals who cause thunder, we have the name He-who-thunders. Similarly we have Walks-with-a-mighty-tread, Shakes-the-earth-down-with-his-face, Comes-with-wind-and-hail, Flashes-in-every-direction, Only-a-flash-

> of-lightning, Streak-of-lightning, Walks-in-the-clouds, He-who-has-long-wings, Strikes-the-tree.
>
> Now the thunderbirds come with terrible thunder-crashes. Everything on earth, animals, plants everything, is deluged with rain. Terrible thunder-crashes resound everywhere. From all this a name is derived and that is my name – Crashing-Thunder.[12]

Each one of the names of the thunder birds which divide up the different elements of the thunder totem is that of ancestors who are perpetually reincarnated. (We even have a story of two reincarnations.)[13] The men who reincarnate them are intermediaries between the totemic animal and the protecting spirit, and the things emblazoned and the rites of the clan or of the great 'medicines'. All these names and bequeathals of 'roles' *(personnalités)* are determined by revelations whose limits, indicated by his grandmother or the elders, are known to the beneficiary beforehand. We discover, if not the same facts, at least the same kind of facts, almost everywhere in America. We could continue this exposition for the world of the Iroquois and the Algonquin, etc.

Australia

It is preferable to revert for a moment to more summary and more primitive facts. Two or three items concern Australia.

Here also the clan is in no way conceived to be entirely reduced to an impersonal, collective being, the totem, represented by the animal species and not by individuals – on the one hand men, on the other, animals.[14] Under its human aspect it is the fruit of the reincarnation of spirits that have migrated and are perpetually being reborn in the clan. (This is true for the Arunta, the Loritja and the Kakadu, etc.) Even among the Arunta and the Loritja, these spirits are reincarnated with very great precision at the third generation (grandfather–grandson) and at the fifth, where grandfather and great-great-grandson are homonyms. Here again it is the fruit of uterine descent crossed with male descent. We can, for example, study in the distribution of names by individuals, clans and exact matrimonial *category* (eight Arunta categories) the relationship of these names to the eternal ancestors, to the *ratapa,* in the form they take at the moment of conception, in the foetus and in the children that they bring to the light of day, and between the names of these *ratapa* and those of adults (which are, in particular, those of the functions fulfilled at clan and tribal ceremonies).[15] The art underlying all these kinds of distribution is not only to arrive at religion, but also to define the position of the individual in the rights he enjoys and his place in the tribe, as in its rites.

Moreover, if, for reasons that will immediately become apparent, I have spoken especially about societies with permanent masks (Zuñi, Kwakiutl), we must not forget that in Australia, as elsewhere, temporary masquerades are simply ceremonies with masks that are not permanent. In these men fashion for themselves a superimposed 'personality' *(personnalité)*, a true one in the case of ritual, a feigned one in the case of play-acting. Yet, as between the painting of the head and frequently of the body, and the wearing of a robe and a mask, there is only a difference in degree, and none in function. In both cases all has ended in the enraptured representation of the ancestor.

What is more, the presence or absence of the mask are more distinguishing marks of a social, historical and cultural arbitrariness, so to speak, than basic traits. Thus the Kiwai, the Papuans of the Isle of Kiwai, possess admirable masks, even rivalling those of the Tlingit of North America, whilst their not very distant neighbours, the Marind-Anim, have scarcely more than one *single* mask, which is entirely simple, but enjoy admirable celebrations of fraternities and clans, of people decorated from top to toe, unrecognizable because of their adornment.

Let us conclude this first part of our demonstration. Plainly what emerges from it is that a whole immense group of societies have arrived at the notion of 'role' *(personnage)*, of the role played by the individual in sacred dramas, just as he plays a role in family life. The function had already created the formula in very primitive societies and subsists in societies at the present day. Institutions like that of the 'retired', seals of the Kwakiutl, usages like that of the Arunta, who relegate to the people of no consequence he who can no longer dance, 'he who has lost his Kabara', are entirely typical.

Another aspect which I am still somewhat ignoring is that of the notion of the reincarnation of a number of spirits that bear names in a determinate number, into the bodies of a determinate number of individuals. Nevertheless, B. and C. G. Seligman have rightly published the papers of Deacon, who had observed the phenomenon in Melanesia. Rattray had seen it among the Ashanti Ntoro.[16] I should like to state to you that M. Maupoil has found in this one of the most important elements in the cult of the Fa (Dahomey and Nigeria). All this, however, I am omitting.

Let us move on from the notion of 'role' *(personnage)* to the notion of 'person' *(personne)* and of 'self' *(moi)*.

III: The Latin 'persona'

You all know how normal and classical is the notion of the Latin *persona:* a mask, a tragic mask, a ritual mask, and the ancestral mask. It dates back to the beginnings of Latin civilisation.

I have to show you how indeed the notion has become one shared also by us. The space, the time and the differences that separate that origin from this terminal point are considerable. Evolutions and revolutions pile up upon one another, this time in history, according to precise dates, for causes, plain to see, which we are about to describe. In one place this category of the mind has wavered, in another it has set down deep roots.

Even among the very great and ancient societies which first became conscious of it, two of them, so to speak, invented it, only to allow it to fade away almost irrevocably. All this occurred in the last centuries B.C. The examples are edifying: they concern Brahmanic and Buddhist India, and ancient China.

India

India appears to me indeed to have been the most ancient of civilisations aware of the notion of the individual, of his consciousness – may I say, of the 'self' *(moi)*. *Ahaṃkāra,* the "creation of the 'I' " *(je),* is the name of the individual consciousness; *aham* equals 'I' *(je):* It is the same Indo-European word as 'ego'. The word *ahaṃkāra* is clearly a technical word, invented by some school of wise seers, risen above all psychological illusions. The *sāṃkhya,* the school which in point of fact must have preceded Buddhism, maintains the composite character of things and minds (*sāṃkhya* actually means 'composition'), esteeming that the 'self' *(moi)* is the illusory thing. For its part, Buddhism, in a first phase of its history, laid down that it was a mere composite, capable of division and of being resolvable into the *skandha,* and sought after its annihilation in the monk.

The great Brahmanic schools of the Upanishads – assuredly predating the *sāṃkhya* itself, as well as the two orthodox forms of the Vedānta which follow them – all start from the maxim of the 'seers' *(voyants),* right up to the dialogue of Vishnu in the Bhagavad Gītā demonstrating the truth to Arjuna: *tat tvam asi,* which corresponds almost word for word to the English, 'that thou art' (the universe). Even the later Vedic ritual and the commentaries upon it were already imbued with these metaphysics.

China

About China I know only what Marcel Granet, my colleague and friend, has been kind enough to inform me. Even today nowhere is more account taken of the individual, and particularly of his social status, nowhere is he more rigorously categorized. What Granet's admirable studies reveal to us about ancient China is the strength and grandeur of institutions comparable to those of the American North-West. Birth-order, rank and the interplay of the social classes settle the names and life style of the individual, his 'face', as is still said, in terms that we are also beginning to employ. His individuality is his *ming,* his name. China has preserved these archaic notions, yet at the same time has removed from individuality every trace of its being eternal and indissoluble. The name, the *ming,* represents a collective noun, something springing from elsewhere: one's corresponding ancestor bore it, just as it will fall to the descendant of its present bearer. Whenever they have philosophized about it, whenever in certain metaphysical schools they have attempted to explain what it is, they have said of the individual that he is a composite, made up of *shen* and *kwei* – two other collective nouns – in this life. Taoism and Buddhism also went down this road, and the notion of the 'person' *(personne)* ceased to evolve.

Other nations have known or adopted ideas of the same kind. Those who have made of the human person a complete entity, independent of all others save God, are rare.

The most important were the Romans. In our view it was there, in Rome, that this latter idea was worked out.

IV: The 'persona'

In contrast to the Hindus and the Chinese, the Romans, or perhaps rather the Latins, seem to be the people who in part established the notion of 'person' *(personne),* the designation for which has remained precisely the Latin word. From the very outset we are transported into the same systems of facts as those mentioned before, but already in a new form: the 'person' *(personne)* is more than an organisational fact, more than a name or a right to assume a role and a ritual mask. It is a basic fact of law. In law, according to the legal experts, there are only *personae, res* and *actiones:* this principle still regulates the divisions between our codes of law. Yet this outcome is the result of particular evolution in Roman law.

Somewhat rashly, this is the way I can envisage this state of affairs to have arisen.[17] It does seem that the original meaning of the word was exclusively that of 'mask'. Naturally the explanation of Latin etymologists, that *persona,* coming from *per/sonare,* is the mask through which *(per)* resounds the voice (of the actor) is a derivation invented afterwards – although we do distinguish between *persona* and *persona muta,* the silent role in drama and mime. In reality the word does not even seem to be from a sound Latin root. It is believed to be of Etruscan origin, like other nouns ending in '-na' (Porsenna, Caecina, etc.). Meillet and Ernout's *Dictionnaire Etymologique* compares it to a word, *farsu,* handed down in garbled form, and M. Benveniste informs me that it may come from a Greek borrowing made by the Etruscans, πρόσωπον ('perso'). Yet it is the case that materially even the institution of masks, and in particular of masks of ancestors, appears mainly to have had its home in Etruria. The Etruscans had a 'mask' civilization. There is no comparison between the masses of wooden masks and of those in terra cotta – the wax ones have vanished – the masses of effigies of sleeping or seated ancestors found in the excavations made of the vast Tyrrhenian kingdom, and those found at Rome, in the Latium, or in Greater Greece (Graecia Magna) – moreover, in my view, these are very frequently of Etruscan manufacture.

Yet if it is not the Latins who invented the word and the institutions, at least it was they who gave it the original meaning which has become our own. This was the process that occurred.

Firstly, among them are to be found definite traces of institutions of the same kind as ceremonies of clans, masks and paints with which the actors bedeck themselves according to the names they bear. At least one of the great rituals of earliest Rome corresponds exactly to the common type whose salient forms we have depicted. This is that of the *Hirpi Sorani,* the wolves of the Soracte (*Hirpi* is the name of the wolf in Samnite). Festus (93, 25) states: *Irpini appellati nomine lupi, quem irpum dicunt Samnites; eum enim ducem secuti agros occupavere.* ('They are called Irpini, the name of the wolf, which the Samnites call *irpus;* following a wolf they arrived at their later domain'.)[18]

Members of the families who bore that title walked on burning coals at the sanctuary of the goddess Feronia, and enjoyed privileges, including exemption from taxation. Sir James Frazer already speculated that they were the remnants of an ancient clan, which had become a fraternity, bearing names, and wearing skins and masks. Yet there is something else: it seems that we are truly in the presence of the very myth of Rome. 'Acca Larentia', the old woman, the mother of the Lares, who was honoured at the Larentalia (December) is none other than the *indigitamentum,* the secret name of the Roman She-Wolf, the mother of Romulus and Remus (Ovid, *Fastes,* I, 55 *ff*).[19] A clan, dances, masks, a name, names, a ritual. I accept that the facts are divided somewhat into two elements: a fraternity which survives, and a myth which recounts what preceded the foundation of Rome itself. But the two parts form a complete whole. The study of other Roman *collegia* would permit other hypotheses. All in all, Samnites, Etruscans and Latins still lived in an environment we have just left, from *personae,* masks and names, and individual rights to rituals and privileges.

From this to the notion of 'person' *(personne)* but a single step needs to be taken. It was perhaps not taken immediately. I imagine that legends like that of the consul Brutus and his sons and the end of the right of the *pater* to kill his sons, his *sui,* signify the acquisition of the *persona* by the sons, even while their father was still alive. I believe that the revolt of the Plebs, the right to full citizenship that, following upon the sons of senatorial families, was gained by all the plebeian members of the *gentes,* was decisive. All freemen of Rome were Roman citizens, all had a civil *persona;* some became religious *personae;* some masks, names and rituals remained attached to some privileged families of the religious *collegia.*

Yet another custom arrived at the same final state: that of forenames, surnames and pseudonyms (nicknames). The Roman citizen had a right to the *nomen,* the *praenomen* and the *cognomen* that his *gens* assigned to him. A forename, for example, might signify the birth-order of the ancestor who bore it: Primus, Secundus. The sacred name – *nomen, numen* – of the *gens;* the *cognomen,* the pseudonym (nickname) – not surname – such as Naso, Cicero, etc.[20] A senatus-consultus decision determined (clearly there must have been some abuses) that one had no right to borrow and adorn oneself with any other forename of any other *gens* than one's own. The *cognomen* followed a different historical course: it ended by confusing *cognomen,* the pseudonym that one might bear, with *imago,* the wax mask moulded upon the face, the πρόσωπον of the dead ancestor kept in the wings of the *aula* of the family house. For a long time the use of these masks and statues must have been reserved for patrician families, and in fact, even more so than in law, it does not appear to have spread very widely among the plebeians. It is rather usurpers and foreigners who adopt *cognomina* which did not belong to them. The very words *cognomen* and *imago* are, in a manner of speaking, indissolubly linked in formulas that were almost in current use. I give below one of the facts – in my view typical – which was my starting point for all this research, one which I found without even looking for it. It concerns a doubtful individual, Staienus, against whom Cicero is pleading on behalf of Cluentius. This is the scene. *Tum appelat hilari vultu hominem Bulbus, ut placidissime potest. "Quid tu, inquit, Paete?" Hoc enim sibi Staienus cognomen ex imaginibus Aeliorum delegerat ne sese Ligurem fecisset, nationis magis quam generis uti cognomine videretur.*[21] Paetus is a *cognomen* of the Aelii, to which Staienus, a Ligurian, had no right, and which he usurped in order to conceal his nationality and to make believe that he was of an ancestry other than his own. Usurpation of 'person' *(personne)*, fictitiousness of 'person' *(personne)*, title and affiliation.

One of the finest documents, and among the most authentic, signed in the bronze by Claudius the emperor (just as the Tables of Ancyre of Augustus have come down to us), the Table of Lyons (48 A.D.) containing the imperial oration on the senatorial decision *de Jure honorum Gallis dando,* concedes to the young Gaulish senators freshly admitted to the Curia the right to the *imagines* and *cognomina* of their ancestors. Now they will have nothing more to regret. Such as Persicus, 'my dear friend' (who had been obliged to choose this foreign pseudonym [nickname]. . . . lacking this senatorial decision) and who can now *inter imagines majorum suorum Allobrogici nomen legere* ('choose his name of Allobrogicus among the "images" of his ancestors').

To the very end the Roman Senate thought of itself as being made up of a determinate number of *patres* representing the 'persons' *(personnes)*, the 'images' of their ancestors.

It is to the *persona* that is attributed the property of the *simulacra* and the *imagines.*[22]

Along with them the word *persona,* an artificial 'character' *(personnage)*, the mask and role of comedy and tragedy, of trickery and hypocrisy – a stranger to the 'self' *(moi)* – continued on its way. Yet the personal nature of the law had been established,[23] and *persona* had also become synonymous with the true nature of the individual.[24]

Moreover, the right to the *persona* had been established. Only the slave is excluded from it. *Servus non habet personam.* He has no 'personality' *(personnalité)*. He does not own his body, nor has he ancestors, name, *cognomen,* or personal belongings. Old Germanic law still distinguished him from the freeman, the *Leibeigen,* the owner of his body. But at the time when the laws of the Saxons and Swabians were drawn up, if the serfs did not possess their body, they already had a soul, which Christianity had given them.

But before turning to Christianity, we must trace back another source of enrichment, in which not only the Latins participated, but also their Greek collaborators, their teachers and interpreters. With Greek philosophers, and Roman nobles and legal experts it is altogether a different edifice that is erected.

V: The 'person' *(personne)*: a moral fact

Let me make myself plain: I think that this effort, this step forward, came about above all with the help of the Stoics, whose voluntarist and personal ethics were able to enrich the Roman notion of the 'person' *(personne)*, and was even enriched itself whilst enriching the law.[25] I believe, but unfortunately can only begin to prove it, that the influence of the Schools of Athens and Rhodes on the development of Latin moral thinking cannot be exaggerated, and, conversely, the influence of Roman actions and of the educational needs of young Romans on the Greek thinkers. Polybius and Cicero already attest to this, as do later Seneca, Marcus Aurelius and others.

The word *πρόσωπον* did indeed have the same meaning as *persona*, a mask. But it can then also signify the 'personage' *(personnage)* that each individual is and desires to be, his character (the two words are often linked), the true face. From the second century B.C. onwards it very quickly assumes the meaning of *persona*. Translating exactly and legally *persona*, it still retains the meaning of a superimposed image; for example, in the case of the figure at the prow of a boat (among the Celts, etc.). But it also signifies the human, even divine, 'personality' *(personnalité)*. It all depends upon the context. The word *πρόσωπον* is extended to the individual, with his nature laid bare and every mask torn away, and, nevertheless, there is retained the sense of the artificial: the sense of what is the innermost nature of this 'person' *(personne)*, and the sense of what is the 'role-player' *(personnage)*.

Everything about the classical Latin and Greek Moralists (200 B.C. to 400 A.D.) has a different ring to it. *πρόσωπον* is no longer only a *persona*, and – a matter of capital importance – to its juridical meaning is moreover added a moral one, a sense of being conscious, independent, autonomous, free and responsible. Moral conscience introduces consciousness into the juridical conception of law. To functions, honours, obligations and rights is added the conscious moral 'person' *(personne)*. In this respect I am perhaps more venturesome, and yet more clear-cut than M. Brunschvicg, who, in his great work, *Le Progrès de la Conscience*, has often touched upon these matters.[26] For me the words designating first consciousness and then psychological consciousness, the *συνείδησις-τὸ συνειδός* are really Stoic, seem technical and clearly translate *conscius, conscientia* in Roman law. We may even perceive, between the early phase of Stoicism and that of the Greco-Latin era, the progress and changes definitevely accomplished by the age of Epictetus and Marcus Aurelius. In one of the original meanings of accomplice, 'he who has seen with one', σύνοιδε, as a witness, we have passed to the meaning of the 'consciousness of good and evil'. In current use in Latin, the word finally takes on this meaning with the Greeks, with Diodorus of Sicily, Lucian and Dionysus of Halycarnassus, and self-consciousness (*conscience de soi)* has become the attribute of the moral person. Epictetus still keeps the meaning of the two images which this civilisation had worked on, when he writes what Marcus Aurelius quotes, 'carve out your mask', put on your 'role' *(personnage)*, your 'type', your 'character', when he suggested to him what has become with us the examination of conscience. Renan saw the importance of this moment in the life of the Mind.[27]

But the notion of 'person' *(personne)* still lacked any sure metaphysical foundation. This foundation it owes to Christianity.

VI: The Christian 'person' *(personne)*

It is Christians who have made a metaphysical entity of the 'moral person' *(personne morale)*, after they became aware of its religious power. Our own notion of the human person is still basically the Christian one. Here I need only follow the excellent book of Schlossman.[28] He clearly saw – after others, but better than they did – the transition from the notion of *persona*, of 'a man clad in a condition', to the notion of man, quite simply, that of the human 'person' *(personne)*.

Moreover, the notion of a 'moral person' had become so clear that, from the very beginning of our era, and even earlier at Rome and throughout the Empire, it was applied to all non-real 'personalities' *(personnalités)* – what we still call by the term 'moral persons' ('legal entities'): corporations, religious foundations, etc., which have become 'persons' *(personnes)*. The word πρόσωπον designated them right up to the New Laws and most recent Constitutions. A *universitas* is a 'collective person' *(une personne de personnes)*, but like a city, like Rome, it is a 'thing', an entity. Indeed as Cicero (*De Officiis*, I, 34) says: *Magistratus gerit personam civitatis*. And von Carolsfeld compares and comments very aptly upon the Epistle to the Galatians, Ch. 3, v. 28: 'You are, with respect to the one, neither Jew nor Greek, slave nor freeman, male nor female, for you are all one person, εἶς, in Christ Jesus.'

The question was raised regarding the unity of the 'person' *(personne)*, and the unity of the Church, in relationship to the unity of God. (εἶς). It was resolved after many discussions. It is the entire history of the Church that would have here to be retraced (cf. Suidas, s.v., and the passages of the celebrated Discourse upon the Epiphany by St Gregory of Nanzianzus, 39, 630,A).[29,30] It is the quarrel concerning the Trinity, the Monophysite dispute, which continued for a long while to exercise men's minds and which the Church resolved by taking refuge in the divine mystery, although however with decisive firmness and clarity: *Unitas in tres personas, una persona in duas naturas,* the Council of Nicea pronounced definitively. Unity of the three persons – of the Trinity – unity of the two natures of Christ. It is from the notion of the 'one' that the notion of the 'person' *(personne)* was created – I believe that it will long remain so – for the divine persons, but at the same time for the human person, substance and mode, body and soul, consciousness and act.[31]

I shall not comment further, or prolong this theological study. Cassiodorus ended by saying very precisely: *persona – substantia rationalis individua* (Psalmum VII). The person is a rational substance, indivisible and individual.[32]

It remained to make of this rational, individual substance what it is today, a consciousness and a category.

This was the work of a long study by philosophers, which I have only a few minutes left to describe.[33]

VII: The 'person' *(personne)*: a psychological being

Here I hope I may be forgiven if, summarising a certain amount of personal research and countless views the history of which might be traced back, I put forward more ideas than proofs.

However, the notion of the 'person' *(personne)* was still to undergo a further transformation to become what it has become over less than one and a half centuries, the "category of 'self' " *(moi)*. Far from existing as the primordial innate idea, clearly engraved since Adam in the innermost depths of our being, it continues here slowly, and almost right up to our own time, to be built upon, to be made clearer and more specific, becoming identified with self-knowledge and the psychological consciousness.

All the long labours of the Church, of churches and theologians, of the Scholastic philosophers and the Renaissance philosophers – disturbed by the Reformation – even brought about some delay, setting up some obstacles to the creation of the idea that this time we believe to be clear. Up to the seventeenth and even up to the end of the eighteenth century, the mentality of our ancestors is obsessed with the question of knowing whether the individual soul is a substance, or supported by a substance: whether it is the nature of man, or whether it is only one of the two natures of man; whether it is one and indivisible, or divisible and separable; whether it is free, the absolute source of all action, or whether it is determined, fettered by other destinies, by predestination. Anxiously they wonder whence it came, who created it and who directs it. And in the arguments between sects, between coteries in both the great institutions of the Church and in the philosophical schools, we do hardly any better than the results achieved in the fourth century A.D. Fortunately the Council of Trent put a stop to futile polemics regarding the personal creation of each individual soul.

Moreover, when we speak of the precise functions of the soul it is to thought, thought that is discursive, clear and deductive, that the Renaissance and Descartes address themselves in order to understand their nature. It is thought that contains the revolutionary *Cogito ergo sum;* this it is that constitutes Spinoza's opposition of the 'extension' to 'thought'.

Even Spinoza[34] continued to hold precisely the idea of Antiquity regarding the immortality of the soul. We know that he does not believe in the survival after death of any part of the soul other than that which is imbued with 'the intellectual love of God'. Basically he was reiterating Maïmonides, who was repeating Aristotle (*De Anima,* 408,6; cf. 430 a; *Generation of Animals,* trans. A.L. Peck [1943], Heinemann [London] and Harvard University Press, II, 3, p. 736 b). Only the noetic soul can be eternal, since the other two souls, the vegetative and the sensory, are necessarily linked to the body, and the energy of the body does not penetrate into the *νοῦς*. At the same time, by a natural opposition that Brunschvicg[35] has effectively highlighted, it is Spinoza who, better than Descartes, better than Leibnitz himself, because he posed above all else the ethical problem, has the soundest view of the relationships of the individual consciousness with things and with God.

It is elsewhere, and not among the Cartesians, but in other circles that the problem of the 'person' *(personne)* who is only consciousness has found its solution. We cannot exaggerate the importance of sectarian movements throughout the seventeenth and eighteenth centuries for the formation of political and philosophical thought. There it was that were posed the questions regarding individual liberty, regarding the individual conscience and the right to communicate directly with God, to be one's own priest, to have an inner God. The ideas of the Moravian Brothers, the Puritans, the Wesleyans and the Pietists are those which form the basis on which is established the notion: the 'person' *(personne)* equals the 'self' *(moi);* the 'self' *(moi)* equals consciousness, and is its primordial category.

All this does not go back very far. It was necessary to have Hume revolutionizing everything (following Berkeley, who had begun to do so) before one could say that in the soul there were only 'states of consciousness', 'perceptions'. Yet he ended up by hesitating when faced with the notion of 'self' *(moi)*[36] as the basic category of consciousness. The Scots adapted his ideas better.

Only with Kant does it take on precise form. Kant was a Pietist, a follower of Swedenborg, the pupil of Tetens, a feeble philosopher but a well-informed psychologist and theologian. He found the indivisible 'self' *(moi)* all around him. Kant posed the question, but did not resolve it, whether the 'self' *(moi), das Ich,* is a category.

The one who finally gave the answer that every act of consciousness was an act of the 'self' *(moi),* the one who founded all science and all action on the 'self' *(moi),* was Fichte. Kant had already made of the individual consciousness, the sacred character of the human person, the condition for Practical Reason. It was Fichte[37] who made of it as well the category of the 'self' *(moi),* the condition of consciousness and of science, of Pure Reason.

From that time onwards the revolution in mentalities was accomplished. Each of us has our 'self' *(moi),* an echo of the Declaration of the Rights of Man, which had predated both Kant and Fichte.

VIII: Conclusion

From a simple masquerade to the mask, from a 'role' *(personnage)* to a 'person' *(personne),* to a name, to an individual; from the latter to a being possessing metaphysical and moral value; from a moral consciousness to a sacred being; from the latter to a fundamental form of thought and action – the course is accomplished.

Who knows what progress the Understanding will yet make on this matter? We do not know what light will be thrown on these recent problems by psychology and sociology, both already well advanced, but which must be urged on even more.

Who knows even whether this 'category', which all of us here believe to be well founded, will always be recognised as such? It is formulated only for us, among us. Even its moral strength – the sacred character of the human 'person' *(personne)* – is questioned, not only throughout the Orient, which has not yet attained the level of our sciences, but even in the countries where this principle was discovered. We have great possessions to defend. With us the idea could disappear. But let us refrain from moralising.

Yet do not let us speculate too much. Let us say that social anthropology, sociology, history – all teach us to perceive how human thought 'moves on' (Meyerson). Slowly does it succeed in expressing itself, through time, through societies, their contacts and metamorphoses, along pathways that seem most perilous. Let us labour to demonstrate how we must become aware of ourselves, in order to perfect our thought and to express it better.

Notes

Mauss's notes have been corrected and elaborated by Ben Brewster, in his translation of Mauss's essays, *Sociology and Psychology* (1979: Routledge and Kegan Paul, London), which we have largely followed in our presentation of the notes here.

1. Two theses of the Ecole des Hautes Etudes have already touched upon problems of this nature: Charles le Coeur, *Le Culte de la génération en Guinée* (vol. 45 of the Bibliothèque de l'Ecole des Hautes Etudes, Sciences Religieuses); and V. Larock, *Essai sur la Valeur sacrée et la Valeur sociale des noms de personnes dans les Sociétes inférieures* (Paris 1932).
2. H. Hubert and M. Mauss, *Mélanges d'Histoire des Religions,* Preface, 1908.
3. On the respective dates of the different civilizations which have occupied this area of the 'basket people', the 'cliff dwellers', the people of the ruins of the 'mesa' and finally of the 'pueblo' (of square and circular shape), a good exposition of likely recent hypotheses is to be found in F. H. H. Roberts, 'The Village of the great Kivas on the Zuñi Reservation', Bulletin of American Ethnology, No. 111, 1932, Washington, p. 23 *ff.* Also, by the same author, 'Early Pueblo Ruins', *Bulletin of American Ethnology,* 1930, No. 90, p.9.
4. Cushing, Frank Hamilton (1896), 'Outlines of Zuñi Creation Myths', *13th Annual Report of the Bureau of American Ethnology to the Secretary of the Smithsonian Institution, 1891–2,* Washington, D.C., pp. 371–2.
5. See also G. Davy, *Foi jurée* (Paris 1922); Mauss, 'Essai sur le Don', *Année Sociologique,* 1923, where I was not able to emphasise, because it was outside my subject, the fact of the 'person' *(personne),* his rights, duties and religious powers, nor the succession of names, etc. Neither Davy nor I were able either to insist on the fact that the potlatch not only comprises 'exchanges' of men and women, inheritances, contracts, property, ritual services, and first, especially, dances and initiations – but also, ecstatic trances, states of possession by the eternal and reincarnate spirits. *Everything, even war and conflicts, takes place only between the bearers of these hereditary titles, who incarnate these souls.*
6. Boas, 'Ethnology of the Kwakiutl', 35th *Annual Report of the Bureau of American Ethnology,* 1913–14, Washington, 1921, p. 431.
7. Boas, Franz (1921), 'Ethnography of the Kwakiutl based on data collected by George Hunt, *35th Annual Report of the Bureau of American Ethnology to the Secretary of the Smithsonian Institution, 1913–14,* p 823.
8. The best general exposition of Boas is to be found in 'The Social Organisation and the Secret Societies of the Kwakiutl Indians', *Report of the U.S. National Museum,* 1895, p.396 *ff. See also* pages 465, 505, and 658.
9. The last shutter opens to reveal if not his whole face, at least in any case his mouth, and most frequently his eyes and mouth. (See Boas article cited in Note 6, p. 628, fig. 195)
10. See Boas article, Note 6, pp. 792–801.
11. P. Radin, 'The Winnebago Tribe', *37th Annual Report of the Bureau of American Ethnology,* V:246, gives the names of the Buffalo clan and in the following pages those of the other clans. Note especially the distribution of the first four to six forenames for men, and those for women. See also other lists, dating from J.O. Dorsey's work.

12. Note also the same fact, set out differently, in Radin, 'The Winnebago Tribe', p. 194.
13. P. Radin, *Crashing Thunder, The Autobiography of an American Indian,* New York, Appleton, 1926, p. 41.
14. Forms of totemism of this kind are to be found in French West Africa and in Nigeria, the number of manatees and crocodiles in such and such a backwater corresponding to the number of living people. Also probably elsewhere individual animals correspond to the number of individual men.
15. Concerning these three series of names, see the bottom of the five genealogical tables (Arunta), in: Strehlow, *Aranda Stämme,* Vol. 5, Plates. One can follow with interest the case of the Jerrambas (the honey-ant) and the Malbankas (the bearers of the name of civilising hero who was the founder of the wild-cat clan), both of which occur several times in these entirely reliable genealogies.
16. See also the article by Herskovits, 'The Ashanti Ntoro', *J.R.A.I.,* LXVII: 287–96. A good example of the reappearance of names in Bantu country has been cited by E. W. Smith and A. Dale, *The Ila-Speaking Peoples of Northern Rhodesia,* London, 1920. C.G. and B. Seligman have been constantly aware of this question.
17. The sociologist and historian of Roman law are still hampered by the fact that we have almost no authentic sources for the very earliest law: some fragments from the era of the Kings (Numa) and some pieces from the Law of the Twelve Tables, and then only facts written down very much later. Of the complete Roman law, we only begin to have a certain idea by legal texts duly reported or discovered in the third and second centuries B.C. and even later. Yet we need to conceive of what was the past for the law and the City. Regarding the City and its earliest history, the books of M. Piganiol and M. Carcopino can be used.
18. A clear allusion to a wolf-totem form of the god of cereals (*Roggenwolf:* Germanic). The word 'hirpex' gave 'herse' (cf. 'Lupatum'. Cf. Meillet and Ernout.)
19. Cf. the commentaries of Frazer, ad loc., cf. ibid., p. 453., Acca lamenting over the corpse of Remus killed by Romulus – the foundation of the Lemuria (the sinister feast of the Lemures, of the souls of the dead lying bleeding) – play of words upon *R*emuria and *L*emuria.
20. We should develop further this problem of the relationships at Rome between the 'persona' and the 'imago', and of the latter with the name: 'nomen', 'praenomen', 'cognomen'. We have not sufficient time here. The 'person' *(personne):* this is 'conditio', 'status', 'munus'. 'Conditio' signifies rank (e.g., 'secunda persona Epaminondae', 'the second person after Epaminondas'). 'Status' is one's standing in civil life. 'Munus' signifies one's responsibilities and honours in civil and military life. All this is determined by the name, which is itself determined by family place, class and birth. One should read in 'Fastes', in the translation and admirable commentary of Sir James Frazer, the passage in which the origin of the name of Augustus is dealt with (II, 1. 476; cf. I, line 589), and why Octavius Augustus did not wish to take the name of Romulus, nor that of Quirinus ('qui tenet hoc numen, Romulus ante fuit') and took one which summed up the sacred character of all the others (cf. Frazer, ad loc., line 40). We find there the whole Roman theory regarding names. Likewise in Virgil: Marcellus, son of Augustus, is already named in limbo, where his 'father', Aeneas sees him.

    Here also should be added a consideration of 'titulus', which is raised in this line. M. Ernout tells me that the word itself might well be of Etruscan origin.

    Likewise the grammatical notion of 'person' *(personne)* which we still use, 'persona' (Greek *πρόσωπον*, grammarians), should be considered.
21. Cicero, Marcus Tullius (1927), *The Speeches, Pro lege Manilia, Pro Caecina, Pro Cluentio, Pro Rabirio perduellionis* (translated by H. Grose Hodge), London, Heinemann, pp. 296–7. ('Then Bulbus, with a smile on his face, approached Staienus and said in his most ingratiating manner: "Hullo, Paetus!" – for Staienus had adopted the

surname of Paetus from the family tree of the Aelii for fear that if he styled himself Ligur, it would be thought that his surname came from his race and not his family'.)

22. Pliny, Natural History, 35, 43, *Iustiniani Digesta* 19.1.17*ff* and Lucretius, 4, 296.
23. For further examples of the usurpation of 'praenomina', cf. Suetonius, *Nero,* 1.
24. Thus Cicero, in *Ad Atticum,* says 'naturam et personam mean', and 'personam sceleris' elsewhere.
25. To my knowledge the best book on Stoic ethics is still Bonhöffer, Adolf (1894), *Die Ethik des Stoikers Epictet,* Stuttgart, Ferdinand Enke.
26. See especially, I, p. 69ff.
27. Renan, Joseph Ernest (1889), 'Examen de conscience philosophique', *Revue des Deux Mondes,* Paris, 94, pp. 721–37.
28. Siegmund Schlossman (1906), *Persona und πρόσωπον, im Recht und im Christlichen Dogma,* Leipzig. M. Henri Lévy-Bruhl introduced it to me a long while ago and in so doing has made this whole demonstration easier. See also the first part of Vol. 1 of Schnorr von Carolsfeld, Ludwig (1933), *Geschichte der Juristischen Person,* Munich, C.H. Beck'sche Verlagsbuchthandlung.
29. Suidas (1935) *Suidae Lexicon* (edited by Ada Adler), vol.1, Leipzig, Teubner.
30. Gregory of Nazianzus (1858) '*Εις τὰ ʾάγια φῶτα* or Oratio in Sancta Lumine', *Patriologiae Cursus Completus, Series Graeca* (edited by J.-P. Migne), Paris, Petit-Moutrouge, V. 36, cols 335–60.
31. Cf. the notes of Schlossmann, loc. cit., p. 65, etc.
32. Cf. the *Concursus* of Rusticus. Cassiodorus Senator, Magnus Aurelius (1958), 'Exposito Psalmorum I–LXX', *Magni Aurelii Cassiodore Senatoris Opera,* para. II, 1, *Corpus Christianorum Series Latina,* Brepols, Turnbolt.
33. Regarding this history, this revolution in the notion of unity, there might be a lot more to say here. Cf. especially the second volume of Brunschvicg, *Progrès de la Conscience.*
34. *Ethics,* Part V, Proposition XL, corollary, Proposition XXIII and scholia, in conjunction with: Pr. XXXIX and scholia, Pr. XXXVIII and scholia, Pr. XXIX and Pr. XXI. The notion of intellectual love comes from Leo Hebraeus, the Florentine Platonist.
35. *Progrès de la Conscience,* I, p. 182 ff.
36. M. Blondel reminds me of the relevance of the notes of Hume, where the latter poses the question of the relationship between 'consciousness and self' *(conscience – moi).* See *Treatise of Human Nature (Of Personal Identity).*
37. *Die Tatsachen des Bewusstseins* (Winter lecture course, 1810–11) A very fine and very brief summary is to be found in Xavier Léon (1927), *Fichte et son temps,* Vol. III, pp. 161–9.

2

The category of the person: a reading of Mauss's last essay

N. J. Allen

The Person, as I shall call it, can stimulate exploration of particular cultures in all sorts of ways, and the more the better. However, there is also much room for reflection simply on the purpose of Mauss's paper as he saw it and on its place within his thought. As it stands, it has a compressed and allusive quality that accounts for part of its charm, but at the same time moves it away from most academic prose in the direction of fine literature, almost poetry (cf. Dumont 1972:18). The full meaning scarcely emerges unless it is read in the light of the rest of his work.[1] Conversely, the essay clarifies, almost epitomizes, a lifetime's thinking by one of the great minds of social anthropology. Although there have been a number of attempts to express what is essential in Mauss's contribution to the subject, none of them takes *The Person* as starting point.[2]

I shall not consider the general theoretical problems of assessing someone's 'thought', but regarding Mauss specifically it needs to be said that much of his early work was published jointly with other members of the Année school. The difficult problem of isolating his own contribution will be touched on only in passing. Indeed beyond a certain point such a separation would be meaningless, as is clear from the important summary of his academic activity (1979), which he prepared (without false modesty) in connection with his candidature for the Collège de France.

The structure of *The Person* is clear. Apart from the introduction and conclusion, the paper consists of an ethnographic section dealing with tribal societies and a historical section dealing with Europe, the latter being introduced by the brief paragraphs on the ancient oriental civilisations. The relationship between the two main sections is frankly evolutionary: tribal societies observed and described within the last century are adduced as representing a type of society which preceded the Greco-Roman and the other historical civilisations. Thus I begin by considering Mauss's evolutionism, an aspect of his thought which is often dismissed as outmoded even by people who admire and use other aspects of his work. He himself was of course aware of contrary trends in the subject, but refused to join in the 'scalp dance' over the collapse of evolutionism (27 III 287).

The label 'evolutionist' is an unhappy one since it covers such a variety of positions. Surprisingly often, it is still understood as connoting the speculations, dogmatism and complacency of nineteenth-century theorists with their now wholly discarded notions of 'primitive promiscuity', 'primitive matriarchy' and the like. Perhaps it would be better to talk rather of Mauss's world-historical awareness, i.e., his habit of assessing particular cultures or social phenomena against the history of humanity as a whole. Such assessments more or less necessitate a concept of types of society ranging from primitive to modern, and this forms a constant background to Mauss's work. In *The Person,* as often, the typology is largely implicit, but even here his assumptions are apparent in the three uses of the word 'primitive' in the tribal half of the essay. Sometimes he is explicit. 'One can classify societies into four great groups', he writes in 1920 (III 580), and goes on to offer a straightforward evolutionary typology of political structures. In the simplest type (segmentary or poly-segmentary), the whole society is divided into totemic clans, and central authority is non-existent.

In most contexts, however, Mauss emphatically rejected the notion of an undifferentiated tribal stage in human history. In his Inaugural Lecture (02 II 231–2), and repeatedly thereafter (e.g., 33 II 233), he consistently presented Australian aboriginal societies as the most primitive that were accessible to history or ethnography (as distinct from prehistoric archaeology). Unfortunately the even more primitive Tasmanians (Aurignacians, as he sometimes called them – M 26, 174) had been destroyed too soon to count as accessible, and it was only the Australians, as survivors from the Palaeolithic age, who could properly be termed primitive (e.g., 23 II 128).

Whatever one thinks of this approach (and the question is not easily settled), Mauss avoided the crudity of certain styles of evolutionism. If Australian societies were primitive in type, it by no means followed that they had merely endured unchanged over the millennia (08 II 201). The point is that they 'allow one, while supposing behind them a long history, to represent to oneself schematically the first human groupings from which the others have originated' (09 I 420). Although he took it as plausible that primitivity in certain respects should be accompanied by primitivity in others (ibid. 427), he was quite clear that the history of particular societies did not necessarily follow the unilineal schemata one can construct for humanity as a whole (01 III 152, 05 I 164). Moreover after the First War he came to realise that in so vast a field premature systematisation was unprofitable (33 III 438), and he warned the fieldworker against searching for the primitive (M 166). In any case rudimentary forms were not necessarily easy to understand: they had their own type of complexity resulting from the mutual interpenetration of elements and meanings which would be distinct in more evolved forms (09 I 396, 34 II 149, M 168).

Like his uncle Durkheim, Mauss saw the study of the primitive as central to the sociological enterprise. In 1909, in the introduction to his thesis on prayer (which concentrated on the Australians), he put the matter clearly: 'I believe that in sociology the study of primitive forms *(formes frustes)* is, and will long remain, more interesting and more urgent, even for the understanding of contemporary phenomena, than the study of the forms that immediately preceded the latter. It is not always the phenomena closest in time that are the profound causes of the phenomena we are familiar with' (09 I 366). It is true that later (possibly under the influence of Granet), Mauss came to think that the pre-war Année had neglected the older literate civilizations and overdone the primitive (27 III 184, 295); but this was a matter of emphasis.

In *The Person* Mauss undertakes to lead us 'from Australia to our European societies', but in fact he starts not with Australia but with the 'far from primitive' North American Indians. The main reason is probably that the relevant Australian phenomena are more summary and less clear-cut (*moins net* 06 II 138) – he often stressed the advantage of studying a social phenomenon in a society exemplifying it in an extreme form. Perhaps he also wanted to start with a society that used masks, since it is the Latin '*persona* equals mask' which bridges the two halves of the essay, and its derivative, *personne,* which is the key word in the title. I suspect too that he had a particular affection for the Zuñi. They were prominent in 1903 in PC, which (excluding book reviews) was his first substantial venture into tribal ethnographic materials, and he was still lecturing on the same people in 1940 (II 268). Moreover he particularly admired Cushing (a 'profound observer and *sociologue génial*' 27 III 185) who had anticipated some of the ideas in PC (04 II 311). Whatever the reasons, the implication of his ordering of the paper is that so far as the category of the person is concerned, the primitiveness of the Australians in technology and other respects makes little difference. To a first approximation all the tribal peoples mentioned (North American, Pacific, African) share a similar notion of the person.

If we ask what exactly is the notion that is supposed to have evolved in the transition from tribal life to Mauss's contemporary Europe, we meet first a terminological problem that constantly recurs in anthropology. We have little alternative but to analyse alien cultures in vocabulary developed in our own, but the result is that terms for social phenomena become systematically ambiguous. Words like 'law', 'religion', or 'kinship' may mean (i) what they are ordinarily taken to mean in English, (ii) the nearest equivalent in some alien society or group of societies, or (iii) what is common to both usages. Thus Mauss is sometimes dealing with the contemporary idea of the person (which we wrongly believe to be innate), sometimes with its nearest equivalent in cultures remote in space or time (Zuñi, Rome), and sometimes with the deeper, more theoretical concept that gives the essay its unity. It is unfortunate that the reader is left to make the distinctions himself, but to do so greatly clarifies the argument. Modern society has a concept of the person (usage i), many tribal societies have or had a related concept (usage ii), and it is the concept in usage iii that has evolved from one to the other, and will evolve further.

Mauss was naturally aware of these distinctions: 'Our music is only *one* music, and yet there exists something which merits the name of "Music" . . . it is the same with all the major classes of social phenomena' (34 II 152). Indeed in his early writings he laid considerable emphasis on preliminary definitions, both in his methodological statements (01 III 164–6) and in his empirical studies (e.g., *Sacrifice* 99 I 205, *Magic* 04 SA 16, *Prayer* 09 I 414), where they are regularly italicised. The object was to avoid prejudicing the investigation by some ethnocentric contemporary category or by some inappropriate would-be native category such as 'fetishism'. The concept of the person, let alone the self, is so close to one that it is apt to blur when one tries to focus on it, and one regrets that he did not follow his early practice of giving an explicit definition of the subject of the essay. However, I think the gap is filled by the statement that the investigation will be entirely one of '*droit et morale*'. These are broad rubrics since in the language of the Année the juridical includes the realm of kinship as well as politics and law, while *morale* (M 161) covers the values and general ethos of a society. Nevertheless we can specify that the essay concerns essentially the *concept of the individual presupposed by or expressed in a society's dominant value system or encompassing ideology*. The emphasis is on the public and institutional domain; a society's theories of the biological, psychological and metaphysical nature of mankind are relevant only in so far as they affect *droit et morale*. Understood as I have defined it, the category of the person is necessarily realised in some form, however indistinct, in any society worthy of the name. It could only be wholly absent in a 'society', presumably pre-human, which lacked values and institutions.

It might be objected that the formulation I offer lays the emphasis too much on the sociology and on the ethnographic half of the essay, too little on the philosophy and the European history. There are several answers to this. The philosophical language is in part a holdover from Durkheim's struggle to establish an academic niche for sociology, to found a discipline combining the empiricism of the natural sciences with the profundity of philosophy. The list of categories was probably little more than a convenient and suggestive device for organising the division of labour among members of the Année school. As for the philosophers, they earn their place in the essay mainly because they articulate the concepts of the person that were expressed in society more or less contemporaneously with them, that is, in the sectarian movements[3] or in the Declarations of Rights – see the treatment in *The Nation* (20 III 592–3) of the writers and philosophers who translated into words what was already present in society. 'The sacred character of the human person' may be important intellectually in the philosophy of Kant and his followers, but it is relevant in *The Person* because it is presupposed by the social and educational ideals of a liberal democratic state. No doubt, in so far as the philosophers suppose themselves to be working a priori, purely by means of reasoning from first principles, they exemplify the characteristic error of non-sociologists who, unaware of the history and pre-history of the fundamental notions with which they operate, naively regard them as natural.

Mauss's fundamental commitment to a sociological approach is well illustrated by his critical attitude to his colleague, Lévy-Bruhl, whose books were widely read and of whom he wrote a warm obituary (39 III 560). A philosopher by training and profession, Lévy-Bruhl had later turned to anthropology and attempted to specify the most general characteristics of primitive thought. As he implies at the start of *The Person,* Mauss thought this approach was too broad: Lévy-Bruhl would have done better to limit himself to studying particular categories. Elsewhere he also criticised the philosopher's insufficient sensitivity to world history, and especially his tendency to abstract an idea from its related social institutions and milieu. For instance, Lévy-Bruhl was perfectly correct in noting that many more or less tribal societies identified an individual's name with his soul, but this was merely to *describe* the facts. 'A sociologist of the strict obedience' – Mauss means a true Durkheimian – would *understand* the belief by showing its foundation in social organisation (23–9 II 125–35). What Lévy-Bruhl saw as a problem in primitive cognition, a topic for psychological and philosophical consideration, Mauss saw as one social phenomenon among others, as something to be related to other aspects of the life of members of societies. He even went so far as to suggest (ibid. 128) that a complete anthropology could replace philosophy 'since it would comprehend precisely that history of the human mind that philosophy takes for granted'. It is this aspect of Mauss's position that explains the brevity of his remarks on India. The ancient metaphysicians invented sophisticated notions of the person closer in character to modern European ideas than to tribal ones, and these even enjoyed considerable currency through religious teaching and writing. But they did not come to dominate *droit et morale;* they were submerged within the encompassing ideology of caste.

The main purpose of the essay, then, is to establish a base-line notion of the person obtaining in tribal society – let us call this elementary form the *personnage* – and then to link it to contemporary notions of the person. Being embedded in beliefs and institutions of various kinds, the concept of the person is not the sort of entity that is immediately accessible. 'Just as the linguist must recover beneath the false transcriptions of an alphabet the true sounds *(phonèmes)* that were pronounced, so beneath the information of the best of the natives, Oceanian or American, the ethnographer must recover the deep phenomena, the ones which are almost unconscious, since they exist only in the collective tradition. It is these real phenomena, these *choses* [i.e. Durkheimian social facts] that we shall try to reach through the documentation' (02 III 369). The brief sketches of the tribes in *The Person* are miniature synchronic analyses, but since Mauss's style is suggestive rather than systematic I try below to summarise and fill out the picture he presents.

1. The *personnage* is a member of a bounded tribal society. While recognising that in practice an ethnographer might find it extremely problematic to identify such a social entity (M 17), Mauss there and elsewhere offered definitions of a society. The essence is a def-

inite group with a sense of attachment to a tract of territory and a shared 'constitution' (10 III 377). The group will be large enough to contain at least two subgroups and several generations, and its sense of wholeness and distinctness from others will generally be expressed in a name, a belief in common origin and an aspiration to internal harmony (M 115, 34 III 306–7, 314–15). Many tribal self-appellations mean something like 'man' or 'human', outsiders being by implication non-man and a fortiori not *personnages*.

2. The tribe is divided into segments which may cross-cut each other (clans, age-sets, sections, etc. – 31 III 11*ff*). The prototypical *personnage* for Mauss would seem to be a member of a totemic clan. Totemism is the commonest religious system in societies where social organisation is based on clans, though it is not possible to say whether all societies have passed through a totemic phase. One should not talk of totemism unless there is a theriomorphic cult practised by clans, each of which bears an animal name, or less commonly, the name of some other natural species (05–6 I 163, 40). Mauss's later definitions also mention a belief in community of substance between the natural species and the members of the clan (or other social unit) such that both are of the same nature and possess the same virtues (M 131, 176).
3. The totemic group possesses a fixed stock of names *(prènoms)* and souls, one for each *personnage*. This is another sense in which the society is closed or bounded.
4. The bearer of a name at any time is regarded as the reincarnation of the original mythical bearer. (Points 3 and 4 seem to be at the very centre of Mauss's concept.)
5. The name may have a meaning relating to the clan's ancestral totem and the associated mythological narratives. These narratives will be acted out at initiation ceremonies (M 178).
6. A name is commonly taken over from a grandfather or great-great-grandfather, though there are other possibilities (Kwakiutl, Winnebago), including divination (as in Dahomey M 185).
7. The bearer of a name has the right and duty at ritual gatherings to represent the original bearer and/or to be possessed by his spirit. This may involve wearing the ancestral mask. However, the identity of performer and ancestor can be symbolised in other ways, and there is no difference in principle between enduring masks and body paintings created afresh for each ritual according to a traditional pattern; anyway masks are often burnt after one use (M 82).

8. The ritual regularly involves dancing, an art often learned at initiation (M 181).
9. Members of a clan are not necessarily *personnages*. This may be because they have had to retire owing to old age or because they are female or too young. It would seem that some clan members otherwise qualified could not be *personnages* because there would not be enough names to go round (unless there were some doubling up). This demographic difficulty seems to be the aspect of the paper that most needs touching up, even in a 'clay model' for a full study. Nor is it clear whether people who are not *personnages* are 'non-persons' in the same sense as the outsiders to the society or as Roman slaves. I suppose not, and this implies the possibility of gradations of personhood.

Despite such uncertainties, one can sum up Mauss's vision as follows: a bounded society consisting of totemic clans, each clan having a fixed stock of names transmitted by recognised procedures, the bearers of a name being reincarnations of their predecessors back to mythical times and dancing out the fact at rituals.

The idea is one that he had been developing for a very long time. Already in 1902 (I 490) he was describing magico-religious birth among the Australian Arunta as a 'truly elementary phenomenon, explanatory of numerous customs', for instance of the frequent practice of recognising a child as some particular ancestor and giving him the latter's name. By 1906 (II 138) the essentials were well established:

> There exists an enormous group of societies, Negro, Malayo-Polynesian, Amerindian (Sioux, Algonquin, Iroquois, Pueblo, North-western), Eskimo, Australian, where the system of reincarnation of the deceased and inheritance of the name within the family or clan is the rule. The individual is born with his name and his social functions. . . . The number of individuals, names, souls and roles is limited in the clan, and the line of the clan is merely a collection *(ensemble)* of rebirths and deaths of individuals who are always the same.

This passage contains most of the elements of the *personnage*, though it does not explicitly mention rituals, dancing, masks, myth or the way in which names characteristically skip one or three generations. Many references to the subject appear about this time. For instance from 1910 one might note the treatment of alternating generations among Pacific coast tribes (III 81), and the Vergilian *Tu Marcellus eris* quoted in a review dealing with West Africa (II 180). Later, in 1925 when reviewing Trobriand and Ashanti materials (III 131–3), Mauss refers to the complex of ideas as more widespread than had been apparent.

The idea of a sociological approach to the categories of the philosophers has an equally long history. It is foreshadowed in 1903 (II 88), and several of the categories, though not the person, are treated together as such in 1908 (I 28*ff,* which builds on 04 SA 111–2). The locus classicus is no doubt Durkheim's treatment of the theory of knowledge in 1912 in EF(12–26, 627*ff*), but although this work discusses the category of the *personnalité* with reference to Australian ideas of the soul, it fails to follow up Mauss's central observation about the finite stock of names and souls.

As for the later transformations of the *personnage,* a few hints appear in early book reviews. In 1905 Mauss noted an interesting treatment of the contrast between the egalitarian individualism characteristic of Christianity and the aristocratic outlook of the Greek philosophers (II 647), while in 1907 he touches on the significance of Jewish sects around the time of Jesus in the development of ideas about the individual and his *conscience* (II 589). In 1920 (III 616–18) he talks more generally of the proselytising religions as evolving and spreading the notion of humanity as everywhere identical; this was the context in which 'the notion of the individual disengaged itself from the social matrix and man gained awareness of himself'. In 1921, building on Fauconnet, he spoke briefly of the development of the notion of liberty, referring to the history of Roman law, to Christian notions of original sin, to 'the appearance of the individual *conscience* of the metaphysical person' and to the Latin *persona* (II 123). In 1929, stimulated by Lévy-Bruhl's insufficient account, already mentioned, of the tribal name-soul connexion, he finally related the *persona* to his pre-war work on the '*personnalité*' (II 132–5). Another stimulus may have been the Indologist Hopkins, whose account of the notions of the soul and self had interested him in 1925 (I 161). Certainly in 1930 he was planning to deal with the topic in a festschrift for the Japanese historian Anesaki (1979: 216).

Thus the central themes of *The Person,* as indeed his attitudes towards evolution and philosophy, had been part of Mauss's thinking for more than three decades. Similarly, many of the less prominent themes can be followed up elsewhere in his work. The brief reference to linguistics relates to his 'Whorfian' interests, to his view of language as giving access to a range of categories additional to those recognised by philosophers. He was particularly influenced by Meillet's study of male/female and animate/inanimate in the gender system of Indo-European (37 III 51, cf. 39 II 166), and he had nourished great hopes for the work on Bantu noun classes of his student Bianconi, who died in the Great War (25 III 491–2, cf. 07 II 97–9). When he referred to 'great' and 'small' as categories (24 SA 309), it was apparently with reference to North-West Amerindian languages (1923/64: 126), or perhaps to Masai (06 II 543). Linguistic categories might of course be related to sociological ones: he once thought he could glimpse a way of relating Marcel Cohen's work on Semitic tenses to Hubert's on time (27 III 192). In *The Person* the footnote reference to the technical use of 'person' in grammar and the problem of deixis alluded to in the Introduction are intriguing (cf. Benveniste 1966). I suspect, from his reference to writing 'the history of abstraction and categorization in human cognition' (*dans l'esprit* – 1923/48: 28), that he had in mind an evolutionary trend towards greater grammatical independence of the speaker from the subject matter of his statement. This would in a general way be parallel to the increasing separation (theoretically) of the legal person from his position in society. Perhaps also there would be a parallel to the relationship of perceiver and perceived: . . . 'until the sixteenth century, following Plato, it was believed that if man could see it was because his eye possessed the ability to project a luminous ray onto things he saw' (M 165).

In the paragraph specifically on pyschology the Introduction distinguishes sharply between a pan-human sense of the self, a biological given, present in everyone, and the variable concepts created around it by each society. However, by the end of the essay the sociological notion of the person is well on the way towards identification with the psychological, and the relationship between the two could be explored at any point in their history. Mauss was particularly interested in the fact that under certain circumstances a healthy member of a tribe may die within days without any apparent illness: 'his vital energy is broken because he has been separated from the pyschological support constituted by the religious society of which he is part' (23 III 282). The phenomenon interested him both for its relevance to Durkeim's work on suicide, and as bringing the social, pyschological and biological into the most intimate contact (26 SA 329–30).[4] It is relevant, too, to note that among primitives moral systems tended not to be interiorised as a *conscience* (M 161), and that in the evolution of prayer and other religious phenomena the two great currents were spiritualisation (i.e., interiorisation) and individualisation (09 I 361). Native theories of individual artistic creation might also be cited. In Greece the work was extracted from the poet by his Muse, while often elsewhere it is revealed to him by spirits (M 190); the active agent is external like the soul reincarnated in the tribal.

This brings us back to the Kwakiutl masquerade, with its components of theatre, ballet and ecstasy. Apart from his personal interest in the arts (Cazeneuve 1968b: 9), Mauss attached great academic importance to aesthetic phenomena, for example, in the *Manual,* thinking that, together with demography and human geography, linguistics and material culture, the subject had been unduly neglected by the pre-war Année (27 III 190*ff*). One might distinguish three aspects to the importance of the arts. The pyschobiological effects of collective rhythmic movement and vocalization attracted his attention early on (03 II 251, 393), for they helped to explain belief in the effectiveness of prayer and oral ritual (04 I 548, 21 II 122). They were the sort of phenomenon that needed to be included in the study of the whole man (24 SA 305), for human sociology was only a component of anthropology, that is, human biology (34 III 313). Secondly, the ethnographer should be particularly sensitive to the *mixture* of the arts (M 171), to the way in which dance may be associated with drama, singing, chanting, music, the decoration of the body or of objects, even with that proto-architecture recognisable in the preparation of a clearing for an Australian initiation (M 86). Above all, Mauss was fascinated by the context in which all these activities typically take place, i.e., the *fête* or ritual gathering, which represented for him the acme both of the sacred and the social.

Consider his well-known contrast between the secular, dispersed lifestyle of the Eskimos in summer, and the concentrated communal life of the winter settlement. The latter is passed, 'one could almost say, in a state of continuous religious exaltation . . . a sort of prolonged *fête*'. Social life is marked with a sort of holiness and is collective in the highest degree. The heightened sense of the oneness of the community sometimes embraces the ancestors, of all generations since mythical times, who are summoned to become incarnate in their living namesakes and to take part in the exchange of gifts (06 SA 444–7). It was this concept of the *fête* that enabled him (with Hubert) to write of 'the identity of the sacred and the social' *(est conçu comme sacré tout ce qui, pour le groupe et ses membres, qualifie la société* – 08 I 16–17).

Of all *fêtes* the type that interested him most was the North-West Amerindian potlatch with its competitive gift exchange and its numerous functions: 'such a syncretism of social phenomena is, in our opinion, unique in the history of human societies' (10 III 33). This led to his best-known book, *The Gift*, and its best-known phrase 'the total social fact' (25 SA 147, 204, 274). By this he meant phenomena which 'assemble all the men of a society and even the things of the society from all points of view and for always' (34 III 329). The conception of society as humans plus things was standard in the Durkheimian tradition, the 'points of view' correspond to the various aspects of the occasion, religious, economic, legal, aesthetic, sportive, and so forth, while the 'for ever' must be a reference to the presence of the ancestors, who will also be reincarnate in descendants. There have been some highly abstract discussions of the total social fact (see Cazeneuve 1968a: ch 8), but Mauss's concept was in fact characteristically concrete.

At the heart of the *fête* was the dance.[5] 'Dance is at the origin of all the arts', and it would be a good starting point for the study of games, with all their psychophysical importance (M77, 74). Under the hypnotic rhythm of the tribal dance individuals as it were merge in mind and body, moving in unity like the spokes of a wheel. It was this sort of context that gave rise to the notion of mana which underlies religion as much as magic (04 SA 125–30).[6] Thus Preuss was largely right in seeing the origin of religion in dance and mimetic ritual (06 II 243). The centrality of dance in tribal culture clarifies the reference in *The Person* to the Kwakiutl and Arunta institutions of compulsory retirement for those too old to participate. More precisely, as Granet had shown for China, dancing was a test or proof of continued possession by the ancestral spirit (31 III 16).

Apart from the masks themselves material artifacts are given more space than one might expect in a crowded essay on *la pensée humaine*. The Kwakiutl boat is used to emphasise the possibility of a macro-historical perspective on tribal cultures, but like the 'almost anecdotal' reference to the Haida pipe, it may have a more general purpose. The essay is explicitly a sample of the work of the French school of sociology, and the post-war Mauss attacked 'the fundamental error of mentalist sociology' (Lévy-Bruhl again? M 164), and emphatically denied that his approach derived all important ideas from social structure, religion and symbolism. For concepts of number and space, for the origins of geometry, arithmetic and mechanics, one should look to the crafts, to weaving, sailing, the potter's lathe . . . (27 III 185), even if the phenomena are often coloured by religious and moral values (34 III 330). In a sense Mauss saw human thought as operating by a sort of bricolage, though he did not actually use the metaphor Lévi-Strauss was to popularise. As an evolutionist he saw the process as cumulative, and to describe it favoured Meyerson's word *cheminer*, 'make one's way' (34 II 149). Thus the early Indian thinkers took the elements of their 'science' from anywhere and everywhere: the notion of universal substance was related to a throw in the game of dice, and 'does not our own philosophy still subsist on words borrowed from all sorts of vocabularies?' (11 II 600). 'Humanity has built up its mental world by all sorts of means: technical and non-technical, mystical and non-mystical, using its mind (senses, affect, reason) and its body . . .' (24 SA 309). These broad formulations stand forcefully near the end of their respective pieces.

The continuity of Mauss's thinking is so striking that Leacock (1954: 69–70), noting the parallels in argument and ethnographic sources between PC in 1903 and *The Person* in 1938, went so far as to conclude that the 'real significance' of the latter lay in its illustration of Mauss's evolutionist conservatism. Mauss himself, however, was well aware of changes in his views. The study written with his uncle concerned the tribals' systematic intellectual constructions of the cosmos, such as constituted the first step towards scientific philosophies of nature (*not* their ability to classify in everyday contexts – 03 II 82). The argument was that the classifications were originally modelled on the structure of society: 'the world view *(mentalité)* of the lower tribes directly reflects their anatomical constitution' (06 SA 4–5, cf. 08 [written 06] I 29). He never doubted the general direction of the argument,[7] but in 1907 (II 95) he recognised that by neglecting subtotems it had given too simple a picture of tribal structures. Among the Hopi the contents of the natural world were parcelled out not only among clans but also among their members, who bore the names of subtotems and were associated with religious roles and hereditary masks; and Mauss relates this to his earlier observations on tribes with finite stocks of names (though one page reference is wrong, as so often). Similarly, in 1913 (II 135), he talks of 'the hierarchy of classifications' among the Omaha descending from totem to subtotem to individual.

Several times (e.g., 27 III 221, M 131), this line of thought led Mauss to develop or recast the views of his uncle who, following Morgan, had exaggerated the amorphousness of the clan.[8] It was necessary to make more explicit the various cross-cutting differentiating factors such as sex, age, generation, and locality (31 III 13). Even in systems of non-competitive total prestations, individual exchange partners are precisely determined according to their place in society (26 III 109n). There is always individualism as well as communism in a society – the problem is to determine their proportions (M 102). Durkheim's concept of the 'mechanical solidarity' of juxtaposed segments, valuable in its time, was too simple to express the nature of tribal social cohesion, just as, conversely, there was an element of amorphousness in modern egalitarianism (34 III 319).

Just as tribal social structure was more sophisticated than he had realised at first, so was tribal cognition. Lévy-Bruhl, ignoring Durkheim's criticism in 1913, had persisted in overemphasising confusions and participations in primitive thought at the expense of contrasts, oppositions and differentiations (23–4 II 126, SA 302). Admittedly (37 II 159), Durkheim, Hubert and he had formerly erred in the same way – he must have regretted expressions like 'the complete lack of differentiation between sign and object, home and person, places and inhabitants' (03 II 16). The so-called 'participations' were not merely confusions, but perfectly deliberate efforts to establish a connection or likeness (Greek *homoiosis* 23 II 130). Indeed Mauss in general put more emphasis than Durkheim on the *active* role of humanity in social phenomena.[9]

By means of their identification with different *personnages* individuals indistinguishable in life-style are rendered qualitatively heterogeneous. This is the exact opposite of the modern egalitarian position that, however obvious the differences in power and wealth, all men are in principle equal in the eyes of the law, and one man's vote is as good as another's. In practice, personhood rarely has this sort of homogeneity beyond the borders of the nation state, and in 1920 Mauss held that, whatever the ultimate truth of the idea of man as 'citizen of the world', it remained utopian and without foundation in real interests or contemporary realities (III 629); he thought national differences in intellectual culture were actually increasing (ibid 594). However, I think that he would have recognised over the next sixty years a further homogenisation of personhood, for instance in sex equality legislation and in international attitudes towards human rights.

In evolutionary perspective (though Mauss never made the point as such) the same ironing out had affected the other categories. For many peoples space is profoundly differentiated, each region having its own affective value and sui generis virtues, whereas for us it is 'made up of parts which resemble each other and are mutually substitutable' (03 II 86). The bloodless classes and taxa of the logician and natural scientist have developed from social groupings that were the object of differential sentiments deriving from religion and kinship (ibid 88 – our society does in fact contrast with most tribal ones in its prescription of more or less homogeneous affection towards all relatives). The scientific view of time as a uniform succession of instants and durations derives from religious calendars in which *fêtes* split up the continuum into periods regarded as qualitatively distinct (07 I 50, summarising Hubert). Numbers, far from constituting a straightforward monotonic series, would in early culture have had rich and varied symbolic values – Mauss might well have thought of Granet (1934: ch 3), for they were intimate friends. As regards substance, the abstruse paper mentioned in *The Person* discusses a decasyllabic Vedic metre which was regarded as food for the gods (11 II 595). Mauss's study was to have focussed on concepts of matter and food, and one might wonder whether the heterogeneity of the *personnages* would once have been conceived in terms of differing bodily substances deriving from differing totemic dietary rules – the tribal initiand is often given the power to eat the sacred animal (39 II 164). Totality, the category par excellence, had been treated in EF (629–35), a passage which Mauss thought unduly neglected (27 III 185) and probably accepted (34 II 150), and which developed 03 II 84. The category was in origin the abstract form of the concept of society and was probably closely related to that of divinity, but with the development of the wider horizons of world religions and internationalism it was becoming ever vaster, more purely cognitive, and more detached from its origins. The world no longer consists of tribes each with its own cosmos, and their dissolution is also a homogenisation, even if logically not of identical type to the process that has affected the previous categories.

As for cause, mana was the attribute, simultaneously material and spiritual (for the distinction was not sharp until Spinoza), of what exerts mystical power (M 167–8, 198, a chapter revised in 1937–8).[10] Perhaps in this case Mauss would have argued that the essential evolutionary trend was a reduction of mystical causation to non-mystical, which would be another sort of homogenisation again. Moreover a compatable reduction seems to apply in the other cases. Despite the deliberate effort of ritual, and the subjective reality that it creates (34 II 151), and even if (as I would argue) early kinship systems in certain perfectly objective senses approximated the individual to a grandparent, the modern person is closer than the *personnage* to what is actually the case. Mauss himself inclined to the view of Hegel and Hamelin that the truest and most fundamental categories appeared late in human history (21 II 124).

Although *The Person* begins with the Aristotelian categories this was only the provisional strategy of the French school. Aristotle had been wrong to think that his logical analysis of the Greek language could by itself constitute the analysis of a universal mode of understanding (*lo-*

gique): there were other concepts and categories still to be discovered (M 165–6), for instance those accessible through linguistics. Some were quite recent, for example, chance, as in 'games of chance' (M 76), or economics – homo economicus really only dated from Mandeville (M 102). We needed the largest possible catalogue of all the categories that mankind could be shown to have used. 'We shall then see that there have been, and still are, many moons, dead, pale or obscure, in the firmament of reason' (24 SA 309, the well-known passage with which Lévi-Strauss ended his introduction to SA).

My purpose has been to understand *The Person* and the mind that produced it rather than to assess the validity of its case. Could it be that, for all the long years of learning that lie behind it, Mauss's *personnage* is really a mirage? It would be a long job to re-examine the evidence on the tribal societies that Mauss mentions,[11] let alone to extend the analysis to others. My own experience and knowledge relate particularly to tribals belonging linguistically to the proto-Sino-Tibetan stock mentioned in *The Person,* but these societies are not very helpful. As one might expect, many isolated elements of the *personnage* complex are to be found, the totemic clans of the Kachari (13 I 594), Tibetan masks (widely diffused – M 82), the reincarnate dancers of ancient China (Granet), and so on, but not (to my knowledge) the finite stock of souls, names, and roles. Mauss would not have been disconcerted – clearly the great majority of societies lie in between the poles he considers, or off to the sides. If the hypothesis could be convincingly established for enough other areas, there would be nothing to prevent one supposing that here, too, sometime in prehistory, the dominant ideology was built around the *personnage.*[12]

On a more theoretical note, the grand evolutionary perspective has largely been left in the background of social anthropology since Mauss's day, and indeed there is much to be said for a degree of humility in the face of the general course of human history, 'a subject so vague and vast that no social anthropologist would be prepared to think it even meaningful today' (Lienhardt 1964: 10). However, academic fashions change, archaeology, Marxism, sociobiology and the work on lexical universals are difficult to ignore entirely, and this aspect of Mauss's approach no longer seems particularly dated. If sociological world history is to be written by anyone, there can have been very few better equipped with the relevant knowledge than he was, and there is a vast amount to be explored in connexion with the framework he suggested. For instance, at the start of his scale, the inheritance of the *personnage* from grandparents is no mere empirical curiosity: it would be the natural concomitant of the simplest logical possibility for kinship systems of the type most characteristic of tribal society, especially Australia, as I have suggested in a preliminary paper which owes much to Mauss (Allen 1982).[13]

Those distrustful of even Mauss's careful evolutionism can of course translate much of what he says into synchronic terms. One of the messages of *The Person* would be that, if one is interested in value systems, the *personnage* in the masquerade is more similar to the voter in the booth or the client in the Citizens Advice Bureau than to the film or television actor on the screen. But however one reads the essay, if one reads it closely, it must be for its length as rich and as 'total' a piece of anthropological writing as one could find.

Notes

1. The corpus as used here consists essentially of (i) the often neglected *Manual* (based on lecture courses given between 1926 and 1939), (ii) the seven texts collected in *Sociologie et Anthropologie* (only six in the earlier editions), and (iii) Karady's three-volume collection. I have not attempted systematically to cover the uncollected writings. Abbreviations: (i) M, *Manual;* (ii) SA, *Sociologie et Anthropologie;* (iii) referred to by volume number only (Karady); also PC for *Primitive Classification* and EF for Durkheim's *Elementary Forms*. References to (ii) and (iii) are usually prefaced by the last two figures of the date, so that 08 I 3 refers to *Oeuvres* vol. I, page 3, a text originally published in 1908 according to Karady's bibliography. Translations are essentially my own; where they are available I have often consulted published ones though without acknowledgement and without necessarily following them.
2. Karady lists some of the secondary literature in III 693, and has followed up his useful introduction to the *Oeuvres* with studies of the Année school as a sociological phenomenon in itself (1982, cf. also Besnard ed. 1979). The 1973 Paris colloquium is of more interest to Africanists than to Maussians (though one might contrast Fortes's reading of *The Person* with the present one). Like most commentators, Diaz (1979) concentrates on the major texts taken one by one. Several commentators seem to me overinfluenced by Lévi-Strauss's interesting but highly personal introduction to SA. Since PC was co-authored with Durkheim, the secondary literature is considerable: One might note Lukes (1973: ch 22) for valuable distinctions, Aston (1978: ch 3) for an interesting treatment of the essay qua text, and Bloor (1982).
3. To a South Asianist, these C. 17–18 movements (whose importance in the development of political and philosophical thought 'can scarcely be exaggerated') recall the Indian sectarian movements whose significance as sources of innovation in Indian history has been so well emphasised by Dumont – cf. note 13.
4. Such a 'total' phenomenon seemed to him incompatible with the dissociated and divided mentality of literate elites (24 SA 306); in spite of progress in recent centuries (22 II 483), the mentality of non-elite Europeans, especially women, remained more unitary. However, by the thirties at any rate, he was stressing the lack of an adequate sociology of women, or, of women in relation to men (31 III 15, 34 III 341, M 173).
5. Mauss's nearest approach to a field trip (ignoring his meeting with some Hopi in Washington – SA 38, M 165) was a three-week visit to Morocco, during which his personal objective was to learn about a certain cultic dance (30 II 565–6).
6. In exploring Hubert's contribution to EF, Isambert (1976: 38) comments on Dur-

kheim's rather sparse acknowledgement of the work of his disciples and I think this is particularly true of Mauss. Mauss used "Elementary Forms of Religious Life" as a title in his Inaugural (02 I 90) and in the *Année* vols. 5–6, and Durkheim's treatment of the relationship between demographic aggregation and religious emotion is close to his own except for the addition of the (characteristically chemical) metaphor of 'effervescence'. Was this part of the reason why Mauss's review of the book was so dry (13 I 186)? Certainly after Durkheim's death Mauss made it clear that his own treatment of mana would have been more nuanced (23 II 129), and he also had his own view of the belief in the soul: in the 1929 preliminary version of *The Person,* the cause of the belief is in part the necessity to name the individual and specify his social position among the dead and the living (II 125). This is considerably more precise than Durkheim's view of the soul as 'the totemic principle incarnated in each individual', or his derivation of 'the notion of person' from an impersonal spiritual principle associated with the group, taken together with the bodily discreteness of the group's members (EF 355–6, 386). By 1933 (II 143) Mauss felt that Hertz (following Robertson Smith) had over-emphasised dualism and that the early Année movement in general had in this respect over-simplified the notion of the sacred. Mauss might also have given less weight to emblems (M 198).

7. The argument would have been clearer if they had distinguished more directly between two possible interpretations of the hypothetical link between society and cosmology: as an evolutionary *event* whereby systematic cosmologies originally came into existence, and as a matter of *co-variation* thereafter, at least in the simpler societies. Mauss (who provided all the ethnographic materials for the essay – 1979: 210) probably supported both interpretations. For his role in converting Durkheim to the use of the ethnographic materials rather than ancient literature, see Condominas (1972: 130).
8. His self-sacrificing work on behalf of deceased Année associates has often been remarked on, but this loyalty did not preclude constructive criticism. The reminiscences of those who knew him (e.g., Waldberg 1970) show an attractive personality, far from austere, in spite of the formidable learning. Clark (1973: 182) transmits the anecdote of Mauss, then around forty, hiding behind an orange tree in a café to avoid being seen by Durkheim when he should have been at work. In his own writing the warmth of character is most apparent in the obituaries, especially those of Sylvain Lévi (35 III 535) and Alice Hertz (1928). For his political attitudes see (as well as the conclusion to *The Gift*) the article on Bolshevism: 'At the risk of appearing old-fashioned and a trotter-out of commonplaces we come back plainly to the old Greek and Latin concepts . . . of that necessary "friendship", of that "community" which are the delicate essence of the City.' One is reminded of the 'delicate and precious' idea of the person, that Idea that could disappear with us.
9. Already in 1901 (III 148*ff*) Mauss saw problems in using Durkheim's 'constraint' as a criterion of the social, preferring to define it as 'all the ways of acting and thinking which the individual finds pre-established and whose transmission takes place generally via education'. He particularly emphasised the notion of expectation *(attente)* with its psychological and quantifiable connotations (04 SA 123, 23 SA 306, 34 II 117–18).
10. For Mauss the prototypical example of mana was perhaps a tribal dance exerting its magical action at a distance. His vivid image of the Dayak women dancing with their sabres constrasts markedly with the extreme abstraction and intellectualism of Lévi-Strauss's treatment of the same topic (SA xlviff). This is characteristic: *The Person* presents, not a composite generalised portrait of the *personnage,* but precise facts on specific societies, even quite long quotations from the ethnographers. We have repeatedly noted his interest in the concrete, the material, the biological. Another side to this realism is his attitude to statistics: he had always had 'an intense certainty, almost a physical awareness, that there is nothing in society except statistical totals . . .' (21 II

125), and as a student he had considered specialising in quantitative studies (1979: 214).

11. Cazeneuve (1958), returning from fieldwork with the Zuñi, argued that the data from that society did not in fact support the argument of PC.
12. In defining the theme of *The Person* I emphasise words like 'public' and 'ideology' because a society's values are not necessarily unitary, and in any case 'that fragment of our life which is our life in society' is not all that needs studying (26 SA 329). Mauss would have been the last to deny a universal psychobiological component, a sense of common humanity, in moral attitudes to the individual. If a toddler has hurt himself and needs comforting, what would it matter who is or is not a *personnage?*
13. Another interesting task would be to relate the work of Mauss to that of his pupil and continuator Dumont. The latter remarks (1979: XXIX, in criticism of some American work): 'I do not think that the comparison of societies should be carried out under the rubric of their conception of the human person, since the latter is in my view something which is fundamental for some societies but not for others, even if every conception of society necessarily implies a certain manner of conceiving men'. Mauss would not necessarily have disagreed, since his essay was concerned not with the comparison of whole ideologies but with the development lying behind the modern form of the conception. One welcomes any attempt (see Collins, this volume) to update Mauss's philosophical vocabulary, but the problem of identifying cultural universals exactly, and of deciding whether or not they are a priori necessary, will no doubt be with us for a long time.

References

Allen, N.J. 1982. A dance of relatives. *J. Anthrop. Soc. Oxford* 13: 139–146.

Aston, M.P. 1978. The French school of sociology 1890–1920. D.Phil. thesis, Univ. of Oxford.

Benveniste, E. 1966. Structure des relations de personne dans le verbe (1946), and De la subjectivité dans le language (1958), Chs. 18 and 21 in *Problèmes de linguistique générale.* Paris: Gallimard.

Besnard, P. (ed). 1979. Les Durkheimiens. *R. franç. sociol.* 20 (1).

Bloor, D. 1982. Durkheim and Mauss revisited: classification and the sociology of knowledge. *Stud. Hist. Phil. Sci.* 13: 267–297.

Cazeneuve, J. 1958. Les Zuñis dans l'oeuvre de Durkheim et de Mauss. *Revue philosophique* 83: 452–61.

1968a. *Sociologie de Marcel Mauss.* Paris: PUF.

1968b. *Mauss.* (Coll. SUP-Philosophes). Paris: PUF.

Clark, T.N. 1973. *Prophets and patrons: the French university and the emergence of the social sciences.* Cambridge: Harvard UP.

Condominas, G. 1972. Marcel Mauss, père de l'ethnographie française. *Critique* 297: 118–39, 301: 487–504.

Diaz-Estevez, J. 1979. The work of Marcel Mauss: an interpretation. D. Phil. thesis, Univ. of Oxford.

Dumont, L. 1972 (written 1952). Une science en devenir. *L'Arc* 48: 8–21.

1979. *Homo Hierarchicus* (édition Tel). Paris: Gallimard.

Durkheim, E. 1912 (5th ed. 1968). *Les formes élémentaires de la vie religieuse: le système totémique en Australie.* Paris: PUF.

Fortes, M. 1973. On the concept of the person among the Tallensi, pp. 283–319 in *La notion de personne en Afrique noire.*

Granet, M. 1968 (orig. 1934). *La pensée chinoise.* Paris: Albin Michel.
Isambert, E.F. 1976. L'élaboration de la notion de sacré dans l' "ecole" Durkheimienne. *Arch. sc. soc. des. rel.* 42: 35–56.
Karady, V. 1982. Le probléme de la légitimité dans l'organisation de l'ethnologie française. *R. franç. sociol.* 23: 17–35.
La notion de personne en Afrique noire. 1973. (Colloques internationaux du CNRS, no. 544). Paris: CNRS.
Leacock, S. 1954. The ethnological theory of Marcel Mauss. *Am. Anth.* 56: 58–73.
Lienhardt, R.G. 1964. *Social Anthropology.* London: OUP.
Lukes, S. 1973. *Emile Durkheim, his life and his work: a historical and critical study.* Harmondsworth: Penguin.
Mauss, M. 1947. *Manuel d' ethnographie.* Paris: Payot.
1950/73. *Sociologie et anthropologie.* Introduction by C. Lévi-Strauss. Paris: PUF.
1923/48. Discussion, pp. 25–8 in A. Meillet, *Linguistique historique et linguistique générale,* Vol. II. Paris: Champion. Translated as 'On Language and primitive forms of classification' by D. Hymes, pp. 125–7 in D. Hymes (ed.), 1964, *Language in culture and society.* New York: Harper and Row.
1968–9. *Oeuvres* (3 vols). Prés. V. Karady. Paris: Editions de Minuit.
1930/79. L'oeuvre de Mauss par lui-même, pp. 209–20 in P. Besnard (ed.), 1979.
Waldberg, P. 1970. Au fil du souvenir, pp. 581–6 in vol. I of J. Pouillon and P. Maranda (eds). *Echanges et communications.* The Hague: Mouton.

3

Categories, concepts or predicaments? Remarks on Mauss's use of philosophical terminology

Steven Collins

I

It is common to find anthropologists, sociologists, intellectual historians and others, as well as philosophers, using the philosophical terminology of *categories of thought* to refer to the more or less fundamental ideas, concepts or simply patterns of thinking which are found in different cultures and different historical periods. When these 'categories' are viewed as organised (more or less) into a system, we are then often said to be confronted with different frameworks, perspectives, world-views, or – more drastically – *different worlds*. The purpose of this chapter is to examine what Durkheim and Mauss might have meant by speaking in this way; and secondarily to raise some general issues relevant to the use of this philosophical vocabulary in cultural or social description and analysis.

The lecture by Mauss to which this volume is devoted was one of the last pieces of work produced by the original *Année Sociologique* group, gathered around and under Durkheim, and Mauss makes clear at the outset his awareness of, and allegiance to this tradition: his paper is, he says,

> an example . . . of the work of the French school of sociology. We have concentrated most especially on the social history of the categories of the human mind. We attempt to explain them one by one, using very simply, and as a temporary expedient, the list of Aristotelian categories as our point of departure. (See Chapter 1.)

In Durkheim's *Elementary Forms of the Religious Life* (hereafter EF) we are offered a sociological account of 'what philosophers since Aristotle have called the categories of the understanding: ideas of time, space, class, number, cause, substance, personality *[personnalité]*, etc.'[1] In fact, as we shall see, it is not Aristotle but Kant – mediated in a particular way by certain French philosophers of Durkheim's own day – whose notion of 'categories of thought' lies behind Durkheim's approach to these problems. Durkheim has often been taken, in a famous phrase, to have 'sociologised Kant'. This can mean many things, but at least one influential interpretation has definitely relativist (and unKantian) implications. Where Kant thought there was but a single and universal set of categories, as the form of conceptual organisation necessary for any human thought, anywhere and at any time, Durkheim is taken to have argued that different categories exist in different societies, and at different times; and that the necessity with which they impose themselves on human minds is not absolute, but particular to, and relative to, the particular society or epoch in question. Thus Ernest Gellner writes that

> Durkheim's main problem, as he saw it, was not to explain religion but to explain conceptual thought, and above all the *necessity,* the compulsive nature of certain of our general concepts . . . It was thus Durkheim who paved the way for modern anthropological fieldwork; it was his view that in observing (say) the rituals associated with a clan totem, we were privileged to observe the machinery which explains the conceptual, logical and moral compulsions of the members of *that* society, compulsions similar, for instance, to our inability to think of the world outside time. [Gellner's italics][2]

Durkheim's influence on anthropology has of course been enormous; and it may not seem a very long way from the characterisation of Durkheimian sociology given by Gellner to the following, and well-known, relativist use of Evans-Pritchard's work by Peter Winch. Speaking not of a set or system of categories, but metaphorically of a 'web of belief',[3] Evans-Pritchard, in Winch's view, explains the lack of general acceptance among the Azande of their (quite commonly expressed) scepticism about magic and witchcraft by arguing that

> Such scepticism does not begin to overturn the mystical way of thinking, since it is necessarily expressed in terms belonging to that way of thinking. [Then quoting Evans-Pritchard:] In this web of belief every strand depends on every other strand and a Zande cannot get outside its meshes because this is the only world he knows. The web is not an external structure in which he is enclosed. It is the texture of his thought and he cannot think that his thought is wrong.[4]

Does a Durkheimian sociology of knowledge imply a relativist epistemology? I think that for Durkheim himself, despite some ambiguities and contradictions, the answer is no; but for Mauss, who would doubtless have considered the question premature, the answer is more likely to be yes, or at least 'not yet decided'. As both Durkheim and Mauss noted, the philosophical term 'category' goes back to Aristotle; but in the text cited by Mauss in note 2, the 1908 joint publication with Hubert, *Mélanges d'Histoire des Religions,* there is – typically[5] – no mention of Aristotle, nor of his list of ten categories. The 'categories' discussed there are *mana,* 'a special category of primitive thought', genre (or class), space and time. Hubert and Mauss claim that the notion of *mana* is an unexamined principle underlying 'the judgements and reasonings' of magic, and that

> These principles of such judgements and reasonings, without which one does not think them possible, are what are called in philosophy categories.
> Constantly present in language, without their being necessarily explicit, they exist ordinarily in the form of determining habits of consciousness, themselves unconscious.[6]

Aristotle is named explicitly in another, and often-quoted remark of Mauss, made in 1924:

> The Aristotelian categories are not indeed the only ones which exist in our mind, or which have existed in the mind and which must be treated. It is necessary first of all to draw up the largest possible list of categories; one must start from all those which it is possible to know that men have used. It will be seen then that there have been and there still are dead or pale or obscure moons in the firmament of reason.[7]

This sort of talk would seem to suggest that Mauss uses the term category simply to refer to certain fundamental and pervasive forms of conceptual organisation, and that – like Aristotle – he neither had nor wanted to have any very definite conception of how these categories were to be ordered into a system or set of systems.

In the quotation from Durkheim's EF given above, the addition of 'etc.' to the list of categories (by no means unusual in such sociological and culture-historical contexts) might seem to suggest that Durkheim thought any such list could be extended and was not systematically ordered or complete. But in fact he, like Kant, has an un-Aristotelian sense of system and order in 'the categories of thought'. In the *Critique of Pure Reason,* Kant had claimed that his own list of categories, unlike that of Aristotle, 'has not arisen rhapsodically as the result of a haphazard search'; and that Aristotle, in whose 'search for these fundamental concepts [there was] no principle, . . . merely picked them up as they came his way, and at first procured ten of them which he called categories'.[8] Kant's own table of categories, on the contrary, was intended to be systematic and complete, derived from (traditional) logic, in which 'the logical functions in all possible judgements', were to be found, so that 'these functions specify the understanding completely, and yield an exhaustive inventory of its powers'.[9] Kant's categories were thus intended to be the universally necessary form or structure of human thought, in all cultures and at all times. Accordingly, Durkheim writes in EF that

> At the root of all our judgements there are a certain number of essential notions which dominate all our intellectual life . . . [These 'categories'] correspond to the most universal properties of things. They are like the solid frameworks which enclose thought . . . Other ideas are contingent and unsteady; we can conceive of their being unknown to a man, a society or an epoch; but these others appear to be nearly inseparable from the normal working of the mind. They are like the framework of the intelligence.[10]

For Durkheim also, the categories of thought have a kind of necessity, which he expresses in high Kantian style: 'it is a special sort of moral necessity which is to the intellectual life what moral obligation is to the will'.[11] In the words immediately preceding this, however, he seems to introduce an un-Kantian notion of variation in categories, which seems to leave open the possibility of there being not just one, but several 'categorial frameworks'.[12] Arguing against both a Humean empiricist, and a Kantian a priori account of the origin of categories, he claims that

> the necessity with which the categories are imposed upon us is not the effect of simple habits whose yoke we could easily throw off with a little effort; nor is it a physical or metaphysical necessity, since the categories change in different places and times.[13]

It is not difficult to find in Durkheim's work as a whole remarks which suggest a quite straightforwardly un-Kantian non-universalist view. Perhaps the most trenchant is to be found in the posthumously edited lecture series *Pragmatism and Sociology,* where he asserts that

> we can no longer accept a unique and invariable system of categories, of intellectual frameworks. The frameworks which have had their *raison d'être* in the civilisations of other times no longer have one today, a fact which, of course, does not take anything away from the value which they had for their epoch.[14]

Part, at least, of the reason for this ambiguity in Durkheim's thought lies in the personal and academic milieu of Durkheim himself. He was concerned, of course, to establish sociology as an independent academic discipline, not subsumable by others, and in particular by philosophy. To this end, he stressed two potentially conflicting roles for the new 'study of society'. On the one hand, he stressed empirical variation in the thought and institutions of different *societies,* in order to argue that philosophical epistemology must necessarily be complemented by historical sociology. In this context, he speaks of categories varying, changing, and so on, across societies and epochs. On the other hand he was concerned to stress the abstract notion of *Society,* of social life as the all-important cognitive and moral force in human consciousness. In this context he speaks of the (i.e., the single and universal set of) categories as *having their origin* in Society. In 1888, Durkheim criticised Comte for 'fixing on Society, not on societies classified into types and species', and claimed that Comte's kind of sociology was 'less a special study of social beings than a philosophical meditation on human sociability in general'.[15] Nonetheless, in many aspects of his own sociology – as I shall try to show in relation to his and Mauss's epistemology – he never clearly separated what was (or might be) true of all societies, as examples of Society, from what was (or might be) true of only some of them.[16] It is worth noting in passing how this affects his political thought – or at least our view of its implications. For him the overwhelmingly important dimension of moral and political values was the fact of collective, social life. Thus where Kant simply considered the categories of thought, in the abstract and for the individual, as constitutive of human nature, Durkheim saw the socially originated categories as constitutive both of social life – 'society could not abandon the categories to the free choice of the individual without abandoning itself' – and of the individual mind: 'does a mind ostensibly free itself from these forms of thought? It is [then] no longer considered a human mind in the full sense of the word, and is treated accordingly'.[17] If we regard this as referring not to the abstract and (indeed) a priori fact of social life as a precondition of human nature but to concrete and empirical facts of particular societies at particular times, then this imposition of 'moral and logical conformity' on the members of that society will produce a very different political temper from Durkheim's own social-democratic individualism. Just before the Second World War, and Mauss's insanity, Léon Brunschvicg said that 'Nuremberg is religion according to Durkheim, society adoring itself'. Mauss, although knowing that this charge was unjustified (as indeed it is), nevertheless felt keenly the 'real tragedy' which Nazism represented for 'Durkheim, and after him, the rest of us'.[18] Of course, on a more theoretical level, it has been precisely the assertion of cross-cultural variability and irreducibility of 'conceptual frame-works', combined with intra-cultural determinism (of a stronger or weaker sort) which has characterised much relativist social science, particularly of the post-Wittgensteinian Winchian sort.

Sorting out these issues in themselves and exhaustively would be a task far beyond the possible range of a single essay, book, or individual thinker. But in seeking to help clarify the Durkheimian tradition in the sociology of knowledge, and of Mauss's contribution to it, three related problems seem to me to be of particular importance.

Are (the) categories of thought empirical or a priori *in origin?*

This is clearly one of Durkheim's main concerns, perhaps his *only* real concern, in EF. He first describes a Humean, empiricist approach, in which each human mind, after confronting experience (seen as a sequence of simple or raw impressions, ideas, sense-data or whatever), then derives from this experience, by some practice of habitual abstraction or generalisation, such notions as causation, the objective existence of things perceived, and personal identity. The philosophically unsophisticated person, on this account, sees these notions as intrinsic and given; the philosophically sophisticated sees these 'fictions' for what they are, but must still rely on them for the commonsense affairs of practical and moral life. Durkheim characterises this view in the light of his attitude to individualism (as a methodological principle): on the empiricist account, he says, the categories of thought 'are constructed and made up of bits and pieces, and . . . the individual is the artisan of this construction'. For the a priori, Kantian view, which Durkheim (following Hamelin) calls the view of a 'divine reason', 'the categories cannot be derived from experience: they are logically prior to it and condition it. They are represented as so many irreducible data, immanent in the human mind by virtue of its constitution'.[19] He rejects this view for a number of reasons. Inter alia, it is unscientific, and in any case 'saying that the categories are necessary because they are indispensable to the functioning of the human mind is simply repeating that they are necessary'.[20] His own solution depends on rejecting the methodological individualism of the empiricist approach: He agrees that all concepts are derived from experience, but insists that this is *collective* experience. Thus, for the individual mind they are a priori, being the quintessential 'collective representations' constructed in and by (and even in some senses *about*) the *conscience collective*. This account has often,[21] and rightly, been taken to anticipate Wittgenstein's argument that concepts must necessarily presuppose the existence of, and operate according to the public rules of, a social milieu, and that a shared public domain of discourse is (in Heidegger's phrase) 'always already there' before individual thought and speech. Of course, Wittgenstein's argument has been taken to be intricately and intrinsically connected with another: that these shared public domains and social milieux are necessarily particular, necessarily only 'forms of life' or 'language-games', which do *not* rest on any one basic logical linguistic structure or categorial framework.

The connexion, in post-Wittgensteinian thought, between the need for shared, socially-elaborated conceptual rules and the denial of any universal set of such rules leads one to the second problem:

Are categories of thought different in different societies, or is there a single, fundamental and universal set?

Durkheim, as I have suggested, is ambiguous here. On the one hand 'each civilisation has its ordered system of concepts which characterises it'[22] and 'the system of concepts with which we think in everyday life is that expressed by the vocabulary of our mother tongue'[23]; on the other hand, as we have seen, *the* categories are 'the solid frameworks which enclose all thought', and whereas we can conceive of other ideas 'being unknown to a man, a society or an epoch', the categories are 'nearly inseparable from the normal working of the intelligence. They are like the framework of the intelligence'. It is arguable that Mauss, on the other hand, made the relativist, or at least anti-universalist claim, with perhaps a greater degree of consistency. As early as 1906 he wrote that:

> When we speak of collective mental states, we are thinking of specific societies, and not of society in general, of the people, of indefinite masses, of a vague humanity where ideas and sentiments would be transmitted from individual to individual, we don't know how . . . [W]e never lose sight of the fact that practices and beliefs are special to certain peoples, to certain civilisations. They always have the particular colour which each phenomenon takes in each society.[24]

In the 1924 'moons in the firmament of reason' passage, in which he argues for the need to draw up a list of all categories, not just Aristotelian ones, Mauss claims that 'mankind has built up its mind', by all manner of means, 'as a random result of *[au hasard de]* choices, things and times; as a random result of nations, their works or their ruins'. It is only 'this sentiment of the present relativity of our reason' which can 'perhaps inspire the best philosophy'. He gives, as examples of things which *have been* categories, the big and the small, the animate and the inanimate, the right and the left; and suggests that the (our?) category of substance has developed through a variety of vicissitudes, one of its ancestors (in India and Greece) being the notion of food.[25] Similarly he speaks elsewhere of *mana* as 'not only a special category of primitive thought' but as the 'prior form [of] other categories which still function in our minds: those of substance and cause'.[26] These kinds of suggestion of change and development in categories of thought leads to the third problem:

Are categories of thought capable of historical change and development?

An a priori account of categories will necessarily hold them to be unchanging (although the way in which they are explicitly and linguistically conceptualised may alter). Both Durkheim and Mauss, taking a specific – sociological – kind of empiricist line, speak of categories developing and changing.[27] In arguing against an a priori 'divine reason' Durkheim claims that the

> categories of human thought are never fixed in any one definite form; they are made, unmade and remade incessantly; they change with places and times. On the other hand, the divine reason is immutable. How can this immutability give rise to this incessant variability?[28]

The categories are not 'very simple notions which the first comer can very easily arrange from his own personal observations', but are 'priceless instruments of thought which human groups have laboriously forged through the centuries . . . A complete section of the history of humanity is resumed therein.'[29] In the 1924 passage, cited earlier, Mauss asserts that in describing and analysing the 'catalogue of categories' the most important form of study is historical.[30] In 1908 he condemned Wundt's *Völkerpsychologie* because it could not explain, nor easily allow for evolution in 'that order of representations which collective psychology studies'. Wundt assumed, he says, 'a common foundation of human mentality' which could never change because it was not connected with changing conditions. Thus it is 'always the same ideas' – he gives the example of 'the soul' *(l'âme)* – which by some mysterious and unaccountable 'inner dialectic' take on different forms in different places. Dismissing this as 'running on the spot' Mauss argues that on his sociological view change is easily explained, since 'all these facts are considered as products of what is properly social life', and 'are related to social factors'.[31] Certainly in the 1938 lecture, he is closely concerned with historical change; and he fears lest the modern and 'delicate' category of the person may disappear.

Durkheim and Mauss, in 1903, had argued in *Primitive Classification* that 'not only has our present notion of classification a history, but this history itself implies a considerable prehistory'. Although primitive classifications differ from modern scientific ones, nevertheless the two 'seem to be connected, with no break in continuity'.[32] Indeed, this stress on historical development – most often, given their evolutionary framework, in the direction of greater sophistication and complexity – makes Durkheim and Mauss, and Durkheim in EF, avoid the simplistic sociological reductionism with which they are sometimes charged. In the conclusion to the latter work, Durkheim has a remarkable passage, which clearly addresses each of the three issues I have discussed: the origin of categories of thought, their cross-cultural variability and their relationship to history and change.

> Attributing social origins to logical thought is not debasing it or diminishing it or reducing it to nothing more than a system of artificial combinations; on the contrary, it is relating it to a cause which implies it naturally. But this is certainly not to say that the ideas elaborated in this way are at once adequate for their object. If society is something universal in relation to the individual, it is none the less an individuality itself, which has its own personal physiognomy and its idiosyncrasies; it is a particular subject and consequently particularises whatever it thinks of. Therefore collective representations also contain subjective elements, and these must be progressively weeded out, if we are to approach reality more closely . . .
>
> [But]the causes which have determined this [historical] development do not seem to be specifically different from those which gave it its initial impulse. If logical thought tends to rid itself more and more of the subjective and personal elements which it still retains from its origin, it is not because extra-social factors have intervened; it is much rather because a social life of a new sort is developing. It is this international life which has already resulted in universalising religious beliefs . . . [In this process] logical organisation differentiates itself from the social organisation and becomes autonomous. That is, it seems, how the bond which right at the start linked thought to particular collective individualities is becoming progressively looser; how, consequently, it [thought] is becoming always impersonal and is universalised. Really and truly human thought is not a primitive datum; it is a product of history; it is the ideal limit towards which we are constantly approaching, but which in all probability we shall never succeed in reaching.[33]

This could almost be taken as a description of the programme of Mauss's 1938 lecture; but before looking at that directly, let me for the moment turn to the intellectual influences on Durkheim's and Mauss's sociology of knowledge, to show something of why and how they wanted to speak of 'categories of thought', and what specific epistemological and political influences shaped Mauss's 'category of the person'.

II

As I have mentioned, Durkheim and Mauss's talk of 'categories of thought' is derived from their view of the philosophy of Kant: *he* would certainly not have countenanced any suggestion that sociologists and field-working anthropologists were necessary to discover or elucidate the categories of the human mind: 'I have to deal with nothing save reason itself and its pure thinking; and to obtain complete knowledge of these, there is no need to go far afield, since I come upon them in my own self'.[34] Of course, the *content* of conceptual organisation might vary; but for Kant its universally necessary *form* is simply available to philosophical introspection. Human experience results from two sources: intuitions *(Anschauungen)* and concepts *(Begriffe)*. 'Objects are *given* to us by means of sensibility *[Sinnlichkeit]* and it alone yields us intuitions; they [i.e., objects] are *thought* through the understanding *[Verstand]* and through the understanding alone arise concepts'.[35] Both intuitions and concepts are necessary for consciousness of the objective world, and both arise through the impinging of external objects, as sensation *[Empfinding]*, on the human mind. The mind has a structure or form, which orders the material of sensation into intuitions and concepts; this structure or form is two-fold, the pure forms of intuition – space and time – and the pure forms of the understanding – the categories.[36] None of these forms of ordering experience could arise *from* experience, in the manner assumed by empiricists like Hume, since they must be presupposed if any recognisable experience can occur at all. Thus they are a priori. They can, however, have no application *outside* of experience; what Kant calls their 'objective employment' is always 'immanent'.[37] The human mind *does* have a propensity to overrun experience, and to think it can know things – and itself – outside of experience, 'transcendentally'; this propensity is natural to human reason, but is fallacious, and gives rise not to objective knowledge of things but merely to 'transcendental' ideas of 'pure reason' *(Vernunft)*, which are illusions. The three classes of 'transcendental illusion' which Kant describes are: in psychology, the supposed knowledge of the thinking subject, the self, as an absolute unity (the Cartesian notion of the soul), in cosmology, the supposed knowledge of the absolute unity of the sum total of all appearances (the universe as a whole), and in theology, the supposed knowledge of the absolute unity of the condition of all possible objects of thought (God). Kant regarded the distinction between the ideas of pure reason and the pure concepts of the understanding (the categories) as the greatest philosophical achievement of his first Critique; and it is because the self, subject or ego *(das Ich)* can be seen in relation both to pure reason (illegitimately) and to the categories (legitimately and necessarily), that its status in Kant's system is very complex and subtle. On the one hand, we read of

> a concept *[Begriff]* which was not included in the general list of transcendental concepts [i.e., categories] but which must yet be counted as belonging to that list, without, however, in the least altering it or declaring it defective. This is the concept, or if the term be preferred the judgement 'I think' *[das Urteil: Ich denke].* As is easily seen, this is the vehicle of all concepts, and therefore also of transcendental concepts, and so is always included in the conceiving of these latter, and is itself transcendental. But it can have no special designation, because it only serves to introduce all our thought, as belonging to consciousness.[38]

Kant speaks elsewhere of 'I' as a concept and as an expression *(Ausdruck);* and of the 'I think' as a proposition *(Satz),* representation *(Vorstellung)* and a thought (*Denken* – this latter in opposition to its being an intuition).[39] Whatever the terminology, the idea is that self-consciousness must necessarily accompany any act or moment of consciousness; and in this 'synthetic original unity of apperception I am conscious of myself not as I appear to myself, nor as I am in myself, but only that I am'.[40] I can know with absolute certainty only *that* I am. I can know myself, know *what* I am, to a greater or lesser degree, in terms of the empirically apparent person or self that I appear to myself to be; but I cannot know anything about *what* I am, in terms of my real self. Any attempt at such knowledge must fail, according to Kant, because it is based on

> the simple, and in itself completely empty representation *"I";* and we cannot even say that this is a concept, but only that it is a bare consciousness *[blosses Bewusstein]* which accompanies all concepts. Through this I or he or it (the thing) which thinks, nothing further is represented than a transcendental subject of the thoughts = X.[40A]

Thus, in at least verbal contradiction with the passages which speak of 'I' and 'I think' as a concept necessarily accompanying all the categories as their vehicle, on this view 'the I is not a concept, but only a designation of the object of inner sense in so far as we know it through no further predicate' since 'if the representation of apperception, the I, were a concept through which anything were thought it could also be used as predicate of other things or contain such predicates in itself. But it is nothing more than a feeling of existence *(Gefühl eines Daseins)* . . .'[41] The distinction between a knowable, empirical and therefore in some sense determined and un-free self, and an unknowable, transcendental, undetermined and free self was of the greatest importance for Kant's ethics; and indeed he considered the main point of his first critique to lie in its making possible a true understanding of ethics.[42] A passage from *Foundations of the Metaphysics of Morals* is worth citing at length, as it shows clearly what Kant's ethical view of the self was; and it was the alleged inadequacies of this ethical view which made Renouvier and Hamelin, influenced by Hegel, take a particular view of 'the category of personality' which they bequeathed to Durkheim and Mauss. For Kant the only way of assuring human freedom, in morality and rational thought, lay in the presupposition of the undetermined, thus free, but unknowable self. There is, he says,

> A distinction, however rough, between the *sensible world* and the *intelligible world,* the first of which can vary a great deal according to differences of sensibility in sundry observers, while the second, which is its ground, always remains the same. Even as regards himself – so far as man is acquainted with himself by inner sensation – he cannot claim to know what he is in himself *[wie er an sich selbst sei].* For since he does not, so to speak, make himself *[er sich selbst nicht gleichsam schafft],* and since he acquires his concept of self *[seinen Begriff]* not *a priori* but empirically, it is natural that even about himself he should get information through sense – that is, through inner sense – and consequently only through the mere appearance of his own nature and through the way his consciousness is affected. Yet beyond this character of himself as a subject made up, as it is, of mere appearances *[über diese aus lauter Erscheinungen zusammengesetzte Beschaffenheit seines eigenen Subjekts]* he must suppose there to be something else which is its ground – namely his Ego as this may be constituted in itself *[sein Ich, wie es an sich selbst beschaffen sein mag];* and thus as regards mere perception and the capacity for receiving sensations he must count himself as belonging to the *sensible* world, but as regards whatever there may be in him of pure activity *[reine Tätigkeit]* (whatever comes into consciousness, not through affection of the sense, but immediately) he must count himself as belonging to the *intellectual* world, of which, however, he knows nothing further.[43]

Thus for Kant, there can be differences in self-perception between individuals, according to their differences in 'sensibility'; and, perhaps, these differences in sensibility might vary systematically across cultures, such that each culture has its own concept of the person, or a pattern of concepts related to the person. But the Kantian self as a category, or rather, as the unknowable but necessary vehicle of all categories, was part of the 'intelligible' or 'intellectual' world *(die Verstandeswelt, die intellektuelle Welt)*, which 'always remains the same'.

III

Although Durkheim certainly knew Kant's philosophy directly, he is said to have 'mistrusted' Kantianism,[44] and it was in fact the neo-Kantian philosophy of Charles Renouvier from which he derived the epistemological basis for his sociology of knowledge. Renouvier was a figure of very great influence in French intellectual life in the latter half of the nineteenth century, as much in his political thought as in his philosophy. Certainly his influence on Durkheim was both political and epistemological. Durkheim wrote that 'if you want to mature your thought, devote yourself to the study of a great master; take a system apart, laying bare its innermost secrets. That is what I did and my educator was Renouvier'.[45] Furthermore, during his twenty-five years at the University of Bordeaux, he was greatly influenced by the Renouvierist philosopher Octave Hamelin, whom he cites as an authority in EF. Renouvier's general political influence on Durkheim lay in his overall espousal of bourgeois-liberal but social-democratic republicanism, his moral and political emphasis on the individual, and his assertion of 'two complementary bases of society: the sacredness of the individual and the fact of human solidarity'.[46] Both Renouvier and Hamelin constructed epistemological systems of categories; but the way in which they did so, and the way their epistemology supported their version of moral and political individualism, owed a great deal to Hegel. Renouvier's system made theoretical reason subordinate to practical reason; and the self or person as a moral agent was no longer an unknowable and presupposed ground, but the knowable concrete empirical individual. This emphasis was so strong in Renouvier that his system came also to be called 'Personalism'.[47]

The two main elements adopted by Renouvier from Hegel were just this emphasis on the concrete, embodied individual; and an historicist view of categories of thought, which allowed for change and development.

In Hegel's system, the immanent cosmic Spirit *(Geist)* comes gradually (and dialectically, through self-contradiction and self-transcendence) to self-knowledge or self-determination *(Selbstbestimmung)* through historical evolution. Categories of thought (*Kategorien*, or *Denkbestimmungen*, 'determinations of thought') are provisional and transient self-embodiments of *Geist*, and are instantiated in different *Volksgeister*, different historical communities, or more generally different cultures.[48] Since for

Hegel the ontological structure of reality is also the conceptual structure of logic, this vision can also be expressed as the progressive evolution to self-consciousness of the basic Concept *(Begriff);* this latter is a self-embodying subject which posits its own objects rather than a representation of a separate objective reality. Thus Hegel rejects Kant's distinction between the world of appearance, phenomena, and things-in-themselves, noumena; and also the distinction between the immanence in appearances of understanding and its categories, and the (illegitimate) transcendence of appearances by Reason. Indeed, he explicitly reverses the Kantian model, extolling Reason as a higher mode of thought than mere understanding, which stays at the level of ordinary experience, where things are divided and separate and no underlying unificatory pattern is detected. In a way which clearly shows his dependence on Kant as well as his disagreements with him, Hegel takes the 'I' or 'I think' as the necessary vehicle of all categories; for him, as Charles Taylor says,

> The best representation of the Concept in the furniture of the world is the 'I'. I may have particular concepts, but 'I' is the pure Concept itself, which as Concept has come into existence . . . for 'I', as Hegel explains, is a unity which is self-identical, and can abstract from all particular determination in order to concentrate on its self-identity. But at the same time, it is particularity, different from others, individual personality. The point is that the particular characteristics of the 'I' are not merely given, but belong to a being who is also capable of abstracting from them and making them over, who is free in the sense of having an identity which is beyond any of them. Hence these characteristics can be seen as affirmed by this universal self-identity. At the same time, while free from any of these characteristics, the 'I' is not free from having some; it cannot be without affirming some character or other, hence the universal must issue in the particular.[49]

In Hegel's own terms,

> Concept is not merely *soul [Seele]* but free subjective Concept that is for itself and therefore possesses *personality [die Persönlichkeit]* – the practical, objective Concept determined in and for itself which, as Person, is impenetrable atomic subjectivity *[der, als Person, undurchdringliche atome Subjektivität ist]* – but which, none the less, is not exclusive Individuality *[Einzelnheit]* but universality and cognition . . . As that with which we began was the universal, so the result is the individual, the concrete, the subject *[das Einzelne, Konkrete, Subjekt]*.[50]

Renouvier and Hamelin, for religious as well as other reasons, rejected what they saw as the 'pantheism' of this view[51]; but they fully accepted the transposition of the 'I' as ground of consciousness from Kant's transcendental unity of apperception to the embodied individual, and they saw the cultural recognition of this – in modern individualism – as the result of an historical process. Put more directly, for them the free, self-determining individual man of western democracies is both the culmination and perfection of the evolution of Man as a whole, and, the perfected expression of that universal structure of human nature and mind which Renouvier's philosophy thought to capture in its timeless essentials.

Most of the details of Renouvier's and Hamelin's systems of categories need not detain us.[52] They saw logic as a dialectically-interrelated network. The first of their categories is Relation itself, with the (Fichtean) sub-divisions of thesis, antithesis and synthesis. Relation, and Personality, the last of the categories, form a circle englobing the others. Relation is intrinsic to all the other categories, since within each category the dynamic movement of thesis, antithesis and synthesis provides both the means of historical development and the connecting link with other categories in the system.[53] Personality, subdivided into Self (*Soi* for Renouvier, *Moi* for Hamelin), Non-Self and Consciousness is similarly intrinsic to all other categories, for two reasons. Firstly, after Kant, consciousness is necessary to all categories, since 'it is present in them all, or rather all of them are present in it. It is only in it, in effect, that representations are given'.[54] Secondly, after Hegel, this consciousness is necessarily an embodied individual subject: for Renouvier, 'consciousness, or to use a perfectly synonymous term, the person, is the synthesis of self and non-self'.[55] For Hamelin, as for Hegel, the self-embodying subject is a *personnalité,* which is an 'active system' *(système agissant),* a 'concrete being' and 'the keystone' of the whole system.[56] Renouvier criticises Kant's view that the free self must exist only in the transcendental world (and thus tries explicitly to refute Kant's arguments concerning the illusions of transcendental reason),[57] arguing that this 'cripples' Kant's own morality of duty.[58] For Renouvier, the ground of all categories and the empirical moral agent – what he calls *la vraie personne*[59] – are the same:

> A person, in effect, is a completely original phenomenon. This individual, who is not only individuated *[individualisé]* because he is a single combination of all the determinations of space, time, quality, etc., but again because he makes himself *[il se fait lui-même]* by virtue of a free initiative; this individual so specially individual is not comparable to any other being. Persons appear as having rights and duties, and consequently as being *obliged* to certain rules in their mutual relations.[60]

By these means, then, Renouvierist philosophy used certain themes from Hegel's philosophy to transform Kant's unknowable transcendental self into the empirically knowable individual – specifically, indeed, the individual of modern liberal society. Confusingly for Renouvier, however, as for Durkheim and Mauss after him, Hegel also bequeathed a profound problem in relation to the historical evolution of these supposed truths. This is a version of a very familiar problem: the self-refutation of relativism and historicism. Philosophers differ as to how vicious is the circularity here, but the argument in simple terms is this: is the system which posits relativism itself only relatively true? If categorial frameworks are only true in relation to their time and place, is the categorial framework which recognises this only true for modern, western culture? There is an imbalance in Hegel between on the one hand his philosophy of history and politics, together with his account of the evolving conceptual self-realization of *Geist,* and on the other his Logic. In the former, he is content to admit that

> Every individual is a child of his time; so philosophy too is its own time apprehended in thoughts. It is just as absurd to fancy that a philosophy can transcend its contemporary world as it is to fancy that an individual can overleap his own age.[61]

That is, any philosophical system is an expression – temporary and transient – of a particular culture, a *Volksgeist,* at a particular time, and the categories of thought it describes or embodies are the categories of *just that* time and place. In his Logic, however, Hegel clearly regards his own system as a final and complete expression of the universally true nature of *Geist.*[62] Similarly, Renouvier's account of the categories of thought was historical and developmental, at least in aspiration, and he sought to avoid the 'disastrous conclusion' of Kantian timeless a priorism[63]; but at the same time, he sought to avoid also a Humean empiricism, in which the categories arise, in some sense contingently, from experience, and in which there could be a variety of category-systems depending on the selection from experience that happens to be made. As Hamelin explains,

> The categories are necessary phenomena in relation to our minds . . . They are necessary truths . . . In Renouvier's words, 'there are laws of the understanding, just as there are laws of nature, laws from which the understanding cannot free itself, which are the condition of its being used'.[64]

In Renouvier, as in Hegel, one part of the approach stresses change, development and historical specificity in categories of thought, while another seems to want to give a universally and necessarily true account of them. Similarly in Durkheim, one side of his thought stresses the uniqueness and modernity of certain conceptions of the person – the sacredness of persons, their individual rights and duties in a free democratic state – while another side derives an a priori and universal account of human personhood from the – universal and necessary – facts of biological and social co-existence.

IV

In EF, the 'category of personality' mentioned in the introductory remarks is dealt with in Book 2, Chapter 8, under the title 'The Notion of the Soul'. This account is essentially identical with that given in the 1914 piece 'The Dualism of Human Nature and its Social Conditions'.[65] The account is well known, and can be briefly summarised. The traditional image of man as *homo duplex,* as an inhabitant of two worlds, must – like all religious beliefs – be regarded as not illusory, but as embodying some reality. The reality here is that man is indeed composed of two parts or factors, but they are to be described in sociological rather than metaphysical terms.[66] One part or factor is the body, the biological individual, along with that 'class of states of consciousness' which has to do with sensory experience of and desire for the material world, for things particular to the individual,[67] and which is constituted by 'vulgar impressions arising from his daily relations with external things'.[68] This part or kind of consciousness is, in Durkheim's highly Comtean terms, egoistic and antisocial rather than impersonal, social and – in both cognitive and moral senses – altruistic.[69] The other part or factor of man is 'the soul'; that is, that part of consciousness which is both moral sense or conscience *(la conscience morale),* and at the same time conceptual awareness. 'The soul' is that which enables individuals (through the public, social medium of language) to rise above their mean and petty individual appetites to the higher life which is social and moral. It is *la conscience collective.* This movement from individual to social is also a move from animal to human; each individual consciousness does – or at least should – recognise that in rising to the level of humanity and human personality it is rising to the level of the social. The traditional idea of the individual soul is both a recognition and a misperception of society's indwelling in the human heart. The sacredness of the soul derives from the sacredness of society, and the idea of the soul's immortality derives from the continuing existence of society beyond the death of its individual members.

This account, parts of which can, as I have noted, be phrased in very modern, Wittgensteinian or even Popperian terms,[70] is importantly, for my present purposes, an account which, if true, is true universally. It arises from the necessary conditions of creatures who are human and therefore social, and is thus – for any given individual – a priori. Without this condition, one would not be human. Thus, Durkheim's account does provide something which might be a Kantian or (in his Logic) Hegelian category.[71] In Durkheim's treatment of the other 'categories' we find a similar account: given the nature of human sociability and its physical conditions, the other categories are universally and necessarily present. *Class* is derived from the experience of the human group as an organised collectivity, *space* from the fact of the group's occupying a territory, *time* from the 'rhythm of social life', *cause* from the idea of 'efficient force', itself a notion based on the force of the collectivity.[72] In none of this do we have that 'incessant mutability' of categories in different times and places, which Durkheim alleged invalidates a Kantian a priorism. What he has done is to show that 'the fundamental notions of the mind, the essential categories of thought are the product of social factors'[73] in the sense that these a priori forms of thought are necessarily connected with a priori forms of social life. When he does investigate change and 'mutability' in a category of thought – in his discussion of space for example – he produces an account not of the category of space itself changing with social conditions, but of the way in which space – once given as a category – is conceived to express a cosmology in correlation with the organisation of society.[74]

Durkheim does have an account of the notion of the person which does emphasise variety and historical change.[75] On this view, the notion of the person has become in modern times quite specific, as a product of specific social factors; and it is a notion which is central and inescapable in modern political and moral life. Through the division of labour, human individuals increasingly recognise and realise their own separate personalities, and this recognition of individuality has become culturally and morally central. Durkheim asserts, with approval, that the sacredness of persons, their individual rights and duties, has become the religion of modern times, a religion in which 'man is, at the same time, both believer and God'.[76] As has often been noted, he thus severs the link, often thought direct and obvious, between individualism as a methodological principle of explanation (to which he was entirely opposed) and individual liberty as a moral and political ideal (to which he was entirely committed). He thinks that these ideas and values have developed historically from Christianity, particularly in Protestantism and the Enlightenment. (In this volume Louis Dumont, a pupil of Mauss, continues this project of historical understanding.) It is of course just this view of the person, and just this account of its historical development, which Mauss espouses in his 1938 lecture. The person, Mauss says, has *become* a category, 'a fundamental form of thought and action' only in modern times. In Mauss's account, this historical process is described largely as an evolution in the history of ideas. Durkheim had offered an explanatory account of the social factors involved, with which Mauss would surely have been in broad agreement:

> As a consequence of a more advanced division of labour, each mind finds itself directed towards a different point of the horizon, reflects a different aspect of the world and, as a result, the contents of men's minds differ from one subject to another. One is thus gradually proceeding towards a state of affairs, now almost attained, in which the members of a single social group will no longer have anything in common other than their humanity, that is, the characteristics which constitute the human person in general. This idea of the human person, given different emphases in accordance with the diversity of national temperaments, is therefore the sole idea that survives, immutable and impersonal, above the changing tides of particular opinions; and the sentiments which it awakens are the only ones to be found in almost all hearts.[77]

Did Durkheim and Mauss regard the evolution of this concept of the person as the gradual unfolding of a truth, of a reality, of something which has *become* a category of the human mind in the general and non-relative sense? The answer seems characteristically ambiguous. Mauss claimed in 1921 that

> A category of thought is not less true because of the fact that it has appeared late in history. Quite the contrary. We are not far from thinking, as (do) Hegel and Hamelin, that the most fundamental ideas are in general those that are discovered last, (those) which the mind has taken longest to arrive at.[78]

In the 1938 piece, however, he alludes to the absence of the category 'throughout the Orient', and to the contemporary denial of individual freedom in western countries (presumably he was thinking of Nazi Germany) and fears that the 'delicate' category might disappear, claiming that 'it is formulated only for us, among us'.[79] Durkheim, as we saw, held that 'really and truly human thought . . . is the product of history'; and he includes in this 'human thought' rational and impersonal science, which 'sees things only in their permanent and essential aspects'.[80] On the other hand, in the article 'Individualism and the Intellectuals' he describes the 'individualist' notion of the sacredness of the person as (merely?) 'the doctrine that is currently necessary.'[81] This sort of phrase might suggest that as history moves on and brings changes in the future, the 'category' of the person embodied in modern individualism will also change, and perhaps disappear.

This ambiguity about the status of the contemporary notion of the person is compounded by the ambiguous relationship between this view and Durkheim's more general *homo duplex* account of the category of personality. Anthony Giddens has commented on this general bifurcation in Durkheim's thought, and has noted that it leads to conflicting assessments, particularly of the moral status of individualism.[82] On the general *homo duplex* view any concern with individual satisfactions is necessarily anti-social and immoral (in theory at least, for obviously the conflict between individual and social aims might on occasion be in practice minor or non-existent). This condemns utilitarianism, which Durkheim sees as positing the reality and value of individuals, who are pre-social, or at least not essentially social in their moral status. On the other hand, in his particular and historicist view of the person in modern times, the satisfaction of individually different desires and aspirations is a cardinal virtue, at least for us. Giddens thinks that 'Durkheim never managed adequately to reconcile these two strands of his thought'. Although he may never have done so in his published work, I think a reconciliation is possible: but it is one which drastically reduces the relativist implications of his sociology of knowledge, and reduces the force of his own claims about the mutability and capacity for development of categories of thought. The *homo duplex* view is a priori and universal, and can reasonably be taken as presenting a sociological account of the *origins* of the 'category' of the person. It answers the first of the three questions I posed in Part I of this chapter. This category is empirical, in that it arises from human experience; but in that it arises from the universal and necessary experience of the conjunction of a biologically individual body with an essentially collective consciousness, it presents a form of experience which is a priori for any individual. Like Kantian categories it defines (the individual's) humanity. This general form of experience cannot be said, accordingly, to vary cross-culturally or develop historically. The historicist account of the modern notion of the person – a notion which clearly arises at a specific point in human historical experience, and is capable of cross-cultural variation and development – thus becomes not an account of the development of a category of thought in itself, but an example of the way in which the general form of human experience described in the *homo duplex* view is given particular content.[83] We are not told in the abstract what role *la conscience collective* plays in human personhood, but rather how the contents of collective consciousness – collective representations

– have changed over time in such a way as to place specific value on certain areas of individual liberty. In Durkheim's words, 'the individual is a product of society [*sc.* is a particular representation in the modern collective consciousness] rather than its cause', since 'individualism is a social product like all moralities and all religions'.[84]

The title of Mauss's lecture speaks of the self and person as a *category* of thought; most often he speaks of them as *notions,* and occasionally as *ideas* or *concepts.* The word for 'self' is *moi;* on two occasions in his lecture he uses *soi.* He says that (due) to the development of the notions of *conscius* and *conscientia* in Latin, 'self-consciousness has become the attribute of the moral person' *(la conscience de soi est devenue l'apanage de la personne morale).* In showing how Christianity gave a metaphysical foundation to this moral-juridical *notion,* before it became a *category* in the last century and a half, he claims that this notion very gradually has 'become identified with self-knowledge and the psychological consciousness' *(la connaissance de soi . . . la conscience psychologique).* (Compare the person first as a 'rational individual substance' and only later 'what it is today, a consciousness and a category'.) Mauss explicitly equates these terms: 'the person = the self = consciousness – and is its primordial category'. According to him, Hume hesitated 'when faced with the notion of self as the basic category of consciousness', while 'Kant posed the question, but did not resolve it, whether the self, *das Ich,* is a category'. (This is, as we have seen, slightly inaccurate.) It was, finally, Fichte who turned 'individual consciousness, the sacred character of the human person' into 'the category of the self, the condition of consciousness and of science, of Pure Reason'. (It is difficult to assess how important Mauss's reference to Fichte is here; certainly Renouvier, whom I have argued to be the main influence on Durkheim's and Mauss's epistemology, acknowledged that his philosophy was derived from Kant through Hegel, in the way I have described.)

In the light of this development of ideas, Mauss's *prima facie* confused use of philosophical terminology becomes, I hope, somewhat less confusing. Ignoring Durkheim's *homo duplex* account, Mauss takes the historicist account of the rise of modern individualism and the sacredness of persons as the gradual unfolding of the category of self very much as did Renouvier and Hamelin. Although this philosophical heritage is crucial in understanding Mauss's terminology, N.J. Allen is surely right (in Chapter 2) to say that the notion of the person is important for Mauss sociologically because 'it is presupposed by the social and educational ideals of a liberal democratic state'. Mauss claims that his discussion is restricted to *droit et morale,* as Allen stresses; but I do not agree that his use of philosophical terminology is as clear, or at least clarifiable, as Allen alleges, and I think that substantial epistemological issues do depend on the terminology used and on what its connotations are thought to be.

Allen argues that Mauss's category of the person 'concerns essentially the concept of the individual presupposed by or expressed in a society's dominant value system or encompassing ideology'. The emphasis is on the public and institutional domain, to the relative exclusion of biological, metaphysical or psychological theories, and this category of the person is 'necessarily realised in some form, however indistinct, in any society worthy of the name'. Any society without the category would lack values and institutions and would be 'presumably pre-human'. Given this view, Allen seeks to distinguish (i) what 'the person' means in English, (ii) the nearest equivalent in other cultures, and (iii) 'what is common to both usages'. This latter is 'the deeper, more theoretical concept that gives the essay its unity' and it is this which 'has evolved from [tribal to modern societies] and will evolve further'. Now it is obviously true, as Mauss was one of the first to point out,[85] despite his own lack of fieldwork, that the practice of ethnography, as of intellectual history, requires a kind of conceptual negotiation, in which *our* concepts and *theirs* – Allen's (i) and (ii) – interact in a dialogue of observer and observed, to the mutual enrichment of both. But if this view of anthropology and the history of ideas as art (or craft) is to lead to anthropology or epistemology as science, as contributing to our knowledge of reality, then the presence of any concept, category or whatever common to all cultures or epochs – Allen's (iii) – is precisely the question here at issue, which cannot be begged by simply assuming it must exist. There seems to me no obvious reason for assuming that the presence of values and institutions necessarily expresses or presupposes any concept of the person. Ethnographic evidence suggests that many simpler cultures have no *expressed* concept of the person; their conceptual configurations seem to omit any relevant item. Even if we were to discover empirically that all societies did have some relevantly analogous conceptual item, this would not of itself show that they necessarily had to do so. The fact that no society lacks an 'X' does not prove that no society could ever lack an 'X'.[86] Presumably this last point is meant to be covered by Allen's suggestion that the common concept is 'presupposed by' and 'necessarily realised in' any system of values and institutions. But the problem then becomes how to characterise this universally presupposed and realised 'category', and what kind of relation social history (or historiography) might bear to it. The same ambiguity found in Durkheim and Mauss is here reproduced: if the category is necessary and universal, and so in a sense a priori, then in just this sense it cannot have a history. Of course particular conceptual 'realisations' of the category must have a social history, and I agree wholeheartedly with Allen when he says that in this sense philosophers (I would add, particularly English-language linguistic analysts) often display 'the characteristic error of non-sociologists who, unaware of the history and pre-history of the notions with which they operate, naively regard them as natural'. I think, however, that there is a correspondingly characteristic error of non-philosophical sociologists, exemplified by Mauss, which consists in removing philosophical terms from their context and placing them in a new sociological perspective, and then naively supposing that their epistemological value can be kept constant.

Mauss explains his concentration on *droit et morale* by differentiating his discussion from psychology (and linguistics). As Michael Carrithers shows in this volume, although he seems to restrict his field in this way, in fact by the end of the lecture he manages by 'amiable cunning' to reintroduce the psychic and philosophical self which he had seemed at first to set aside. I think this cunning – and more directly the philosophical heritage he preserved so piously in Durkheim's memory – deceived Mauss also, as it might his readers. He differentiates his subject from psychology and linguistics thus:

> In no way do I put forward the view that there has ever been a tribe, a language, in which the term 'I', 'me' *(je–moi)* . . . has never existed, or that it has not expressed something clearly represented . . . nor shall I speak to you of psychology any more than I shall of linguistics. I shall leave aside everything that relates to the 'self', the conscious personality as such. Let me merely say that it is plain, particularly to us, that there has never existed a human being who has not been aware *[n'ait eu le sens]* not only of his body, but also at the same time of his spiritual and physical individuality.

Thus, he claims, he treats not 'the sense of "self" ', *le sens du 'moi'*, but 'the notion, the concept that men in different epochs have made of it'; and he speaks of his lecture as a 'catalogue of the forms that the notion has assumed at various times and places'. What is universal, on this account, is the *sense* of self, the immediate 'here-and-now' consciousness expressed in human language in the first person singular. This can easily be seen in Durkheimian fashion as a 'social fact', if we accept the need to presuppose a social milieu with public and objective rules if human consciousness – cognitive and moral – is to be possible at all. This 'social origin' of the human *sense* of self can, like Durkheim's *homo duplex* view, be seen as categorial in a Kantian way: its origin is the (empirical) fact of society, but it is a priori for any given individual, and its essential authority over human thought derives from its being essential to the possibility of human thought at all. Different from this universal *sense* of self are Mauss's 'notions', which are necessarily particular to specific times and places, and which develop in history. N.J. Allen suggests that the relevant notions here are public and institutional ones; Michael Carrithers argues in this volume, rightly in my view, that there can be private and non-institutional notions – what he calls '*moi*-theories' – which are similarly elaborated differently in different milieux, and equally have a social history. Whether or not we wish to catalogue different varieties of Maussian 'notions' in this way, the fact remains that they are all – unlike his 'sense' of self – merely conceptual forms, which cannot be categories in the Kantian sense. Their authority, of whatever force, is contingent; it is quite possible to be human, to think in a human manner without any particular 'notions' of the person. If we wish to describe such notions – which might be overwhelmingly and unavoidably important in particular times and places – as 'categories' of thought, it can only be in that general, descriptive and non-epistemological manner to which I referred at the start of the chapter.

The question at issue here is not merely a terminological one – how is it best to use the word 'category'? This can be brought out by considering a standard criticism of Durkheim and Mauss's *Primitive Classification* – a work with many similarities to Mauss's 1938 lecture – and the recent defence of it by David Bloor.[87] The criticism is that Durkheim and Mauss could not show that human classification of nature and things, in logical and linguistic classes, arises from the social experience of organised human groups – in their words that 'the classification of things reproduces the classification of men' – for the simple reason that any organisation or classification of men presupposes the ability to classify. This circular argument, so it is held, confuses the *capacities* of the mind with its *contents:* one must first have the capacity to organise experience spatially, for example, before one can have any particular notions about what space is (Euclidean ones, for example, which Kant himself thought to be of universal application).

The reply to this criticism depends on distinguishing between the pragmatic capacity to draw those 'rudimentary distinctions in the flux of experience'[88] which must be assigned even to animals, and the conceptually and linguistically represented classifications which form part of human knowledge- and belief-systems. In *Primitive Classification* the former are referred to as 'technological classifications', which relate to the negotiation of immediate experience of the environment – 'this is to the right, that to the left, that is past, this is present'[89] – while the latter are part of the non-immediate, objective and necessarily public domain of human conceptual thought. In EF, Durkheim argues that 'the feeling of resemblances is one thing, and the idea of class is another', and distinguishes, for example, between animals' ability to orient themselves in space – 'to find the road which leads to places with which they are familiar' – and that 'self-conscious organisation' which human social and conceptual classifications impose on experience.[90] The non-conceptual, pragmatic or 'technological' classifications are properties of any individual organism, whereas conceptual classifications are necessarily 'collective representations'. Bloor, using modern arguments for the public nature of conceptual systems, argues that what Durkheim and Mauss sought to explain was the origin and maintenance of these public systems, and that it is the regular classifications made in these conceptual 'networks' to which we are directed by the term 'categories'. Bloor claims that

> Durkheim's use [of the word 'category'] and my gloss upon it correspond closely to the meaning of 'category' as it occurs in present-day analytical philosophy. Here it refers to any classification that is deemed so important that a violation of it must be specially sanctioned . . .[91]

However, it is crucial in assessing the epistemology of Durkheim and Mauss to see that the philosophical import of the word 'category' has undergone a vital change from Kantian to modern. (It may be, indeed, that Mauss himself had, even before his uncle's death, a more modern and non-Kantian view of what a 'category' is, and that it was this unexpressed difference of emphasis between his and Durkheim's view which was productive of much of the epistemological ambiguity of the *Année Sociologique*'s work.)

In the modern use of the term 'category', the authority and necessity of such forms of thought is quite different from that in Kant. Now, rather than the categories being necessary to human thought a priori, and having authority over individual minds because without them there would be no human mind, any particular forms of thought, any 'categories', have a quite contingent authority, which arises in and from the facts of human culture and history. The authority which such particular forms of thought might have can be the passive 'obviousness' of common sense and everyday culture (this is most seen, perhaps, in traditional pre-scientific cultures, but not only there); or it can be the authority which is maintained by, and for, vested economic, political, religious or other interests. The unmasking of these forms of cultural authority is indeed a vital task for the sociology of knowledge. But it is not the Kantian task, and not, I think, what Durkheim thought he was doing (though it may arguably be the best way of developing his thought).

If Bloor is right about Durkheim's use of the term 'categories', then we must discard, or seriously revise, our notion of the 'sociological Kantianism' of Durkheimian sociology. It is clear that Durkheim, and Mauss after him, had not separated out the various implications and connotations of their use of philosophical terminology. Once we have done so, we cannot then simply enlist their work, as does Bloor, in support of a relativist epistemology. We need other, and separate arguments, and ones which do not repeat their confusions.

VI

I think that some progress can be made in elucidating these issues, and in assessing Mauss's contribution to our understanding of the notions of self and person, by speaking not only of human and animal non-conceptual classificatory capacities and human conceptual representations, but also of human *predicaments* (I leave aside the issue of animal predicaments). To clarify this a little, let us look at these three areas in terms of the questions I raised in Part I: (i) are categories of thought empirical or a priori in origin; (ii) can they vary cross-culturally; and (iii) can they develop historically?

In the case of non-conceptual classificatory abilities, the answers seem to be (i) that for individual members of a species they are given a priori, as defining its nature as a particular organism. Over long periods of evolutionary time, the kind and nature of these capacities might also arise from experience – but from the experience of the species as a whole (see [iii]). (ii) They can vary across species (although there might be limitations on our imaginative capacity to make sense of this).[92] There may perhaps be some sub-set of such capacities which we would want to regard as necessary, as defining what it is to be an organism in the relevant sense. (iii) As in (i) above, these capacities might develop historically, as the species as a whole evolves through adaptation to its environment. For an individual organism, these capacities might be regarded as categorial in Kant's sense, as defining the possibility and parameters of experience. Some sub-set necessary to all organisms, if such could be found, might be regarded as timelessly a priori in the fullest Kantian sense.

In the case of conceptual classifications, 'categories' in the non-Kantian or modern sense used by Bloor's version of Durkheimianism, the answers seem to be that (i) they are obviously empirical in origin, whether developed by whole societies or, as in the case of scientific or political theories, by sub-groups (conceivably even individuals) within societies. (ii) They are obviously variable cross-culturally and (iii) capable of historical change and development. There seems, on this view, no reason to assume that any such classifications need to be presupposed and hence universal. However much, and for whatever reasons, the influence of these conceptual 'networks' might in practice be authoritative, it cannot be the case that they can play the role assigned to them by Kant, or by Durkheim in his Kantian manner – it will always be possible in principle to escape, ignore or change them without ceasing to be human. As Bloor notes, Durkheim equivocates on the kind of authoritativeness involved, by saying that if someone 'rids himself of these fundamental notions', he is no longer *considered* human, and that we *have the impression* that abandoning them is to cease to think in a truly human way.[93] It is arguable whether any societies, however primitive, have ever had quite such a rigid and inescapable unanimity;[94] but the theoretical point is separate and crucial. If these categories define what it is to be human only in the metaphorical sense of being more or less essential to continuing and successful membership of a particular group, the whole force of their Kantian necessity is lost when thus transposed into the intra-cultural domain.

A human predicament, as I wish to define it, need be conceived neither in terms of (individual) psychological capacities nor in terms of socially constructed conceptual representations, but as a given situation or situations arising from the interaction of the human biological constitution with its geophysical and technological (and perhaps other) circumstances. Doing this may enable us, for certain purposes only, to bypass the philosophical problems involved in construing translation from one conceptual scheme and language into another.[95] As Nicholas Rescher has recently put it:

> By now some four thousand natural languages have evolved on the planet, and the remarkable thing about them is not so much that it is difficult for the speakers of one language to penetrate the thought-framework of another, but that it is *possible* to do so. And this is so, in the final analysis, not because their inherent conceptual schemes are identical, but because their users, endowed with a common biological heritage, face the same sorts of problems in making their way in the world.[96]

It may be that, as Robin Horton has recently argued, technological, economic and social changes might condition the rise of predicaments or problems which are not universal, but specific to particular times and places[97]; but I think it will also prove possible to make out some predicaments to be universal and necessary in the required rationalist, or Kantian sense – I shall try to sketch out such a 'predicament' of personhood in a moment.

In general, how does the conception of human predicaments answer the three questions about categories I have posed? If we assume, as I think we can, that there is a set of basic predicaments which define what it is to be human, then they will neither vary cross-culturally nor develop historically. As to their origin, we may claim, with Durkheim, that in so far as some of them are inextricably linked with the existence of society (as, for instance, personhood) they may be said to arise from the empirical fact of society, but to be given in this way a priori to individuals. In so far as some predicaments may be at the mercy of a variety of non-universal, perhaps historical factors, they may be said (i) to originate empirically, (ii) to vary cross-culturally (take, for instance the varying ways in which the geophysical environment imposes limits on human activity in different places), and (iii) to develop historically. For the last, take even so basic a predicament as the reproductive process. The facts of biology might reasonably be taken to impose some necessary features on human reproduction, which in turn might generate specific constraints on logically possible kinship relations. But even here, technological changes in biochemistry – notably in test tubes – might introduce novelty even here. Similarly, the use of speech for human communication, mutual identification and cooperation could perhaps also be construed as a basic predicament. But again, technological changes – in the past the transition from oral to written culture, in the future possible transformations of information technology – might cause 'categorial changes' in language-using human organisms. If these sorts of technological change can plausibly be seen to introduce changes in basic predicaments – and, by occurring differentially in different cultures, cross-cultural variation as well – we should beware the too-easy identification of bio-social universals. If there were such changes, however, they would be available not to individuals, but – like evolutionary changes in the non-conceptual capacities of a species – only to collectivities.

Having sounded a note of caution, let me try to sketch out a universal and necessary predicament of personhood. It has, I think, two necessary aspects:

1. The body is a necessary but not sufficient condition of personhood. Personhood must be completed by some psychological identity, the possibility of which essentially depends on social relations. In logi-

cal terminology persons are physical particulars but psychological *relata*.

2. No specific psychological/social completion of physical identity can be regarded as necessary. (Although perhaps certain kinds of radical psychological disunity or discontinuity might be seen as endangering even physical continuity.)

To use the philosophical terminology of Kant and Hegel: Kant's Transcendental Unity of Apperception is the body, or rather the fact that connecting experiences as part of one consciousness requires their being related to a spatio-temporally concrete and continuous body.[98] Hegel's 'I', which can 'abstract from all particular determination' (by ignoring spatio-temporal location and concentrating on the mere fact of subjectivity) but also must be 'particularity, different from others, individual personality' is then simply the necessarily individuated 'here-and-now', of consciousness (rendered in language by 'I') necessarily associated with the body, which does the individuating. Further, if personhood consists in the (universal) fact of a body needing psychological and social 'completion', it will be necessarily the case, as Hegel saw, that any completed realisation of personhood will be particular, dependent on the – contingent – conditions of a specific time and place.[99]

If we see the 'completion' of personhood in human psychology, language and consciousness as necessarily taking place in a social milieu, we can preserve the one sense in which Durkheim and Mauss retained a Kantian notion of categories: Durkheim's *homo duplex* account, and Mauss's 'sense of self', which is universal and always 'clearly represented', both required a social milieu, but as an a priori condition. So too will my account of personhood as a predicament; and for that reason, it might be regarded as a categorial predicament.[100]

Other contributions to this volume can help in expanding this approach. If some social completion of identity is a necessary part of personhood, but no particular social identity is in itself necessary, then there will always be at least a potential gap between private consciousness and public character. Michael Carrithers demonstrates how this privacy or innerness, as an individual relationship to the natural and (more arguably) spiritual cosmos, has been elaborated in the 'moi-theories' of the literate cultures of India at the time of the Buddha, and Germany in the nineteenth century. Mark Elvin shows how in China the tension between views which stress individual character and experience, and those which emphasise social status and duties, has been a constant source of debate for nearly 3,000 years; while Alexis Sanderson shows how the extraordinarily rich and complex intellectual tradition of Kashmir has explicitly formulated the difference between metaphysical and social identity, and has produced systematic accounts of the relationship between the two as forms of consciousness. Even in the relatively unsophisticated oral cultures of Africa, Godrey Lienhardt reminds us, the distinction between private and public is well-recognised, as is its moral significance. Jean La Fontaine explores the relationship between biological *individuals* and social *persons,* and shows how individuals, howsoever incorporated into or debarred from those systems of institutionalised authority which confer, and are embodied in, social personhood, must necessarily also be capable of certain relations – notably of power and practical influence – which derive from their individual character. In a simple and common case (which Mauss seems to take as paradigmatic) where the social *personae* of a tribe, and the concomitant statuses and powers, are restricted to (a possibly finite set of) male adults, then there will be many ways in which the real human relationships between persons (*qua* biological individuals, child or adult, male or female) will be wider than the narrower sphere of relations between *personae,* and the moral and psychological vocabulary of any given group will reflect this.

Charles Taylor and Martin Hollis offer philosophical – and universally applicable – accounts of how the 'body plus . . .' predicament affects our view of the place of language and role-playing in the notion of personhood. In Taylor's case, specifically human consciousness and agency are differentiated from those of animals and machines by the presence of language, which creates specifically human significances in articulated self-consciousness. But language is also the disclosure of a 'public space', in the moral and psychological as well as physical sense. This public space is the locus of a great many 'human significances' – shame, for example – which cannot be reduced to the 'vital and sentient'. Thus, 'I become a person and remain one only as an interlocutor'. The fundamental insight here seems very similar to, if not identical with, Durkheim's view of an individual body coming to human, and therefore social consciousness in the moral and conceptual space of the collectivity.

Martin Hollis argues that we can only make sense of the notion of a social role if we distinguish between role and role-player, since roles can always be played well or badly, and so 'the distinction between man and office [is] built into the role itself'. In a phrase he has used elsewhere, Hollis suggests that roles both constrain and enable self-expression. They constrain because they particularise – even where, as with Antigone, the particularisation involves a choice between two conflicting roles – but they also enable, for without *some* role the notion of self-expression is empty. It would be far too simplistic to see the body as the role-player, and social identity (or personhood) as the role(s). Bodies, on their own and (logically) previous to social identity cannot be said to be capable of *acting*. It is only human beings, already in some role or set of roles, who can be said to be *agents* in the relevant sense. But neither should we search for some intrinsically psychological (or worse, spiritual) individual to be the role-player. Psychological individuals, on their own and (logically) previous to their embodiment, cannot be said to exist, leave alone be capable of acting. It is, rather, the predicament of 'body plus . . .' which creates the distance between role and role-player (perhaps better, role-playing), and which generates Hollis's 'puzzle' about self and role. Of course, the solution of this, and many other puzzles in this area, still lies before us as a task; and in doing it, however stimulated and enlightened by Mauss's lecture we may be (and should be), we must learn to distinguish more clearly than he does between a properly philosophical epistemology and a sociologically-informed history of ideas. It is precisely the confusion of these two areas which his use of the term 'category of thought' achieves; and which I have tried to help dispel.

Notes

I should like to thank Nick Allen, Claude Grangier and Steven Lukes for helpful comments on an earlier draft of this paper.

1. EF, pp. 12–13; translation (1915), p.9. (English versions are emended where necessary.)
2. Concepts and Society, in Wilson (1970), pp.22–3.
3. *Web of Belief* was also the title of a work by Quine and Ullian (1970). Quine argues on purely philosophical grounds for a form of relativism, although the book in question is intended explicitly as 'a study of rational belief'.
4. Understanding a Primitive Society, in Wilson (1970), p.90, quoting Evans-Pritchard (1937), p.194.
5. Many commentators have noted the sometimes surprising degree to which the *Année Sociologique* writers lapsed from the usual scholarly standards of reference, citing of evidence, and the like.

   Aristotle's categories were: substance, quantity, quality, relation, time, place, posture, state, action, passion.
6. 06 I 28–9. (For the method of referring to Mauss's work, see N.J. Allen, Chapter 2, Note 1, this volume.)
7. SA 309.
8. *Critique of Pure Reason* A81/B107 (Kemp Smith's translation).
9. *Critique of Pure Reason* A79/B105. Kant's categories are: *Of Quantity:* unity, plurality, totality. *Of Quality:* reality, negation, limitation. *Of Relation:* of inherence and subsistence, of causality and dependence, of community (reciprocity between agent and

patient). *Of Modality:* possibility–impossibility, existence–non-existence, necessity–contingency.

10. EF, pp. 12–5; translation, p.9.
11. EF, p. 25; translation, p.18.
12. A phrase taken from Körner's book of that name. In this work Körner himself does not try to settle the issue of whether there is 'only one true, correct, or wholly adequate categorial framework' (Körner [70], p.10).
13. EF, pp. 24–5; translation, pp.17–18.
14. Durkheim (55), p. 149. He agrees with pragmatism that this is a fact to be explained, but differs in his explanation of it.
15. Cited in Lukes (73), p. 82. The second quotation is from Comte.
16. Compare Lukes (77), Ch. 4 on Durkheim's concept of *anomie.*
17. EF, p. 24; translation, p.17.
18. Lukes (73), pp. 338–9 and notes.
19. EF, p. 18; translation, p. 13. On Hamelin, see pp. 58–62.
20. EF, p. 23; translation, p. 17.
21. For example by Gellner (64), pp. 183–4, and in Wilson (70), p.22; and by Lukes (73), pp. 436–7.
22. EF, p. 622; translation p. 435.
23. EF, p. 619; translation, p. 433. Mauss makes some very incisive remarks about the lack of fit between 'the categories of collective thought [and] the categories of language', Mauss (23) in Hymes (ed.) (64). See N.J. Allen in this volume.
24. 06 I 37. He is attacking Wundt's *Völkerpsychologie.* See p. 53 and note 31.
25. SA 309–10.
26. 06 I 29.
27. They would, I think, disagree with the pragmatist C.I. Lewis, who argued that 'categories and concepts do not literally change; they are simply given up and replaced by new ones . . . Any contradiction between the old truth and the new is *verbal* only, because [e.g.] the old word "disease" has a new meaning [in the change from description in terms of 'disease entities' to one in terms of 'adjectival states of the organism induced by changed conditions such as bacteria']. The old word is retained but the old concept is discarded as a poor intellectual instrument and replaced by a better one'. (*Mind and the World Order,* pp. 268–9 apud Rescher [82], p. 271, n. 14.)
28. EF, p. 21; translation, p. 15.
29. EF, p. 27; translation, p. 19.
30. SA 309.
31. 08 II 225–6.
32. 03 II 15 and 82 (translation Durkheim and Mauss [63], pp. 5 and 81, respectively).
33. EF, pp. 634–5; translation p. 444–5. The English version omits the sentence 'That is . . . is universalised'. See also his remarks on the historical evolution of Greek and Roman religion, Durkheim (53), p. 31.
34. Preface to the first edition of the *Critique of Pure Reason* (hereafter CPR), p. xiv. On Kant, Hegel, and other writers of the period, see P. Gardiner (1981).
35. CPR A19–20/B33–4. Italics in original.
36. In Kant, space and time are pure forms of intuition rather than categories for the following sorts of reason: they are not general concepts, admitting of a plurality of instances, like the concept blue being instantiated in various blue things, but are necessarily dimensions of a single and directly experiencable reality. We experience objects as extended *in* space and time, in a literal sense; whereas in the case of categories, causation for instance, we do not directly and literally experience one object or event causing another.

Durkheim follows Hamelin in arguing that space and time are categories, on the rather vague grounds that 'there is no difference between the role played by these ideas in intellectual life' and that played by categories like cause. (EF, p. 13 n. 1; translation, p. 9, n. 1).

37. CPR A327/B383.
38. CPR A341–2/B399–400.
39. 'I' as *concept/expression,* CPR A341–2/B399–400; 'I think' as *proposition,* A348/B406; as *representation,* B131; as *thought,* B157.
40. CPR. B157.

40A. CPR A346/B404.

41. *Prolegomena to Any Future Metaphysics,* p. 46 and footnote. (Translation, Gray-Lucas [53], p. 98). When Kant speaks here of categories as predicates, it should be remembered that he considered categories not only to be 'forms of the mind' in a psychological sense, but also, like Aristotle, as basic predicates in a more objectivist epistemological manner.
42. See, for example, his remarks in the introduction to the second edition, B xxv, and the discussion of the freedom of the soul, B xxvii–xxviii.
43. *Foundations of the Metaphysics of Morals,* p. 106. (Translation, Paton [48], pp. 111–12.) Italics in original.
44. Cited in Lukes (73), p. 54 n. 48; and cp. ibid, pp. 435–6.
45. Cited in Lukes (73), p. 54.
46. Soltau (31), p. 307.
47. Renouvier (03).
48. Taylor (75), pp. 380*f.*
49. Taylor (75), pp. 298–9.
50. *Hegel's Science of Logic,* Book 3, Section 3, Chapter 3. (Translation adapted from Miller [69], pp. 824,837.)
51. See Hamelin (07), pp. 32–4, and cp. Renouvier on Fichte's pantheism, Renouvier (27), p. 214. On Renouvier's religious attitudes see Soltau (31), pp. 311–12, and Scott (51), pp. 57,75.
52. Their schemes are as follows (Renouvier's is taken from Hamelin [27], p. 110; Hamelin's is adapted from chapter headings in Hamelin [07]).

RENOUVIER

Categories relation	*Thesis distinction*	*Antithesis identification*	*Synthesis determination*
Number	Unity	Plurality	Totality
Position	Point (limit)	Space (interval)	Extension
Succession	Instant (limit)	Time (interval)	Duration
Quality	Difference	Class (genre)	Species
Becoming	Relation	Non-relation	Change
Causality	Act	Power	Force
Finality	State	Tendency	Passion
Personality	Self (*Soi*)	Non-self	Consciousness

HAMELIN

Relation	Thesis	Antithesis	Synthesis
Number	Unity	Plurality	Totality
Time	Instant	Space of Time	Duration

Categories relation	*Thesis distinction*	*Antithesis identification*	*Synthesis determination*
Space	Point	Distance	Line
Movement	Abode	Displacement	Conveyance
Quality	Positive	Negative	Particular
Alteration	Persistence	Change of nature	Transformation (of Quality)
Specification	Class	Difference	Species
Causality	Cause	Effect	Action
Finality	End	Means	System
Personality	Self (*Moi*)	Non-self	Consciousness

53. Hamelin (07), pp. 31–2; (27), p. 112; Renouvier (03) p. v.
54. Hamelin (27), p. 158.
55. Cited by Hamelin (27), p. 159.
56. Hamelin (07), p. 326. In the same work, however, he rejects Hegel's 'pantheism'. He also rejects a doctrine which must be taken to be Durkheim's:

    'Certain sociologists hold, if we are not mistaken, that there is, apart from individual consciousnesses, a social consciousness; that nevertheless this consciousness must not be postulated apart from individual consciousnesses; that it has each of these consciousnesses as its support'.

    In this view, however, 'individuality vanishing with consciousness and the freedom which is inseparable from it', we are again led to pantheism; and so Hamelin prefers theism, and an irreducibly real plurality of individual consciousnesses.
57. Renouvier (06), pp. 229*ff*.
58. Renouvier (03), pp. iv–vi.
59. Renouvier (03), pp. iv–vi.
60. Hamelin (27), p. 160.
61. *Hegel's Philosophy of Right*, translation, Knox (52), p. 11. Compare the remark at the end of his *Philosophy of History*, 'that is as far as consciousness has reached'. (Cited in Mure [50], p. 324.)
62. See Mure (50), pp. 327–8, and Taylor (75), pp. 131, 218–29, 391.
63. Hamelin (27), p. 100.
64. Hamelin (27), pp. 89, 95.
65. Translated in Wolff (60), pp. 325*ff*.
66. Durkheim was, ontologically, a psycho-physical dualist. Indeed, he based the irreducibility of society to its individual component members explicitly on an analogy with the irreducibility of the mind to the brain. See Durkheim (53), Ch. 1.
67. In Wolff (60), p. 327.
68. EF, p. 376; translation, p. 263.
69. Compare his remarks in 1913, cited in Durkheim, *Textes*, vol. II, pp. 30–1.
70. See Note 21; and Bloor (74) and (82), p. 295 n. 80, for the similarity between Durkheim's view of collective consciousness and representations, and Popper's World 3 of objective knowledge.
71. There are also some rather striking parallels between Durkheim's and Hegel's thought which have not, I think, been adequately noticed. Just as for Hegel, the universal *Geist* is not a separate, transcendent reality but is immanent in the process of its own self-realization through empirically individual embodiments, so for Durkheim the 'soul' of society, its sacred 'spiritual principle' can only be a reality through its instantiation in

empirically, biologically individual beings (e.g., EF, pp. 317, 495–6; translation, pp. 221, 347, and compare Hamelin's remarks cited in Note 56 above). Equally, and ambiguously, just as for Hegel, *Geist* is embodied differently not in different individual beings but in different cultures or collectivities, *Volksgeister,* so for Durkheim in his more historicist moments, the notion of Society is necessarily instantiated in different societies (see, for example, his remarks on Comte cited in the text and Note 15).

72. See, for example, the summary in EF, pp. 627–8, translation, pp. 439–40. Individual categories are treated at greater length in the main body of the work.
73. EF, p. 206, translation, p. 145.
74. EF, pp. 15–17, translation, pp. 11–2, and Durkheim and Mauss (03) passim.
75. It is most clearly expressed in his article 'Individualism and the Intellectuals', translated and discussed by Lukes (69).
76. Lukes (69), p. 22.
77. Lukes (69), p. 26. See Durkheim (33), *The Division of Labour in Society,* translation, pp. 402*ff.* N.J. Allen points out (this volume, Chapter 2) that Mauss's stress on primitive heterogeneity as opposed to the modern homogeneity of persons complicates Durkheim's simple distinction between mechanical and organic solidarity.
78. 21 II 124; cf. N.J. Allen, this volume, Chapter 2.
79. This volume, Mauss's essay. Given what the First World War did to the *Année Sociologique* group, the events of the 1930s in Germany and elsewhere must have been an intolerable strain on Mauss's nerves – he was, of course, Jewish – and can plausibly be connected with his mental breakdown, which occurred at the start of the War.
80. EF, pp. 633–5, translation, pp. 444–5, cited in part earlier and in Note 33.
81. Lukes (69), p. 26. See also the remarks from 'Pragmatism and Sociology', at Note 14.
82. Giddens (1977), Chapter 8. Quotation in text from p. 286.
83. Compare Tiryakian (62), pp. 51–2.
84. Lukes (69), p. 28 and Note 1.
85. See Dumont (72).
86. On this point, see Martin Hollis in Hollis and Lukes (82), p. 84.
87. Bloor (82), especially pp. 293–6. He is answering criticisms made, for example, by Needham in the Introduction (p. xxvi–xxix) to Durkheim and Mauss (63). Cp. Lukes (69), pp. 447–8.
88. Bloor (82), p.295, adapting a phrase, and an argument, of Durkheim and Mauss (03) (in the translation [63] p. 7).
89. Durkheim and Mauss (03), pp. 81 n. 1 and p. 7, respectively.
90. EF, pp. 208, 632, translation, pp. 147, 443, respectively. (Also see EF, p. 15 n. 1, translation, p. 11, on 'the difference which exists between the group of sensations and images which serve to locate us in time, and the category of time'.)
91. Bloor (82), p. 294 n. 74.
92. See Thomas Nagel (79) on 'What is it like to be a bat' (Chapter 12).
93. Bloor (82), p. 294 n. 74, referring to EF, p. 24, translation, p. 17.
94. See, for example, Robin Horton in Hollis and Lukes (82), pp. 222*ff.*
95. As addressed influentially by Donald Davidson. See, for example, his paper, and David Lewis's reply, in *Synthese* (1974), vol. 27, pp. 309–23 and 331–44, respectively.
96. Rescher (82), p.37. Italics in original.
97. In Hollis and Lukes (82), pp. 201*ff.*
98. See, for instance, Bernard Williams (78), pp. 95–100.
99. I mention Kant and Hegel here because of their importance to Durkheim and Mauss. More generally, this view of the predicament of personhood might be seen as a development of Strawson's view, following Robin Horton's advice (in Hollis and Lukes [82] p.233) to avoid 'the Teutonic mists' and return to 'the clearer air of home'. See also his use of Strawson in Brown (ed.) (79), pp. 197*ff.*

100. In this sense I would agree with Martin Hollis, in Brown (79), pp. 229*ff*, against Robin Horton, that this kind of assertion is not an empirical hypothesis, but an a priori question.

Bibliography

Bloor, D. 1974. Popper's Mystification of Scientific Knowledge, in *Science Studies*, vol. 4.

(1982) Durkheim and Mauss Revisited: Classification and the Sociology of Knowledge, in *Studies in History and Philosophy of Science*, vol. 13, no. 4.

Brown, S.C., ed. 1979. *Philosophical Disputes in the Social Sciences*, Brighton.

Dumont, L. 1972. La Science en devenir, in *L'Arc*, vol. 48.

Durkheim, E. 1912. *Les Formes Elementaires de la Vie Religieuse*, 6th edition. Presses Universitaires de France, 1968. English translation by J. Swain, 1915, London.

1933. *The Division of Labour in Society*, translated by G. Simpson. New York.

1953. *Sociology and Philosophy*, translated by D.F. Pocock. New York.

1955. *Pragmatisme et Sociologie*. Paris.

1975. *Textes* (3 volumes). Paris.

and Mauss, M. 1963, originally 1903. Translated by R. Needham. *Primitive Classification*. London.

Evans-Pritchard, E.P. 1937. *Witchcraft, Oracles and Magic among the Azande*. Oxford.

Gardiner, P. 1981. German Philosophy and the rise of relativism, in *Monist*, vol. 64, (2).

Gellner, E.A. 1964. *Thought and Change*. London.

Giddens, A. 1977. *Studies in Social and Political Theory*. London.

Hamelin, O. 1907. *Essai sur les éléments principaux de la Representation*. Paris

1927. *Le Système de Renouvier*. Paris.

Hollis, M. and Lukes, S. 1982. *Rationality and Relativism*. Oxford.

Hymes, D.H., ed. 1964. *Language in Culture and Society*. New York.

Kant, I., ed. 1933. *Critique of Pure Reason*, 2nd ed., translated by N. Kemp Smith. London.

1948. *The Moral Law*, translated by H. Paton. London.

1953. *Prologomen to any future Metaphysics*, translated by P. Gray-Lucas. Manchester.

Knox, T.M. 1952. *Hegel's Philosophy of Right*. Oxford.

Körner, S. 1970. *Categorial Frameworks*. Oxford.

Lukes, S. 1973. *Emile Durkheim*. London.

1977. *Essays in Social Theory*. London.

and Lukes, J. 1969. Durkheim's 'Individualism and the Intellectuals', in *Political Studies*, vol. 17.

Mauss, M. 1968–9. *Oeuvres* (présentation de V. Karady). Paris.

1950. *Sociologie et Anthropologie*. Paris.

Miller, A.V. 1960. *Hegel's Science of Logic*. London.

Mure, G.R.G. 1950. *A Study of Hegel's Logic*. Oxford.

Nagel, T. 1979. *Mortal Questions*. Cambridge.

Quine, W.V.O. and Ullian, J.S. 1970. *The Web of Belief*. New York.

Renouvier, C. 1903. *Le Personnalisme*. Paris.
1906. *Critique de la Doctrine de Kant* (Paris).
1927. *Les Dilemmes de la Metaphysique Pure* (Paris).
Rescher, N. 1982. *Empirical Inquiry*. London.
Scott, J. 1951. *Republican Ideas and the Liberal Tradition in France 1870–1914*. New York.
Soltau, R. 1931. *French Political Thought in the Nineteenth Century*. London.
Taylor, C. 1975. *Hegel*. Cambridge.
Tiryakian, E.A. 1962. *Existentialism and Sociologism*. New Jersey.
Williams, B. 1978. *Descartes*. London.
Wilson, B.R., ed. 1970. *Rationality*. Oxford.
Wolff, K.H., ed. 1960. *Emile Durkheim 1858–1917*. Ohio.

4

Marcel Mauss and the quest for the person in Greek biography and autobiography

A. Momigliano

I

One of the most obvious features in the analysis of the idea of the person by Marcel Mauss is that it leaves out the classical Greeks almost entirely. He introduces Greek philosophy only in its late stage as a factor in the interiorization of the Roman notion of *persona*. The decisive moment in the creation of this notion is for him the transition which happens in Rome from *persona* as mask to *persona* as a juridical notion.

Though Mauss adroitly uses a few texts which seem to associate the Roman *cognomen* with the *imagines maiorum,* I very much doubt whether these survivals (if that is what they are) of archaic rituals about the dead can be compared in importance with the role played by Greek historiography, and especially biography, in developing the idea of the person. This role was of course known to the Romans at least from the middle of the third century B.C. onwards.[1]

What seems to me interesting in the historiographical approach of the Greeks is the effort to develop the description of the person on the basis of evidence. The person was to the Greek historians and biographers not so much a datum or an entity as an approximation to be reached by using the available evidence. The person is defined, as far as possible, by reliable evidence. If a letter of Brutus is not authentic, essential details about his relation to his wife will have to be modified (Plutarch, *Brutus* 53,7).

It is unnecessary to add that if Mauss did not pursue the connection between biography and the theory of the person, classical scholars and students of Greek philosophy did. But it is not impossible that the results they reached confirmed Mauss in his decision, in which he was encouraged by the works of L. Schnorr von Carolsfeld and S. Schlossmann, to place the emphasis on the Roman juridical notion of *persona*.[2] About ninety years ago Ivo Bruns, who had Burckhardt's study of the individual in the Renaissance before his eyes, asked himself how the Greeks produced literary portraits in the fifth and fourth centuries B.C. He included not only historians, but also tragedians and orators. Almost immediately afterwards he produced what he considered a supplement to his previous research by extending it to later historians from Polybius to Tacitus. In fact the very title of his supplement, *Die Persönlichkeit in der Geschichtsschreibung der Alten,* indicated that he had meanwhile become more conscious of the special contribution of classical historiography to the search for the person.[3] Bruns established a distinction which is, I believe, still valid between direct and indirect characterization of persons in Greek and Roman histories. Although some historians, like Herodotus and Polybius, characterized and evaluated an individual directly by making a pen-portrait of him, others, like Thucydides and Livy, chose the indirect approach. They narrated the events in which a man was involved and avoided subjective evaluations of what the man did. Strangely enough, in his second volume Bruns did not include biography and autobiography in his exposition: in discussing Tacitus he did not examine the *Agricola*. Consequently the only biographies examined by him were Isocrates' *Euagoras* and Xenophon's *Agesilaos*.

A far more thorough analysis of ancient biography and autobiography was undertaken, respectively, by F. Leo (1901) and by G. Misch (1907).[4] The former was mainly concerned with the contribution of Aristotle's school to the creation of biographical schemes; and the latter, who was a pupil of Dilthey, extended to Antiquity his master's interest in literary self-revelation. In addition to Bruns, they made fundamental contributions to the study of how the person is represented in Greek and Latin historiography. In being explicitly concerned with biography and autobiography they came nearer to the central preoccupation of Mauss. Yet Leo was more interested in techniques of organizing the biographical material (narration in chronological order versus systematic characterization of individual traits) than in its implications for the understanding of the person. Misch, on the other hand, who was primarily interested in the problem of the person, reached the conclusion that no man before St. Augustine had enough "inner life" to write an authentic account of his own. Though such a conclusion was a decisive correction of Burckhardt's theory that individualism begins in the Renaissance, it confirmed Dilthey's view that interiority, and therefore personality, is a new feature of

Christianity. Autobiographies by pagans were not comparable with what Christians were able to do from St. Augustine to Rousseau. While Bruns seemed to have raised hopes that pagans were persons, Misch, though a Jew, followed his Protestant teacher Dilthey in denying personality, in the sense of inner life, to pagans and Jews. Whether he may have helped to persuade Mauss to leave the Greeks out is an open question. Mauss was well informed about classical studies, but if there is any allusion to Leo and Misch – or indeed to Bruns – in his collected works it has escaped me.[5]

II

Thus the question to ask is not whether the Greeks (or the Romans) knew what a person was, but what specific contributions classical historiography made to the description of the person by trying to build up images of individuals from given evidence. Finer distinctions – such as those between person and personality, character and attitudes, soul and mind – would of course be premature. Other Greek literary genres, from epic to tragedy, did not take evidence (as distinct from generic experience) into account in the presentation of individuals. Greek and Roman historians had to control their imagination by reference to evidence.

When we say that Greek historians felt that they were conditioned by the available evidence we are not implying that they would quote chapter and verse for every statement they made. Ancient readers of historical books were spared footnotes. What we imply is that from the end of the sixth century B.C. a group of writers became conscious of a problem of evidence about events of the more or less remote past. Certain accounts came to be considered more reliable than others according to some more or less consistent and coherent criteria. Truthfulness of the witnesses, intrinsic persuasiveness of the accounts, personal observation of the historian himself and other criteria, which no doubt had long been current in tribunals and political assemblies, were now used regularly to select, transmit and comment upon versions of past events. Hence the inherent necessity of being able to justify one's own account whenever the received version was challenged. But neither Herodotus nor Thucydides nor any of their successors felt obliged to explain in every case why they considered their own account to be reliable. In fact the severe Thucydides, who clearly took responsibility for everything he said, was less inclined than Herodotus to indicate the alternatives to his own choice. But even Herodotus, who had been more forthcoming than Thucydides about the sources of his information and the value he attributed to some of his stories and who had enjoyed collecting stories for their own sake, would no doubt have considered it ridiculous to have to explain in every case whether and why he believed in the truth of what he was telling.

Formulated in this general way, the rule of evidence applies both to the (political) historian, who was chiefly concerned with wars and internal politics, and to the biographer. However, the use of evidence produced some specific problems for the biographers. It is therefore appropriate at this point to emphasize that from the beginning of the fifth century B.C. some distinction existed in Greece between writing history and writing biography. It is also the moment to add that autobiography offers some problems of its own which will require special attention later.

In this early stage the distinction between (political) history and biography was perhaps not so sharp. Herodotus used in his history biographical accounts he had read or heard about the Persian Kings Cyrus and Cambyses and about the Athenians Miltiades and Themistocles. What he tells us about Miltiades and his ancestors can in fact be put together to form a short, self-contained biography. Though no self-contained biography belonging to the fifth century is preserved, we are told on good authority that such works had existed. Theagenes of Rhegium did research on the life of Homer about 500 B.C. About the same time Skylax of Caryanda, a famous explorer in the service of Darius I, wrote a life of his contemporary Heraclides tyrant of Mylasa. We are told that Xanthos (presumably Herodotus' contemporary, Xanthos, the historian of Lydia) wrote a monograph on Empedocles with biographical details. We also have some attractive biographic (and autobiographical) fragments by Stesimbrotos of Thasos and Ion of Chios, who wrote about the middle of the fifth century.[6] It will be noticed that this early biographical and autobiographical information, whether in forms of independent monographs or incorporated into the ample framework of Herodotus' histories, refers to, and is reported by, men who lived on the borders of the Persian Empire and may ultimately well be influenced by Oriental biographical models. This question does not concern us here.

Biography became more of a separate literary genre in the fourth century. It was then explicitly asserted that certain details about individuals are unsuitable for registration in books of political history. Thucydides, unlike Herodotus, already excludes such personal details, even about Pericles: his few exceptions are for the main part in excursuses outside the main narrative text. In keeping with his example, Xenophon apologizes in his Greek History (2,3,56; cf. 5,1,3) for introducing details about the behaviour of Theramenes before his execution. Another indication that biography and history are by now sharply separated is provided by the same Xenophon. He dealt twice with King Agesilaos of Sparta – once in the context of his Hellenic history and then again in a separate pamphlet. Though a definite distinction between history and biography is perhaps made for the first time in our sources of Polybius (10,26) – and then repeated by Cornelius Nepos *(Pelopidas* 1,5) and by Plutarch (*Alexander* 1,2) – it was apparently presupposed by the whole development of historical writing in the fourth century.

This distinction may well be reflected in the different attitude to evidence observable in the two genres. The most ancient complete biographies we happen to have (Isocrates' *Euagoras* and Xenophon's *Agesilaos*) were explicitly considered encomia by their authors. No fourth-century historian, in my recollection, ever presented his history as an encomium, even if his aim was to extol a party or a city or (as Thucydides paradoxically did) an individual politician like Pericles. Even when the biographer related nothing that was not in his evidence, he might consider it appropriate to suppress something that was in it – not because it was irrelevant, but because it was not in agreement with his encomiastic purpose. We may even wonder whether the boundary between imagination and evidence was less well marked in biography than in history. The classic case is Xenophon's *Cyropaedia*. The conclusion reached long ago by scholars is that the *Cyropaedia* is a philosophic or historical novel with an educational purpose. This is indeed what it is, and perhaps no fourth-century reader ever asked himself whether it was anything else. But the fact remains that in the book, which is about a real King of Persia, fact and fancy are freely mixed without warning. The author does not tell us where biography in our sense ends and invention begins. True enough, the same might be said about some unscrupulous historians who existed even in the fourth century B.C. The older contemporary of Xenophon, Ctesias, who dealt with analogous Oriental themes from a political point of view, did not exactly have a reputation for truthfulness. What, however, creates a presumption or suspicion that the biographers felt in principle much freer than the historians in their use of evidence is that I cannot recall a single passage of an ancient biography which tells us that the writer is unable to describe or judge a certain aspect of his hero because of lack of evidence. I may of course have overlooked or forgotten important passages, but I am under the strong impression that the ancient biographers tried to look extremely well informed about their heroes – even when the hero was Romulus.

These remarks about evidence must not be construed as a denial of the basic fact that ancient biographers wrote on evidence. What I want to say is that the use of evidence in Greek biography is lacking consistency and therefore seems to us even less satisfactory than the use of evidence in Greek political historiography.

Whether this is correct or not, there remains in any case one capital difference between biography and history in relation to evidence. An event is an event. People will see a battle or a revolution and report on it. The task of the historian will ultimately be to collate and evaluate such reports (even if he himself was present at the event) and to draw his own conclusions. But the biographer has the additional task of inferring from external details the mental state of the individual about whom he is writing. In so far as he was involved in biographical sketches, Herodotus was well aware of this difficulty. He tells several stories he has heard about Cambyses and then concludes triumphantly: "I hold it then in every way proved that Cambyses was very mad; else he would never have set himself to deride religion and custom" (III, 38, trans. A. D. Godley, Loeb). In Isocrates' *Euagoras* and *Xenophon's Agesilaos* we see two different attempts to grapple with the problem of how to connect external events with a man's inner character.

Isocrates combines in a continuous context the chronological account of events with reference to inner qualities. Xenophon separates the chronological account from character description: the second section of his pamphlet is non-chronological, systematic, and claims to be based on the preceding section.

Later Greek and Roman biography had continuously to wrestle with this problem of how to use external details of a life to build up a character – or, if you prefer, a person. As Cornelius Nepos says in the life of his contemporary and friend Pomponius Atticus: *Difficile est omnia persequi et non necessarium. Illud unum intelligi volumus, illius liberalitatem neque temporariam neque callidam fuisse* (11, 2–3: "It is difficult to enumerate everything, and needless besides. This one thing I wish to make clear, that his generosity was neither time-serving nor calculated," trans. J. C. Rolfe, Loeb). Conversely, the biographer lives to explain events from character: *suos cuique mores plerumque conciliare fortunam* (19, 1: "it is the character of every man that determines his fortune"). The reputation of Plutarch is based to a great extent on the ability, or rather simplicity, with which he presents episodes of life as evidence of character. At the same time Plutarch has an ingratiating way of registering inconsistencies without looking for an explanation. Character is to him what emerges from a majority of situations.

A special case of the relation between evidence and character is notoriously offered by the ancient biographies of writers – especially of poets.[7] How would one evaluate, for instance, the relation between Euripides' tragedies and Euripides' character? No doubt, a tragedy was an event: it could be seen, as the battle of Marathon could be seen. But could one infer the character of Euripides from his tragedy *Hippolytos* in the same way in which the Athenians inferred the character of Miltiades from his performance at Marathon, after which "the fame of Miltiades which had before been great at Athens was increased" (Herod. 6, 132)? Euripides' ancient biographers explained the attitude to women in the play *Hippolytos* by the alleged unfaithfulness of Euripides' wife Choirile. Even Plato in the *Phaedrus* explains Stesichoros' palinode about Helen by telling the story that the poet was struck blind for slandering Helen and had to recant in order to regain his sight (243 a–b). The Greek biographers faced the question of how the character of a poet could be deduced from his poems in the same spirit in which they faced the problem of how the character of a general could be deduced from his victories on the battlefield. Though deductions of this kind are more likely to be disastrous in the case of a poet, there have been honourable men (one such perhaps was Tolstoi) who doubted the value of the inference even more in the case of generals. In both cases what is at stake is the validity of inferences from events to character.[8]

III

I have assumed rather than argued that Greek and Latin biographers described what we can recognize as a person. It is my impression that Greek and Roman historians, and especially biographers, talked about individuals in a manner which is not distant from our own. Our style of describing persons derives from the classical tradition of biography and accepts its basic presuppositions about the need of evidence and about the techniques of transition from external signs to internal qualities. After all, the terminology of ancient biography is not so different from our own. Rhetorical theory, accepting and developing the distinction between history and biography made by the historians, spoke of a *genus narrationis quod in personis positum est* ([Cic.] *ad Herennium* 1, 9, 13) so that not only events, but also the conversations and mental attitudes of the characters can be *seen (personarum sermones et animi perspici possent,* Cicero, *De inventione,* 1,19,28). Even dreams were included among those mental performances which allowed inferences about character and personality (for instance Plutarch, *Demetrius* 4, where a dream is an illustration of the natural inclination of Demetrius Poliorcetes towards kindness and justice). True enough, characterizing dreams are in Plutarch far less common than dreams predicting the future: in the *Lives of the Philosophers* by Diogenes Laertius such characterizing dreams are, if I am not mistaken, entirely absent. All the same, Plutarch's "heroes" and Diogenes' philosophers look like persons to me.

If any doubt lingers about the existence of "persons" in Greek biography, may I refer to the first chapter of Plutarch's life of Aemilius Paulus (which through an error of judgement is transposed to the beginning of the parallel life of Timoleon in the Loeb edition)? There Plutarch welcomes each of his heroes in turn as his guest and favourably compares this company "of the most noble and estimable" with the enforced associations of daily life. Whether or not Plutarch was one of those who, in Mauss's words, "ont fait de la personne humaine une entité complète, indépendante de toute autre, sauf de Dieu," his biographies would not have become the influential model they were (and still are) for the Christian world throughout the centuries if his perception of the individual had not satisfied men educated to Christian inner life. At a lower level one can still see Cornelius Nepos behind Aubrey's *Brief Lives.*

However, we may well ask legitimately whether autobiography was separated from biography by a wider gulf in the classical world than in the modern world. Before St. Augustine – or at least before Gregory of Nazianzus, as G. Misch pointed out[9] – it is difficult to find autobiographies with the purpose of describing oneself, one's own character and inner life. The earliest extant Greek autobiographies are speeches in self-defence, such as Isocrates' *About the Exchange* (c. 354 B.C.) and Demosthenes' *On the Crown* (c. 330 B.C.). Four centuries later Flavius Josephus was still writing his autobiography or life ("bios") in self-defence. His work belongs to a tradition of judicial speeches. The author's moves are conditioned, if not determined, by the accusations of his enemies. The purpose of immediate self-defence creates a real difference from biographies dictated by curiosity and sympathy for the persons concerned, such as we can see in Plutarch.

Yet this effort of explaining oneself and one's own purposes to a personal audience, if not to one's own direct accusers, may well have been a decisive contribution to the recognition of the self as a person with a definite character, purpose and achievement. After all, in so far as they express a relation to gods or God, confessions have an element of self-defence which links them to judicial speeches.[10] Unfortunately, we are less well-informed about pagan confessions than about Christian ones;

and we are of course dominated by St. Augustine's book, which is a rather unique document even for Christianity.

Plato's Seventh Letter is better left aside in this context, not because the question of authenticity is still undecided, but because the text still belongs to the tradition of judicial self-justification of the fourth century B.C. It is a mixture of information and apology. It contains, as we all know, some important reflections about the inadequacy of the written word, but it does not even start to be an analysis of the self or a meditation on the self.

Marcus Aurelius's *Thoughts* are a different matter. The element which prevails is a dialogue with oneself. At the same time the Emperor's long list of debts to his relatives, teachers and friends presupposes awareness of a co-existence of persons, each with his own marked features, each different, but not isolated, each capable of contributing to the education of others. The sociality of the self is strongly emphasized by Marcus Aurelius (e.g., 9,23). The foundation of both sociality and interiority is the mind *(nous)* which alone is "in any true sense thine" (12,3). Reflection upon one's self and a relation to the others are equally fundamental in such a notion of man (11,8). Mauss is of course right in underlining with Renan the importance of Epictetus and Marcus Aurelius as witnesses to an early form of "notre examen de conscience." But he does not seem to attribute enough importance to the fact that this happens in an autobiographical context which has a long tradition of search for outside evidence. The search began, if I am correct, for the purpose of self-defence and was turned into a quest for self-knowledge only slowly and – for good reason – incompletely. Even in an autobiography which included dreams, self-analysis was insufficient. It had to be supplemented by knowledge of past events and of other individuals. Autobiography referred back to biography, and biography to history.[11]

Notes

1. M. Mauss would now be able to rely on important new research on Roman personal names and in general on the function of these names in other ancient cultures. I shall only mention, as examples, the French collective work *L'Onomastique latine* (N. Duval, ed.), Paris, C.N.R.S., 1977 and the seminal book by J. J. Stamm, *Akkadische Namengebung,* Leipzig, Himrichs, 1939. The question of the name had already been raised by Mauss in 1929: see *Oeuvres* II, 1969, 131–5.
2. See especially L. Schnorr von Carolsfeld, *Geschichte der Juristischen Person* I, München, Becu, 1933; S. Schlossmann, *Persona und prosopon im Recht und im christlichen Dogma,* Kiel, Lipsius 1906, quoted by Mauss himself. For further literature, e.g., M. Kaser, *Das Römische Privatrecht,* München, Beck, 2nd ed., 1971, I, 271.
3. I. Bruns, *Das literarische Porträt der Grieschen im fünften und vierten Jahrhundert vor*

Christi Geburt, Berlin, Hertz, 1896; *Die Persönlichkeit in der Geschichtsschreibung der Alten,* Berlin, Hertz, 1898 (reprinted together, Hildesheim, Olms, 1961).

4. F. Leo, *Die Griechisch-römische Biographie nach ihrer litterarischen Form,* Leipzig, Teubner, 1901; G. Misch, *Geschichte der Autobiographie,* 1st ed., Leipzig-Berlin, Teubner, 1907; idem, 3rd. in two volumes, Frankfurt, Schulte-Bulmke, 1949–50 (English translation, *A History of Autobiography in Antiquity,* London, Routledge & Kegan Paul, 1950). For more recent work, see K. J. Weintraub, *The Value of the Individual: Self and Circumstance in Autobiography,* Chicago University Press, 1978. It is important to remember that for Dilthey, death, and death alone, imposes unity on the person: I. N. Bulhof, *Wilhelm Dilthey,* The Hague, Nijhoff, 1980, 120–1.
5. Studies known to me on Mauss, however valuable, do not give enough information. Nor does the autobiographical sketch by Mauss published in *Revue Française de Sociologie,* 20, 1979: 209–220. See, for instance, V. Valeri, "Marcello Mauss e la nuova antropologia," *Critica Storica* 5, 1966: 677–703; J. Cazeneuve, *Sociologie de Marcel Mauss,* Paris, P.V.F., 1968; S. Lukes, *International Encyclopedia of the Social Sciences* 10, 1968: 78–82. Some useful hints will be found in R. Di Donato's chapter on Usener and French sociologists, in the volume edited by me, *Aspetti di Hermann Usener filologo della religione,* Pisa, Giardina, 1982.
6. For the main facts on Greek biography see my book *The Development of Greek Biography,* Cambridge, Mass., Harvard University Press, 1971, with a large bibliography. See my paper, "Second Thoughts on Greek Biography," *Meded. Kon. Nederl. Akad.* 34, 1971, no. 7. The Italian translation, *Lo sviluppo della biografia Greca,* Torinto, Einaudi, 1974, comprised both texts.
7. It will be enough to refer to Mary R. Lefkowitz, *The Lives of the Greek Poets,* London and Baltimore, Duckworth, 1981, with an excellent bibliography.
8. Biographers use, of course, mottoes, sayings, and speeches as elements of characterization. But speeches (whether founded upon authentic evidence or freely composed) are more frequently used by political historians to analyse a situation than by biographers to characterize a man. The whole use of speeches in ancient biography needs reassessment. Letters and testaments are also to be found in biographies (testaments are a feature in Diogenes Laertius), but less often than we might expect.
9. See Gregory of Nazianzus, *Carmen de Vita Sua,* p.37 and see also the commentary by Chr. Jungck (*Gregor von Nazianz, De Vita Sua,* Heidelberg, Winter, 1974).
10. See, for instance, R. Pettazzoni, *La confessione dei peccati,* Bologna, Zanichelli, I–III, 1929–1935. Confession was practised in the sanctuary of Samothrace and perhaps among Epicureans. The traces of it in Orphic circles are too vague. For the sanctuary of Epidauros, see F. Kudlien, *Medizinhistorisches Journal* 13, 1978: 1–14.
11. Biography and autobiography are not examined in the very valuable contributions by J.-P. Vernant ("Aspects de la personne dans la religion grecque") and by M. Détienne ("Ébauche de la personne dans la Grèce archaïque") to the volume edited by I. Meyerson, *Problèmes de la Personne,* Mouton, Paris, 1973 (the papers were written in 1960). Détienne, who partly depends on R. Hirzel, "Die Person," *Sitz. Bayer, Ak.,* 1914, 10, explicitly denies autobiography to the Greeks (p. 47). I found Vernant's remarks about the heroes especially illuminating. Among the other essays of this volume J. Daniélou, "La Personne chez les Pères Grecs," is suggestive. Further bibliography may be found in the essay by P. Hadot in the same volume (pp. 123–4). I have a further debt to the discussion with Sally Humphreys.

5

A modified view of our origins: the Christian beginnings of modern individualism

Louis Dumont

The study is in two parts. The main part bears on the first centuries of Christianity, when the first stages of an evolution are perceived. A complement or epilogue shows the evolution coming to a conclusion, long afterwards, with Calvin.

The outworldly beginnings

In the last decades, some of us have become increasingly aware that modern individualism, when seen against the background of the other great civilisations that the world has known, is an exceptional phenomenon. Now, if the idea of the individual as a value is as idiosyncratic as it is fundamental, there is by no means agreement on its origins. For some scholars, especially in countries where nominalism is strong, it has always been everywhere; for others it originated with the Renaissance or with the rise of the bourgeoisie. Most commonly perhaps, and according to tradition, the roots of the idea are thought to lie in our classical as well as in our Judeo-Christian heritage, in varying proportions. For some classicists, the discovery in Greece of 'consistent discourse' was the deed of men who saw themselves as individuals. The mists of confused thinking have dissipated under the Athenian sun. Then and there myth surrendered to reason, and the event marks the beginning of history proper. There is undoubtedly some truth in such a statement, but it is so narrow as to appear parochial in today's world and surely it needs, at the least, some modification. To begin with, the sociologist would tend to give prominence to religion as against philosophy, because religion encompasses the whole of society and relates immediately to action. Max Weber did this.

As for us, let us leave aside all considerations of cause and effect and consider only configurations of ideas and values, ideological networks, to try and reach the basic relations on which they are built. To state the thesis in approximate terms, I submit that something of modern individualism is present with the first Christians and in the surrounding world, but that it is not exactly individualism as we know it. Actually, the old form and the new are separated by a transformation so radical and so complex that it took at least seventeen centuries of Christian history to be completed, if indeed it is not still continuing in our times. In the generalisation of the pattern in the first place, and in its subsequent evolution, religion has been the cardinal element. Within our chronological limits, the pedigree of modern individualism is, so to speak, double: an origin or accession of one sort, *and* a slow transformation into another. Within the confines of this essay I must be content to characterise the origin and to point out a few of the earliest steps in the transformation. Let me apologise at the outset for the condensed abstraction of what follows.

To see our culture in its unity and specificity we must set it in perspective by contrasting it with other cultures. Only so can we gain an awareness of what otherwise goes without saying, the familiar and implicit basis of our common discourse. Thus, when we speak of man as an individual we designate two concepts at once: an object out there, and a value. Comparison obliges us to distinguish analytically these two aspects: one, the *empirical* subject of speech, thought, and will, the individual sample of mankind, as found in all societies; and, two, the independent, autonomous, and thus essentially non-social moral being, who carries our paramount values and is found primarily in our modern ideology of man and society. From that point of view, there emerge two kinds of societies. Where the individual is a paramount value I speak of individualism. In the opposite case, where the paramount value lies in society as a whole, I speak of holism.

In rough and ready terms, the problem of the origins of individualism is very much how, starting from the common type of holistic societies, a new type has evolved that basically contradicts the common conception. How has the transition been possible, how can we conceive a transition between those two antithetic universes of thought, those two mutually irreconcilable ideologies?

Comparison, in the instance of India, offers a clue. For more than two millennia Indian society has been characterised by two complementary features: society imposes upon every person a tight interdependence which substitutes constraining relationship for the individual as we know him, but, on the other hand, there is the institution of world-renunciation which allows for the full independence of the man who chooses it.[1] Incidentally, this man, the renouncer, is responsible for all the innovations in religion that India has seen. Moreover, we see clearly in early texts the origin of the institution, and we understand it easily: the man who is after ultimate truth forgoes social life and its constraints to devote himself to his own progress and destiny. When he looks back at the social world, he sees it from a distance, as something devoid of reality, and the discovery of the self is for him coterminous, not with salvation in the Christian sense, but with liberation from the fetters of life as commonly experienced in this world.

The renouncer is self-sufficient, concerned only with himself. His thought is similar to that of the modern individual, but for one basic difference: we live in the social world, he lives outside it. I therefore called the Indian renouncer an individual-outside-the-world. Comparatively, we are individuals-in-the-world, *inworldly* individuals, while he is an *outworldly* individual. I shall use this notion of the outworldly individual extensively, and I beg to draw your full attention to that strange creature and its characteristic relation to society. The renouncer may live in solitude as a hermit or may join a group of fellow-renouncers under a master-renouncer, who propounds a particular discipline of liberation. The similarity with Western anchorites and between, say, Buddhist and Christian monasteries, can go very far. As an instance, both congregations invented independently what we call majority rule.

What is essential for us is the yawning gap between the renouncer on the one hand and the social world and the individual-in-the-world on the other. To begin with, the path of liberation is open only to those who leave the world. Distance from the social world is the condition for individual spiritual development. *Relativisation* of life in the world results immediately from world renunciation. Only Westerners could mistakenly suppose that some sects of renouncers would have tried to change the social order. The interaction with the social world took other forms. In the first place, the renouncer depends on that world for his subsistence, and would instruct the man-in-the-world. Indeed a whole dialectic, a specifically Indian dialectic, set in, which must be disregarded here. What must be borne in mind is the initial situation as still found in Buddhism. Short of joining the congregation, the layman is taught only a relative ethic: to be generous towards the monks and to avoid deleterious and self-abasing actions.

What is invaluable for us here is that the Indian development is easily understood and indeed seems 'natural'. On the strength of it we may surmise: if individualism is to appear in a society of the traditional, holistic type, it will be in opposition to society and as a kind of supplement to it, that is, in the form of the outworldly individual. Could we then say that individualism began in the same way in the West?

That is precisely what I shall try to show: that, notwithstanding the differences in the content of representations, the same sociological type that we found in India – the outworldly individual – is unmistakenly present in Christianity and around it at the beginning of our era.

There is no doubt about the fundamental conception of man that flowed from the teaching of Christ: as Troeltsch said, man is an *individual-in-relation-to-God:* for our purposes this means that man is in essence an outworldly individual. Before developing this point let me attempt a more general one. It can be argued that the Hellenistic world itself was so permeated with the same conception among the educated, that Christianity could not have succeeded in the long run in that milieu if it had offered an individualism of a different sort. This is admittedly a strong thesis, which seems at first sight to contradict well-established conceptions. Actually, it is a mere modification and allows for bringing together a number of discrete pieces of evidence better than the current view does. It is commonly admitted that the transition in philosophical thought from Plato and Aristotle to the new schools of the Hellenistic period shows a discontinuity, a great gap – the surge of individualism (see Sabine 1963:143). Self-sufficiency, which Plato and Aristotle regarded as an attribute of the *polis,* becomes an attribute of the individual (*ibid.:* 128) that is either assumed as a fact or posited as an ideal by the Epicureans, Cynics and Stoics. But I must go straight to my point. It is clear that the first step in Hellenistic thinking has been to leave the social world behind. I could quote at length, for instance, Sabine's standard *A history of political thought* from which I have already reproduced some formulations, and which characteristically distinguishes the three schools as different varieties of 'renunciation' (*ibid.*: 137). These schools teach wisdom, and to become a sage one must first renounce the world. A critical feature runs throughout the period in different forms: it is a thorough dichotomy between wisdom and the world, between the wise man and the unenlightened men who remain in the throes of worldly life. Diogenes opposes the sage and the fools: Chrysippus states that the soul of the sage survives longer after death than that of ordinary mortals. Just as, in India, truth is attainable only by the renouncer, so according to Zeno only the sage knows what is good; worldly actions, even on the part of the sage, cannot be good, but only preferable to others: accommodation to the world is obtained through the relativisation of values, the same kind of *relativisation* that I underlined in the case of India.

Accommodation to the world characterises Stoicism from its inception, and increasingly during its middle, and then late phases. It has certainly contributed to blur, in the view of the later interpreters, the outworldly anchorage of the doctrine. The Roman Stoics assumed heavy duties in the world, and a Seneca was felt as a closely related neighbour by medieval minds, as well as by Rousseau, who borrowed extensively from him. Yet, it is not difficult to detect the permanence of the Stoic cleavage: the self-sufficiency of the individual remains the principle, even when he acts in the world. The Stoic must remain detached, he should maintain indifference even to the sorrow he tries to allay. Thus Epictetus: 'He may sigh (with the suffering man) provided his sigh does not come from the heart'.[2]

This feature, to us so strange, shows that, even if the Stoic has returned to the world in a manner foreign to the Indian renouncer, it represents for him only a secondary accommodation while at bottom he still defines himself as a stranger to the world.

How can we understand the genesis of this philosophical individualism? Individualism is so taken for granted that in this instance it is commonly seen without more ado as a consequence of the ruin of the Greek *polis* and of the unification of the world – Greeks and foreigners or barbarians confounded – under Alexander. Now this tremendous historical event can explain many traits, but not, to me at least, the emergence of the individual as a value, as a creation *ex nihilo*. We should look first of all to philosophy itself. Not only have Hellenistic teachers occasionally lifted out of the Presocratics elements for their own use, not only are they heirs to the Sophists and other currents of thought that appear to us as submerged in the classical period, but philosophical activity, the sustained exercise of rational inquiry carried out by generations of thinkers, must by itself have fostered individualism, because reason, universal principle, is in practice at work through the particular person who exercises it and takes precedence, at least implicitly, over everything else. Plato and Aristotle, after Socrates, were able to recognise that man is essentially a social being. What their Hellenistic successors essentially did was to set up a superior ideal, that of the wise man detached from social life. Such being the filiation of ideas, the vast political change, the rise of a universal empire opening the gate to the intensification of interrelations, will no doubt have favoured the movement. In that environment, direct or indirect influence from the Indian type of renouncer is not entirely to be ruled out, but the data are insufficient.

If a demonstration was needed of the all-pervading pattern of otherworldliness among educated people in the times of Christ it can be found in the person of the Jew, Philo of Alexandria. Philo showed to the later Christian Apologists the way to accommodate the religious message to an educated pagan audience. He tells in glowing terms of his predilection for the contemplative life of the recluse, to which he yearns to return, having interrupted it to do political service to his community – which he did with distinction. Goodenough has precisely shown how this hierarchy of two modes of life and that of Jewish faith and pagan philosophy are reflected in Philo's double judgement on politics – exoteric and apologetic on the one hand, esoteric and Hebraic on the other (see Goodenough 1940).

Turning now to Christianity, let me first say that my main guide will be the sociological historian of the Church, Ernst Troeltsch. In his extensive work, *The social teachings of the Christian churches and groups,* published in 1911, which I consider to be a masterpiece, Troeltsch had already given a relatively unified view, in his own words, of 'the whole sweep of the history of the Christian Church' (Troeltsch 1922). While Troeltsch's treatment may of course have to be completed or modified on some points, my effort will be in the main to take advantage of the comparative perspective I have just outlined in order to reach a still more unified and simpler view of the whole, even if we are concerned for the moment with only a fraction of it.[3]

The subject matter is familiar, and I shall only isolate schematically a few critical features. It follows from Christ's and then Paul's teaching that the Christian is an 'individual-in-relation-to-God'. There is, Troeltsch says, 'absolute individualism and absolute universalism' in relation to God. The individual soul receives eternal value from its filial relationship to God, in which relationship is also grounded human fellowship. Christians meet in Christ, whose members they are. This tremendous affirmation takes place on a level that transcends the world of man and of social institutions, although these are also from God. The infinite worth of the individual is at the same time the disparagement, the negation in terms of value, of the world as it is: a dualism is posited, a tension is established that is constitutive of Christianity and will endure throughout history.

Here we must pause and ponder. For the modern man this tension between truth and reality has become most difficult to accept or to value positively. We sometimes speak of 'changing the world', and it is clear from his earliest writings that the young Hegel would have preferred Christ to declare war on the world as it is. Yet, in retrospect, we see that had Christ done so as a man, the result would have been poor as compared with the consequences his teachings have led to throughout the centuries. In his maturity Hegel has made amends for the impatience of his youth by fully acknowledging the fecundity of Christian subjectivism, that is, of the congenital Christian tension.[4] Actually, in a comparative perspective the idea of 'changing the world' looks so absurd that we come to realise that it could ever appear only in a civilisation which had for long implacably maintained the absolute distinction between the life promised to man and the one he actually lives. This modern folly has its roots in what has been called the absurdity of the cross. I remember Alexandre Koyre opposing in conversation the folly of Christ to the good sense of Buddha. And yet they have something in common, precisely the exclusive concern for the individual coupled with, or rather founded on, a devaluation of the world.[5] That is how both religions are truly universalistic, and therefore missionary, and have spread and endured, how they have brought solace to innumerable men, and how – if I may venture so far – both are true in so much as, for human life to be bearable, especially in a universalist view, values must be maintained well beyond the reach of events.

What no Indian religion has ever fully attained and which was given from the start in Christianity is the brotherhood of love in and through Christ, and the consequent equality of all, 'an equality that exists purely', Troeltsch insists, 'in the presence of God'. Sociologically speaking, the emancipation of the individual through a personal transcendence, and the union of outworldly individuals in a community that treads on earth but has its heart in heaven, may constitute a passable formula for Christianity.

Troeltsch stresses the strange combination of radicalism and conservatism that results. It is advantageous to look at the matter in hierarchical terms. There are a whole series of similar oppositions – between this world and the beyond, body and soul, state and church, the old and the new dispensations – which are the basic framework used by the early Fathers and which Caspary (1979) calls the 'Pauline pairs' (see his analysis in a remarkable recent book on the exegesis of Origen). It is clear that the two poles in such oppositions are ranked, even when it is not obvious on the surface. When Christ teaches to 'render unto Caesar the things that are Caesar's, but unto God the things that are God's the symmetry is only apparent, as it is for the sake of God that we must comply with the legitimate claims of Caesar. In a sense the distance thus stated is greater than if the claims of Caesar were simply denied. The worldly order is relativised, as subordinated to absolute values. There is an ordered dichotomy: outworldly individualism encompasses recognition of and obedience to the powers of this world. If I could draw a figure, it would represent two concentric circles, the larger one representing individualism in relation to God, and within it a smaller circle standing for acceptance of worldly necessities, duties and allegiances: that is to say, the accommodation to a society, pagan at first and later Christian, which has not ceased to be holistic. This figure – encompassing the antithetical worldly life within the all-embracing primary reference and fundamental definition, and subordinating the normal holism of social life to outworldly individualism – can accommodate economically all major subsequent changes as formulated by Troeltsch. What will happen in history is that the paramount value will exert pressure upon the antithetical worldly element encapsulated within it. By stages worldly life will thus be contaminated by the outworldly element, until finally the heterogeneity of the world disappears entirely. Then the whole field will be unified, holism will have vanished from ideology, and life in the world will be thought of as entirely conformable to the supreme value, the outworldly individual will have become the modern, inworldly individual. This is the historical proof of the extraordinary potency of the initial disposition.

If only I had time, I should like to add at least a remark on the millenarist aspect. The first Christians lived in the expectation of the imminent 'Second Coming' of Christ who would establish the Kingdom of God. The belief was probably functional in helping people to accept at least provisionally the uncomfortable position of holding a belief which was not immediately relevant to their actual predicament. It so happens that the world has recently known an extraordinary proliferation of millenarist movements often called 'cargo cults', in conditions very similar to those prevailing in Palestine under Roman domination. The main sociological difference lies perhaps precisely in the outworldly climate of the period and first of all the outworldly orientation of the Christian community which kept the upper hand against extremist tendencies, whether of the rebel Jews or of the Apocalyptic writers, of Gnosticism or Manicheism. From that angle, early Christianity would seem to be characterised by a combination of millenarism and outworldliness with a relative predominance of the latter over the former.[6]

Schematic and insufficient as this development has been, I hope at any rate to have made it likely that the first Christians were, all in all, nearer to the Indian renouncer than to ourselves, more or less snugly ensconced in the world which we think to have accommodated to ourselves. In actual fact, we have conversely – also? – accommodated ourselves to it. This is my second point which I shall now turn to by singling out some of the early stages of that accommodation.

How was the outworldly message of the Sermon on the Mount brought to bear upon life in the world? The institutional link was the Church, which may be seen as a sort of foothold or bridgehead of the divine, and which spread, unified itself, and extended its sway only slowly and by degrees. But there had to be also a conceptual tool, a way of thinking which concerned earthly institutions in the light of outworldly truth. Ernst Troeltsch laid great stress on the borrowing from the Stoics by the early Fathers of the idea of Natural Law, which was to serve as this indispensable instrument of adaptation. What was this pagan 'ethical Law of Nature'? I quote:

> Its leading idea is the idea of God as the universal, spiritual-and-physical, Law of Nature, which rules uniformly over everything and as universal law of the world orders nature, produces the different positions of the individual in nature and in society, and becomes in man the law of reason which acknowledges God and is therefore one with him. . . . The Law of Nature thus demands on the one hand submission to the harmonious course of nature and to the role assigned to one in the social system, on the other an inner elevation above all this and the ethico-religious freedom and dignity of reason, that is one with God and therefore not to be disturbed by any external or sensible occurrence (1960:64).

As regards the special relation to the Stoics, it could be objected that by our time such conceptions had become widely diffused, and that Philo and, some two centuries later, the Apologists borrowed as much or perhaps more from other schools of thought. Troeltsch has replied in advance: 'the concept of an ethical law of nature from which are derived all juridical rules and social institutions is a creation of the Stoa' (1925: 173–74). And it is on the level of ethics that the Church will construct her medieval social doctrine, 'a doctrine which, albeit imperfect and confused from a scientific viewpoint, was to have practically the utmost cultural and social meaning, was indeed to be something like the Church's dogma of civilisation' (1922:173). The borrowing appears quite natural once we admit that both Stoicism and Christianity were wedded to outworldliness, and to the concomitant relativisation of the inworldly. After all, the message of Buddha to the man-in-the-world as such was of the same nature: subjective morality and ethics constitute the interface between worldly life and its social commands on the one hand, truth and absolute values on the other.

Let us return to the founder of the Stoa three centuries before Christ, in whose teaching we find the principle of the whole later development. For Zeno of Kition, who was more a prophet than a philosopher according to Edwyn Bevan,[7] the good is what makes man independent of all external circumstances. The only good is internal to man. The will of the individual is the source of his dignity and self-containment. Provided he adjusts his will to whatever destiny has in store for him, he will be safe, immune to all attacks from the outside world. As the world is ruled by God, or the law of nature, or reason – for nature becomes reason in man – this command is what Troeltsch called the absolute Law of Nature. Now, while the sage remains indifferent to external things and actions, he is nevertheless able to distinguish among them according to their greater or lesser conformity to nature, or reason: some actions are by themselves relatively commendable as against others. The world is relativised as it should be, and yet values, *relative values,* may be attached to it. Here is *in nuce* the relative Law of Nature that will be extensively used by the Church. To those two levels of the Law correspond two pictures of mankind, in its ideal and in its real state. The former is the state of nature – as in Zeno's ideal cosmopolis or in the later utopia of Iambulus (see Bidez 1932: vols. 18–19, 244*ff*) – which the Christians identified with the condition of man before the Fall.

As to the real state of mankind, the close parallelism between Seneca's justification of institutions as results of and remedies to men's viciousness and similar Christian views is well known. What Troeltsch considers essential is the rational aspect: that reason could be applied to actual institutions, either to justify them in view of the present state of men's morality, or to condemn them as contrary to nature, or again to temper or better them in the light of reason.

Thus Origen held against Celsus that positive laws that contravene natural law are not laws in any sense of the term (Caspary 1979:130), to such effect that Christians were justified in refusing to worship the Emperor or to kill under his orders.

On one point Troeltsch needs an addendum. He has missed or bypassed the importance of sacral kingship in Hellenistic times and later on. Natural law as 'unwritten' or 'animate' law (empsychos) is incarnate in the ruler. It is clear in Philo, who wrote of 'incarnate and rational laws', and in the Fathers. According to Philo, 'the wise men of ancient history, the patriarchs and fathers to the race present in their lives unwritten laws, which Moses wrote later. . . . In them the law was fulfilled and it became personal' (Troeltsch 1922, note 69, quoting Rudolf Hirzel). And Clement of Alexandria wrote of Moses that he was 'inspired by the law and therefore a royal man' (Ehrhardt 1959–69: Band 2, 189). This is important because we are here in contact with the primitive, sacral type of sovereignty, that of the divine king or priest-cum-ruler, a very widespread representation, present in the Hellenistic world and later on in the Byzantine Empire (see Dvornik 1966). We shall encounter it again later on.

The views and attitudes of the early Fathers on social questions – the State and the ruler, slavery, private property – are mostly considered by the moderns in isolation and from an inworldly viewpoint. We can better understand them by focusing on outworldliness. We should remember that everything was seen in the light of the individual's relation to God and of its concomitant, the brotherhood of the Church. At first sight the ultimate end entertains an ambivalent relation with life in the world, for the world through which the Christian is on pilgrimage in this life is both an impediment to salvation and a condition of it. But we had best think of the whole configuration in hierarchical terms, for life in the world is not simply refused or negated, it is only relativised in relation to man's destiny of union with God and outworldly bliss. The orientation to the transcendent end, as towards a magnet, introduces a hierarchical field, in which we should expect every worldly thing to be situated.

The first tangible consequence of this hierarchical relativisation is a remarkable degree of latitude in most worldly matters. As such matters are not important in themselves but only in relation to the end, there may be a great range of variation according to each pastor's and author's temperament and more importantly according to the circumstances of the moment. Rather than searching for hard and fast rules we should ascertain in each case the limits of permissible variation. They are clear in principle: first the world should not be condemned out of hand, as by the Gnostic heretics; secondly it should not usurp the dignity that belongs to God alone. We should, moreover, expect the range of permissiveness to be narrower in more important matters than in those of lesser significance and value.

One author has recently stressed the kind of flexibility I am referring to. Studying the exegesis of Origen, Caspary has admirably shown how what seems to me the fundamental opposition plays on a variety of levels and in a variety of forms, and constitutes a network of spiritual meaning, a hierarchy of correspondences.[8] What is true of Biblical hermeneutics is similarly applicable to the interpretation of the rough data of experience. I said a moment ago that things of the world can be taken as hierarchised according to their relative import for salvation. There is no systematic statement to that effect in our sources: yet there is at least one major point on which the difference in valuation should be taken into account. I have shown elsewhere that the modern world has reversed the traditional primacy of relationships of men as against relations of men to things. On this point the attitude among the Christians is unmistakable, for things can only be means or impediments to the attainment of the Kingdom of God, while relations between men involve subjects made in the image of God and predestined to union with Him. This is perhaps the place where the contrast with the moderns is the most marked.

We thus may surmise and we verify that the subordination of man in society, whether in the State or in slavery, poses more vital questions for the early Christians than does the permanent attribution of possessions to persons, i.e., private property in things. The teaching of Jesus concerning wealth as an impediment to, and poverty as an asset for, salvation is addressed to the individual person. As to the social level, the perennial rule of the Church is well known: it is not a rule of property, it is instead a rule of use. It matters little to whom the property belongs provided it is used for the good of all, and in the first place of those most in need, for, as Lactantius put it (in *Divinae institutiones,* III, 21) (against Plato's communism), justice is a matter of the soul and not of external circumstances. Troeltsch happily shows how love within the brotherhood involved detachment from possessions (Troeltsch 1922: n. 57; 1960: 115*ff,* 133*ff*). For all that we know we may suppose that, in the absence of dogmatic stress in the matter, the small and largely autonomous early Churches may have varied in their actual treatment of property, some perhaps having all in common at some time, while only the basic injunction to help destitute brethren was uniform.

The equality of all men had been declared by the Stoics and others as grounded in their common endowment with reason. Christian equality was perhaps more deeply rooted, set at the core of the person, but it was similarly an outworldly equality. 'There can be neither Jew nor Greek. . . . neither bond nor free, . . . no male and female, for ye are all *one man in Christ Jesus*', said Paul, and Lactantius: 'No one, in *God's sight,* is a slave or a master . . . we are all . . . his children.' Slavery was a matter of this world, and it is indicative of the gulf that separates those men from us that what for us strikes at the root of human dignity and independence was seen by them as a contradiction inherent in worldly life, and which Christ himself had assumed in order to redeem mankind, thus making humility a cardinal virtue for all. All the effort to perfection was turned inside, was internalised, as becomes the outworldly individual. This is readily seen, for instance, in Origen's 'tropological' level of exegesis where all Biblical events are interpreted as happening in the inner life of the Christian (see Caspary 1979).

As regards political subordination, Troeltsch's treatment can perhaps be bettered. He follows A.J. Carlyle; the attitude to the laws is governed by Natural Law conceptions, but the power that decrees the laws is seen quite differently and regarded as divine.[9] Actually, Natural Law and sacral kingship are not such perfect strangers. We are again faced with a case where a hierarchical view does better. The cardinal point is found in Paul: all power is from God, but within this overall principle there is room for restriction of contradiction. This is clear in a comment on Paul by the great Origen in *Contra Celsum:*

> He says 'There is no power but from God'. Then, someone might say: What? That power also, that persecutes the servants of God . . . is from God? Let us answer briefly on that. The gift of God, the laws, are for use, not for abuse. There will indeed be a judgement of God against those who administer the power they have received according to their impieties and not according to the law divine. . . . He [Paul] does not speak of those powers that persecute the faith: for here one must say: 'it is fitting to obey God rather than men, he speaks only of power in general' (Troeltsch 1922: n. 73).

We easily see that here a relative institution has overstepped its limits and come into conflict with the absolute value.

As it was contrary to the ultimate Christian value, political subordination was attributed to the Fall of man, that is, it was justified in terms of the relative Law of Nature. Thus Irenaeus: 'men fell from God . . . [and] God imposed on them the restraint of the fear of other men . . . lest they devour each other like fishes.' The same view was applied by Ambrose to slavery somewhat later, perhaps because it appeared as an individual matter while the State confronted the whole Church as a threat. It is noteworthy that a similar explanation is not given of private property, except by John Chrysostom, an exceptional character. Once more there is room here for some variation. On the one hand, the State and its ruler are willed by God as is everything on earth. On the other, the State is to the Church as the earth is to heaven, and a bad ruler may be a punishment sent by God. In general we should not forget that in the exegetical perspective life on earth since Christ is a mix: he has ushered in a transitional stage between the unredeemed state of men under the Old Dispensation and the full accomplishment of the promise in the Second Coming (see Caspary 1979: 176–7). In the meantime, men have the Kingdom of God only within themselves.

Let me now make an apology. Reluctantly, I am going to leave Saint Augustine out of consideration, although his thought is central to our problem, as his genius points unerringly to the whole future development. But his very greatness discourages summary treatment. Within the present limits, I must focus on a more limited object: the evolution of the relation between the Church and the State, that epitome of the world, up to the crowning of Charlemagne in the year A.D. 800. I shall isolate a remarkable formula of that relation, and show how it was subsequently modified.

In the first place, the conversion to Christianity of the Emperor Constantine at the beginning of the fourth century, besides forcing the Church to a new degree of unification, created a redoubtable problem: what was to be a Christian State? The Church was willy-nilly brought face-to-face with the world. She was glad to envision an end to persecutions, and she became an official, richly subsidised institution. The Church could not go on devaluing the State as absolutely as she had done hitherto.

The State had after all taken one step out of the world and towards the Church, but by the same token the Church was made more worldly than she had ever been. Yet the structural inferiority of the State was maintained, albeit nuanced. The latitude to which I have drawn attention was increased, in the sense that a more or less favourable assessment of the State could be made depending on circumstances and temperaments. Conflicts were not ruled out, but they would henceforth be internal, both to the Church and to the Empire. It was inevitable that the heritage of Hellenistic sacral kingship would collide occasionally with the claim of the Church to remain the superior institution. The frictions that subsequently developed between the Emperor and the Church – and particularly with the first of the bishops, that of Rome – were chiefly around points of doctrine. While the Emperors, mostly for the sake of political unity, insisted on proclaiming compromises, the Church, its ecumenical councils and especially the Pope, was keen on defining the doctrine as the basis for orthodox unity, and resented the rulers' intrusion in the preserve of ecclesiastical authority. A succession of doctrinal divergences obliged the Church to elaborate a unified doctrine. It is noteworthy that most of those debates which issued in the condemnation of heresies (such as Arianism. Monophysitism, Monothelism) centred – predominantly in the East, around the ancient sees of Alexandria and Antioch – on the difficulty of conceiving and properly formulating the union of God and man in Christ. This is precisely what appears to us as the core, the secret of Christianity considered in its full historical development; namely, in abstract terms, the assertion of an effective transition between the outworldly and the inworldly, the *Incarnation of Value*. The same difficulty is reflected in the later iconoclastic movement, where it was perhaps catalysed by the puritanical Muslim influence (the sacred cannot be 'imaged'). At the same time, there was clearly a political imperial interest in Arianism and in iconoclasm. Peterson has shown that the adoption of the dogma of the Holy Trinity (Council of Constantinople, A.D. 381) had tolled the bell of political monotheism (Peterson 1951).[10]

Around A.D. 500, after the Church had led an official life in the Empire for some two centuries, Pope Gelasius made a theoretical statement about the relation between the Church and the Emperor which was subsequently enshrined in tradition and abundantly drawn on. Yet modern interpreters do not seem to have done full justice to Gelasius. His clear and lofty pronouncement is widely treated as stating the juxtaposition and cooperation of the two powers, or, as I would say, of the two entities or functions. That it contains an element of hierarchy is somehow admitted, but seeing as the moderns are uneasy in that dimension, they misrepresent it or are unable to see its full import. On the contrary, the present comparative perspective should allow us to restore the high stature and logical structure of the Gelasian theory.

The statement is contained in two texts that complement each other. Gelasius says in a letter to the Emperor:

> There are mainly two things, August Emperor, by which this world is governed: the sacred authority of the pontiffs and the royal power. Of these, priests carry a weight all the greater, as they must render an account to the Lord even for kings before the divine judgement . . . [and a little further on] you must bend a submissive head to the ministers of divine things and . . . it is from them that you must receive the means of your salvation.[11]

The reference to salvation clearly indicates that Gelasius deals here with the supreme or ultimate level of consideration. We note the hierarchical distinction between the priest's *auctoritas* and the king's *potestas*. After a brief comment Gelasius goes on: 'In things concerning the public discipline, religious leaders realise that imperial power has been conferred on you from above, and they themselves will obey your laws, for fear that in worldly matters they should seem to thwart your will.' That is, the priest is subordinate to the king in mundane matters that regard the public order. What modern commentators fail to take fully into account is that the level of consideration has shifted from the height of salvation to the lowliness of worldly affairs. Priests are superior, for they are inferior only on an inferior level. We are not dealing either with mere 'correlation' (Morrison 1969:101–5) or with mere submission of kings to priests (Ullmann 1955:20*ff*) but with *hierarchical complementarity.*

Now, I found exactly the same configuration in ancient, Vedic, India. There, the priests looked at themselves as religiously or absolutely superior to the king while materially subject to him.[12] Thus, with some difference in the wording, the configuration is exactly the same as in Gelasius. The fact is astounding, given the vast differences in the respective backgrounds. On the Indian side there was no corporate unity of the faithful, nor any unitary organisation of the priesthood, nor, in the first place, was there any stress put on the individual. (The renouncer, of whom I spoke previously, had not yet appeared.) I am thus emboldened to surmise that the configuration in question is simply the logical formula of the relation between the two functions.

The other main text by Gelasius is found in a treatise *(De anathematis vinculo.)* Its main interest for us lies in the explanation of the differentiation of the two functions as instituted by Christ. Before him (I must excerpt) 'there actually existed – though in a prefigurative sense – men who were concurrently kings and priests', such as Melchisedech. Then 'the One came who was truly King and Priest' and 'Christ, mindful of human frailty . . . has separated the offices of the two powers[13] by means of distinctive functions and dignities . . . intending that His own [people] should be saved by salutary humility. . . .' It is only the Devil that has imitated the pre-Christian blend of the two functions 'so that', says Gelasius, 'pagan emperors caused themselves to be called sacred pontiffs'. There may well be here an allusion to what remained of sacral kingship in Byzantium. For the rest we may find in this text a quite sensible surmise on the evolution of institutions. It is not unreasonable for us to suppose that the original sacral sovereignty (for example, that of ancient Egypt or of China), has in some cultures differentiated into two functions, as it did in India.

It would be enlightening to discuss at length the commentators' difficulties, but I must pick and choose. A recent author, Father Congar, argues that the hierarchical formula of authority versus power is only occasional (see Congar Yves 1968). In fact we have heard Gelasius, when dealing with the differentiation, speak only of 'the two powers'. But is not the distinction the best expression of what Gelasius is saying all along? Congar (*ibid.*: 256) is right in stating that here the Church does not tend 'to a temporal realisation of the City of God'. As in the Indian case, hierarchy is logically opposed to power: it does not claim, as it will do later on, to transcribe itself in terms of power. But Congar (*ibid.*: 255–56) also argues that Gelasius does not subordinate imperial to sacerdotal power, but only the Emperor to the bishops with regard to the *res divinae,* and he concludes that, although the Emperor, as one of the faithful, was within the Church, the Church itself was *within the Empire* (his italics). Now, it is not apposite here to introduce a distinction between the function and its bearer which would in fact ruin Gelasius' argument, and of which Carlyle (1903: 169) admits in his own way that it is often disregarded in our sources. Actually the Empire culminates in the Emperor and we must understand Gelasius as saying that, if the Church is *in* the Empire with respect to worldly matters, the Empire is *in* the Church regarding things divine. On the whole, the interpreters seem to apply to the statement of A.D. 500 a later and quite different mode of thought. They reduce the rich, structural, flexible use of the base opposition (to which Caspary draws our attention) to a unidimensional, substantial matter of either-or, or black and white distinctions. These will appear only, in Caspary's words, when 'with the freezing of political positions as the result of the [investiture] controversy and, more importantly, owing to the slow growth of scholastic and legal modes of thinking, the second half of the twelfth century slowly lost this sort of flexibility. . . . and emphasised clarity and distinctions rather than interrelationships' (1979:190).

We have studied an important ideological formula. It should not be imagined that Gelasius' dicta have either settled all conflicts between the two main protagonists or even received, whether durably or not, the agreement of all concerned. Gelasius himself was led to his pronouncements by an acute crisis following the promulgation by the Emperor of a formula intended to reconcile his Monophysite subjects, the Henotikon. In general, the Patriarchs of Eastern Christendom did not follow blindly the Vicar of St. Peter, and the Emperor first of all had his own viewpoint in the matter. There are signs that something of Hellenistic sacral kingship always remained in Byzantium, at least for the Emperor's own use and in the imperial palace (see Dvornik 1966). Moreover, some Emperors pretended to concentrate in their hands not only temporal but also spiritual supremacy, and sometimes succeeded in doing so. Not only Justinian before the time of Gelasius, but after him in the West, in different manners, Charlemagne and Otto I assumed the supreme religious functions as part and parcel of their rule.

It would be difficult to imagine a more glaring contradiction to Gelasius' doctrine than the policy the papacy developed from the middle of the eighth century. In A.D. 753–54 Pope Stephen II, in an unprecedented move, left Rome, crossed the Alps and visited the Frankish king Pippin. He confirmed him in his kingship and gave him the title of 'Patrician of the Romans' and the role of protector and ally of the Roman Church. Fifty years later, Leo III crowned Charlemagne as Emperor in St. Peter's at Rome, on Christmas Day A.D. 800.

How the Popes had been led to adopt such a drastic course of action may be understood from their general predicament. We may almost say with Carlyle that it 'was forced upon them' by circumstances. On an immediate level, what has happened may be summed up in two points. The Popes have put an end to a situation of humiliation, oppression, and danger by turning their back on Byzantium and exchanging a remote, civilised but assuming protector for another who is nearer, more efficient, less civilised but therefore hopefully more docile. At the same time, they have taken advantage of the change to press their claim to sovereign political authority in a part of Italy. The Western Emperors may later prove to be less docile than expected, and to begin with, Charlemagne probably looked at the political rights he guaranteed to the Pope as only a kind of autonomy under his own paramountcy. He did assert his duty not only to protect but to direct the Church.

What is essential for us is the papal assumption of a political function, which is clear from the start. In the words of Professor Southern (1970:60) commenting on the pact with Pippin: 'for the first time in history the Pope had acted as a supreme political authority in authorising the transfer of power in the Frankish kingdom, and he had emphasised his political role as successor to the Emperors by disposing of imperial lands in Italy'. The appropriation of imperial territories in Italy is not quite articulate to begin with: the Pope obtains from Pippin, and later from Charles, the recognition of the 'rights' and territories of the 'Republic of the Romans' without any clear distinction being made between private and public rights and powers, but this includes the Ravenna exarchate. We cannot yet speak of a papal State, although there is a Roman political entity. A forged document, of perhaps somewhat later date, the so-called Donation of Constantine, clearly states the papal claim. There, the first

Christian Emperor is made to transmit to the Roman See in A.D. 315, along with the Lateran 'palace', extensive patrimonial estates and the religious 'principate' over all other sees as 'universal pope', imperial rule over Roman Italy and imperial regalia and privileges (see Southern 1970:60; Partner 1972: 21–23).

What is of primary importance from our viewpoint is the ideological change that is here initiated and will be fully developed later on, independently of what will happen in fact to the papal claim. With the claim to an inherent right to political power, a change is introduced in the relation between the divine and the earthly: the divine now claims to rule the world through the Church, and the Church becomes inworldly in a sense it was not heretofore.

The Popes have, through a historical choice, cancelled Gelasius' logical formula of the relation between the religious and the political function and turned to another. For Gelasius' hierarchical dyarchy is substituted a monarchy of unprecedented type, a spiritual monarchy. The two agencies or realms are unified while their distinction is relegated from the fundamental to a secondary level, as if they differed not in their nature but only in degree. The distinction is henceforth between the spiritual and the temporal, as we have known them ever since, and the field is unified, so that we may speak of spiritual and temporal 'powers'. It is characteristic that the spiritual is conceived as superior to the temporal *on the temporal level itself,* as if it was a superior degree of the temporal, or so to speak, the temporal raised to a superior power, that is a 'squared temporal'. It is along this line that later on the Pope will be conceived as 'delegating' the temporal power to the Emperor as his 'deputy'.

As compared with Gelasius' theory, the superiority is here stressed at the expense of the difference, and I would venture to call this disposition a perversion of hierarchy. Yet a coherence of a new type is achieved. The new unification represents a transformation of an older unity. For if we remember the archetypal model of sacral kingship we see here substituted for it what we might call kingly priesthood.

This new disposition is pregnant with meaning and with further historical developments. It should be obvious that, in a general sense, the Christian individual becomes here more intensely involved in this world. But to remain on the level of institutions, the movement is, as similar previous movements, double-edged; if the Church becomes more worldly, conversely the political realm is made to participate in absolute, universalist values. It is, so to speak, consecrated, in quite a new manner. And we can thus descry a potentiality that will be realised later on, namely, that a particular political unity may in its turn emerge as a bearer of absolute values, as the modern State. For the modern State is not in continuity with other political forms: it is a transformed Church, as is readily seen in the fact of its not being made up of different functions or orders, but rather of individuals, a point which even Hegel failed to admit.[14]

I cannot even sketch out this further development here. Let me say only that the shift I have just underlined will be followed by other shifts in the same direction, and that this long chain of shifts will issue finally in the full legitimation of this world, together with the full transfer of the individual *into* this world. This chain of transitions can be thought of in the image of the Incarnation of the Lord as the progressive incarnation or embodiment in the world of those values which Christianity had initially reserved to the outworldly individual and his Church.

To conclude, I have proposed that we abstain from projecting our familiar idea of the individual onto the first Christians and their cultural environment; that instead we should recognise a notable difference in the respective conceptions. The individual as value was then conceived as apart from the given social and political organisation, outside and beyond it, an outworldly individual as opposed to our own inworldly individual. Helped by the Indian instance, I argued that individualism could not possibly have appeared in another form and developed otherwise from traditional holism, and that the first centuries of the history of the Church showed the first lineaments of the accommodation to the world of that strange creature. I stressed at the start the adoption of the Stoics' Law of Nature as a rational instrument for the adaptation to worldly ethics of outworldly values. Then I turned to a single but highly significant dimension, the political. Initially the State is to the Church as the world is to God, and therefore the history of the conception by the Church of its relation to the State is central in the evolution of the relation between the bearer of value, the outworldly individual, and the world. Subsequently, after the conversion of the Emperor, and then that of the Empire, had forced upon the Church a closer relation to the State, a logical, that is, truly hierarchical, formula was reached by Gelasius, which we may call a hierarchical dyarchy. Yet the truth-value of that formula should not blind us to the fact that, as the Indian parallel shows, it bears no relation whatsoever to individualism. Then, in the eighth century, comes a dramatic change. By a historic decision, the Popes snap their tie with Byzantium and arrogate supreme temporal power in the West. This momentous step was invited by the hopeless situation that had developed, but cannot be explained by it. It expresses a subtle but fundamental ideological shift. The Church now pretends to rule, directly or indirectly, the world, which means that the Christian individual is now committed to the world to an unprecedented degree. Other steps will follow in the same direction but this one is decisive in general and especially with regard to future political developments. We have thus seen some stages of the transformation of the outworldly individual into the inworldly individual.

The main lesson upon which to meditate is perhaps that the most effective humanisation of the world has issued in the long run from a religion that subordinated it most strictly to a transcendent value.

Calvin

It is a weakness of the present study that it stops at the eighth century. I imagine that the thesis would be strengthened if the subsequent developments were followed, as they should, down to the Reformation. I am unable to do so for the present, but in order to remedy the shortcoming in some measure, I propose here a brief consideration of the terminal stage of the process as represented by Calvin.[15] Accepting Troeltsch's account, I shall try and show that it is best reformulated in the language used heretofore.[16]

In what sense can Calvin be taken as standing at the end of a process? In a general sense the process goes on beyond the man. The inworldliness of the individual will progress in the sects, in the Enlightenment, and further on. But from the point of view of what I have tried to highlight – that is, the conceptual interrelation between the individual, the Church and the world – Calvin marks a conclusion: his Church is the last form that the Church could possibly take without disappearing. Moreover, when I say Calvin, what I mean is the Reformation as culminating – from our viewpoint – in Calvin. Calvin built on Luther; he was conscious only of making Luther's stand explicit, articulate, and drawing its logical consequences. We may thus, for the sake of brevity, avoid considering Lutheranism in itself and retain only those of Luther's views that are presupposed in Calvin, while leaving aside his other views as superseded by Calvin's.

My thesis is simple: with Calvin, the hierarchical dichotomy that characterised our field of consideration comes to an end: the antagonistic worldly element that individualism had hitherto accommodated disappears entirely in Calvin's theocracy. The field is absolutely unified. *The individual is now in the world, and the individualist value rules without restriction or limitation.* The inworldly individual is before us.

Actually, this recognition is nothing new, for it is present in every page of Troeltsch's chapter on Calvin, even if it is not expressed in exactly the same words. Early in the book, at the end of the chapter on Paul, Troeltsch pointed forward to this unification: 'This principle of the mere juxtaposition of given conditions and ideal claims, that is the mixture of conservatism and radicalism, is first broken only by Calvinism' (1922: 81–82, 1960:88). The sequence of the passage suggests the possibility of two alternative views: as a consequence of the unification, either, as with Calvin, the spirit animates the whole of life, or, conversely, material life commands spiritual life. Hierarchical dualism is replaced by a flat continuum governed by an either/or choice.

Calvin thinks he is following Luther and yet he produces a different doctrine. Let us therefore start from his particular character or temperament. Troeltsch says that Calvin has a peculiar conception of God. Well, this conception closely corresponds to Calvin's inclinations, and in general he projects everywhere his deep personal inspiration. Calvin is not of a contemplative temper, he is a rigorous thinker whose thought is oriented to action. Actually he ruled Geneva as a skilled statesman, and there is in him a legalistic bent. He likes to promulgate regulations and to discipline himself and others. He is possessed by the will to act in the world and brushes aside through consistent arguments the received ideas that would block his way.

Such a personal disposition throws light on the three fundamental interrelated elements in Calvin's doctrine: the conceptions of God as *will*, of predestination, and of the Christian city as the object on which bears the will of the individual.

For Calvin, God is essentially will and majesty. This implies distance: God is here more remote than hitherto. Luther had removed God from the world by rejecting the mediation institutionalised in the Catholic Church, where God was present by proxy in men singled out as intermediaries (Church dignitaries, priests endowed with sacramental powers, monks devoted to a higher type of life).[17] But with Luther God was accessible to individual consciousness through faith, love, and, to some extent, through reason. With Calvin, love falls into the background and reason applies only to this world. At the same time, Calvin's God is the archetype of the Will, or the affirmation by proxy of man himself as will, or finally the strongest affirmation of the individual as opposed to, or superior to, reason. Of course, the stress on the will is central in the history of Christian civilisation as a whole (from Augustine to modern German philosophy), not to mention freedom in general nor the link with nominalism (Ockham).

The paramountcy of the will is dramatically expressed in the dogma of predestination. The root of it lies in Luther's rejection of salvation through works, which was in the first place meant for the destruction of the Catholic Church, its ritualism and the domination it had established upon the individual soul. Luther had replaced justification by works with justification through faith, and had in the main stopped at that point, leaving to the individual some margin of freedom. Calvin went further, maintaining with iron consistency the complete impotence of man in the face of the omnipotence of God. At first sight, this appears a limitation rather than a development of individualism. Troeltsch therefore sees Calvinism as a particular sort of individualism rather than as an intensification of it (1922: n.320). I shall try to show that it is an intensification, insofar as the relation of the individual to the world is considered.

God's inscrutable will invests some men with the grace of election, and condemns others to reprobation. The task of the elect is to work for God's glory in the world, and faithfulness to this task will be the mark and the only proof of election. Thus, the elect relentlessly exercises his will in action, and in so doing, while absolutely subjected to God, he will in actual fact participate in Him in contributing to the implementation of His designs. I am trying, no doubt imperfectly, to sum up the nexus of subjection and exaltation of the self found in the configuration of Calvin's ideas and values. On this level, that is, within the consciousness of the elect, we find again the hierarchical dichotomy with which we are familiar. Troeltsch warns us against interpreting Calvin in terms of unfettered atomistic individualism. And it is true that divine grace, the grace of election, is central to the doctrine and that Calvin has nothing to do with man's freedom. He holds that 'the honour of God is safe, when man bows under His law, whether his submission is free or forced'. Yet, if we see here the emergence of inworldly individualism, and if we think of the intrinsic difficulty of this attitude, we might as well look on the individual elect's subjection to God's grace as the *necessary condition* for legitimating the decisive shift.

In effect, until then the individual had to recognise in the world an antagonistic factor, an irreducible alter that could not be suppressed but only subjected, encompassed. This limitation disappears with Calvin, and we find it replaced, so to speak, by his peculiar subjection to God's will. If such is the genesis of what Troeltsch and Weber called inworldly asceticism, we had best speak of ascetic, or conditioned, inworldliness.[18]

We may also contrast Calvin's active participation in God with the traditional contemplative participation that is still Luther's. Instead of taking refuge from this imperfect world in another which allowed us to cope, it would seem we had decided that we should ourselves embody that other world in our determined action upon this one. What is of paramount importance is that we have here the model of modern artificialism at large, the systematic application to the things of this world of an extrinsic, imposed value. Not a value derived from our belonging in this world, such as its harmony or our harmony with it, but a value rooted in our heterogeneity in relation to it: the identification of our will with the will of God (Descartes' man will make himself 'lord and master of nature'). The will applied to the world, the end sought after, the motive and inner spring of the will are extraneous; they are, to say the same thing, essentially outworldly. Outworldliness is now concentrated in the individual's will. This fits in with Tönnies' distinction of spontaneous will and arbitrary will *(Naturwille* and *Kürwille*), and it shows where the arbitrariness, (the *Willkür*) has its ground. To my mind it also underlines what Weber called modern rationality.

Our view of Calvin allows for correcting or deepening the paradigm that we used hitherto. Outworldliness is now concentrated in the individual's will. This recognition leads to thinking that modern artificialism as an exceptional phenomenon is understandable only as a distant historical consequence of Christian outworldly individualism, and that what we called the modern inworldly individual has in himself, hidden in his internal constitution, an unperceived but essential element of outworldliness. There is thus more continuity between the two kinds of individualism than we had initially supposed, with the consequence that a hypothetical direct transition from traditional holism to modern individualism appears now not only improbable but impossible.[19]

The conversion to inworldliness has in Calvin noteworthy concomitant features. I noticed the recession of mystical and emotional aspects. They are not entirely absent from Calvin's writings, but conspicuously so from his dogma. Even Redemption is seen in a dry legalistic way, as satisfaction of God's offended honour. Christ is the ruler of the Church (in place of the Pope), the paradigm of Christian life, and the seal authenticating the Old Testament. Christ's own distinctive teaching was not adequate to the regulation of a Christian earthly commonwealth and therefore the Sermon on the Mount largely disappears behind the Decalogue. The Covenant is between God and the Church, and it had been between God and ancient Israel. Choisy stressed the change from Luther's 'Christocracy' to Calvin's nomo- or logocracy.

Similarly, most features corresponding to otherworldliness lose their function and therefore disappear. The Second Coming had already for long lost much of its urgency. The Kingdom of God is essentially, we may say, to be built up piecemeal on earth through the efforts of the elect. To one who is unremittingly struggling with men and institutions as they actually are (the stress on the state of nature or of innocence), the distinction between the absolute and the relative law of nature appears as idle speculation.

But can we really assert that the individualist value now rules without contradiction or limitation? At first sight, this does not seem to be the case. Calvin keeps the medieval idea according to which the Church should dominate the State (or the political government of the city), and in the first place he still thinks in terms of *the* Church identified with the global society. Troeltsch was careful to underline the fact: although many features of Calvinism inclined it towards the sect, and whatever the future developments in the same direction or in that of the 'Free Churches', yet Calvin strictly adhered to the idea of the Church as regulating all activities within the social community as a whole. Indeed, he put into effect such a strict regulation in Geneva. This being so, it might be surmised that all trace of holism cannot have disappeared, that with Calvin, as before, some counterweight to individualism would result from the necessities of social life. Troeltsch tells us explicitly that it is not so:

> The idea of community has not been evolved out of the conception of the Church and of grace, like the Lutheran ecclesiastical idea; on the contrary it springs from the same principle which appears to give independence to the individual, namely from the ethical duty of the preservation and making effective of election, and from abstract biblicism . . . (1922:625–6; 1969:590–2).

Troeltsch quotes Schneckenburger: 'The Church does not make the believers what they are, but the believers make the Church what she is', and adds: 'the conception of the Church is placed within the setting of predestination' (1922: n. 320). Through predestination the individual takes the upper hand over the Church. This is of course a fundamental change. It becomes more understandable once we realise that Luther, while keeping the idea of the Church, as he thought, unchanged, has already in fact emptied it of its vital core. It remained as the institute of grace or salvation *(Heilsanstalt)*, but Calvin's predestination deprived it even of that dignity; actually if not in principle. What remained of the Church was an instrument of discipline acting on individuals (the elect as well as the reprobate, for they are practically indistinguishable) and on the political government. More precisely it was an institute of sanctification *(Heiligungsanstalt)*, effective in the christianising of the life of the city. The whole of life – in Church, family and State, society and economy, in all private and public relationship – had to be moulded by the Divine Spirit and the Divine Word as intimated by the Ministers of the Church (and eventually confirmed by the Consistory where laymen were represented in addition to the Ministers). In point of fact, the Church was now the organ through which the elect were to rule over the reprobate and to carry out their task for the glory of God. It kept some features of the old Church, which distinguished it from a sect, but at the same time it had become, for all practical purposes, an association composed of individuals.[20]

To sum up, Calvin did not acknowledge either in the Church or in the society or commonwealth, the Republic or City of Geneva – the two being coterminous in terms of membership – any principle of a holistic kind that would have limited the application of the individualist value. He acknowledged only imperfections, resistances or obstacles to be handled in the appropriate way, and a unified field for the exercise of the elect's activity, that is for the glorification of God.

Notwithstanding the vast chronological gap that remains, let me attempt a provisional conclusion. With Calvin the Church encompassing the State has dissolved as a holistic institution.

Yet Calvin's deed, the unification of the field and the conversion of the individual to this world, was made possible only by the secular action of the Church. It is clear that until then the Church had been the great agent of the transformation we are studying; something of an active mediator between the outworldly individual and the world, which is society at large and in particular the Empire or State.

We are thus enabled, in principle, to replace our initial model with a more precise one. But I must be content with a thumbnail sketch. Between the encompassing value – the outworldly individual – and earthly necessities and allegiances, we have to posit the Church. We see the Church throughout the centuries busy on two fronts – asserting itself against the political institution, and also, so to speak, against the individual. In other words, the Church has been growing on both sides: *(a)* by subordinating to itself, in principle at least, the Empire, and *(b)*, through the Gregorian reform and the doctrine of the sacraments in particular (Penance) by taking upon herself certain functions and capacities by means of which she smoothed the way to salvation of the common man, but which with the Reformation the individual will later on claim to recover. Luther and Calvin attack in the first place the Catholic Church as an institution of salvation. In the name of the self-sufficiency of the individual-in-relation-to-God they cancel the division of religious labour instituted by the Church. At the same time they accept, or rather Calvin most distinctly accepts, the unification obtained by the Church on the political side.

As a result of this double attitude the field already unified to a large extent by the Church falls by a single stroke under Calvin's inworldly individualism. The Reformation picks the fruit matured in the Church's lap.

In the general continuous process, the Reformation is a crisis marked by reversal on one level: the institution that had been the bridgehead of the outworldly and had conquered the world is itself condemned as having become inworldly in the process.

Notes

The first part is a slightly expanded version of the 1980 Deneke Lecture given at Lady Margaret Hall, Oxford. I am thankful to the College for the opportunity to return to a previous study which had remained uncompleted (see *Annuaire de l'Ecole pratique des Hautes Etudes, 6e section,* for 1973–4). The general hypothesis presented here was sparked off by a *Daedalus* colloquium on the first millennium B.C., and I am much indebted to the participants – mainly Arnaldo Momigliano, Sally Humphreys and Peter Brown – for their criticism and some suggestions (see *Daedalus,* Spring 1975, for the first and restricted form of the hypothesis, which the criticisms have contributed to modifying and widening).

The complement on Calvin was proposed in a seminar on the category of the person (Oxford, Wolfson College, May 1980).

This essay was first published in French in *Le Débat,* 15, Sept.–Oct. 1981; in English in *Religion,* 12, 1982, p. 1–27 (see the discussion in *Religion,* pp. 83–91).

1. See my essay 'World renunciation in Indian religions' first published in French in 1959, and then in English in 1960, now reprinted as Appendix B in Dumont 1980.
2. Quoted in Bevan 1927:63. The same author has noted the similarity with Indian renunciation. He quotes at length from the *Bhagavad Gita* to show the parallelism with Stoic maxims on detachment (*ibid.*: 75–9). Actually what the *Gita* exposes is renunciation accommodated to the world; cf. my paper (Note 1), section 4.
3. The distance is small between Troeltsch's inspiration and the present formulation. Thus Benjamin Nelson, no doubt a perceptive sociologist, noting that the interest not only of Troeltsch but of leading German thinkers in the nineteenth and twentieth centuries, from Hegel onwards, had focused on 'the institutionalisation of primitive Christianity', formulated their problem alternatively as 'how the charismatic fellowship of the apostolic Church had been bureaucratised' or, *'how an otherworldly "sect" gave rise to the Roman Church'* (Nelson 1975:232 n.; emphasis added).
4. See Hegel 1907:327*ff*,221;30; in English translation by Knox 1971:283*ff*, 152–65. The young Hegel was carried away by his revolutionary zeal and his fascination with

the ideal *polis* (*ibid.*: 163–64, 297–302,335; English: 81–83, 248–52, 293). Yet he slowly came to a better recognition of Jesus ('The spirit of Christianity'). For his mature views, see Theunissen (1970: 10–11 *passim*).

5. That the devaluation is relative here, radical there, is another matter. The more restricted parallel set up by Edward Conze between (Mahāyāna) 'Buddhism and Gnosis' clearly rests on the underlying presence on both sides of the outworldly individual (see especially the concluding developments and the last footnote in Conze 1967: 665*ff*).
6. Sir Edmund Leach has drawn attention to the millenarian aspect, but he saw it unilaterally and somewhat indiscriminately as a model of 'subversion' (Leach 1973:5–14; see also Note 10).
7. See Note 2.
8. Actually Caspary distinguishes four dimensions of contrast or 'parameters', of which he gives only one as hierarchical (1979: 113–14), but it is easy to see that hierarchy extends to all of them.
9. In his otherwise invaluable book, A.J. Carlyle (1903) had treated in two separate chapters 'natural equality and government' and 'the sacred authority of the ruler'.
10. Leach linked Arianism with millenarism (see Note 6 above).
11. The texts of Gelasius are taken from Carlyle (1903:190–1) (but see Note 13). The translation follows mostly Dvornik's (1966: vol. 2, 804–5).
12. See 'The conception of kingship in ancient India', (esp. § 3), now in Dumont 1980: App. C. (cf. Note 1 above).
13. On this point our authors' texts seem (variously) corrupt. We read with Schwartz: *officia potestatis utriusque* (Schwartz 1934:14).
14. See Hegel's *Philosophy of Right,* Part III, section iii, and his impatience in 1831 at seeing the Revolution threatening to burst out anew. ('The English Reform Bill' in *Political writings, in fine,* and correspondence.) Cf. Habermas' 'Nachwort' in Hegel 1966:364–65, and the pointed reference to *Philosophy of Right* (actually §258: 'If the State is confused with civil Society . . .').
15. I hope to produce an account of the process as a whole at some later date.
16. This epilogue is thus no more than an exercise on Troeltsch's text. If an excuse is needed for not considering wider literature, I shall say that, judging from a few incursions – as into the books by Choisy to which Troeltsch refers, or into Calvin's own *Institutes* – one finds that the questions at issue can easily be univocally answered: there is no twilight, no zone that would call for another angle of vision or another kind of lighting: the contours have been drawn with a firm hand and there is no mistaking them. Indeed there is something slightly uncanny in Calvin's assurance and decisiveness. In this as elsewhere he is quite modern: the rich, complex and fluctuating world of structure has been banned.
17. This feature seems largely neglected in the history of ideas. Such a type of transcendence will later appear unbearable to German philosophers. Colin Morris happily contrasts Karl Barth's statement that there is no point of contact between God and man with the close presence of God in St. Bernard and with the Cistercian effort 'to discover God in man and through man' (1972:163).
18. Max Weber said very much the same thing in 1910 in a discussion following Troeltsch's lecture on Natural Law: he opposed 'the forms of world-rejecting religiosities' to the 'Calvinistic religiosity which finds the certitude of being God's child in the to-be-attained "proving of oneself" *(Bewahrung)* . . . within the given and ordered world'; or again on the one hand the 'community' of acosmic love characteristic of the eastern Church and Russia, on the other, the 'society' or 'the formation of the social structure upon an egocentric base' (Nelson 1973:148).
19. The two parts of our initial paradigm had been developed more or less independently and could appear as mutually inconsistent. To put the matter briefly, the hol-

ism/individualism distinction supposes an inworldly individualism, while in the inworldly/outworldly distinction the outworldly pole is not opposed to holism (at any rate, in the same manner as the inworldly pole). Actually, outworldly individualism is hierarchically opposed to holism: superior to society, it leaves society standing, while inworldly individualism negates, destroys the holistic society and replaces it (or pretends to do so). The continuity we have now described between the two types, especially in the instance of Calvin, reinforces their unity and qualifies their difference. It thus confirms the initial paradigm.

20. See Note 18.

References

Bevan, Edwyn. 1927. *Stoïciens et Sceptiques.* (Translated from English.) Paris, Belles-Lettres.

Bidez, J. 1932. "La Cité du monde et la Cité du soleil chez les Stoïciens". *Bulletin de l'Académie royale de Belgique,* Lettres, série V, vols. 18–19, pp. 244–94.

Carlyle, A.J. 1903. *The second century to the ninth,* vol. 1 in R.W. and A.J. Carlyle, *A history of mediaeval political theory in the West.* Edinburgh and London, Blackwood.

Caspary, G. 1979. *Politics and exegesis: Origen and the two swords.* Berkeley, University of California Press.

Congar, Yves M.J. 1968. *L'Ecclésiologie du haut moyen âge.* Paris, Editions du Cerf.

Conze, Edward, 1967. "Buddhism and Gnosis", in Anonymous: *Le origini dello gnosticismo.* Colloquio di Messina, April 13–18, 1966. Leiden, Brill.

Dumont, Louis. 1960. "World renunciation in Indian religions". See Dumont 1980, Appendix B.

1962. "The conception of kingship in ancient India". See Dumont 1980, Appendix C.

1980. *Homo Hierarchicus. The caste system and its implications,* University of Chicago Press.

Dvornik, F. 1966. *Early Christian and Byzantine political philosophy, origins and background.* 2 vols. Washington, Dumbarton Oaks Center.

Erhardt, Arnold A.T. 1959–69. *Politische Metaphysik von Solon bis Augustus.* 3 vols. Tübingen, Mohr.

Goodenough, E.R. 1940. *An introduction to Philo Judaeus.* New Haven, Yale University Press.

Hegel, G.W.F. 1907. *Hegels theologische Jugendschriften,* edited by von H. Nohl, Tübingen, Mohr. English translation by T.M. Knox, *Hegel's early Theological Writings,* 1971. University of Pennsylvania Press.

1942. *Philosophy of Right,* translated by T.M. Knox, Oxford University.

1964. *Political Writings.* Oxford University Press.

1966. *Politische Schriften.* Frankfurt, Suhrkamp.

Leach, Edmund. 1973. "Melchisedech and the Emperor: Icons of subversion and orthodoxy." *Proceedings of the Royal Anthropological Institute for 1972.* London, pp. 5–14.

Morris, Colin. 1972. *The discovery of the individual, 1050–1200.* London, SPCK.

Morrison, Karl F. 1969. *Tradition and authority in the western Church, 300–1140.* Princeton University Press.

Nelson, Benjamin. 1973. "Max Weber on church, sect and mysticism". *Sociological Analysis,* 34, 2.

1975. "Weber, Troeltsch, Jellinek as comparative historical sociologists". *Sociological Analysis,* 36, 3.

Partner, Peter. 1972. *The Lands of St. Peter.* London, Eyre and Methuen.

Peterson, Erik, 1951. "Der Monotheismus als politisches Problem" *Theologische Traktate.* München, Kösel, pp. 25–147.

Sabine, George H. 1963. *A History of Political Thought,* 3rd ed. London, Harrap.

Schwartz, E. 1934. "Publizistische Sammlungen". *Abhandlung der BayerischerAkademie,* Philologie–Historisch Abteilung, NF 10. München.

Southern, R. 1970. *Western Society and the Church in the Middle Ages.* Harmondsworth, Penguin.

Theunissen, Michael. 1970. *Hegels Lehre des absoluten Geistes als theologisch–politischer Traktat.* Berlin, de Gruyter.

Troeltsch, Ernst 1922. *Die Soziallehren der christlichen Kirchen und Gruppen,* in *Gesammelte Schriften.* Band I. Tübingen, Mohr. English translation by O. Wyon. *The social teaching of the Christian churches and groups.* New York, Harper Torchbooks, 1960.

1925. "Das stoisch-christliche Naturrecht und das moderne profane Naturrecht". *Gessammelte Schriften,* IV. Tübingen, Mohr.

Ulmann, Walter, 1955. *The Growth of Papal Government in the Middle Ages.* London, Methuen.

6

Person and individual: some anthropological reflections[1]

J.S. La Fontaine

In the paper reprinted in this volume, Mauss argues that the idea of the individual is unique to Western thought. He uses an evolutionary method which was, even at the time which he wrote (1938), somewhat old fashioned, to trace the development of the idea and to set out a contrast between the social and moral significance of the individual in Western society and the absence of such a concept in other societies. Dumont, his pupil, makes this contrast the basis of the opposition set out in *Homo Hierarchicus,* between hierarchy, the fundamental principle of Indian society, and equality, which is a Western idea, rooted in individualism. However, Mauss's essay appears to have made little impact on British anthropology until comparatively recently.[2] The earliest article on the subject by Read (1955) offers empirical confirmation of the French view, arguing that the New Guinean people he studied lack a concept of the person, a term he, like Mauss, attributes uniquely to Western thought, though strangely Read does not mention Mauss. Read's article remained an isolated example of British work on this topic until an important contribution by Fortes (1973), which takes the opposite view: that all societies have a concept of the person. Other anthropologists have contributed ethnographic data which can be used to further a discussion which, with a revival in Britain of anthropological concern with systems of thought, has once again become of central interest.

This chapter has two aims: to discuss Mauss's conclusion in the light of subsequent ethnographic evidence and then to advance an explanation for the manifest variation in concepts of the person which the ethnography demonstrates. My view is that such concepts cannot be considered out of context. In particular I shall be arguing that social representations of society itself, and the nature of authority within society, give a characteristic form to related notions of the person.

It is already clear that the Western concept of the person needs clarification, for the terms person and individual have been used as though they were interchangeable although they are not (cf. Beattie 1980:313–14). Mauss starts by distinguishing between the social concept of the person and any human being's self-awareness, which he regards as universal, as manifest in language and largely the concern of linguists and psychologists. He thus contrasts consciousness of self, which he sees as compounded of awareness of the body and of the spirit, an 'individuality, both spiritual and physical' with a social concept. The social concept, the idea of the person, is a compound of jural rights, and moral responsibility; it also includes what Mauss attributes to the Greek roots of our civilisation, a notion of the actor behind the mask, the unique and transient human being. This is translated by Christianity into the idea of the soul to arrive finally at the notion of a unity, of body and soul, mind and conscience, thought and action which is summed up in the concept of the individual which Mauss labelled 'the person', *'la personne morale'*. Dumont, in building on Mauss's work, uses the term 'individual' rather than person, but he refers to the same idea: the social concept of a unique and indivisible unity. Alan MacFarlane in his recent book, *The Origins of English Individualism,* describes it as: ". . . the view that society is constituted of autonomous, equal units, namely separate individuals and that such individuals are more important, ultimately, than any larger constituent group. It is reflected in the concept of individual private property, in the political and legal liberty of the individual, in the idea of the individual's direct communication with God" (MacFarlane 1978:5). The Western concept of the individual thus gives jural, moral and social significance to the mortal human being, the empirically observable entity. This entity, its constitution, acts and motivation receives some form of social recognition in all societies.

In order to compare the variability of social forms against the universal human being of which they are representations, some clarification of terms is essential. Mauss uses the term 'person' to refer to one distinct variety of such collective representations, the Western idea, which Dumont and MacFarlane, following an earlier tradition, have labelled 'individualism'. If the self is an individual's awareness of a unique identity, the 'person' is society's confirmation of that identity as of social significance. Person and individual are identified in contrast to the self.

Radcliffe-Brown, the source of many of the contributions from British anthropologists, makes a sharp distinction between individual and person, from a theoretical stance which ignores both awareness of self and the collective representations. His characteristically lucid exposition asserts:

> Every human being living in society is two things: he is an individual and he is also a person. As an individual he is a biological organism. . . . Human beings as individuals are objects of study for physiologists and psychologists. The human being as a person is a complex of social relationships. . . . As a person the human being is the object of study for social anthropologists (1940:193–4).

The concept of the person is thus a technical term which abstracts certain features, roles in social relationships, from the empirical reality, Mauss's self-conscious unity of mind and body. There seems no possibility of confusion; but Radcliffe-Brown is aware that in common parlance no such clear distinctions are made. He continues in a later passage:

> If you tell me that an individual and a person are after all really the same thing, I would remind you of the Christian creed. God is three persons, but to say that He is three individuals is to be guilty of a heresy for which men have been put to death. Yet the failure to distinguish individual and person is not merely a heresy in religion: it is worse than that; it is a source of confusion in science (1940:194).

Radcliffe-Brown is himself guilty of falling into this confusion. As his critics have pointed out, in his article on The Mother's Brother in South Africa, he explains the social relationship between the roles Mother's Brother and Sister's Son as though it were a relationship between individuals. It is a fault of which methodological individualists, who use their society's concepts as though they were analytical tools, have also been accused.[3] Clearly, for Western Europeans the distinction between the individual and person is hard to make.[4]

Radcliffe-Brown ignores the problem of how society conceptualises the self but Fortes, in an article written for a conference devoted to considering Mauss's paper (Fortes 1973), transposes Radcliffe-Brown's term 'person' from theoretical anthropology to ethnography, using it as a label for the social representation. For him then, Mauss's *'personne morale'* is merely a special case of a concept common to all societies: he argues "that the notion of the person in the Maussian sense[5] is intrinsic to the very nature and structure of human society and human social behaviour everywhere" (1973:288). This is because such a concept is concerned with "the perennial problem of how individual and society are interconnected" (ibid); the context of the article shows that 'individual' clearly means what Radcliffe-Brown means by the term. Since I use Fortes's approach here I shall also accept his wider, ethnographic, definition of person.

In what follows I shall use the term 'individual' to refer to the mortal human being, the object of observation, and 'person' to refer to concepts such as that of the Tallensi which lend the object social significance. This usage has the advantage of an attempt to maintain the distinction between individual and person, the difficulty of which was commented on by Radcliffe-Brown and Dumont. It still allows us to use the term 'individualism' or 'individualist' to refer to the Western variety of the concept of person which, I shall argue, is indeed different from those found in the four exemplar societies to whose ethnography I now turn.

All four societies: the Tallensi of Ghana, the Lugbara of Uganda, the Taita of Kenya and the Gahuku-Gama of Highland New Guinea are agricultural peoples, lacking centralised political institutions, in the absence of which, patrilineal descent organises local communities, though in different ways. There are many differences in their concepts but the similarities reveal that overall they resemble one another in their concepts of 'person' more than they resemble the individualist West. It should be clear, then, that my conclusions differ from Fortes, though I use his approach to the problem.

In these four societies human beings are seen as composite creatures; in all four the individual human being is composed of material and immaterial components. Neither aspect is necessarily simple; indeed, as Beattie remarks (1980), the concepts of other societies often seem immensely complex by comparison with the ethnographer's own. Like our own, however, concepts of the person serve to identify and explain a wide range of behaviour, emotions and events. None of the concepts are strictly comparable with the concept of person which characterises individualism, for the elements are not unified into a whole which of itself has significance. There is a difference in the degree to which material or immaterial elements are emphasised; where the immaterial components of the person are of greatest significance some human beings are not persons at all. This is true of the Tallensi and Lugbara, whose concepts of the person distinguish most clearly between the transient reality of human life and social significance.

Living beings and social roles

To take the Tallensi concepts first: a human being has *sii,* which is not life itself, but that which constitutes the living body as a unique entity, an individual in our terms. An individual's possessions are imbued with his (or her?) *sii;* the taboos which an eldest son must observe towards his father's possessions are said, by Tallensi, to prevent conflict between the *sii* of the son and that of his living father, for it is *sii* which accounts for the state of personal relations between individuals. The attraction and repulsion of the *sii* in each individual engenders liking or dislike. It would seem that the *sii* vanishes at death, when it is detached from the body *(pooni);* this possibility of detachment is not identical with the body's mortality, for the *sii* may be detached temporarily and harmlessly in sleep, although it is also vulnerable to mystical injury.

The living body is what distinguishes persons *(niriba)* from ancestors, ghosts and non-human spirits on the one hand; the immaterial aspects distinguish men from animals. However, certain sacred crocodiles, which are manifestations of the ancestors, are persons for they combine the human spiritual aspects with a living body; not all crocodiles are persons, merely those which satisfy these essential prerequisites. Individuals are distinguished from one another by their distinct *sii;* names do not have this effect, for they identify the individual, first with "an event in the life history of his family" (the public name), and secondly with an ancestral guardian (the private name). These distinguish him first from other individuals, by reference to a family, and secondly from among his agnates. The shrine which Fortes calls a Personal Destiny shrine, embodies the fate already prepared for its owner and is associated with a set of ancestors; it thus distinguishes him as an individual but in terms of a "place in a system of social relations" (Fortes 1973:315). A human being's unique identity is thus determined from the first by his place in society.

To the Lugbara human beings are bodies, animated by and infused with *adro* spirit. This spirit is a refraction of Spirit, the capital letter being used by Middleton to represent the "immanent aspect of divinity" (1973:494); it is responsible not only for life itself but also for an individual's desires and wishes. Women's *adro* is responsible for their erratic behaviour, their yielding to personal whims and their association with the bush which is the location of Spirit. This is because women lack *orindi,* a spirit of responsibility which enables an individual to control his egoistic *adro; orindi* grows with age, it is weak in small boys and strongest in old men, although individuals vary in the amount they manifest. "A man who behaves contrary to this expected [male] behaviour does so because his spirit is too strong and out of control and if it is too blatant he may be thought a witch" (Middleton 1973:503). It is this quality of responsibility, *orindi,* which accounts, in Lugbara views, for the authority of men and the jural minority of women. It is thus intelligible that it is *orindi* which is transformed into *ori* (ghost), or rather *a'bi,* that element of the ghost (for they are composite beings too), which is responsible for and responsive to, its descendants. It is thus, as Middleton states, *orindi* which confers personhood on Lugbara men, though not on all. There are significant categories of Lugbara men who are not persons, as we shall see.

Bodily idioms and concepts of the individual

Concepts of biology are believed by those who hold them to represent the empirical reality of human beings; in some societies, they may locate elements of human behaviour in organs of the body, linking human physiology and psychology. Thus the Taita individual, according to Harris, is "an entity made up of various components and capacities, some of them surviving death and connected with bodily parts and processes" (Harris 1978:49). The head is associated with the total individual being: (Harris's phrase is the 'total person'). It is seen as the locus of consciousness, speech, memory and knowledge. Women's heads are held to be weaker than men's, their hearts more prone to disturbance. The heart is the seat of emotion, in particular emotions which affect others, of which the most important is anger. It is also the source of life, for when the heart is 'finished', the individual is dead. Because of the heart, in its mystical aspect, human beings male and female, can become ancestors and affect their living descendants; in living individuals the anger of the heart may cause misfortune to the one who arouses it. Taita rituals normally involve a blessing to cool and cast out anger from the heart; the term for this act, *butasi,* is also the Taita name for their religion.

In similar vein the Tallensi also attribute various emotions to different organs of the body. They distinguish between head and heart but in different terms from the Taita. The quality *yam,* which Fortes glosses as wisdom or good judgement, increases with age and progressively enhances its owner's personhood, and is located in the abdomen. Fortes also tells us that the terms for the various emotions are compounds of the root word indicating the bodily region with which they are identified. However, it is among the Gahuku-Gama as described by Read (1955) that the material (what we would call the biological) aspect of the individual receives its greatest emphasis. Read writes: "To an extent which it is perhaps difficult for us to appreciate and understand, the various parts of the body, limbs, eyes, nose, hair, the internal organs and bodily excretions are essential constituents of the human personality, incorporating and expressing the whole in each of their several parts. It follows that an injury to any part of the body is also comparable to damage to the personality of the individual sustaining the injury" (1955:265). Among the Gahuku-Gama a whole range of behaviour, from everyday greeting to the rituals of mourning when hair is cut, follows from this premise.

A feature of Gahuku-Gama ideas which I shall set out at more length is the significance of 'skin', a notion which includes the fleshy covering of the body; it represents the whole range of characteristics of the individual. Cultural differences, as manifest in individual behaviour, are referred to as skins of the same or different kind; "indebtedness involves having a debt 'on one's skin'." Moral evaluations can also be expressed in this way; individuals can be described as having good or bad skins. A bad skin may also refer to a social state; a state of mourning is 'having a bad skin'. It is consistent with all these attitudes to the body, as Read argues, that relationships are expressed in frequent and intimate touching, bodily contact and fondling. The frequent rites associated with the development of children are directed to their physical growth and development. By comparison the *meni,* the immaterial element which gives life to the body and which is described by Read as "the essential principle of human nature, the whole self or personality – this element is of negligible significance. At death it simply ceases to exist; what remains is something so insubstantial as to have no characteristics and no individuality" (Read 1955: 265).

Read argues that among the Gahuku-Gama there is "no essential separation of the individual from the social pattern; social roles and social status are not distinguished from the individuals who enact them" (1955:276). The incorporation of non-physical attributes into the 'skin' of the living human being makes the same point in Gahuku-Gama terms. In a telling passage, Read shows that the lack of a concept of friendship follows from these same premises. In Western Europe the notion of friendship is defined as a relationship between two unique individuals, not by virtue of any socially defined relationship such as that of neighbour or kinsman, but as social persons in the Maussian sense. The Gahuku-Gama could not grasp this idea; it was impossible for them to conceive of a relationship apart from one defined in social structural terms. It was not, as Read points out, that in their daily life they did not show personal preferences, interact more with some people than others, but such behaviour was not conceptualised as a relationship between persons.

Read's paper is argued towards an explanation of the relativisitic moral code of the Gahuku-Gama, which he claims rests on the lack of a concept of the person. He does not cite Mauss, but his detailed discussion of the Christian origin of the idea makes it clear that he is making the same point: that the idea of the person is peculiar to a particular society or civilisation. By contrast, among this New Guinean people: "Individual identity and social identity are two sides of the same coin" (Read 1955:276).

The bodily idiom used by the Gahuku-Gama should perhaps be seen as the conceptual mechanism whereby these people obliterate the distinction between an individual and his social roles by incorporating the latter into his physical self, into the skin. Yet this is an ethnocentric formulation for it implies a prior distinction between self and society, actor and role which does not seem to exist among the Gahuku-Gama. It would be more accurate to say that the Gahuku-Gama do not distinguish clearly the material and immaterial (including the social) attributes of persons. Their concept of the person is totally particularised. Since there is no awareness of relationships unstructured by recognised roles, which are part of each individual, there is no general category of personhood, merely distinct personalities, defined by their particular social relations. These particular sets of roles are unique combinations of relationships which, like the body, cease to exist at death. It is not surprising to find Read emphasising the strong sense of self and the violent aggressive behaviour of Gahuku-Gama, for their concept of the person implies that bodily strength is social power.

Social continuity, responsibility and concepts of the person

If the Gahuku-Gama seem to recognise no generalised concept of personhood, this is clearly not true of the other societies I am considering, although their concepts of personhood do not extend to all individuals. As I have pointed out, most Lugbara women and some Lugbara men are not persons. Rainmakers and diviners, who are often women, are associated with *adro,* spirit and hence with the bush, not the settlements where ancestral shrines are located. They are thus outside society in some sense, since they do not participate in the association of the living and the dead which constitutes the continuity of social life, society itself. The personhood of women among the Tallensi is of a lesser order than that of men for women lack the domestic and lineage authority of men. For the Taita, Harris notes that the full range of ritual powers is not open to women so that they reach the limits of their achieved personhood sooner than men. In all three societies children are, by definition, not persons; Taita children are treated as extensions of their parents and referred to as 'somebody's child', a phrase which may also be used of adults when their ritual and social dependency is being stressed. (It may perhaps be noted that a phrase which recurs frequently in English discussions of the emancipation of women is 'a person in her own right' which suggests that sexual differentiation in personhood is not entirely alien to Western Europe!) Autonomy and responsibility thus seem vital to the concept of personhood and certain individuals by virtue of their sex, or their specialist roles, are excluded. They are individuals and may wield considerable power; they are not persons.

It is the Tallensi ethnography which indicates most clearly that the concept of person there refers to what Harris calls a 'moral career' (1978:48), using this term to refer to an essentially similar situation among the Taita. Among the Tallensi an individual is first identified by birth into a particular lineage, his public name associates him with an event in his family's history and his private name, together with the ancestors in his Personal Destiny shrine, distinguish him among his agnates, though not to society at large. It is the completion of a proper life which qualifies an individual for full personhood, for marriage and the birth of children are essential prerequisites. Fortes emphasises that no individual qualities of behaviour or temperament can disqualify a parent from personhood; conversely, no matter how loved and admired an individual may be, if he or she fails to fulfil the ideal pattern of life and leaves no children, then full personhood has not been attained.

Lugbara women can never become full persons for they lack *orindi,* the sense of responsibility, although some old women may have power in their own right; unlike the Lugbara, the Taita do accord full personhood to women but this quality is developed over the course of an individual's life. To be more precise the ritual recognition of the accumulation of roles and statuses marks the progress of Taita men and women towards full personhood. The process starts at initiation when the boy or girl ceases to be "somebody's child" and becomes an adult, a transition fully accomplished at marriage. Married adults become, in a sense, the equals of their parents; Taita express this by saying that a man becomes a brother to his father. As householders they are equal. However a man whose father is alive, like a Tallensi or Lugbara man in the same situation, is still not fully independent and capable of autonomous action. A husband and wife may still be referred to as 'somebody's children' in ritual where this dependency is vital. Harris sees ritual in Taita life as helping "to create personhood by ritually conferring its elements upon the individual and transforming happenings in the life-cycle into moral events" (1978:76). It is the long-drawn-out character of this transformation of the individual into a person which characterises non-Western societies. In Western societies the conferring of a name serves to achieve the same end; personhood and individuality are thus identified from the beginning.

By contrast, for the Tallensi, personhood is finally validated at the death of the individual. Fortes lays great stress on this element in Tallensi thought. At death, the Tallensi divine to discover the cause of death to reassure themselves that the death was such as to confer personhood on the deceased, that he was not, for example, a bush sprite masquerading as a human being. A "good death" for the Tallensi is one which derives from the ancestors and which follows the assumption of the full range of statuses proper for the individual, in particular that of parent. The essence of Tallensi personhood is thus continuity, as it is for the Lugbara, for even Lugbara men cannot become significant ancestors (ghosts in Middleton's terminology) unless they have sons, although the *orindi* of any man survives after death as part of the nameless dead, the ancestors as a collectivity. According to Fortes, personhood is conferred by society on the individual. There are two aspects of the matter to be borne in mind, he argues: the awareness of its bearer of socially generated personhood, that is, the assemblage of roles and statuses and, secondly, the qualities and powers associated with personhood that are conferred on individuals. Here personhood is explicitly associated with office in the Weberian sense; Fortes tells us, what is also clear from the other accounts, that "an individual is *invested* with the capacities of personhood specific to defined roles and statuses" (1973:287, my italics). The completed person, whether Tallensi, Lugbara or Taita is the product of a whole life. By conferring personhood on the individual such societies also, though implicitly, distinguish between person and individual, conferring moral worth not on the individual but on the social form, which includes as a vital element the maintenance of continuity. The concept serves to fuse the finite span of a human life with the unlimited continuity of social forms, by identifying personhood with self-reproduction.

How far can we say that Mauss's conclusion has been validated by subsequent ethnographic investigation? *Pace* Fortes, I would say that it has been. The use of Radcliffe-Brown's concept of the social personality enabled Fortes to classify Tallensi ideas, and allowed me to classify Taita and Lugbara ideas, too, as concepts of the person. However, the concept of the person as manifest in individualism, the '*personne morale*' makes it clear that it does not refer to the sum of statuses; Mauss uses the term *personnage* for such a concept. The person in individualism implies a general moral status accorded individual human beings by virtue of their humanity, which recognises their autonomy and responsibility for their actions.[6] It is, as Mauss argued, the extension into the moral sphere of the concept of the unique nature of the individual. By contrast, the ideas I have been discussing here particularise, they do not generalise. In spite of general terms such as the Tallensi *niriba,* which serves to distinguish people both from animals and disembodied spirits, personhood varies according to social criteria which contain the capacities of the individual within defined roles and categories. Indeed, one might say that where personhood is a status reserved for defined categories of people, parents or men, by implication those who are not persons are individuals and such concepts may be said to distinguish more clearly between these two ideas than most Western versions. There is evidence from the three African societies to support this contention. Fortes reports that when an elder is invested with linear office he is left alone for one night with the insignia of office; if he is unworthy of the responsibility the office may kill him (Fortes, 1973). In similar vein, Lugbara elders inflict with illness those who defy their authority; however it is tressed by Middleton that an elder should not use his powers to punish offences committed against him as an individual but only those which attack his office (Middleton, 1973). His powers are thought to derive from the ancestors who are concerned, not with individuals, but with the maintenance of social order. The Taita doctrine of the anger of hearts is similar in its effects, although the powers of anger are not restricted to lineage elders among the Taita; even a child may cause harm by its anger. Taita believe that proneness to anger is a natural human characteristic, although they recognise that some individuals are more quickly roused than others. In particular it is thought that anger is provoked when an individual sees the rights pertaining to his socially defined status being ignored or denied. Thus the anger of individuals defends the rights by which a person will be defined; 'casting out anger', the ritual to repair the harm caused by anger, thus emphasises the rights pertaining to roles and statuses, confirming the individual incumbency of them. It is important to note, though, the direction of attack by such mystical harm: anger causes harm to the person defined as responsible in the relationship in which it occurs. Anger among Taita is thus a sanction against the improper use of authority.

Beattie has noted that the "abstract and immaterial components of the person . . ." have in common that they are conceived as "forces, powers or potentialities of some kind" (Beattie 1980:315). The Lugbara concept of *tali* confirms this view; it also serves to underline the distinction between individual and office, for *tali* refers to the ability of an individual to influence others as an individual, and not an office-holder. All Lugbara are believed to have *tali,* which grows with age, being weak in children and strongest in powerful elders. Old women, particularly the elder sisters of lineage elders, have strong *tali,* even though they are not persons and cannot exercise authority like their brothers. *Tali* is also responsible for the powers of other categories of non-person: rainmakers and diviners. *Tali* is clearly a quality of individuals; it is a direct manifestation of Spirit, although it is connected with lineage organisation for the lineage has a pool of *tali* to which the *tali* of members is added when they die. Agnates can therefore augment the lineage pool or store of *tali* if their own is strong. It is significant that Tallensi by contrast know of believers in powers conferred directly on individuals through possession or the direct intervention of spirits, and do not credit them (Fortes 1979:68). In the Tallensi system of collective representations there is no room for individual powers, for powers are exercised by individuals only as the authority of office.

The distinction between individual and person, and the nature of the constituent elements of the person seem connected with the degree to which office and office-holder are distinguished, the degree to which such offices are in fact institutionalised. All Tallensi, Lugbara and Taita are individuals but not all are recognised as full persons; those that are exercise powers and must accept responsibilities, which are attributed to the office; office is legitimised in a variety of ways, which we can call traditional, in Weberian terms. By contrast, the Gahuku-Gama appear to make no distinction between actor and role, individual and person; the bodies of living beings are, at the same time, both private selves and social persons. There seem to be no offices in this society and the only authority is that of senior kinsmen.

The link between the nature of authority and the concept of the person is suggested by Beteille in an article on inequality (1980:5). He attacks the association of equality with individualism which is made by Dumont (and see the quote from MacFarlane earlier in this chapter). He goes on to point out that individualism is most developed in those societies where achievement is considered of great importance and competition is the means by which individuals acquire power and office. By contrast, in hierarchical societies, ascription assigns the social and political roles of individuals and inequalities inhere in social roles. Hence, by a paradox, Western societies conceive of natural man, the individual, as equal in order to disguise the inequalities of achievement; Indian society, the locus of Dumont's *Homo Hierarchicus,* is free to acknowledge equality emerging from individual behaviour, since inequality is ascribed. Dumont and Beteille are using a much broader canvas than I attempt to cover; however, if we apply their approach to the four societies I have used as examples in this paper, there are interesting results.

While all four societies are similar in some respects, as I indicated earlier, the axis along which they conspicuously vary is that of the nature of authority. Among the Tallensi strict succession by agnatic seniority is the principle by which the authority of office is allocated; the political unit is defined by a genealogy which also establishes a hierarchy among agnates.[7] Power inheres in the traditional office; there is a clear indication that this is so in the Tallensi belief, cited earlier, that if an unworthy individual allows himself to be invested with office, it will kill him. Personhood, like office, is a fulfilment of social roles and, significantly, is finally validated only when the individual ceases to exist, at death. Among the Taita a measure of achievement allows some men to surpass their fellows; there are no offices conferring authority on their incumbents. Instead a hierarchy of shrines, medicines of increasing power, is associated in its lower ranks with the life-cycle as bench-marks on the route to full personhood. The successful progress further and faster along this route than the insignificant; the more powerful the shrines, the fewer the elders entitled to own them. The summit of attainment is a ritual few achieve, which in some sense confers ancesterhood on a man before his death. In a manner totally alien to the Tallensi, a married Taita man achieves a measure of equality with his father; thereafter his personhood increases with his success, though at each stage it must be ritually validated, by his seniors. Authority increases throughout a successful moral career. The Lugbara represent another variation: as among the Tallensi, the politically significant unit is constituted genealogically and seniority is a matter of agnatic succession; however, the concept of powers derived from Spirit introduces a new element: charismatic authority. Rainmakers and diviners are non-persons, outside the normal structure of traditional authority. They are individuals possessing *tali,* the power to influence others and their specialist powers are received direct from Spirit as individuals. One could argue, against Middleton, that such people are not non-persons, they are persons in the Western sense, except for the fact that they are exceptional, abnormal. Moreover their powers are not entirely outside the lineage framework.[8]

It seems clear that as far as these three examples are concerned, that the greater the emphasis on traditional office, the clearer is the distinction between individual and person, and, that where individual achievement of influence is recognised, as among the Lugbara and to some extent the Taita, then more than one concept of the person may co-exist. Recognition of individuality exists in all three African societies, but among the Tallensi and among the Taita full personhood is the attainment of a whole life, a moral career, which is not achieved by all; the influence of the actor on his role receives recognition in the Taita doctrine of the anger of hearts, and they do not attribute authority to clearly-defined office but to a ladder of achieved ritual powers. Each new rung of the ladder must receive public recognition by ritual investiture. The Lugbara appear to have a double concept of power, *tali* and the ancestral power of invocation exercised by elders, and it is consistent with this that there are possibilities of exercising social influence outside the hierarchy defined by genealogy.

None of the three African societies can be said to have systems of competitive leadership; there are kinship and descent principles which rank individuals. By contrast the Gahuku-Gama present the very picture of free competition. There we find the pattern of aggressive achievement, of shifting alliances and Big Men striving to hold together followings which are vulnerable to the vagaries of war or the success of others (the pattern made familiar by the ethnographers of Highland New Guinea). Where the Taita dislike violence and seek to prevent and control it, among these Highlanders it is "the warp of the cultural pattern and is manifest alike in many day to day situations as well as many institutional contexts" (Read 1955:254). Read states: "The majority of social rewards go to the physically strong and self-assertive; to the proud and the flamboyant and to the extroverted warrior and orator who demands, and usually obtains, the submission of his fellows. As a result we find that people are markedly aware of themselves as individuals" (Read 1955:254). Read administered special tests, devised by Nadel, to check his findings and these confirmed the personality characteristics his impressions suggested. Yet he argues that the Gahuku-Gama view of man does not distinguish between the individual and his social roles. If, as Beteille has argued (1980), individualism reflects a competitive society, one would expect the Gahuku-Gama to hold a concept of the person more akin to that of the West. The fact that they do not suggests that something is missing in the initial formulation, a crucial element which accounts for the unique character of the individualist concept of the person.

What has been overlooked in discussions of the Western notions is that they exist in the context of a particular concept of society as a whole: the idea of the nation-state. The idea of the whole is integral to MacFarlane's definition of individualism with which I began: "society is constituted of autonomous equal units" and, equally, the individual is a constituent unit of society. The institutions which reflect the idea of the (individualist) person are established and maintained by a society organised on the rule of law, the state in which persons are citizens. In such a society all members, even rulers are, ideally, subject to the law. As Weber pointed out long ago, this principle is the defining characteristic of bureaucratic organisation. The main features of such structures are: a clear distinction between office and office-holder, and hence between an individual and his social role, and the allocation of authority on the basis of fitness for office, fitness being of course a quality of individuals. The equality of persons and competition for office are thus integral to the structure of Western society. Hierarchy and inequality are conceptualised as attributes of social roles; all individuals are equal as persons.

By contrast, all the other societies I have been discussing base their concept of society on the idea of tradition, established once and for all. Society is the projection over time of the original founders, heroes or ancestors. From the outsider's point of view, this means that the boundaries of society are established by the genealogy which relates living people to these original beings. The genealogy creates a structure in which the relations of individuals to the whole are mediated through a series of more and more inclusive links. The farther removed in time the ancestor, the wider the group that recognises its identity by reference to that focal point. The widest referent may not be the same as that which might be defined by a common language. The significant feature is that, ideally, in such a society each new baby has a position defined at birth, which relates it to this structure and the succession of generations. Only full siblings have the same social identity and even they may be ranked in order of birth, as they are distinguished by sex. Personhood in such a society is, as Radcliffe-Brown pointed out, a complex of social relationships. As more social relations are added through life, personhood approaches completion, but the critical feature is the social relation with the next generation whereby society is continued into yet another generation. Not every individual is fully a person, or even a person at all, in societies which define human beings by their place in a social chain linking past with present.

The Gahuku-Gama seem to lack all concepts of a social whole. Little of myth or legend exists among them to establish a traditional identity and genealogies are shallow, serving to organise small groups which are vulnerable to warfare and other demographic accidents. They live in a social world of change and instability. There are no fixed units of allegiance nor offices which confer authority, wider than that of senior kinsman. Warfare is endemic; residential and social groupings change with the shifting alliances that are organised by competing leaders. In accordance with this weakly developed notion of the social whole and its continuity, the Gahuku-Gama concept of the human being emphasises the transient physical form. Even cultural differences, such as those of ritual practice or language, are seen in terms of individual characteristics, as different kinds of 'skin'. 'Skin', the outer covering of the self, is the means by which the social is represented. Human beings may embody various social roles but they cannot be distinguished from them; society as such barely exists beyond the interactions of living individuals. Thus the competitive basis for leadership among Gahuku-Gama is different from that in Western society, for the distinction made in the latter between the office and the qualities of the individual incumbent that legitimise his or her tenure, requires competitors to be conceptualised apart from their other social roles, as persons. Among the Gahuku-Gama, by contrast, competition takes place between social selves, seeking power and dominance, not selection for office.

In his concluding paragraph, Mauss warns us that the idea of the person characteristic of our society is neither universal nor immutable. "It is formulated only for us, among us". In comparing the concepts of the person in four non-Western societies with our own, I have tried to suggest how we may understand their variant forms. The key to such understanding is, I suggest, the recognition that concepts of the person are embedded in a social context. In particular they relate to the degree of institutionalisation of offices and the nature of authority. The existence of an office logically entails a distinction between the powers and responsibilities pertaining to it and their exercise by different incumbents. Hence some concept of the individual as distinct from the office is established. However, the way in which an individual is accorded the moral status of personhood depends on other social features. As Fortes points out, the concept of the person relates mortal, transient human beings to a continuing social whole. Ideas of society, variously conceptualised, and the nature of the concept of the person are thus interdependent. In modern states with their bureaucratic hierarchies, society is conceived of as an organisation of competing individuals, citizens of the state. Continuity lies in a structure of offices and roles to which individuals accede according to their personal qualities. In such societies person and individual are virtually indistinguishable. By contrast, where society is seen as the descendants of founding ancestors, personhood is the fulfillment of a socially significant career, of which the crucial elements are parenthood and paternal authority. In these societies, not all individuals are persons.

Societies based on a principle of patrilineal descent are not identical, as the examples discussed here have shown. Their concepts of the person vary according to the particular principles by which authority is legitimised. Among the Lugbara or Taita the legitimate exercise of power by particular individuals is recognised; among the Tallensi it is not. Their concepts of the person vary accordingly. The final example, that of the Gahuku-Gama, shows how a weakly elaborated sense of social continuity and the absence of institutionalised offices require no concept of the person. Social characteristics of individuals are represented by images of the living body, not by concepts of the person. The Western concept resembles none of those described so far in other societies. Its unique character is not simply the result of greater sophistication or elaboration of conceptual thought but, as Mauss has made us aware, it derives from a particular social context.

Notes

1. Earlier versions of this paper were read at the Departments of Anthropology in Durham and Oxford and at a seminar in Wolfson College. I am grateful to colleagues at both those places and at the London School of Economics for comments which have helped me clarify the argument. They cannot be held responsible for this final form.
2. See Beattie (1980) for a similar point.
3. Notably by Dumont (1970) in which he criticises a certain school of sociology for sociocentrism in making this individual the centre of sociological analysis. He includes in his strictures (rightly to my mind) certain strands in recent anthropological thought. Of course Radcliffe-Brown cannot really be included as a methodological individualist but the paper mentioned has in common with that view a concern with motivation. As John Beattie has reminded me, Radcliffe-Brown's later answer to the problem of the Mother's Brother is in terms of social structure.
4. As the English phrase "a real person" indicates.
5. Since Mauss restricts the term 'person' *(personne morale)* to one variety of such concepts, Fortes's use of the term is not strictly Maussian.
6. However, even individualism allows for greater or lesser personality. I am grateful to Rosine Perelberg for reminding me of this; however, the negative connotation of the phrase 'cult of personality' seems to indicate that there should be limits to the recognition of individual differences in this way.
7. I am here, as throughout this paper, concerned with the social representations of these units, not the composition of actual political groups.
8. Unlike those of Lugbara prophets who have appeared in exceptional crises in Lugbara history. They represent a more developed form of charismatic authority, which I cannot deal with here.

Bibliography

Beattie, J. 1980. Review article: "Representations of the Self in Traditional Africa". *Africa* 50(3).

Beteille, A. 1977. *Inequality among Men*. Basil Blackwell, Oxford.

1980. "The Idea of Natural Inequality". Auguste Comte Memorial Trust Lecture, The London School of Economics and Political science, London.

Dumont, L. 1966. *Homo Hierarchicus,* English edition (1970). Weidenfeld and Nicholson, London.

1970. "The Individual as Impediment to Sociological Comparison and Indian History", in *Religion, Politics and History in India: Collected Papers in Indian Society*. Mouton, The Hague.

Fortes, M. 1973. "On the Concept of the Person among the Tallensi", in *La Notion de la Personne en Afrique Noire,* ed. G. Dieterlen. Editions du Centre National de la Recherche Scientifique, Paris.

1979. "Coping with Destiny, Among the Tallensi", in *Fantasy and Symbol,* ed. R. H. Hook. Academic Press. London

Harris, G. 1978. *Casting out Anger: Religion among the Taita of Kenya*. Cambridge University Press.

MacFarlane, A. 1978. *The Origins of English Individualism*. Basil Blackwell, Oxford.

Middleton, J. 1973. "The Notion of the Person among the Lugbara", in *La Notion de Personne en Afrique Noire,* ed. G. Dieterlen. Editions du Centre de la Recherche Scientifique, Paris.

Radcliffe-Brown, A.R. 1940. "On Social Structure" in *Structure and Function in Primitive society*. Cohen and West, London.

Read, K. 1955. "Morality and the Concept of the Person among the Gahuku-Gama". *Oceania* 25(4).

7

Self: public, private. Some African representations

Godfrey Lienhardt

At the very beginning of Lévy-Bruhl's book *L'Ame Primitive* (1927) (translated as *The 'Soul' of the Primitive,* and those quotation marks around *Soul* mark it as an area of the translator's uncertainty), the author took it for granted that his 'primitives' would be confused if asked about those aspects of themselves which now concern us:

> It is scarcely likely that primitives have ever given a form, however indefinite, to the more or less implicit ideas they have of their own personality. At any rate it would be quite useless to question them about it, for ambiguity and misunderstanding would be the only result.

He suggests that his readers, by contrast, would have more clearly formulated answers ready. Yet in the year in which *L'Ame Primitive* was published, Aldous Huxley, reflecting on Proust's phrase 'the intermittence of the heart', observed that:

> The number of completely unified personalities is small. Most of us go through life incompletely unified – part person, the rest a mere collection of discontinuous psychological elements.

And Ouspensky, of course, had gone much further. In a lecture given in 1922 he is reported on as follows:

> Man misunderstood himself: he thought he had a permanent self, a master 'I', which integrated and controlled his thoughts and actions. But this was an illusion. Instead of the single 'I' there were innumerable I's, many of which said contradictory things. Then Ouspensky got up and drew a circle on the blackboard, and divided it by criss-cross lines until it looked like a fly's eye seen under a microscope. In each little space he put an 'I', and said 'this is a picture of Man'.

Academically more central though, and nearer to our own time, place and intellectual habits, the Waynflete Professor of Metaphysical Philosophy in Oxford, Gilbert Ryle, reflected in *The Concept of Mind* on the 'enigmas . . . which all turn on what I shall call the systematic elusiveness of the concept of "I".' It was ultimately this elusive 'I' which St. Augustine in the *Confessions* sought in God, and which Mauss in 'The Category of the Person' sought in a history of Man's self-image.

Early in his essay, Mauss distinguished his own investigation – 'entirely one of law and morality', he says – from those of contemporaneous linguists and psychologists. 'In no way do I maintain', he wrote for the linguists,

> that there has ever been a tribe, a language, in which the term 'I', 'me' *(je–moi)* (you will note that we still decline it with two words) has never existed, or that it has not expressed something clearly represented.

In the seemingly casual aside – ' "I", "me" . . . (you will note that we still decline it with two words)' – he allows for subtle difficulties of translation, and hints, perhaps, that some languages have been better equipped than others for making the particular moral, philosophical, legal and theological distinctions which then interested him. In relation to academic psychology he added:

> I shall leave aside everything which relates to the 'self' *(moi)*, the conscious personality as such. Let me merely say that it is plain, particularly to us, that there has never existed a human being who has not been aware, not only of his body, but also of his individuality, both spiritual and physical.

Indeed there is much more to the idea of the self than Western ideas of legal and moral personality; and I do not think that ideas of the self can be so readily separated from the sense of simultaneously mental and physical individuality as Mauss's purpose then required. The 'average', 'archaic' or 'total' man, as Mauss called those outside the academically educated classes of modern society (and from whom he thought those educated classes had much to learn), does not think about himself as though he were examining an intellectual construct; and even that sense of mental and physical individuality appears to be dissolved or surrendered in trances, mystical experiences, spirit possession and contemplative prayer; and even those who have had none of these experiences may have had, in dreams, some intuition of the transformation of the self – of 'the conscious personality' – those experiences are said to involve. Certainly, to consider African ideas of the 'I', we have to begin by allowing 'the self' to be more labile than are the ideas of it in Mauss's essay.

Let us take our bearings, then, not from Mauss but from African forms of self-expression not elicited by questions put by foreign observers in a foreign philosophical and psychological idiom. Here is a summary of a West African, most probably Yoruba, folktale:

> The king invited the animals to a great feast, and offered a prize to the best dancer. The animals danced energetically before him, each showing off its own most striking qualities – the elephant its grave dignity, the leopard its beautiful coat and sinuous agility, the gazelle its spectacular leaps and so forth. When, at the end of the dance, they gathered around the king to hear his judgment, to their surprise and displeasure he awarded the prize to the tortoise. Answering their complaints, the king asked them who had provided the feast, and who was giving the prize, to which they could only reply 'It is you, O king!'. 'And so it is that I award the prize to the tortoise', said the king, 'for it is only I who can see the dance of the tortoise: his dance is entirely inside him'.

In much West African folklore, the tortoise represents intelligence, resourcefulness, trickery and luck. Thus for those who tell this tale, the success of the slow, ungainly tortoise is an extreme example of the deceptiveness of outward appearances, though the moral is not that hidden intellectual agility is preferred, as such, to physical display: both are parts of the dance. The tortoise too, now public and exposed, now withdrawn and hidden, is a fitting and subtle image for the self.

Otherwise the story is immediately comprehensible without anthropological or literary comment to any thoughtful child; and since folktales in Africa as elsewhere contribute to the education of children, it may be assumed that from childhood the Yoruba are not only supposed to have an idea of a hidden, private self – here an inner *activity,* you will have noted – but to understand that it may ultimately be more important than the outer activity, the *persona,* or mask, in Mauss's terms, presented to others. There are many other African stories about tricksters – the spider, the hare and the others besides the tortoise – who often admirably succeed, but sometimes ludicrously fail, by being, as we might say, 'all out for themselves'.

I emphasise this because much of what has been written about African ideas of self, rightly putting to the fore the importance of a person's group and status – the public self – for defining what and who he or she is, can deflect interest from this African concern, also, on occasion, with individuals as individuals. Professor John Beattie has drawn my attention to what Burckhardt wrote about pre-Renaissance man in Europe in this connection: 'Man was conscious of himself only as a member of a race, people, family or corporation – only through some general category'; and he quotes for comparison the modern French Africanist Professor Roger Bastide: 'It is clear that the African defines himself by his position. . . . When one asks him what he is, he places himself in a lineage, he traces his place in a genealogical tree'. Lévy-Bruhl, whose 'primitive mentality' subsumes all mentality except that of his most rationalist readers, earlier made a generalization which, with more or less qualification, has underlain many interpretations of African thought:

> If primitive mentality pictures the individual as such, it does so in a way that is wholly relative. The individual is apprehended only by virtue of his being an element of the group of which he is a part, which alone is the true unit.

This collectivist philosophy, so to call it, appeared as characteristically 'African' very recently in a pamphlet put out to explain African values in the Rhodesian-Zimbabwe elections. It is summed up at a religious level of interpretation (to which in a somewhat different way I shall later return) in Fr. Placide Tempels's almost mystical recreation of a traditional African metaphysic:

> For the Bantu, man never appears in fact as an isolated individual, as an independent entity. Every man, every individual, forms a link in a chain of vital forces, a living link, active and passive, joined from above to the ascending line of his ancestry and sustaining below the line of his descendants.

So, it might be said, at a more mundane level, do all who take the idea of incorporation seriously – members of royal houses, for example, or ancient Colleges. 'Bantu philosophy' here corresponds to that of the Bourbons, the Hapsburgs, the Tudors, and innumerable families established as the 'so-and-so's' of their local communities, whose secure conviction of their hereditary status, far from inhibiting individuality, has sometimes led them to indulge and exploit it.

Much humour and drama in African (as in other) oral literature and history, derive from a keen perception of individual eccentricities, the deliberate or accidental flouting of convention, slips of the tongue which reveal private reservations, clever calculations of personal advantage, and selfish obsessions (often represented in Africa as gluttonous greed), all of which defy or subvert accepted standards of judgment and behaviour. Many African songs are also, contrary to what was once supposed about their anonymous, communal 'folk' origins, usually assigned to their individual composers, who hold the copyright, as it were, and they contain images and allusions which are incomprehensible (though they may be exciting in the context of performance) without a knowledge of intimate local and personal experience of the composer himself. In this respect, like much of the best poetry, they make the private self public, while retaining a sense of privileged admittance to its privacy.

Dr. Francis Deng, himself a Dinka, writing of the Dinka of the Sudan, describes how songs voice experiences, attitudes and emotions which people keep to themselves in the course of daily conversation. His account of the relationship between private self-esteem and public esteem (and it is clear to anyone who has taken part in a dance that up to a point the dancers are dancing for themselves) recalls the Yoruba dance of the tortoise:

> The power of group song lies largely in the chorus, even though the role of the individual solo is a pivotal one, showing that the significance of the individual is not overshadowed by this group demonstration. The fact that there are points in dancing when every individual chants his own *mioc* [individual praises, or 'he does his thing'] shows the significance of songs and dances to the ego of each person. Even the group reference to 'I' [when the choral singers refer to themselves together as 'I' and not as 'we'] indicates that group solidarity is fundamentally a construction of individual egos.

Evans-Pritchard pointed out in 1928, *contra* Radcliffe-Brown's doctrinally sociologizing interpretation of dancing as an expression of, and training in, social harmony and conformity, that Zande dances were often turbulent affairs, involving '. . . slanderous songs, sexual indiscretions, competition (for self-display is essentially aggressive when thwarted)', and referred to the airing of private grievances at large public gatherings, with several hundreds of dancers.

I have said perhaps more than enough to suggest that one can lay too much one-sided stress on the collectivist orientation of African ideas of the person. Obviously, the less differentiated a people are by occupation, interests, ideals, and origins (and the readers of Mauss and Lévy-Bruhl were by comparison with most Africans of the time very differentiated indeed), the more of their private, as well as public, values and resemblances they may be expected to share; but the recognition of the importance of an inner, mysterious *individual* activity, comparable to what is meant by speaking in English of 'what goes on inside' a person is attested by many proverbs.

The 'what goes on inside' a person may not be fully grasped by that person himself, as is recognized in a Fipa (Tanzanian) proverb: 'What is in the heart, the heart alone knows', glossed by Dr. Roy Willis as 'We don't know everything about ourselves through our intellect', which accords with psychoanalysis and with some African notions of witchcraft, for a witch may not always be thought conscious of being so. Fr. Tempels, with all his mystique of the collective, quotes a Congolese proverb, 'None may put his arm into his neighbour's inside', meaning 'The neighbour's conscience remains inviolable even for his closest friend'. The most quoted of all Zande proverbs according to Evans-Pritchard is 'Can one look into a person as one looks into an open-wove basket?', the open weaving being contrasted with close weaving, which conceals what is inside – as when a Zande also said, 'Our bodies are like a man who builds a hut to reside in. Our real person is the strength [or breath] which is in our bodies and is the soul *[mbisimo]*'. Such statements, and many more – the Fante proverb, 'One never knows what is in another person's heart', the Dinka proverb, 'What is inside a person is like what is in the forest or the river' (i.e., hidden, often dangerous, and unpredictable) – all allude to the importance, no matter how much store may be set by social role and status, of individual, private, intellectual and emotional activities: the private self. The real difficulties of translation arise when we ask (and we may ask mistakenly, for the question presupposes particular kinds of answer) for a description of the private self that acts and is acted upon, and where that action is located.

There is now for Africa (as there was not in Mauss's time) an extensive literature on the vocabularies used by African peoples to describe the emotional and intellectual attributes of human beings, attributes often represented in that literature as separate 'components' of the total person of personality. It appears from much of that literature that some African peoples (and naturally some of the most articulate in this respect come from Francophone Africa with its inheritance of French education) formulate their indigenous metaphysical systems more clearly than others; have reflected more than others on the nature of the self, for example; and have their own men of learning to enter into debate about it. Also, whether in the nature of the information or in its interpretation, there are, in any language, difficulties in deciding whether some expressions are to be taken more literally or more metaphorically, since in all societies some people are bound to be more literal minded than others. My close Fanti friend, who gave me the proverb, 'One never knows what is in another person's heart', added (for even their friends never know what anthropologists may make of their information), 'Of course this doesn't refer to the physical heart'.

I now return particularly to the Dinka of southern Sudan, for among them I had that experience of daily conversation which enables one to discriminate, as we take for granted in the language into which we were born, between what people mean and what they say. Then one learns also what kinds of questions, formulated in an alien mode of thought, might receive answers – but answers which, though grammatically, syntactically and even semantically plausible, do not represent, and may positively misrepresent, indigenous and spontaneous interests and ideas.

The Dinka were indifferent to many of the metaphysical speculations and distinctions which comparative studies in Africa and elsewhere might lead one to seek among them. The commonest answer to a foreigner's questions of a speculative kind is 'I don't know'. In the first, and even now outstandingly competent, grammar and vocabulary of the Dinka language, published almost exactly a hundred years ago, the great missionary-traveller Fr. Giovanni Beltrame gave samples of dialogue in the 1870s between the missionary and the Dinka. Despite imposing upon the Dinka some conspicuously Christian eschatologial doctrines about heaven and hell which were clearly being fed back to him, the missionary truthfully represents in the dialogue the frequency of the answer 'We don't know'. But it is an assertion of agnosticism in the strict sense, a doubt about the questions, not a confession of ignorance. It does not mean 'but we should like to learn', but rather 'The answer means nothing to us'.

According to the literature again, some African peoples have ideas of a soul–body dichotomy analogous to that which is generally assumed in Christian Europe, but differing from it, importantly, in allowing for the presence of several distinct 'souls' in each person. It might be possible to make some sort of translation of the belief into Dinka, but it would make no traditional sense; for the word by which 'soul' would have to be translated is the word for breath and breathing, and for the presence of life which breathing signifies. To suggest therefore that a person might have several 'breaths' with different attributes would be as odd to the Dinka as the notion of a plurality of different souls in one of their number would be to the other fellows of All Souls College, Oxford. Missionaries, using *weei*, breath and life, as the best approximation to translate 'soul', have presumably successfully reshaped the Dinka word for their converts – reshaped it into a unitary term for a moralised and spiritualised self-consciousness of each separate individual in relation to a personalised God.

I hope that further research, especially among converts, will tell us something about how this translation of conscience intimately takes place.

In Dinka traditional thought, the breath/life comes from and in some way returns to God, but otherwise little resembles the 'soul', understood as a ghostly counterpart of the living person, the 'ghost in the machine' as Ryle called it, which atheists as well as theists could imagine to be morally good or bad, and doctrinally consigned to heaven or hell. There is a Dinka word, *atyep,* which might adequately translate 'ghost', but not 'soul' for it means primarily a shadow, image or reflection, and may properly be regarded as the image of the dead as reflected in the memories and experiences of the living. The *atyep* is not 'something inside' a living person.

I shall now imagine (and with some misgivings, for the experience upon which I base it is some thirty years behind me) that a Dinka without recourse to the vocabulary of European philosophy or theology were to contribute to this discussion in traditional Dinka idiom; and I shall try to represent what might be said by using the nearest literal equivalents in English to Dinka expressions, leaving the Dinka words for footnotes in a later publication. The Dinka word for 'person' has strong masculine overtones, but in some contexts may mean 'mankind' as when we use the capital 'm' for 'Man'. A living person has a body which is animated by breath/life, but body and breath are not in apposition as 'body and soul' are in English. Dinka would not normally say what would be translated word for word as 'a dead body'. For 'corpse' they might perhaps say 'the body of a person who has died', but the natural expression would be simply 'a person who has died'. What is then left is not strictly the 'body', which also means 'self' as we shall see, but flesh and bones and the rest. The breath/life is stronger in the more vigorous, whether people or animals; is weaker in the old, in children and in the sick; and departs when a person dies. In prayer and sacrifice God is asked to give and support the breath/life of people and cattle, but this breath can scarcely be regarded as a 'component' of human personality, since it differentiates humans only according to their degree of vitality, has no moral qualities, and merges the human self-image with what is in the nature of all sentient beings, perhaps especially cattle. Further, breath is obviously both inside and outside our bodies, whereas the qualities of personality are spoken of as in the body. The 'what is inside' a person is in general spoken of as 'in the belly', though the reference may specify that particular part of the body more or less according to context. (The 'what is inside', it is interesting to note, seems to be cognate with the Dinka word for 'truth'.)

It is through metaphors based primarily upon the head and the heart (and more from the heart than from the head) that most moral, affective and intellectual states are expressed. Like many other peoples, the Dinka tend to relate thinking to the head (though not to the brain, and cleverness is shown in the eye) and feelings to the heart. But many mental activities much more complex than sensations and affections are referred to the heart – doubt and suspicion, for example. There are numerous expressions using the words for 'heart' and 'head' with adjectival qualifications. Here are a few examples taken from the entries under *pwou*, 'heart', in Father Nebel's little Dinka dictionary. I give my literal translations of the Dinka entries. Fr. Nebel translates the word *pwou* generally as 'heart, chest, mind, intention', and then includes: 'my heart is there' (or 'in it') for 'I agree, I like'; 'my heart is not there' (or 'in it') for 'unwillingly'; 'heart lost' for 'to forget, to lose control of oneself' (though for 'to forget', 'my head has lost' would be more usual); 'to forbid the heart to someone' as 'to be heartless to' (perhaps 'to harden one's heart' would be as close in the English idiom); 'to have the heart darken' as 'to be startled, frightened or sorry'; a phrase which may mean 'not to have enough heart' or 'heart not to suffice' as 'to be suspicious'; 'to have a small heart' as 'to be discreet, humble'; 'to have a big heart' as 'to be proud' – for 'magnanimous' I think one would have to begin by saying simply 'good-hearted', and add words for generosity, nobility, forgivingness and so on. The most commonly used expressions are 'sweet (or tasty) heart' for 'happy' or probably more accurately 'contented', and 'bad heart' for 'aggrieved'.

Even from this short list it will be seen that the metaphorical associations of the Dinka word *pwou*, heart, for defining human characteristics, thoughts and feelings, often do not coincide with the English idiom, and in another context it might be interesting to consider the implications of such cultural and linguistic differences. ('Lionheart', for example, could literally in Dinka suggest a were-lion who changed form in order to devour people.) But here my interest is of another kind. Although like ourselves sometimes, the Dinka often put the hand to the heart, or the head, when speaking of conditions associated with those parts of the body, the linguistic usuages are consciously metaphorical. To take and use the physical heart of a victim in order to possess oneself of its qualities (as is sometimes reported to happen in ritual murders in other parts of Africa and elsewhere) would appear as evilly superstitious and wicked to the average Dinka as to the average European, though that is not to say that there are no superstitious and wicked people either in Dinka land or in

Europe. Those whom Europeans call 'psychopaths' are those whom the Dinka call by words translated as 'witch' or 'sorcerer'. But for most Dinka, the distinction between the metaphorical and the literal resembles that of an ethnically related people, the Southern Luo of Kenya, for whom the indigenous distinction between the physical and the moral content of metaphors is quite explicitly and deliberately emphasized by a Luo author, A.C.C. Ochalla-Ayayo:

> The heart, *Chuny* according to the Luo, is the site of the intellect and ethical emotions and wisdom of a person. They consider emotions of attitudes, evil thoughts, pure feeling, wisdom, hospitality and generosity as invoked from the heart, *Chuny*. The Luo make a distinction between physical heart, which they call *Adundo,* and the spiritual heart, *Chuny*. It does not appear that *Chuny* which also means liver is (in that meaning) referred to in this context, since the positions they point at when asked for physical *Chuny* (in the sense of liver) and spiritual *Chuny* of a human being do not correspond. The spiritual heart is situated somewhere beneath the end of the central cartilage, a spot believed to be occupied by the physical heart. Yet they do not call it *Adundo* when ethical emotions are implied, but *Chuny,* spiritual heart.

The Dinka do not have two words for heart, but otherwise this distinction – and also connection – is implicit in their usage.

Such are some of the ways in which Dinka speak about themselves and others, and these forms of self-expression clearly represent that 'sense' of the simultaneously mental and physical which it was not part of Mauss's intention to dwell upon, but without considering which we should have little to say about their ideas of human personality. It seems to me that the Dinka language, unlike modern, educated, and for the most part metropolitan English, compels its speakers to integrate the moral and physical attributes of persons together within the physical matrix of the human body. In modern English, moral and mental conditions are spoken of in more or less abstract terms (anger, suspicion, forgetfulness and so on), cut off, for most, from their etymological roots. We say 'I trust him', for example, and could ask in a Platonic way, 'What is trust?'. In Dinka, one would have to say 'I know his heart', and should the question then arise of what it means to know someone's heart, it would be necessary to return to what is meant by 'heart' in other contexts. It may be that the disjunction, for most modern English speakers, between abstract terms and concrete imagery has something to do with the complex foreign origins of the English language. Non-literate Africans can explain the etymology of words as non-literary English speakers cannot, but that is beyond my province. The difference is however consistent with the absence, among (in this case) the Dinka, of the mind–body dichotomy which many writers of this century have wished to resolve. D.H. Lawrence is perhaps the most fervid of many who attacked what Eliot called the 'dissociation of sensibility', the separation of thinking from feeling, in modern civilisation, and (like Mauss) attributed some ideal undivided self to American Indians (he read a good deal of anthropology), peasants, workers and others whose lives and language had not been corrupted by bookish education – among people who, like Matthew Arnold's Scholar Gypsy, had escaped:

> . . . this strange disease of modern life,
> With its sick hurry, its divided aims,
> Its heads o'er tax'd, its palsied hearts.

And still an integration of thought and feeling in metaphor and imagery is what we seek to have recreated for us in the best literature. We go to the theatre to hear Cordelia say:

> Unhappy that I am, I cannot heave
> My heart into my mouth. . .

not, 'Even on this distressing occasion I cannot bring myself to display my emotions'.

The importance of the bodily matrix in Dinka notions of self is shown finally in the very word most often used where we should use 'self', for that indeed is the word *gwop,* 'body'. 'I myself' is literally 'I body', 'yourself' is 'you body'. Body here is obviously not like 'self', a pronoun, but a noun intensive of the personal pronoun. Body, *gwop,* is incorporated in many metaphors, for example 'light body' for 'healthy', 'sweet body' for 'lucky', 'body afraid' for 'shy, embarrassed or timid', 'body heavy' for 'sick'. There is also a real reflexive pronoun for 'self', quite different from the word for body, and which signifies also 'apart from others' or 'separated from others'. Thus 'look after yourself' ('take care') uses the reflexive pronoun *rot* as does 'to kill oneself', and 'to love oneself' – that is, to be a selfish, self-interested and self-indulgent person. If one were to translate Shakespeare's line, 'Sin of self-love possesseth all my soul' into Dinka, it would have to be something like 'I have been very wrong (mistaken, missed the mark, as in aiming) because I have loved myself very much' using the reflexive pronoun *rot* again. But that is enough of a discussion which does no justice to the poetry of the Dinka language, by reducing it to something that sounds like a dull form of pidgin. I introduced translations to give an impression of the way in which at almost every point the Dinka language allows for a wide range of intellectual and moral discriminations without leading into a seemingly autonomous world of abstractions. Words, as it were, must return to base.

And here I return to Professor Ryle, for the Dinka mode of thought and expression has correspondences in the work of a distinguished English academic. Consider Professor Ryle's account of his elusive concept of 'I':

> Like the shadow of one's own head, it will not wait to be jumped on. And yet it is never far ahead, indeed sometimes seems not to be ahead of the pursuer at all. It evades capture by lodging itself inside the very muscles of the pursuer. It is too near even to be within arm's reach.

Thus in the use of bodily imagery, the Dinka (and probably other African peoples), and one of the most reformist of modern British philosophers, come together – the Dinka never having been entangled in the 'entities and quiddities' of European metaphysics, the Waynflete Professor of Metaphysical Philosophy in Oxford having determined to get rid of them, as did Samuel Butler in satirizing his omniscient philosopher more than 300 years ago:

> Beside he was a shrewd philosopher
> And had read every Text and gloss over . . .
>
> He could reduce all things to Acts,
> And knew their Natures by Abstracts,
> Where Entity and Quiddity,
> The Ghosts of defunct Bodies, flie;
> Where Truth in Person does appear,
> Like words congealed in Northern Air.

If our imaginary Dinka were to be given a course in Descartes, he might well conclude, like another of Descartes's critics, A.J. Krailsheimer:

> The *Cogito* is achieved at the price not only of severing all the traditional bonds by which man has been joined to other men and the world around them, but also of splitting in two the personal union of mind and body and expelling the instincts of the latter.

Mauss seems to have sensed (to use that word) this strain placed upon European intellectuals of his time; but one fact seems strange to me. Mauss was in very close collaboration with Henri Hubert, especially in writing of religion; and it is reported that on one occasion, when that doyen of Catholic studies of comparative religion in the Vatican, Pater Schmidt, referred somewhat slightingly to Hubert and Mauss as 'two Jewish authors', Mauss replied: 'I accept for myself, but not for Hubert, who is descended from Pascal'. With his awareness of, perhaps even pride in, an indirect connection with Pascal, it does seem odd that one of the three most famous statements in French about *'le moi'* (the others being *'L'Etat c'est moi'* and *'Après moi le déluge'*) is not seriously considered, as far as my reading has gone, by Mauss: that is Pascal's aphorism *'Le moi est haïssable'*.

For what follows from that aphorism in the *Pensées* would certainly be taken for granted by those whom Mauss contrasted with enlightened philosophical (or philosophized) man:

> In short, the self *(moi)* has two qualities: it is unjust in itself, in that it makes itself the centre of all; it is offensive to others, in that it wishes to enslave them; for each self *(moi)* is the enemy, and would wish to be the tyrant, of all others.

Mauss may too easily and optimistically have described that Pascalian self as an aberration from the idealised self of his essay, directed by only the most altruistic and rational categorical imperatives:

> I shall show you how recent is the world 'self' *(moi)* used philosophically; how recent "The category of 'self' " *(moi)*, "the cult of the 'self' " *(moi)* (its aberration); and how recent even the respect of 'self' *(moi)*, in particular the respect of others (its normal state).

He does not really take much account of the part played by religious conviction in moulding ideas of the self, though surely how men see themselves must be influenced by how, or if, they see the gods. Dr. Deng represents for the Dinka what could be found in one form or another in, I should think, all African ethnography. Referring to the Dinka myth of creation, to which I shall shortly turn, he writes that it

> addresses itself to the question 'Where is God?' which the Dinka sometimes wonder about, and not to the question 'Does God exist?'. Among the Dinka the latter is never posed. Should it be posed, as it is now with the introduction of inquisitive Western culture, the immediate answer would be 'Who created you?'.

And if egotism and egoism were condemned among the Dinka, as they certainly traditionally were, it is not because of some democratic and secular ideal of the quality and brotherhood of man (though equality and brotherhood were probably actually achieved among them more than among many who politically profess them), but because of the profoundly religious orientation of their thought, their respect for the gods.

God and Man begin to be mutually defined in a myth recounting that in the beginning, God created a man and a woman, whom he kept close to him. He forbade them to pound more than one grain of millet a day which sufficed, but because they were 'greedy', the woman pounded more, and in doing so raised up her long pounding pestle (as women do now when pounding). The pestle struck God, who then withdrew into the above, and must now be brought near to help human beings by prayer and sacrifice. So human beings, quite usually referred to as 'the ants of God', are as tiny and helpless in relation to God as ants are to men. God's transcendence ultimately reduces all merely human persons to the same level, and since in Dinka thought God and gods are quite different in kind from Man (scarcely any less anthropomorphic or more abstract representations of divinity could be found in Africa), the virtual deification of human beings and human qualities is quite alien to Dinka thought. There are no man-made representations of the divine.

But this distant God (like Professor Ryle's elusive 'I') though out of reach can be *interfused* (I may say this is not sociopsychological jargon, but comes from Wordsworth), with the human person and the human body. In states of possession, which any Dinka may experience and all must certainly have seen in others, divinities 'seize' or 'capture' the human person, body and all. The self is then temporarily replaced by a god, both subjectively and objectively, for it appears that the person possessed has no subjective experience of possession. He (or she, for it often happens to women) is replaced by a spiritual being, a being of another order. People appear temporarily to lose 'self-control'.

It will have been apparent from what I have said earlier that the Dinka are a very rational, even in some ways rationalist, people, especially when confronted with the non-rational constructs of foreigners. It is not difficult for the most part to share, or at least give a notional assent, to their way of talking about themselves. But here, in the acceptance of the interpenetration from time to time of the human and the divine (and of the divine as defined, of course, by their tradition), there appears an experience into which foreigners cannot really enter, for while still living in the same political and social world, they do not belong to it by descent, and descent itself has a profoundly religious value.

This is brought out clearly in the relationship between the members of Dinka clans and what I have elsewhere called the 'divinities' of those clans, for which the commoner anthropological term is 'totem'. The Dinka comprise a large number of such clans, of which the members are all the generations of the descendants of an ancestor in the male line. Each clan has its divinity or divinities, inherited through all the fathers. The divinities are figured as plants, animals, natural forms, and so forth, which clan members take care not to injure; but for the Dinka, they are not themselves these material emblems, but spiritual beings. The clans are religious corporations, and the Dinka themselves speak of clansmen as being related to, and through, their divinities, and of being 'joined' or 'united' in those divinities. From the Dinka point of view, though all clansmen are equivalent in certain situations – in blood feud, for example – this clanship does not diminish the individuality of its members by making them mere units or cells of the larger organization, as some of what I earlier quoted about the predominance of the collectivity in African thought might suggest. Rather it adds something to each individual, as (on a rather shaky analogy) a strong sense of belonging to an Oxford college does not diminish the individuality of its members.

The archetypical clan-divinity, that of the most respected clans of priests, is Flesh itself, represented by the flesh of sacrificed oxen, held to be intermittently immanent in the bodies of its clansfolk, but also, like other divinities, transcendent. It is both within those who inherit it, and outside and above them; the most spiritual aspect of the self is embedded in flesh and blood. The clan-divinities are most commonly called upon in invocations and prayers as 'that [quality, possession, very nature] of the father', and brings to mind, figured in the divinity, the life they have inherited, embody, and pass on – some vital power which indeed is part of each clansman, but does not come from him or her alone, and which informs each successive generation. When, at sacrifices, the divinity Flesh 'awakens' (in the Dinka term) in the flesh of some of those who venerate it, they become possessed. Sometimes they produce a kind of glossolalia. Occasionally they may break into short staggering runs. For the most part they appear withdrawn into themselves, their eyes unfocussed and unseeing, their muscles twitching and quivering. According to the Dinka, when thus possessed they are literally 'not themselves'.

On such occasions, there appears a dimension of the Dinka self into which an outsider cannot really enter, excluded as he is from the intensely felt relationship of clanship which in part, at least, possession by the divinity seems to represent. The individual 'I', both public and private, is temporarily submitted to and replaced by the clan 'we', and perhaps only Dinka can tell us further what this entails.

8

Between the earth and heaven: conceptions of the self in China

Mark Elvin

To what shall I compare myself, so blown by the winds?
To a lone sand-gull between the Earth and Heaven.
Duh Fuu (eighth century A.D.)

Mauss puts forward two main arguments in his famous essay. The first is that the human actor as a carrier of roles, rights, and responsibilities is not an innate idea but a social creation, and hence subject to variation. The second presents as a historical process, distinctively unique to Western Europe, the gradual internalisation from 'person' to 'self', the latter becoming the 'individual' as a category of law, religion, philosophy, and perhaps indeed also of experience. My concern here is only with the second of these arguments, and only in so far as it concerns China. It can, I think, be shown to be substantially mistaken.

To imply that the Chinese in classical and medieval times did not make the human actor *(personne)* "a complete entity independent of any other except God" does not do justice either to the radical individualism of Yang Ju, or to the sense of personal isolation expressed by the poet Chiu Yuan, extreme but revealing cases discussed below. Likewise, to argue that "an Orient that has not attained to our understandings" has never made the self – as the West has – into "a sacred entity . . . a fundamental form of thought and action" is to ignore one of the two main traditions of Neo-Confucianism, that of 'mind' *(shin)*. For thinkers like Luh Shianqshan (thirteenth century) and Wang Yangming (sixteenth century), the mind of the individual was not unlike Mauss's conception of the self in the Western Enlightenment. It was the carrier of conscious awareness, knowledge, and reason, as well as being the source of moral judgement and even, in a Berkeleyan sort of way, of the world's existence.

Mauss also denies China any historical development. Its culture, he says, "conserved the notions of archaic times." On the contrary, as in the West, older strata were constantly being overlaid and metamorphosed, even destroyed altogether. To take a small, specific example: Mauss alludes to the archaic re-use of personal names by descendants. By imperial times (the third century B.C.) this practice had died out; and its earlier extent is uncertain. What Mauss does not mention is that, ever since, Chinese personal names have been almost unique to the individual, a stock of perhaps several million appellations.[1] By comparison, our limited repertoire of 'Johns' and 'Marys' is meagre.

Mauss's one-sentence encapsulation of China, namely that "nowhere is the individual more taken into account, in particular as a social being, and nowhere is he more subject to classification," does neatly evoke the Confucian feeling that a person was what he or she was as the node of a multiplicity of specifically defined social relationships. But there were other, equally compelling, ways of thinking about the self in China. It is a mistake to equate 'Chinese' with 'Confucian'.

In what follows I shall make little further reference to Mauss directly, though I shall have his concerns in mind. My purpose is to build up for the reader a preliminary sense of the Chinese reality so that he may make whatever modifications to Mauss's thesis seem appropriate.

The image of the self in ancient poetry

Let us begin with a commonplace. The ancient Chinese everyday view of the self, when it first becomes clear to us during the second quarter of the first millennium B.C., is neither strange nor inaccessible to the modern Western imagination. Consider, as an illustration, this autobiography in verse from the *Scripture of Poetry* (Karlgren, *Odes,* no. 58, retranslated). It was written by a woman, and tells the story of her marriage to a husband who was her social inferior:

> Man of the people! How you kept me laughing,
> Hemp-cloth in your arms, come to barter for silk.
> But skeins of silk were not what you were after.
> – You were there with schemes to make me come with you.
>
> And so – I went with you. Across the Chyi River,
> To the Mounds of Duenn, we went together.
> Don't tell me it was I put off our day for marriage;
> You'd found us no one to serve as a go-between.

Then, when I urged you to put away your anger,
We fixed the date for a day in autumn.

I climbed the crumbling wall.
I watched the toll-barrier for you to come back to me.
I watched the toll-barrier, but could not see you.
My tears fell and fell.

Once I had seen you return to the barrier,
We laughed, then we talked.
You burnt cracks in tortoise-shell, cast stalks of milfoil –
No word of ill-luck.

Before leaves fall from the mulberry tree
They are glossy and green.
Doves! Don't eat of the mulberry fruits!
Girls! Don't pleasure with gentlemen!
If a man has his way, he'll be excused.
If a girl has hers, there's no excuse.

When leaves drop off from the mulberry tree,
They lie brown and discoloured.
In three years with you,
I have eaten poor food.

Chyi's water swell and flood.
Our carriage hangings are wet.
Nothing I've done has not been straight,
Nothing of yours but bent.
You set no limits to what you did
– Man of too many inner selves.

Three years a wife!
Effort no effort,
Getting up early, late to bed,
No day for myself.
– It is finished now.
My brothers ignore me
With biting laughter.
I think in silence,
Sad for myself.

I came to you to grow old with you.
We grew older. You made me resent you.
Chyi at least has its shorelines,
Marshes their edges.
– When my hair was still up, as a girl's is,
How we talked, how we laughed our contentment,
Vowed good faith so intently,
Not thinking it all might be altered,
The change that was not to be thought of,
This change that has happened.

So far as we can judge across the millennia, these lines show a feeling for the individual self not far removed from that which we have today in the non-philosophical and non-devotional parts of our lives.[2] The speaker has a clear inward vision of herself as a relatively coherent, enduring, and self-contained entity that makes decisions, carries responsibilities, is possessed by feelings, and in general has a fate, a fortune, and a history.

What may be the earliest example of critical self-evaluation in Chinese prose literature refers to the middle of the sixth century B.C., and comes from the somewhat later *Records of Tzuoo* (first year of Shiang-gong). Muh Jiang, the mother of a former ruler of the state of Luu, has consulted a divining-manual to see whether she will ever leave a palace where she seems to have been under some form of house-arrest. The diviner has put a favourable gloss on the outcome, but she rejects his views, concluding:

> However, [the good qualities that you impute to me] must be authentic and not simulated. For this reason, although *swei* [the hexagram obtained through the divination] signifies 'without blame', in this case I am a woman and have played a part in [the creation of] disorder. The fact of the matter is that I occupy an inferior status and, having no sensitive concern for others, cannot be called 'good'. I have not brought peace to the state, or to the [ruling] family, and cannot be said to have 'exerted a [beneficial] influence'. In my actions I have been hurtful to myself, and cannot be deemed to have 'brought advantage' [to myself or others]. I have abandoned [the conduct proper to] my status and acted immorally, and so cannot be called 'constant' [in virtue]. Those who [really] have these four virtues are *swei* and without blame. I have none of them. How could I be *swei*? I have chosen evil. How could I be 'without blame'? I am certain to die here. I shall not be able to leave.

The individual is conceived of here as a distinct locus of decision-making, and experiencing a life that is partly pre-determined and partly the consequence of her own choices. Whether or not it is an accident that both these early examples refer to women, I do not know.

By the end of the classical age, in the fourth and third centuries B.C., we can see a conscious tension between the individual and society, between ideals and an inadequate reality.[3] Once again the clearest expression is in poetry. Chiu Yuan's "Inescapable Sorrow" *(Li sau)* is a psychological self-portrait. Liberally sprinkled with the word 'I', unlike much later Chinese verse, it evokes the isolation felt by the egoistic type of suicidal personality. The poem is too long to quote in full, or even summarise, here. We can only consider those parts that relate to our theme.

He starts with self-praise, describing his "inner beauty." The passing of time haunts him. He fears he will be unable to put right his ruler's faulty understanding of affairs. He denounces the corruption of the court in his native state of Chuu:

Factions thieve pleasure for themselves.
Dark are their paths. They take dangerous ways.
What matter that I am in dread and peril?
I fear the overthrow of the Chariot of State.

His efforts to follow the good rulers of antiquity have been misunderstood by the king:

The Fragrant One could not see my motives.
He listened to slander, hot his anger against me.

The poet is unsurprised. He knows that "frank, loyal speaking brings disaster". He describes the plans he has promoted and the subordinates whom he has brought forward as his "flowers," concluding sadly:

Mine are now withered. It matters little.
My grief's the weeds grown over *all* sweet scents.

As for the people at court:

Merely from greed they all fight for preferment.
To be full does not sate them. They want more and more.
Just from feelings they know in themselves they judge others.
And, envy-swollen, their appetites grow.

He knows he is different:

What *they* gallop after in hasty pursuit
And what I yearn for are not the same.
Slow, slow is the coming of age, but will have me soon,
And gone then my hopes of a lasting fame.

He values his inner integrity:

Let what I feel be honest and beautiful,
With nothing in it not essential.
Of what account, then, my shrunken pallor?

He accepts that he is "not in accord with the men of the present day":

Though I love what is good, curb and bridle myself,
Mornings I meet with insult, at nightfall am tossed away.

Even so, he is unrepentant:

I shall never regret what my heart approves of,
Though death for it come to me nine times over.

Already his inclinations are half suicidal:

> Heartache. Foreboding. There is no way forward.
> Who else cares what happens, here in our world?
> I'd rather be dead – done – dissolved in the waters.
> To act as *they* do could not be endured.

He makes a last effort. He recalls that

> Subduing one's heart, repressing ambitions,
> Enduring wrong, keeping free from shame,
> Staying inward unstained, so dying upright,
> This was in truth what the Sages acclaimed.

But he cannot face being wronged again. His mood turns to dismissive disdain:

> That none understand me shall no more concern me,
> So long as my feelings are sweet and sincere.

In a passion of self-exaltation he reflects:

> Something there is gives each man his delight.
> To be pure – mine alone! And to stay so ever.
> Tear my body apart! Still I could not alter.
> And even so torn, could my mind be hurt?

His elder sister[4] criticises him. What is the use of trying to stand apart from the weed-filled court? How, she asks, can he go around saying to everyone, "Please look at my inner feelings?"

> "Normal people act together. They like to have friends.
> Why keep to yourself and not listen to me?"

He ignores her scolding and goes off to make clear his "inner correctness" by stating his case to the long-dead sage-emperor Shuenn at the latter's grave.

At this point the poem changes gear. Chiu departs on two supernatural journeys, perhaps the reflections of his experiences in trance or in meditation. In the first he rises in a phoenix chariot to the walls of Heaven, but his quest ends in frustration:

> I told God's porter to unlock the gates,
> But he leant on the portals and simply looked at me.

Thus the world of men is hateful and Heaven will not have him. After other unhappy adventures of a supernatural kind he comes back to his original complaint. It is anguish to be unable to make one's views heard:

> So deep are the inner palace apartments
> That the king of discernment has not yet awoken.

My thoughts remain in me. I cannot convey them.
How can I endure to be thus for ever?

He consults a god, who tells him:

"Exert yourself! Search the heights and deeps
For him whose standards are your own . . .
If what you feel within you be sweet
What need have you then of a go-between?"

But in Chuu the situation is worse than ever. Even those of whom he once had had a good opinion are now contaminated with evil:

Many and many are time's changes!
Why should I stay among them more?
The sweetness from the orchid fled,
And rank and foul the iris grown. . . .

Flow with the stream – that's the
way of our world.
Who can stay in it untransformed?

Feeling totally alone, he resolves to leave:

Hearts that are alien – what have I to do with them?
I shall go – go far away – till we are sundered.

He embarks on his second magical journey. Flying dragons carry him across the Milky Way, and he comes to the uttermost West. But –

I mounted up to the dazzling light of Heaven,
And cast down a glance at the land once my home.
O the grief of my charioteer! My horses, pining,
Turned their necks to look back. They went no further.

Sorrow is inescapable. Chiu Yuan ends:

I must go to Perng Shyan, to his mansion beneath the waters.

And he drowns himself.

Self and cosmos

In the archaic period there was a fear that nature was hostile, an anguished apprehension that God and the ancestors might not be benevolently disposed towards humankind. This feeling may be found in a lament traditionally ascribed to an official of the ninth century B.C. (Karlgren, *Odes*, no. 258, retranslated):

Drought overwhelms us.
Streambeds and mountains are dry and lifeless.

The drought fiend scourges us.
All seems aflame, all seems on fire.
  We curse the heat.
  Fear burns in our hearts.
O long-dead rulers, you do not hear us!
Majestic Heaven! O God above us!
Why do you make us cower in terror?

During the last century or so before the empire, the belief in a supreme God or a conscious Heaven, and in the lesser deities presiding over particular phenomena and places, faded from the minds of learned men. So did the belief that the ancestors had a major power to regulate the world's affairs. A little later new hierarchies emerged: Buddhist (as Buddhism, half-understood, trickled into China) and Dawist. Popular religion was fecund in the promotion of new gods. But among the sophisticated a new vision appeared, with a changed attitude to nature, as significant as it is hard to explain the reasons for it. This vision drew men into a quest for the mystical absorption of the individual into a unified and basically benevolent universe. Here is part of a suite of verses by Wang Shijy, who lived in the fourth century A.D., setting forth this new world-view (Obi, reconstructed text, pp. 205–6):

I Far-flung and numberless move the Great Patterns,
Returning in sequences that never cease.
– Shaping and changing not in our hands to fashion,
Beyond our mastery to bid them come or leave.

Where was their generation? What commands them?
– Self-caused fulfilment, following Inner Logic.
Those who have minds, but still lack understanding,
Stumble entangled in mere loss and profit.

Give yourself up to each encounter.
Roam unattached. Find good in each conjuncture.

II In March bud forth diversity of kinds.
Each swells, is stirred by Inborn Being.
I lift my eyes to gaze at the horizon,
Head lowered, watch this green bank by this stream.

Silent, bright, limitless the vision that remains!
Transient in what I see, World-Order unfolds Itself.
How great is what It does, maker and changer
Of differences many and many, accordant in their arrangements!

Innumerable Its pipes, and though so various
V Are ever well met, ever part of us.[5]
. . . .
Gathering, dissolving – both sure in their constancy.

Perfecting had no first moment. Nor did decay.
Instant on instant new things are given existence,
That, once departed, come not forth again.

What sticks, then stays, resembles dust or lees.
Only in now, and now, and now is spirit-power.
Who cannot but regret hopes unachieved?
Dissolve them in the search for Guiding Structure.

And what one is, if words remain, is not cut off.
Clear too the river that nowhere stops.

This universe was not made by an external creator. It was subject only to transformations guided by immanent patterns and forces. Nature embodied an Inner Logic (*lii,* archaic* *lieg*[6]), which may also be translated, as above, as World-Order or Guiding Structure. One achieved understanding by seeing through to the essence of this Inner Logic, surrendering one's will to it, and becoming identified with it.

For the poets, the faculty that put one in touch with nature was *shaangshin,* the 'delighting heart' or 'responsive mind'. It led one to that state of sensitive awareness in which one is, to use Wordsworth's phrase, "alive to all things and forgetting all." The term was coined by Shieh Liingyunn (A.D. 365–433), a poet and lay devotee of Buddhism. As he put it, didactically:

Feelings work through responsive delight to make beauty.
Dark are phenomena. Who can discern them?
Once this is seen, objects no more concern one.
In one instant enlightened, one has what one pursued.

Perhaps this absence of alienation from the world gave the self in China slightly less sharply defined margins than it had in the West. For the Chinese, this life was neither a vale of tears, nor a testing-ground, but a home.

Individual and society in the philosophy of antiquity

When we turn to the philosophers of Chinese antiquity we find concerns different from those of the poets. The crucial conflict that developed here was between those who emphasised the relative autonomy of man's inner being and those who thought that what was significant in a personality was the creation of social forces working on it from outside, especially education and/or rewards and punishments.

A conscious awareness of an inner self was present, at the latest, by the sixth century B.C. Thus Tzyy-chaan, prime minister of the state of Jenq, is said to have observed, "Men's hearts are no more alike than their faces." Confucius, who lived slightly later, was also concerned with the problem of penetrating beneath the surface. "Discover what brings him content," he said with regard to the problem of evaluating a person, "and can the man's real worth remain hidden from you?" For Confucius the supreme virtue was *ren*. The conventional translations of this term are 'goodness' and 'benevolence', but its meaning is closer to 'a sensitive concern for others'. The sage exemplified this virtue in his own behaviour, for example by not eating his fill when seated next to someone in mourning; and it was in response to a request for a definition of *ren* that he gave the negative form of the Golden Rule: "Do not do to others what you would not wish for yourself."

It is in the works attributed to Moh Dyi (later fifth century B.C.) that we first meet the idea that society and the state are – or, perhaps, should be – the creators of the individual's values, giving this term both a moral and a semantic meaning, the latter applying to the very words he uses. Before the formation of government there had been chaos, each person having his own particular morals and his own particular values for words. It was the duty of the head of each family, each community, and each state to unify the values of those beneath him. It was the emperor's duty to do this for the world as a whole. "If superiors and inferiors do not share the same values, rewards and fame will not be enough to encourage people to act well, nor will punishments be adequate to prevent violence." Moh Dyi envisaged a corporatism that was very different from the Western ideal of democracy when he expressed the hope that the members of the state would become united with the ruler to the point that they came to resemble extensions of his organs of perception, communication, and thought.

In the second half of the fourth century B.C. there was a philosophical crisis in China. One aspect of it was the opposition posited by the individualist Yang Ju between human nature and the demands of society. His doctrine was to act "for myself". Personal pleasure was real and fame inane. Social institutions were a form of torture (Legge, *Mencius*, prolegomena, pp. 96–7, retranslated):

> There are the things forbidden under pain of punishment, and the things we are urged to do with the promise of rewards. Concern for our reputation drives us on, and the laws hold us back. We fretfully struggle for an hour of empty glory. We calculate the fame that will be left to us after we are dead. With the greatest circumspection we . . . worry about what is right and what is wrong in our conduct and thoughts. In vain we lose the true pleasure that is suited to our years, unable to follow our inclinations for a moment. How is this different from being in a prison with many walls and shackled with irons?

Yang urged men to act "in accordance with their hearts" (*shin,* a term that may also be taken as "minds"), and with their inner natures.

In the later fourth century Mencius (Menqtzyy) tried to resolve this crisis by arguing that man's heart (or mind) was innately good. This heart, which he also called "the heart of a child," took pleasure in a sensitive concern for others, and in morality generally, just as the mouth took pleasure in the flavours of food and the eyes in sexually attractive bodies. "There is no greater delight," he said, "than to reflect upon oneself and to be conscious of one's perfect sincerity." Just as all men had the same essential physical constitution, so they all had the same essential moral constitution. The innately good heart-mind could be corrupted in the way that the wooded slopes of a hill could be deforested by the hacking of axes, but this degraded state was not "what is essential to man." As proof, he gave the example of a baby crawling towards an open well. "All men have a heart that cannot bear to see others suffer. Who could be so inhuman as not to rush forward to save it?"

Mencius also propounded the ideal of "self-cultivation." One had to study, so as to "seek for the heart that one has abandoned," and to nurture one's "moral vitality" through the steady accumulation of good behaviour. Eventually one's heart could become immovable in its resistance to pressure from outside, but supremely capable of transforming others. Mencius was also the first to see the individual as, in some sense, a microcosm. "All the things in the world," he said, "are already complete in us."

For Juang Jou, the first and greatest of the Dawist philosophers, the self was as real (or unreal) as other objects distinguished by convention, but the artificial divisions created by words prevented us from seeing that "things have neither development nor decay, but return into each other and interpenetrate to form a single whole." Dreams provided evidence that things were constantly turning into other things, a process that he compared to molten bronze taking first one shape then another in the hands of a master-smith. His vision of the self in this flux of continual transformation can be found in the famous anecdote of the butterfly *(Juangtzyy jyishyh,* chyiwuh luenn):

> Once Juang dreamt he was a butterfly, a butterfly delighted with itself, doing whatever it felt like doing, and unaware it was Juang Jou. Suddenly he woke up, and realized with a shock that he *was* Juang Jou. He had no idea if he was the Juang Jou who had dreamt that he was a butterfly, or the butterfly dreaming he was Juang Jou. There was assuredly a difference between Juang and the butterfly. This is what is meant by 'the transformation of things'.

But there was no necessary continuity of memory or awareness. "When one's body is transformed in death, one's heart goes with it in the same way." The wise man, "unable to know what will come after, submits to the transformations that make him what he is, and so waits for the next unknowable transformation."

Juang also thought that individuals differed, both in what they were capable of understanding and in their ideas of true and false, a position that was at variance with that of Mencius. Thus (*Juangtzyy jyishyh*, shiauyauyou):

> The blind have no way of joining us in the seeing of patterns. The deaf have no way of joining us in hearing the sounds of drums and bells. Why should there only be bodily blindness and deafness? It is likewise the case with knowledge.

Failure to understand might also be caused by lack of experience. It was pointless to talk about the ocean to a frog who lived in a well, or to summer insects about the winter's ice.

If one could achieve what Juang called "great" or "true" knowledge, one became absorbed into the Daw, or Way, which may be thought of as the pervasive, autonomous, amoral functioning of nature. "Fish," he said, "forget themselves in the lakes and rivers. Men forget themselves in the Way." The ultimate aim was an all-encompassing indifference (*Juangtzyy jyishyh*, chioushoei):

> There are no limits to the sizes of things, no endpoints to their possible durations, no constancies in the divisions between them. Their ends and their beginnings are not to be forcibly determined. So great knowledge keeps in view both the distant and the close at hand. The small does not seem inadequate, nor the great excessive, since it knows the limitlessness of sizes. It draws its proofs from both present and past. The long-enduring causes it no dull stupor, nor does the transitory make it flustered, since it knows that there are no terminal points to possible duration. It scrutinizes the full and the empty. Gain brings no pleasure and loss no grief, for it understands the inconstancies of divisions. The path of tranquillity is clear to it. Life seems no happiness and death no disaster, since it knows that ends and beginnings cannot be forcibly determined.

This passage hints at one of the paradoxes of later Dawism (a world that I do not have the knowledge adequately to explore[7]). Adepts sought for physical immortality through the practice of both external and internal alchemy, yet this perpetuation of the self seems often to have been conceived as akin to its absorption into the workings of nature.

The most forceful expression of the view that man was the product of social conditioning was put forward by Shyun Ching early in the third century B.C. (*Shyuntzyy jyijiee*, chyuanshyue):

> Children born among the Hann and Yueh people of the south and among the Yi and Moh barbarians of the north cry with the same voice at birth. As they grow older they follow different customs. Indoctrination causes them to be thus.

Man became what he was through acquiring a stock of socially accumulated wisdom. "To attempt to do everything your own way is like a blind man trying to distinguish colours." Morality had to be learnt. "When a man is born, he is certainly an inferior man." Teachers and models were indispensable.

Shyun Ching justified morality on practical, socio-biological grounds (*Shyuntzyy jyijiee*, wangjyh):

> When morality effects a differentiation of roles there is a correct proportionality. A correct proportionality makes for unity, and unity for the multiplication of strength. The multiplication of strength means the ability to conquer other beings.

Human emotions had to be conditioned both through "ritual" (a term which had the usual sense and also that of appropriate behavior in specific social situations) and through music. Rituals had two functions: they crystallized and made clear the meaning of various aspects of human life, and they defined what should distinguish people in different positions from each other. Music summoned up feelings of mutual solidarity (like a pipe-band or a rock concert), and overcame the feelings of alienation that could arise from too much differentiation. "The conjunction of rituals and music," said Shyun, "dominates the hearts of men."

Some of the Chinese theorists of statecraft known as 'legalists' or 'realists' went far beyond Shyun Ching in their subordination of the individual to the collectivity. They argued that the welfare of the state, or of society as an organised whole, required standards and values diametrically opposed to those regarded as admirable in individual relationships, and which the Confucianists (such as Mencius and Shyun Ching) saw as also being the natural foundations of a good society and polity. The *Book of Lord Shang* (early third century B.C.) asserted (*Shangjiun shu*, chiuhchyang):

> A state that uses good people to govern the wicked will always suffer from disorder until it is destroyed. A state that uses the wicked to govern the good will always enjoy order, and so become strong.

It was vital, in their view, that individuals should not be psychologically stronger than the law. "States are thrown into disorder by people having numerous private opinions as to the nature of their duty." This justified the destruction of the culture and learning that were the foundations of such opinions. It may be doubted if the pre-modern West ever produced so extreme a disregard for the individual as this.

The mainstream view, as it developed towards the end of the first millennium B.C., was very different. It can be found most succinctly expressed in the syncretistic metaphysics of the various commentaries that had gathered around the old core material of the *Scripture of Changes (Yihjing),* the divining-manual of the Jou dynasty. At its heart was a science of sequential situations, expressed in terms of the transitions from one to another of sixty-four archetypal situations, the "Great Patterns" of Wang Shijy's poem quoted previously. These archetypes were symbolised as hexagrams of complete and broken lines derived from a multidimensional dualism of "bright" and "dark," "hard" and "soft," "male" and "female," and so on. It found its justification in the supposed existence of a vast network of correspondences that linked the aspects of the world into varying degrees of kinship. The oracle was believed to work because of a presumed resonance between the archetypes governing the situation asked about by the enquirer, and his action in casting stalks of milfoil or coins. As one commentary put it, "Similar frequencies will respond in resonance to each other. Similar vital forces will seek each other out." The crucial point for our present purposes is that this scripture (which was perhaps the most revered of all) concerned itself with the practical mediation of the relationship between the individual and the moral–material universe. (An example is Muh Jiang's divination recounted above.)

In this relationship the individual counted for something. The oracle was by no means rigidly deterministic. It offered a real if limited scope for choice. The overall trend of a situation was given by the pattern of the prevailing archetypes, but within this trend one might act wisely or foolishly, and so be effective or impotent. The self could live, through the insights provided by the sages, in a magical rapport with the cosmos (*Jouyih Yaushy-shyue,* shihtsyr shanq):

> The *Changes* constitutes a model of Heaven and Earth. . . . It is for this reason that we can know the causes of what is obscure and what is visible. . . . We are similar to Heaven and Earth, and thus not in conflict with them. Our knowledge embraces the Ten Thousand Things, guiding and benefitting the world. . . . We are at ease on the Earth, firm in our concern for others, and so able to express love.

The interaction of Buddhism and the Chinese tradition

The coming of Buddhism from India during the first half of the first millenium A.D. marked a watershed in Chinese thought. For our present concerns, and these only, perhaps its most important long-term effects were to accentuate the tendency to identify the self with the cosmos in one way or another, and to infuse what might be loosely termed a certain 'democratic' or 'egalitarian' quality into Chinese thought, where it existed in a state of tension with the hierarchicalism congenial to purely Confucian ideas.

This may seem surprising to those only familiar with Indian Buddhism. Part of the explanation lies in the differences between the basic orientations of the Chinese tradition and Indian thought at the time of the Buddha and some centuries after. For the Indian, suffering was an intrinsic property of life. For the Chinese, it was secondary: either accidental or brought unnecessarily by the human actor onto him- or herself. Pain *(dukkha)* is not a basic Chinese philosophical concern. Equally, the Indian believed in a continuous cycle of rebirths among living beings into lives of suffering, the wheel of *saṃsāra*. The Chinese believed, by and large, in a unique personal existence, no doubt fortified by the concept of a structure of kinship ascendants and descendants, stretching indefinitely back into the past and indefinitely forward into the future, in which the individual occupied his unique place. The Chinese recycled hexagrams, not selves. Likewise, the Indians sought some type of 'salvation', some escape from rebirth into suffering. The Chinese, for whom birth and life were positive goods, felt no such need. They were, until the coming of Buddhism, innocent of soteriology.

The Indians also devalued the impermanent, as being in some sense unreal. The Chinese, on the contrary, celebrated flux. The Daw and the sixty-four archetypes of the *Changes* were, in a sense, outside time, but they expressed themselves through change and were inconceivable apart from it. Similarly, the Indians, or at least their philosophers, distrusted the senses. For the Buddhist, the senses pertained to Māra, the evil one. They were the conduits of illusion. For the Chinese, it was through perception that one apprehended the real, the immanent pattern-principle(s). Hence it is not surprising that Indian Buddhism was pervasively transformed in Chinese hands, and that the reactions to it only responded to certain of its elements.

A key question to be answered about early Buddhism concerns the nature of its concepts of self *(attā)* and non-self *(anattā)*. The entities of which the world appears to consist were regarded as composed of aggregates *(khandhas)*. A crude analogy is with a television screen, on which changing collections of coloured dots fleetingly call up an illusion of people, animals, and landscapes. Such entities are void *(suñña)* in that they lack essential reality. The usually accepted view is that this analysis also applied to the self, which thus likewise lacked essential reality. An alternative view is that in its early stages the religion posited a core self that remained after the inessential 'non-self' elements, such as attachments and desires, had been stripped from it. The basis for this latter view is that it makes intelligible the many positive references to the *attā* in early Buddhist writing, and explains what it was that attained to *nibbāna*. This state may be approximately described as a pure, permanent, desireless and painless perfection freed of any of the causal-effectual characteristics resulting from the moral-material consequential chains running through existence after existence, as postulated by the doctrine of *kamma*. Without adjudicating on this dispute (which is outside my abilities), it may be agreed that orthodoxy soon placed a decisive emphasis on the view that there was no permanent ego or self. A typical simile that was offered relating to the sequences that are normally perceived as a personality was the impress of a seal on clay, in which only pattern is transferred.

From early Buddhism, the mainstream of Chinese philosophical tradition took up first and foremost a concern with the theory that (in the words of the Hwayan school) the world of apparent objects is "created by the artist in one's own mind." The *Long Scroll*, written in the late sixth century, is an early Charn (Zen) expression of this view (Jorgenson, pp. 13–14):

> It is as if there were a great rock in the front of the courtyard of your house on which you had the habit of sitting or snoozing. You have no fear of it. Suddenly the idea comes into your mind to make it into a statue. So you employ a sculptor to carve it into a statue of the Buddha. Your mind interprets it as being a Buddha, and you no longer dare to sit on it, fearing it to be an offence. . . . How can there be anything that is not constructed in your imagination?

From the Mahāyāna Buddhism of Nāgārjuna the mainstream Chinese tradition acquired a sense that everything is ultimately related to everything else, a view that is derived from the idea of "dependent co-origination" (Sanskrit *pratītya–samutpāda*), but has been given a characteristically Chinese concrete interpretation. According to Faatzanq (643–712), there was a "complete interfusion" *(yuanrong)* and "interpenetration" *(shiangruh)* of all phenomena. In his structuralist-relativist theory of being, each thing, as it flickers instantaneously in and out of existence, is only what it is by virtue of its relationship to every other thing; and it, in its turn, contributes in comparable fashion to making them what they are. The soteriological implication is that, because all beings are affected by each other's moral qualities, both good and bad, no being can be fully released from suffering and illusion until all are. The Bodhisattva (who stays behind in the world to help others) acts as he does not from choice but necessity.

The Neo-Confucianism that took shape in the eleventh century was a rationalist, secularist reaction to this sort of Buddhism. It was rationalist in that it implicitly accepted that words, arguments, and symbols can adequately grasp reality, and secular in that it maintained the moral worth of the everyday world. Jang Tzay, for example, formulated a metaphysics that, while having obvious Dawist antecedents, was basically a materialist reinterpretation of Buddhism. He says (*Jang Herngchyu jyi,* jenqmeng):

> The Great Potentiality [*tayshiu,* literally 'Great Void'] contains no specific shapes. It is the basic state of matter-energy. Its congealing and scattering are no more than transient non-intrinsic shapes subject to transformations. A profound calm unaffected by responses is our nature in its profoundest original state. Knowledge and awareness are no more than transient non-intrinsic responses due to interaction with things.

At the same time he extended the notion of *ren* (a sensitive concern for other people) until it had more the sense of 'a sensitive awareness of all other beings'. The opening lines of his *Western Inscription* read (*Jang Herngchyu jyi,* shiming):

> The Creative I designate my Father, and the Receptive I designate my Mother.[8] Compared to them I am of no significance, but I live intimately together with them in their midst. The all-filling plenum of Heaven and Earth is my body. The commands of Heaven and Earth are my nature. [All] people are my brothers. [All] things are my companions.

Jang's younger contemporary Cherng Mingdaw went even further when he said: "By *ren,* Heaven and Earth and the innumerable things are regarded as one substance, so that nothing is not oneself; and, when this is recognized, there is nothing one will not do for them." The attempt by Jang and Cherng to uphold Confucian values at the same time, for example by describing the sovereign as "the eldest son of our Father and Mother," immediately introduced a conflict between the older sense of hierarchy and this newer feeling for equality, which was to continue to affect later thinkers.

Jang also stressed that the congealing and scattering of matter-energy was "subject to pattern-principle *(lii),*" therefore "obeyed laws" and was "not arbitrary." He disagreed with what he described as "the Buddha's theory that mountains, rivers, and the great earth itself are a sickness in one's perceptions." Cherng Ichuan, Mingdaw's younger brother, extended the function of pattern–principle still further, making it both natural *and* normative, both descriptive *and* prescriptive. "A thing," he said, "must have a reason why it is as it is, and a rule to which it should conform." *Lii* determined both why fire was hot and how a son should behave towards his father.

This attempt to define morality in terms of what was 'natural' brought predictable problems. It was possible, to a certain extent, to finesse the dilemma of unnatural behaviour by arguing that if an entity has to have a given property to be a proper something, then, if it does not have this property, it is simply not that something (and hence not behaving unnaturally). Beyond this, the question of evil was resolved (in so far as it could be) by adopting Mencius's position that human nature was intrinsically good, but adding that its *lii* could be obscured by turbid matter-energy. The simile used was of a pearl lying in muddy water. This implied dualism between principle and matter tended to push the former in the direction of a transcendental realm, and left the strategy of deriving morality from nature in ruins.

An alternative approach was the moral intuitionism developed by Luh Shianqshan in the twelfth century. He identified pattern-principle *(lii)* with mind *(shin),* and avoided arbitrariness of intuition by positing a universal mind, of which the individual's was a part, gaining access to the whole by the faculty of intuitive moral knowledge *(liangjy)* except when contaminated by selfishness, which explained the occurrence of immoral actions by some individuals. Wang Yangming (1472–1529), who extended Luh's ideas, asserted that "outside the mind, there are no pattern-principles. Outside the mind there are no phenomena." He was not quite a solipsist, as he thought that mind had to have, so to speak, something to work on. "If my intelligence were separated from the universe, the spirits, and the manifold things, it too would lose its existence."

The radical, not too say revolutionary, aspects latent in this manner of thinking, and due in great measure to an interaction with Buddhist ideas, came to the surface in some of the more heterodox thinkers of the sixteenth century. Perhaps a belief in universal mind had made it safe for Wang Yangming to say, "I will not hold to be true a principle that my mind judges to be false, even if this principle has been enunciated by Confucius," since divergence was unlikely. But Lii Jyh (1527–1602) saw no valid grounds for supposing that all individuals would necessarily intuit the same values, and found the established social morality philosophically arbitrary. Her Shinyiin (1517–1579) thought friendship the only fully morally satisfactory relationship, and hoped that even if the relationships of ruler and minister and of father and son continued to have a formal existence, they would lose any substantive content, transformed by a feeling of amity. He also dreamed of a universal psychic intercommunication, an interlinking of all minds. These subversive notions, and others, were largely suppressed in the seventeenth and eighteenth centuries, but they were to be woken into life again by contact with the modern West.

If we had to sum up in a very general way the self as conceived of by the mainstream Neo-Confucian thinkers, we might say that it had the status of a microcosm reflecting a macrocosm. In the words of Ju Shi, the synthesizer of orthodoxy in the twelfth century, "Heaven . . . is totally immanent in nature." While this gave the self an irremovable centrality as the carrier of moral action, it also meant that any distinctive individuality (which would usually be associated with impure matter-energy or selfishness) was for the same reason morally somewhat suspect.

The self in modern Chinese thought

When we come to the philosophers of the later nineteenth and early twentieth centuries, we meet a paradox that is partly the result of a resurgence of traditional heterodox ideas and partly of Western influence. They begin with a search for the liberation of the self, but end with the desire for its extinction: for its absorption into a collective consciousness, the homogenization of its individuality, its perpetuation as a fragment of a greater Social Self, or its assimilation into the flow of a progressing human history.[9]

Tarn Syhtorng (1865–98) exemplifies this more clearly than anyone else. His *Study of Sensitive Concern for Others* reveals his hatred for the constraints imposed on the individual by accepted values (*Renshyue,* p. 2):

> From the time I was young until the time I was grown up, I everywhere encountered the afflictions of the bonds and relationships [of conventional morality]. I swam deep in their bitterness. It was almost something a living person could not endure. The burden was deadly, yet one did not die.

The old relationships had to be destroyed (*Renshyue,* p. 3):

> First we must break through the net of profits and remuneration. Then we must break through the net of conventional scholarship. . . . Then we must break through the net of having rulers. Then we must break through the net of moral norms. Then through the net of [believing in] Heaven. Then through the net of the world's religions. Last of all, we must break through the net of Buddhism.

He attacked the Confucian doctrine of 'names', or what we should call 'prescriptive definitions'. Their chief use was to define the roles that each person should act in social life.

> Names [wrote Tarn] are created by men. Superiors use them to control their inferiors, so that they are obliged to accord them respect. . . . Rulers use names to hobble ministers. Officials use names to keep the people on the [desired] track. Fathers use names to oppress their sons. Husbands use names to keep their wives in bondage. . . . How can the slightest feeling of sensitive concern for others survive in them? (*Renshyue,* pp. 11–12)

Equally abhorrent was ritual, the moralised manners that governed interpersonal relations. The old moral code graded one's obligations, and the intensity of the appropriate accompanying feelings, according to the proximity of the relatives concerned. Tarn would have none of this (*Renshyue,* p. 24):

> If a distinction is made between 'closeness' and 'remoteness', there come into being the prescriptive definitions on which ritual is based. . . . The heart is forced into that in which it takes no delight. The body is bound to do that which incommodes it.

In the utopia of the future, he maintained, there will be "no 'fathers' and no 'sons'. How much less will there be 'rulers' and 'ministers'! None of the prescriptive definitions with which despots, those robbers of the people, have coerced and bound them will any longer exist."

The ideals in whose name Tarn was demanding the demolition of Confucian values were equality and personal freedom. This is evident from his praise of friendship (*Renshyue,* p. 59):

> The least harmful to human life of the Five Relationships, and the most beneficial, with no trace of bitterness and a delight like that of fresh water, is friendship. . . . Why is this so? First, it is equal. Second, it is free. Third, its only object is [mutual] development. To summarise what this means, it is simply that the right to personal autonomy is not lost.

In politics, these new values led him to an anarchism modified only by a hint of the old concept of an all-embracing world-order (*Renshyue,* p. 76):

> In the government of the world, there should be an All-Under-Heaven but no nation-state. . . . Since everyone is free, no one should be the citizen of any particular state. If there are no states, then boundaries will dissolve, wars cease, suspicions end, distinctions between self and others vanish, and equality appear.

Thus far, the category of an independent self is central to Tarn's argument. But the context is missing. When supplied, it alters the perspective dramatically. Everything in Tarn's thinking found its reason for being, and its proper place, in what might be called a 'materialist mysticism'. Consider the following (*Renshyue,* pp. 7–8):

> Throughout the world of laws, the world of space, and the world of all that lives, from the vast to the microscopic, there is something that fills them all, everywhere holds them together, coordinates them, and weaves them into one. It cannot be seen, or heard, or tasted, and there is no way to give it a name, but I designate it 'the ether'. Confucius termed its manifestation in actions 'sensitivity to other individuals', the 'primal', and the 'basic nature'. Moh Dyi called it 'loving [mankind] as a whole', the Buddha the 'sea of the true nature' and 'compassionate sorrow'. Jesus spoke of it as the 'spiritual soul', 'loving others like oneself', and 'regarding enemies as friends'. Scientists name it 'chemical affinity' and the 'force of attraction'. This entity is all of these. . . . It is the ether that lets the eyes see, the ears hear, the nose smell, the tongue taste, and the body touch. . . . If you were to split an atom down to nothing, and to observe what it is that holds it together, that would be the ether. . . . The moon and the earth attract each other and do not fly apart. The eight planets . . . and the countless asteroids and comets all attract each other and do not scatter. . . . The starry clusters of the Milky Way, whose number is as the sands of the River Ganges, attract each other and do not scatter. . . . All this attraction is what I call the ether. . . . Only when scholars have clearly recognized its substance and function may they go on to talk about a sensitive concern for others.

We are all part of a flux of forces (*Renshyue,* p. 8):

> Just as people know that the nerves carrying the forces of the brain join the five sense-organs and the skeleton into a single body, so they ought to know that electrical forces join Heaven and Earth, all creatures, others and ourselves, into a single body. . . . My mind has the power to affect others, so that they share my thoughts. . . . In the last analysis, there is no barrier between others and one's self, for which reason the innermost feelings are as if open to view. Scholars should also recognize clearly that electricity is the same as brain. Since electricity is present everywhere, one's self is present everywhere. When foolish divisions are made between others and one's self, sensitive concern for others disappears.

The structure of human relationships should be dissolved (*Renshyue,* pp. 60–61):

> According to Buddhist teaching, all alike – regardless of whether they are rulers or ministers, husbands and fathers or wives and mothers, or sons, or elder or younger brothers – should leave the family and take vows, becoming members of the monastic community. . . . There is nothing that can be called a state. It is as if all were one family. There is nothing that can be called a body. It is as if all were one body.

It is at this point in Tarn's thinking that the self, after being liberated, begins to disappear again. The better to understand its extinction, we must leave the mysticism for a moment and look at the materialism. Tarn's study of Western science had taught him that the difference between "sweet smells and stinking odours" was no more than "a slight difference in the arrangement of the atoms." Hence it was a mistake to think of anything as having "a fixed and unchanging nature." The conservation of matter in chemical reactions seemed to him to prove that, much as Jang Tzay had argued earlier, "existence and non-existence are concentration and dispersion. There is no creation and destruction [of matter]." Why then should we fear death?

> To love life [he wrote] may be called a great delusion and a lack of understanding. It results from being blind to non-creation and non-destruction. . . . If people cannot overcome their fear of death, and are shrinking, confused, and without the courage to act, they will be even less fit to deal with the human predicament. They will more and more abandon themselves to evil, pay unceasing attention to making a favourable impression, but be ill-at-ease everywhere and think of nothing but their own pleasure and peace of mind. How can All-Under-Heaven be brought under good government again? . . . If they think only of their lives or, as one might say, of those few decades so swiftly gone, their minds will remain fixed on eating, drinking, copulating, possessions, income, reputation, and status. . . . Did Heaven give birth to men merely to furnish them with amusement and then forthwith to destroy them? (*Renshyue*, p. 20)

After setting forth a theory of the chemical reincarnation of the body, in which the atoms of a corpse reassemble to "become new people and new things," Tarn declares "how much less does the essence that is in the bodily soul pay regard to birth and destruction!" And he cites with approval the opinion of the seventeenth-century philosopher Wang Fujy that "when a sage dies, his vital essence divides and becomes a multitude of men of worth."[10]

Tarn's goal was a collective enlightenment, to achieve which every self had to be extinguished in a totality. Consider these words from his closing pages (*Renshyue*, pp. 73–4):

> The fundamental reason why others and the self cannot intercommunicate is that the way in which the ethers of the brain move are different for each of us. Whenever I am in a state of peaceful introspection, I can see the movements of the ethers of my brain. Their colour is a pure white, their light clear and sparkling. They are as fine as silken threads, their shapes sinuous and twisting. This is how they move: they alter all the time in an undetermined way between long and short, plentiful and sparse, existent

> and non-existent, with a swiftness for which no words are adequate, like flashes of lightning among the clouds, free from the least imperfection.
>
> It is my belief that the brain is electricity. At first I thought that it moved at random. Later I perceived that this is not so. When the multitude of thoughts is transparent, they are hidden in their tranquillity and not visible to the eye. If, by some chance, a thought emerges, patterns of electricity appear, and thought tirelessly follows thought, their movements never ceasing. When thoughts change, the movements are likewise very different; and the more thoughts, the more differences. They accumulate in so much complexity, and so intermingle, that they no longer form patterns. One can deduce from the different movements that accompany different thoughts that the manner of movement is determined by the thoughts, and is of a specific type. . . .
>
> The movements of the ethers of the brain constitute consciousness. Since the ways in which the ethers of the brain move have countless dissimilarities, and consciousness is borne along upon them, confusion arises. As every person, every place, every time, and every phenomenon is different, how can there be a means whereby others and the self can communicate? The fault lies in the mutual incompatibility or, in other words, in consciousness. If we now seek intercommunication between them, we must *extinguish consciousness*. If we want to extinguish consciousness, we must change the way in which the ethers of our brain move. Contact with the outside must be cut off. Internally, we must return to simplicity. We must become simpler and simpler until nothingness is reached, at which point consciousness will have been destroyed. When consciousness has been destroyed, the self will have been removed along with it. When the self has been removed, differences will have been annihilated. When differences have been annihilated, equality appears. When equality has been attained, every entity will be penetrated by an awareness of every other entity, with not the least barrier between them. This is the culmination of the intercommunication of self and others. . . . This is a sensitive concern for others!

The goals of Confucianism and Buddhism, *ren* and *nibbāna,* have been identified, through a materialism based on Western science.

The legatees of the self: society, culture, and the future

Tarn Syhtorng was unusual in the ruthlessness of his conclusions, but elements of the ideas just discussed can be found in most modern Chinese philosophers, with an important exception. The objective of a psychological simplification of the self to a totally undifferentiated state vanishes. Instead the self tends to find its ultimate meaning as a distinctive component of a vaster structure that extends across space and time: a society, a culture, or a future. Let us look at a few cases.

Kang Yeouwei (1858–1927) was best known in his life as a political reformer, but is mainly remembered today as the author of *The Great*

Uniformity,[11] a blueprint for utopia, partly drafted in the 1880s but only published in full in 1935. Kang believed that Heaven had given him his talents in order to cure the agonies of mankind. His emotional orientation was that of a bodhisattva who had become a Benthamite. The cruelty of life haunted him. "The azure Heaven and the round earth are nothing but a great slaughter-yard, a great prison." Progress was to "reduce men's pain and to increase their pleasure."

Avoidable or remediable unhappiness, thought Kang, was due to inequalities created by nature and by man. Thus having different states caused wars, and as a cure Kang advocated a world government and a world language. Having social classes bred bitterness and hindered the development of the talents of those in the less privileged groups. So – no more classes. Complete physical and mental uniformity was essential to happiness. Therefore different ethnic groups had to be homogenized by means of population transfers and mixed marriages. Eventually everyone was to be of the same colour, the same shape, and the same intelligence.

Women had suffered from the subservience they were expected to show towards men on no better grounds than sexual difference. Except in matters relating to the bearing of children, men and women were therefore to be treated as equals. On all formal occasions they were to wear unisex clothing. The family was a source of small-scale collective selfishness, and was to be abolished. Children could then be brought up in identical fashion in institutions. "Otherwise," he said, "people's characters will not be of the same kind." Men had varying dispositions and had to be "smelted and forged," a process most easily effected when they were young. In this way, he concluded, "morality may easily be unified and behaviour made identical." The economy was to be run by the state, to prevent the re-emergence of rich and poor. Kang remained beset by the fear that exceptional and charismatic personalities might reappear. So he ordained that such people were to be thrown into prison.

The wilderness was to be municipalised and homogenised. All animals harmful to man were to be exterminated. The others were to be domesticated, kept in zoos, or employed as servants. Birds would perform as choristers. Universal economic development – the irrigation of deserts, the levelling of mountain ranges, and the building of artificial islands on the seas – would create a global parkland with every consumer amenity. The human spirit would be kept alive (he hoped) by a modest emulation between administrative units in productive output, the advancement of knowledge, and the practice of altruism.

Kang repeatedly affirmed that "all men have a right to freedom conferred on them by Heaven." Yet his recipe for general happiness was the destruction of all that makes an individual individual.

In Ferng Yeoulan's *A New Examination of Man* (1943), the drama is psychological rather than social. For Ferng, man's most distinctive characteristic is conscious awareness. Personal development consists in the enhancement of this conscious awareness. According to its level, a man lives in one of four spiritual realms: the Realm of Nature, the Realm of Utility, the Realm of Morality, and the Realm of the Universal. Each corresponds to a mental state (*Shin yuan ren,* p. 37):

> In the Realm of Nature, men do not know that there is a self. . . . In the Realm of Utility, men have a self. In this realm, all a man's actions are selfish. . . . In the Realm of Morality, man is without self. He acts morally, for the sake of morality. . . . In the Realm of the Universal, man is likewise without the self, but this selflessness must be called the 'Great Selflessness'.

In his view, morality derives from man's being a member of society. Moral actions are defined as those consciously directed to seeking the happiness of others, without any thought of personal advantage therefrom. "A man," he says, "must sacrifice himself in order to seek the benefit of others."

As awareness advances, one realises that one is not just a part of society, but also of the Universe. "Man," he says, "must contribute not only to society but also to the Universe." The enlightened person sees his own life and all phenomena as "parts of the embodiment of the Way." This term, he says is "a general name for all transformations," or the "Great Phenomenon that has no beginning and no end," or even "the flux of operational effects." Such a man is not only aware that he is part of the Great Totality, he actually becomes identified with it, even identical to it. "When a man has become identified with the Great Totality," says Ferng, "for him the distinction between self and non-self no longer exists."

He then imagines a sceptic asking how a part, that is to say, man, can be identified with a whole, that is to say the Universe. The answer is "mind." He quotes Wang Yangming's view that intelligence pervades the Universe, so that there are no divisions between the self and other entities. "Man's mind," says Ferng, "may likewise be a part of the Cosmos, but the range of its thoughts is not restricted to part of the Cosmos." To materialists who argue that the mind is no more than the movements of the brain, he retorts that the mind depends on the brain but only in the way that a picture depends on paints and paper for its existence. Furthermore, "when one becomes identified with the Great Totality, the self is by no means entirely extinguished." What happens is, rather, "an unlimited expansion of the self." "In this unlimited expansion the self is in fact the ruler of the Great Totality." Finally, "religions consider God to be the ruler of the Universe, but the man who is in the realm of the universal is aware that his self is the ruler of the Universe. If the ruler of the Universe is God, then his self is God."

The man in the realm of Utility is ruled by the pursuit of pleasure, income, and publicity. His life is "the continuation of the existence of the self," and his death "the destruction of its existence." For the man in the realm of Morality, death is merely the end of his obligations. His acts have an exclusively social significance, so personal extinction is of no great importance. The man in the realm of the universal is "one with the Creative Force" (in the words of Guo Shianq, a fourth-century commentator on the Dawist scriptures). He is "without beginning and without end." The self, identified with the Great Totality, exists across all space and time.

Freedom is not a matter of one's actions. "The man in the realm of the universal," says Ferng, "has in no sense to act differently from the mass of the ordinary people." Indeed, "it is the special characteristic of the Neo-Confucian to seek the realm of the universal in the actions of his everyday life." One's obligation is only "to fulfil the duties arising from one's personal relations and one's job." Like an actor who has been assigned a part in a play, one must accept one's role and play it to the best of one's ability. He does not consider that one might question the casting and the script.

Just as Kang's brave new world is in some respects an update of Moh Dyi (probably but not provably inspired by the Western utopian socialists of the nineteenth century), so Ferng's vision is a fusion of the ideas of the 'mind' school of Neo-Confucianism with elements of Dawism, transformed by an internalization of significance that seems to derive from German idealism.

Quite different is the doctrine of social immortality espoused by Hwu Shyh (1891–1962). It is summed up in his reflections on the death of his mother (Kwok, pp. 103–104):

> As I reviewed the life of my dead mother, whose activities had never gone beyond the trivial details of the home but whose influence could be clearly seen on the faces of those men and women who came to mourn her death . . . I came to the conclusion that everything is immortal. This line of reasoning led me to what may be called the religion of social immortality, because it is essentially based on the idea that the individual self, which is a product of the accumulated effects of the social self, leaves an indelible

> mark of everything it is and everything it does upon that larger Self which may be termed Society, or Humanity, or the Greater Being. . . . This Great Self lives forever as the everlasting testimony of the triumphs and failures of the numberless individual selves.

He distinguished this theory from the traditional idea that a select few survive through the memory of their virtues, achievements, and writings. He ascribed social imperishability to every action of every person, trivial as well as exceptional, evil as well as good. He argued that this was not "revering Society and annihilating the individual" since, though "the world of today is what it is through the accumulated virtues and sins of our predecessors, the world of the future depends entirely on the virtues and sins that we ourselves accumulate." This is a secular, collectivist version of the doctrine of *kamma*.

With Jang Dongsun (1886–1965) we find Culture replacing Society and the appearance of the Future as the supreme validating principle of morality and meaningfulness. In his *Fledgling Philosophy* (1929) Jang describes the universe as a spatial structure, composed of the "interweaving of countless structures," that evolves through time. The distinguishing feature of this "evolutionary process" is an "increased intercooperation throughout the entire entity." From this he argues that "if a man's life has any value, that is because man's life in the universe has a relatively . . . progressive place. . . . If it does not . . . then one can deduce that that man's life is valueless." Strictly speaking, he adds, value is relative and man's life lacks any absolute value or purpose. In a sense one can regard its purpose as the immanent one of the self-completion of the personality.

In *The Philosophy of Morals* (1931) Jang says that the goal of each individual's life is to break free from immediate existence in the here and now. Culture and civilisation represent a collective effort by humanity to achieve this objective for their members. "What is noble in man," Jang says, "is that he can mark out a domain independent of the natural world in which the laws of nature reign, a domain in which he can put into effect laws at variance with the laws of nature."

Knowledge and awareness are what permit civilised man to take part in this process of collective self-realisation. Jang uses the metaphor of two lamps in a dark room. "The lamps," he says, "cannot have their existence in common, but their light can." People are like lamps, irreducibly individual, but knowledge, which is "the value of life" as opposed to its mere existence, is like the light, and belongs to a shared, objective domain, that of culture. He concludes: "The reason I say that human life has a purpose is because there is knowledge; and it is possible for it to change a purposeless natural existence into a purposeful idealistic existence." Underpinning this faith is Jang's conviction that the advance of knowledge is "absolutely irreversible."

Jang's starting-point is the individual. "If," he says, "the spirit of an individual can create something that will add to the existing general stock of culture, this creation represents the forward march of culture." But, he warns, if it is too individualistic then it will have no value. What he calls the "lesser self" or the "false self" can only attain any value if its sublimation of selfish desires can lead it to an awareness of the "greater" or "true" self. What is society, then? Is it a super-being in its own right, or just an association for the benefit of individuals? Jang says he is a follower of Wundt here: the social mind is more than an agglomeration of individual minds.[12] The appearance of an inherited tendency to moral behaviour he explains on the socio-biological grounds of its survival value for the group.

The individual attains immortality only in terms of his actions. In *A Fledgling Philosophy* Jang wrote (*Shin jershyue luenntsorng*, p. 63):

> [If there is no undying soul] does that not mean that once we are dead we are finished? No. It does not. If, indeed, our universe is a complex, living structure, then every one of our actions has consequences in its remotest parts.

In the *Philosophy of Morals* he elaborated (*Dawder jershyue*, pp. 614–15):

> Since mankind came into being, all creations of the spirit . . . have been a struggle to find immortality. . . . The individual seeks to extend the domain of his life so that he may exist for ever. The accumulation of [such] endeavours is culture. . . . Every individual dies, but the culture that he has produced is comparatively immortal.

Subject to the proviso that it is progressive. "If," says Jang, "a person is stationary with respect to the advance of human life in the universe . . . or even goes against the current, then – even if his person and actions are known to a great number of people – he does not merit the designation 'imperishable'."

Here are the structuralist metaphysics of Faatzanq (see earlier discussion of "complete interfusion" and "interpenetration") set in motion by a future-worship inspired by German idealism.

Revolutionary emotion and revolutionary theory

Nowhere does the tension between the desire for ecstatic self-expression and ecstatic self-immolation show itself so clearly as in the early writings of the left-wing poet and scholar Guo Mohruoh. Here he is talking about poetry (Roy, p. 87):

> Only a poem which is a pure manifestation of the poetic feelings and images in the mind, a strain flowing from the well of life, a melody played on the lute-strings of the heart, a tremor of life, a cry of the soul, can be a true poem, a good poem, a well-spring of human happiness. . . . Whenever I encounter such a poem . . . I only wish I could swallow it, book, paper, and all.

Here he is on children (Roy, p. 90):

> There is not a moment of the day when [a child] does not devote his entire self to the tasks of creation, expression, and enjoyment. The life of a child is the life of a genius in miniature.

Guo wanted to become a superchild.

Little by little, though, he came to feel that self-realisation was an illicit indulgence until it was equally accessible to everyone. In 1923 he declared (Roy, p. 155):

> Until the economic systems of the world have been transformed, such things as the manifestations of Brahmā, the dignity of the self and the gospel of love can only be the morphine or cocaine of the propertied and leisured classes, while the members of the proletariat are left to soak themselves in sweat and blood.

Personal freedom had to be renounced, in a mortification of the spirit, so that others might enjoy it later.

Romanticism and revolutionary impulse fused into a cult of action (Roy, p. 135):

> If all natural phenomena are manifestations of God, and I also am a manifestation of God, then I am God, and all natural phenomena are manifestations of me. When a man has lost his Self and become one with God, he transcends time and space, and sees life and death as one. . . . Energy is the source from which all things are created; it is the will of the Universe. . . . If one can achieve union with this energy, one will be aware only of life and not death, only of constancy and not change. . . . With the same energy with which a lion strikes its prey, with the whole body and the whole soul, one must seek self-realization in every moment.

So he became a revolutionary writer, hating the beauties of the world as an illusion, raging at songbirds that they should dare to warble in the gardens of the rich, and seeing his work as the artistic equivalent of the activist's bomb.

This pattern of revolutionary emotion had no counterpart in Chinese revolutionary theory. In the most systematic exposition of Mauist Communism, the *Philosophy of the Masses* by Ay Sychyi (1910–66), there is no commitment to the self-realisation of the individual but, rather, views like the following (*Dahjonq jershyue,* pp. 125–126):

> We have revolutionary thoughts and actions. We exert ourselves to serve the great people. This is the main side of our character, and an aspect of the path of development of the distant future. But we also often contain dregs of the thought of petty-bourgeois individualism, and even the dregs of the consciousness of the other exploiting classes. We often make calculations for our own private profit, which prevents us from serving the people with whole heart and whole will. This is the reverse side of our character, the rotten side that must be smashed.

Independence of thought or perception is an illusion. Thought has a class character. There are no purely rational grounds, therefore, for deciding the validity of an argument. What proves an idea erroneous is its defeat in practice (by implied analogy with an experiment in a laboratory). Any failure on the part of a revolutionary therefore indicates that his mind is not reflecting reality properly, since knowledge is a reflection of the material world about us.[13] Only the minds of those who have a working-class standpoint can reflect reality unimpaired by selfishness. (Compare the Neo-Confucian idea that selfishness could block the individual mind from contact with the universal mind.) So Ay says – and this really is what he says – (*Dahjonq jershyue,* p. 57):

> If you are resolved to become a very good camera, and able to have an accurate knowledge of everything, then you must first resolve a basic question, namely you must take the standpoint of the workers and the broad mass of the people. . . . You must be able to make yourself wholeheartedly, whole-mindedly loyal to the interests of the people, that is, you must resolve that all your work and all your ability shall be used for the task of liberating the broad mass of the people, and that you will sacrifice all, without begrudging it, to the achievement of this goal. . . . If you are able to be like this, without the slightest individual selfishness, and in no degree affected by the influence on thought of the selfishness and vileness of the large landlord or large bourgeois classes, then, when you examine a question, you will have no prejudices, no anxieties, to impede your understanding the true nature of the question to the bottom, and you can obtain a correct knowledge of everything.

The individual remains of significance only as the locus of an ever-renewed moral struggle whose aim is the extinction of individuality.

By taking the working-class point of view, and so escaping from the realm of bourgeois utility, the mind can gain the understanding of the laws that give it freedom and power. According to Ay (*Dahjonq jershyue*, p. 202):

> If we have not the slightest knowledge of the laws of development of society, then our actions are entirely conditioned by our own class interests. . . . If, on the contrary, we know the laws of the development of society . . . we can escape from blindness and consciously tread the road of inevitable victory.

What is more, "If a man's thinking can be in accord with the laws of reality, and if he can know the laws in appropriate fashion, then he can wield very great strength, and make use of the knowledge of these laws to change the reality of the world." In short, "He can control the world."

Of course reality is always changing. So the truth in the revolutionary's mind must alter in corresponding fashion. This, to cut short a familiar story, is what dialectics is about. Ay Sychyi's vision, then, is of an ever-changing reality and an ever-changing correct theoretical interpretation perfectly attuned and interacting, in which the selfless yet omnipotent revolutionary becomes one with the simultaneous forward march of progress and truth. The assumptions about class and progress are new, but the underlying style of thought, which is predicated on the existence of an exact correspondence between reality and a symbolic system, and the power accruing to those who can comprehend it, has much in common with that of the *Scripture of Changes*.

Final observations

Chinese ideas about the self from late archaic times to the present day were extraordinarily varied. If, however, a broad contrast may be tentatively made with comparable ideas in Europe over the same span of time it is probably best brought out by focussing on the Middle Ages and the early modern period, when it emerges most clearly. In spite of the purgatories and paradises of popular Buddhism, the Chinese were not on the whole obsessed with the personal fate of the soul (which is the crucial aspect of the self in this context) in an afterlife to anything like the same degree as the Europeans. Nor was there in China any condition comparable to the isolation of the European soul, either from other souls or, above all, from an omnipotent, ultimately incomprehensible, transcendent deity.

Notes

Thanks are due to the Australian National University for permission to make extensive use of material from the author's G.E. Morrison Lecture, *Self-Liberation and Self-Immolation in Modern Chinese Thought* (Canberra: Australian National University, SocPac Printery, 1978). Professor Wang Gungwu generously helped improve the translations from Tarn Syhtorng. Professor D.T. Roy and Harvard University Press kindly consented to the quotation of substantial passages from *Kuo Mo-jo: the Early Years.* Dr Jorgenson agreed to the quotation of a passage from an unpublished seminar paper on early Charn Buddhism. To all these scholars I am most grateful.

1. One reason for this is presumably the need to compensate for the severely restricted number of Chinese *surnames.*
2. The only reference that may puzzle the modern reader is that to the doves. They were thought to become intoxicated from eating mulberry leaves, like girls from making love before they married. The literal sense of "man of too many inner selves" is "two and three [i.e., various] your characteristic virtue," where 'virtue' indicates the quality that makes something what it is.
3. For a detailed discussion see M. Elvin, "Was there a transcendental breakthrough in China?", in S. N. Eisenstadt, ed., *The Axial Age and Its Diversity* (forthcoming, 1985).
4. If we follow the traditional commentators. Modern scholarship is not so sure.
5. Read *chyn* for *shin* in this line.
6. Hypothetical form.
7. There is an excellent introduction in K. Schipper, *Le corps taoïste* (Paris: Fayard, 1982).
8. The Creative and the Receptive are the first two hexagrams of the *Scripture of Changes.*
9. For a somewhat fuller account, see M. Elvin, *Self-Liberation and Self-Immolation in Modern Chinese Thought,* 39th G. E. Morrison Lecture (Canbèrra: Australian National University, SocPac Printery, 1978).
10. This is a theme briefly noted by Mauss, namely the tendency of the Chinese to think of the self or soul as in some respects divisible.
11. This non-standard translation is justified by the contents of the book in question. A more conventional rendering would be *The Great Concord.*
12. Much of Jang's later work was to be concerned with the cultural development of the basic concepts of systems of thought, concepts that we recognise as essentially undefinable since, in the last resort, the definable may always be replaced by its definition, and at some point regress must stop.
13. Elsewhere Ay does note that these reflections need to be interpreted by a theory.

References

References in the text to the classics are by section rather than page, because of the multiplicity of editions, except for English/Chinese parallel texts.

Ay Sychyi. *Dah jonq jershyue* [The Philosophy of the Masses]. N.p.: Shinhwa, 1949. 2nd edition.

Billeter, J-F. *Li Zhi, philosophe maudit (1527–1602).* Geneva: Droz, 1979.

Cook, F. *Hua-yen Buddhism.* Philadelphia (University Park): Pennsylvania State University Press, 1977.

Couvreur, S. *Tch'ouen Ts'iou et Tso Tchouan. La chronique de la principauté de Lou* [Chinese text and French translation]. Ho-kien-fou: mission press (?), 1914. Reprinted, Paris: Cathasia-France, 1951. 3 vols.

Ferng Yeoulan. *Shin yuan ren* [A New Examination of Man]. Shanghae: Shangwuh, 1943, reprinted 1946.

Graham, A. C. *Two Chinese Philosophers, Ch'eng Ming-tao and Ch'eng Yi-ch'uan.* London: Lund Humphries, 1958.

Guo Chinqfarn, ed. *Juangtzyy jyishyh* [The *Juangtzyy* with Collected Explanations]. Beeijing: Jonghwa, 1961. The 'inner chapters', which are generally agreed to be beyond doubt by Juang Jou himself, are translated in A. Graham, *Chuang-tzu: The Seven Inner Chapters and Other Writings . . .* (London: Allen and Unwin, 1981).

Jang Chwenyih, ed. *Mohtzyy jyijiee* [The Works of Mohtzyy Annotated]. Shanqhae: Shyhjieh, 1931. See also Y. P. Mei, *The Ethical and Political Works of Motse* (London: Probsthain, 1929).

Jang Dongsun. *Shin jershyue luenn tsorng* [Collected Essays on the New Philosophy]. Shanqhae: Shangwuh, 1929.

Dawder jershyue [The Philosophy of Morals]. Shanqhae: Jonghwa, 1931.

Jang Herngchyu jyi [The Works of Jang Tzay]. Shanqhae: Shangwuh, 1926. 3 vols.

Jorgenson, J. "The Philosophy of Early Ch'an," unpublished seminar paper, Australian National University, 1978.

Jou Yih Yaushyh-shyue [The *Changes of Jou,* annotated by Yau (Peyjong)]. Mid-nineteenth century. Reprinted, Tairbeei: Shangwuh, 1965. 3 vols. See also R. Wilhelm, trans. C. Baynes, *The I Ching or Book of Changes* (New York: Bollingen/Pantheon, 1950. 2 vols in 1).

Kang Yeouwei. *Dahtorng shu* [The Book of the Great Uniformity]. Beeijing: Guujyi, 1956. There is a partial translation in L. Thompson, *Ta T'ung Shu, The One-World Philosophy of K'ang Yu-wei* (London: Allen and Unwin, 1958).

Karlgren, B. *The Book of Odes* [Chinese text and English translation]. Stockholm: Museum of Far Eastern Antiquities, 1950.

Kwok, D. W. Y. *Scientism in Chinese Thought.* New Haven: Yale University Press, 1965.

Legge, J. *The Chinese Classics, I: Confucian Analects, The Great Learning, and the Doctrine of the Mean* [Chinese texts and English translations]. (Oxford University Press, 1893.) See also A. Waley, *The Analects of Confucius* (London: Allen and Unwin, 1938).

The Chinese Classics, II: The Works of Mencius [Chinese text and English translation]. London: Trübner, 1861.

Obi Kōichi. *Chūgoku bungaku ni arawareta shizen to shizenkan* [Nature and the View of Nature as Revealed in Chinese Literature]. Tokyo: Iwanami, 1962.

Schipper, K. *Le corps taoïste.* Paris: Fayard, 1982.

Shangjiun-shu Critical Annotation Committee of Beeijing Broadcasting Institute, etc., ed., *Shangjiun shu pyngjuh* [The Book of Lord Shang with Critical Annotations]. Beeijing: Jonghwa, 1976. See also, J. Duyvendak, *The Book of Lord Shang* (London: Probsthain, 1928).

Tarn Syhtorng chyuan jyi [The Complete Works of Tarn Syhtorng]. Beeijing: Sanlian, 1954.

Wang Shianchian, ed. *Shyuntzyy jyijiee* [The Works of Shyuntzyy Annotated]. Shanqhae: no pub., *circa* 1891. See also H. Dubs, *The Works of Hsuntze* (London: Probsthain, 1927).

Wang Wencherng chyuanshu [Complete Works of Wang Yangming]. Shanqhae: Jongiang, 1925. 4 vols.
You Gwoen, ed. *Li sau tzoanyih* [Collected Interpretations of 'Inescapable Sorrow']. Beeijing: Jonghwa, 1980. There is an English translation in D. Hawkes, *Ch'u Tz'u. The Songs of the South* (Oxford University Press, 1959).

9

Purity and power among the Brahmans of Kashmir

Alexis Sanderson

Mauss recognises India as the scene of man's first formal conception of the self as an individual conscious entity. Seeing that this discovery was not followed by the developments which lead in his evolutionist scheme to the perfection of the category of the person in the minds of Europeans, he seeks an explanation for this failure and finds it in the influence of the Sāṃkhya dualists, Buddhist impersonalists and Upanishadic monists.[1] Since these doctrines belong to the earliest accessible stratum of Indian metaphysics, gaining prominence in the middle of the first millennium B.C., it appears to Mauss that the proper growth of the Indian self was prevented at its birth by views which recognized it only to reject it as a fiction constitutive of an undesirable worldly consciousness.

What is striking in his cursory treatment is not so much his evolutionism as the inadequacy of his evidence and his lack of sociological and historical perspective. Firstly the relevant intellectual culture of India was much more than these three renunciationist doctrines. They were important; but they were also vigorously opposed. Secondly Mauss presupposes that it is reasonable to approach the category of the person in India through metaphysics alone, overlooking the dimensions of social personhood which are, as it were, the raw material out of which these metaphysical systems were cooked. In order then to go beyond Mauss's conclusions we must not only consider a wider range of doctrines. We must also go beneath the surface of philosophical and theological abstractions to the theory and prescription of social roles and, beneath this level, to materials whose aim was not to prescribe the construction of social personhood but to describe it or expose its presuppositions. For if we are to offer a picture of the category of the person in India which is more than a catalogue of unlocated and unrelated theories of the referent of the "I"-cognition, then we must seek those principles implicit in social life which gave soteriological sense to these idealizations and make comprehensible their coexistence in awareness of each other.

Now these theories must be located and related in as well-determined a context as possible. It is not sufficient to contextualize them within Indian society in the abstract. These soteriological discourses in representing the raw materials of personhood may draw on prescriptive texts which suppress in a characteristically Sanskritic manner all awareness of their origins in time and space; but we must not be drawn by this ideological feature into presupposing like Mauss that Indian culture was a single homogeneous whole. We must look at the way in which these levels of self-representation, for all their claims to universality, coexisted in a particular community at a particular time. We will not be able to conclude that what we find was the case throughout India at all times; but we will have a basis from which to work towards greater generality. Among various possibilities Kashmir from the ninth to the thirteenth centuries stands out as particularly promising for such an investigation. This period in India is one in which the materials at all levels have achieved great sophistication and mutual consciousness, while Kashmir, particularly well documented historically and then at the height of its creativity and intellectual reputation, gives us access through its literature to a uniquely broad perspective on the presuppositions and realities of Indian self-reference. It was the scene of maximum inclusion; for it saw the entry into sophisticated discourse of religious systems which the orthodox consensus considered impure,[2] visionary and magical cults seeking superhuman power. Nowhere else at any time did this fundamental element in Indian society find so articulate a voice, and as it grows in strength we witness the strategies by which certain groups within these radical sects were brought in from the visionary fringe to accommodate areas of orthodox self-representation. This accommodation is of particular interest because the visionary power of the heterodox self is recoded in order to be inscribed *within* the orthodox social identity and in such a way that it reveals the latter as a lower nature within the one person. Thus we are provided with a unique view of the presuppositions of Indian personhood: for the tradition sustains its 'power' behind the appearance of conformity by means of philosophical arguments and coded rituals which demonstrate to the initiate that all other doctrines of the "I"-cognition are no more than the making explicit of the instinctive levels of self-representation which are the parameters of this lower nature. This tradition, by deriving its power from this ability to contain and transcend all others, reveals more than any other the principles underlying their diversity and interaction. We see that the forces of self-representation in the Kashmirian community of this period, manifest in the poles of this duality of the orthodox and the heterodox and in the dialectic of their convergence, were contained within a fundamental structure of values which, arguably, underlies a far wider range of cultural forms in the kingdoms of medieval India. Its terms are purity and power. At one extreme are those who seek omnipotence and at the other those who seek depersonalized purity. The former are impure in the eyes of the latter and the latter impotent in the eyes of the former. The former seek unlimited power through a visionary art of impurity, while the latter seek to realize through the path of purity an essential unmotivatedness which culminates, in the most uncompromising form of their doctrine, in the liberating realization that they have done and will do nothing, that the power of action is an illusion. The absolute of the impure is absolute Power; that of the pure is inert Being.[3]

The path of purity

The ideal Brahman

The way into this chiasmic structure was necessarily through the path of purity. For those Brahmans[4] who opted for the path of power did so in the consciousness that it could be entered only by transcending the identity-through-purity embodied in the orthodox consensus and embedded in themselves.

Brahmanhood in its orthodox form as the basis of the path of purity was of two levels, the physical and the social. The first, conferred by birth from Brahman parents and seen as an inalienable property of the body,[5] is necessary but not sufficient for the second, participation in the society of Brahmans through the study of Vedic revelation, marriage and commensality. This could be achieved, maintained and perfected only by conformity to the corpus of rules derived directly or indirectly from the infallible Veda[6] and embodied in the conduct of the orthodox.[7] This functional Brahmanhood entailed a life of exacting ritual and duty, which required the relentless avoidance of the forbidden and contaminant in all aspects of the person's existence: in his relations with his wife, in his food, drink, sleep and natural functions, in his dress, speech, gestures and demeanour, and in all his contacts, physical, visual and mental, with substances, places and with persons differentiated not only permanently by their castes but also at any time by degrees of purity determined by the same or similar criteria. The Brahman could maintain his privileged position at the summit of the hierarchy of nature only by conformity to his dharma, to the conduct prescribed for him in accordance with his caste and stage of life. The vast catalogue of rules extricating the pure from the impure and enjoining the acts by which he could establish his identity illumined for him a perilously narrow path through a dark chaos of possibilities excluded by absolute and, for the most part, unexplained interdictions. The ideal Brahman was alone with no companion but his balance of merit through conformity.[8] His greatest enemy was the spontaneity of the senses and his highest virtue immunity to emotion in unwavering self-control.[9]

The atheistic autonomism of the ritualists

Dogmatic anthropologies defined for this orthodox subject of injunction, epistemological and ontological frameworks adequate to his personhood. We will examine the two extremes within these orthodox theories, the Mīmāṃsaka and the Vedāntin or Upanishadic. For while there was much Brahmanical theory which cannot be identified with either, these two marked out the fundamental lines of force within which Brahmanical thought operated. The divergence of their categories records a tension within the orthodox which the theories of the extremes sought to minimize. This middle ground, even if it expressed the self-representation of the majority of Brahmans, only emphasises, with its sacrifice of theoretical coherence for the sake of an uneasy peace, the truth-value of the more radical positions.

First, the Mīmāṃsaka ritualists,[10] specialists in the interpretation of the Vedic texts as the sole authority for the duties of the twice-born, required the orthodox person to recognize as his a world in which all form is external to consciousness. He was not to view ideas and language as a field of internal construction, an inner depth coming between him and the world in itself. For such a formulation would have undermined his realism, causing him to doubt whether he was in fact in contact with an external world at all.[11] Cognitions, said the Mīmāṃsakas, are not formed entities: they are acts, which by their very nature produce in their objects the quality of being known. We therefore know that we know only by inference from this effect, not by introspection.[12] Thus the objective world was to confront the orthodox Brahman pre-arranged, with no contribution from his side, in an eternal[13] taxonomy of universals[14] and values.[15]

If his cognition as pure act was to have no object-form, so that the world it revealed might have absolute objectivity, then it must also surrender any claim to subject-form, so that he as its agent might have unquestionable reality. The "I" of his constant intuition[16] was not to be some noetic pole within cognition. It must point to an independent self, self-existent and enduring as the knower, linked to a manipulable external world by its inherently active nature.[17] The orthodox Brahman was enjoined to know himself therefore as the turbid[18] variable constant[19] of the worldly "now", always changing on the side of the states which were the reflexes of his actions, but always the same on the side of the fact of his consciousness per se.[20] The intuition of this latter fact was to show that he was an eternal and omnipresent spiritual essence; for he was to see that this intuition contained no notion of spatial or temporal limitation.[21] His contact with the here and now through a mind and senses was to be explained by the theory of motivated action (*karma*). Such actions generate inescapable retributive potencies which perpetuate such limitation through their fruition into future experiences. This series of causes and effects is beginningless, projecting the agent from contact to contact in life after life and determining the position of these contacts in the hierarchy of nature.[22]

If his self had not been eternal and omnipresent, the Veda which guaranteed his survival beyond death and his relation with ever new spatial contexts for the experience of the fruition of his dharma-born merit, would have been false. This possibility was however excluded by the ritualists' ultra-realist epistemology. Cognition being a formless act was not such that it could ever fail to be veridical: error and illusion were to be understood not as characteristic of certain cognitions in themselves but as due to deficiencies in the instruments of cognition or the indistinctness of their objects.[23] Thus cognitions being valid in themselves simply by virtue of their occurrence, he could not doubt the validity of the Veda.[24] For did he not cognise the eternal (unauthored) sound-units which were its substance? Were not the injunctions which it comprised unambiguous and did they not inform him of matters inaccessible to the sense-bound faculties of man, for example, that one desiring heaven should sacrifice? How then could their cognition contain that element of doubt that accompanies all cognitions of human utterances; and how, for the same reason, could they ever be contradicted?[25] Thus the Vedic injunctions were to incite him to act in the certain knowledge that the rewards of which they spoke would be enjoyed by him in the life to come, or for the more radical Prābhākaras, simply by virtue of their injunctive form, in the manner of categorical imperatives.[26]

So the Mīmāṃsaka defined the orthodox self as active, individual and eternal, but devoid of all creativity. The Brahman was not to see himself as having the capacity to constitute his own values or as able to have cognitions which were not purely the making manifest of that external world which was the sphere of his enjoined actions and the receptacle of the values which these injunctions entailed (purity/impurity, etc.). For were he to have conceded even one case of non-objective perception, of perception perceived, his faith in the veridicality of cognition[27] and therefore in his identity-determining cognition of the Veda would have been undermined.[28] What, he feared, would prevent the implosion of his world into the contemplative intrinsicism of the Buddhists, enemies of the Veda, deniers of the efficacity of sacrifice? For they held that "self" and "object of action" are not external to each other and related by momentary acts of formless cognition, but simply the way cognition reveals itself. For them there were neither selves nor an external world but only constructs of agency and externality within each momentary constituent of a flux of self-cognising cognitions. It is this flux that the worldly man clings to as a stable self, believing that it illumines a world of external facts on which he can act in his own interests.[29]

Securing the category of action from the language-dissolving void to which it was consigned by the Buddhist theory of impersonal flux,[30] the Mīmāṃsaka ritualist defined for the orthodox a self that was not only real but also absolutely self-determining. In harmony with his conviction that the Vedic rituals were mechanisms dependent for their results only on the exactitude of their performance[31] and that these results would accrue to him alone as their agent,[32] he held that his present experience and all the perceptible aspects of his identity were the outcome of nothing but his own actions.[33] Just as the gods had no existence for him apart from their names, affecting the outcome of the rite only in as much as their utterance was part of the sacrificial mechanism,[34] so he admitted the existence of no omnipotent and omniscient controller of his destiny, no superhuman entity privy to the balance of merit and demerit which he had accumulated and for which he alone was responsible.[35]

Thus in his self-representation, the most orthodox of Brahmans was the most individual of individuals.[36] For him there were no external powers which moulded his life. His "deity", his miraculous power of cosmic consistency, was nothing but the law of his action. By this alone each individual "created" his own world within an eternally unchanging set of possibilities.[37] Yet at the same time he exemplified all that was non-individual: he was the perfect man of the group. This contradiction, that of the "solipsistic conformist", was his self-representation as ritual agent. The notion of autonomous agency individualised the person, but his determination by a world of revealed duties, his wish to conform to the Brahmanical ideal, depersonalised this individual, purging him of all independent motivations.[38] Thus it was that the orthodox anthropologies idealised two antagonistic values in the person: on the one hand his individuality as the agent of the sacrificial causality which sustained the world of rites and held it outside of him as the receptacle of absolute values, and on the other an impersonality devouring his sense of agency from within so that it progressively permeated the extrinsicist perception of the parameters of action with a sense not of their inwardness but of their unreality.

For all the orthodox soteriologies were the validation of this depersonalisation. There were fundamental differences on the metaphysical plane, as we shall see, but these are unified by a common concern to define the relation between the outer sphere of individual action and this inner impersonality. The Mīmāṃsakas' devotion to the former precluded their recognising a depersonalisation whose cultivation could dispense at any point with the Brahman's ritual duties and the irreducible, if merely numerical, individuality which they and an injunctive Veda entailed. In their view the Brahman was to achieve his depersonalisation *within* the scrupulous execution of his obligatory rites through the renunciation of all personalising motivation. For it was motivated action alone that tied the eternal and omnipresent "I" to its beginningless and potentially endless series of births into the here and now. Therefore, abandoning all attachment to the results of his actions, he would be liberated from life when his karma-stock no longer growing had exhausted itself in a long but finite series of lives passed in unmotivated conformity to dharma.[39] There the perfected Brahman would be, omnipresent without contact or cognition (since these were the result of the forces of actions now spent), a mere ens, forever in an eventless now, coextensive with others but unaware of their presence.[40]

The inactive being of the renunciationists

Facing the Mīmāṃsaka ritualists within the orthodox camp were the Vedāntins.[41] They spoke for the extreme according to which the outer, though the necessary context for the inner's development,[42] was finally devoured by it altogether, leaving in the place of the depersonalised individual an individuality-obliterating intuition of inherent non-agency.[43]

All plurality, of selves, cognitions and objects, was to be seen as the work of a beginningless ignorance.[44] It was this which veiled the twice-born's nature, creating the false appearance of an individual agent subject to ritual duties and transmigration. This veil binding his self-representation to the categories of action would dissolve if he constantly reinforced the knowledge of his true nature as proclaimed in the Upanishads,[45] revealing the essential self "in the beauty of an endless, absolute, self-illumined and innate bliss",[46] as the non-relational, pure Is-ness which is the substratum of imagined diversity, the prediscursive absolute in the source of all cognitive appearances, timelessly conscious, with no content but its own inert non-dual essence, the only reality.[47]

This realisation, even if it could be cultivated within the life of the householder, could dispense with that life once it reached a critical degree of maturity.[48] Thus the Vedāntins diverged from the ritualists[49] in upholding the institution of renunciation, in which the depersonalised individual would move forth from the domain of his illusory agency into a life of solitary mendicancy and contemplation. The impassivity and self-control which had led him within his life of ritual duty to the intuition of its emptiness, would become outside of it the sum of his dharma. The comparatively dispersed path of agency, by means of which the Brahman sustained his individuality amid the personalising ties of worldly life, was compressed into an adamantine essence, which permeating his consciousness would dissolve these bonds and with them his residual individuality.[50]

The inaction in action of the middle ground

The Brahmanism of the middle ground sought to reconcile these two extremes on the line of conformity to Vedic dharma, the Mīmāṃsaka and the Vedāntin. It offered the Brahman householder a monism for the ritual agent which admitted renunciation but tended to confine it to the last quarter of a man's life[51] (after the payment of the three debts[52]), and at the same time made it an unnecessary option by propagating a doctrine of gnostic liberation within the pursuit of conformity to the householder's dharma.[53] This compromise excluded both the illusionism of the Vedāntins and the atheistic autonomism of the ritualists.[54] Thus the world of relations in action, individual agency and the rest, was perceived here, not as a mirage inexplicably concealing the inactive impersonality of a prediscursive absolute, but as the real self-differentiation of the One.[55]

The householder Brahman was to reconcile the antithesis of motivation and conformity within his ritual agency by seeing the world of objective values and his own autonomy as respectively absolutised[56] and negated[57] by their subsumption within an all-inclusive Supreme Being. He was enjoined to contemplate the convergence of the parameters of action into an underlying unity in the very process of his Veda-directed activities,[58] cultivating the conviction that it was not he that acted but the self-limiting absolute.[59] This introjection of agency from the ritualists' "I" into a non-individual essence of consciousness (a Vedāntic super-self), an "inner controller" accounting for and validating the sense of impelledness within the world of objective values, added to his absolute an element of divine personality.[60] The inclusivist Brahman of this predominantly Vaiṣṇava theistic middle ground was to perfect himself through disinterested conformity to God's will manifest as his dharma. He was to act not out of desire for the rewards of his ordained actions, but in a withdrawn contemplation of a personal-cum-impersonal absolute as the causative agent of his actions and cognitions.

The path of power

The transcendence of orthodox inhibition and extrinsicism: the Kālī-self

We have seen the Vedic construction of the self from the inside, from the points of view of those who sought to formulate metaphysical anthropologies adequate to the personhood of the orthodox ritual agent within the antitheses of motivation and conformity, of individuality and depersonalised consciousness, of agent and non-agent. Let us consider now this same construction from the inside of the inside, through the vision of the Kashmirian Tantric Brahmans, who objectivating this subjective identity within themselves saw the orthodox metaphysics "from above" as its transmigration-bound and transmigration-binding truth.

These heterodox[61] visionaries derived the extrinsicist doctrines of Brahmanism from an undesirable and transcendable psychological condition, from a state of anxious inhibition tied to the acceptance as objective and concordant of the vast and complex body of prescriptive dichotomies enshrined in the Vedic literature.[62] The conscientiousness essential to the preservation of purity and social esteem[63] was to be expelled from his identity by the Tantric Brahman as impurity itself,[64] the only impurity he was to recognise, a state of ignorant self-bondage through the illusion that purity and impurity, prohibitedness and enjoinedness were objective qualities residing in things, persons and actions.[65] The consequence of this degrading extrinsicism of values[66] was identified as impotence,[67] blindness to an innate power of consciousness and action considered infinite in its fullest expansion.[68] This inhibition, which preserved the path of purity and barred his entrance into the path of power,[69] was to be obliterated through the experience of a violent, duality-devouring expansion of consciousness beyond the narrow confines of orthodox control into the domain of excluded possibilities,[70] by gratifying with wine, meat and, through caste-free intercourse, with orgasm and its products the bliss-starved circle of goddesses that emanated in consciousness as his faculties of cognition and action. Worshipped in this lawless ecstasy they would converge into his consciousness, illumining his total autonomy, obliterating in the brilliance of a supramundane joy the petty, extrinsicist selfhood sanctified by orthodox society.[71]

The strength of this lower nature is revealed by the Tantric's account of the process of this implosive liberation. The celebrant of this sensual worship[72] was to experience in the end a twelve-phased retraction of his power of cognition, from its initial self-dichotomisation in which it represents itself as projecting an object external to itself, through the resorption of this object and its own reversion through deeper and deeper levels to its autonomous and universal source pulsating from beyond time and individuality in the emission and resorption of the relations of agent, act and object of cognition that constitute the universe of experience. Significantly the extrinsicist inhibition, which the adept had tried to annihilate through the observance of his vows[73] and the contemplation of its irrationality,[74] reasserts itself even here, at the deep levels of this final liberating insight. It resists the dissolution of individuality by setting up oscillations in the midst of this implosion between "this new awareness vibrating in essential radiance, free of the contraction of laws, untouched by injunction or prohibition"[75] and a regressive anxiety for some aspect of Brahmanical externalised values. Only when awareness of autonomy had evaporated this inhibition (in stage 4) and its recalcitrant latent traces (in stage 7) would the faculties dissolve into the ego, the ego into the representation of individual agency which sustained it and individuality itself finally implode into the abyss of transindividual consciousness and the infinite power of cosmic projection and resorption in the zero-point at its inexpressible end, the goddess Kālī.[76]

Thus though the description of the twelve phases of retraction was the visionary affirmation of a metaphysics of being, a twelve-phased realisation that the world exists only as its representation in consciousness[77] (the opposite of the Mīmāṃsakas' view), it reveals at the same time that this realisation meant first and foremost victory over the deep urge within the Brahman to establish his identity through a system of values determining him from without. It is as though the world was external to his consciousness only in as much as it was the substratum of these values. Thus for the Tantric devotee of the Kālī-self the cosmos-projecting power and this slavery within himself to Vedic injunction were identical.[78] He represented his consciousness as projecting itself to appear as though other than itself,[79] facing and determined by what it was not[80] and manifesting in the same movement the injunctive and metaphysical systems of the followers of the powerless path of purity as the formalised reflection of this contracted mode of awareness.[81] His idealism in the Tantric domain was the evocation of an omnipotent, all-containing identity immune to this self-imposed tyranny of extrinsicist inhibition.[82]

Power through impurity: the culture of the cremation grounds

When we go beneath the surface of this orgasmic Tantric idealism into the scriptural literature which it claimed to represent, we find that we have entered a world which at first sight bears little relation to that we have left. Here at the ground-level of the cults of Bhairava and Kālī the Tantric deities reveal to us another aspect. They are not the projections of the inner power-structure of an autonomous consciousness,[83] but rather regents of hordes of dangerous and predominantly female forces[84] which populated the domain of excluded possibilities that hemmed about the path of purity, clamouring to break through the barrier protecting its social and metaphysical self.[85] Externally this barrier was the line between pure and impure space,[86] on the largest scale that which separated the caste-ordered community from the pollutant cremation-grounds at its edge. Internally it was maintained by conformity to his dharma.[87] Any relaxation of the inhibition and self-control that this conformity required was seen as opening up a chink in the armour of the integral self through which these ever alert and terrible powers of the excluded could enter and possess, distorting his identity and devouring his vital impurities, his physical essences.[89]

It will readily be recognised that the orthodox anthropologies were in themselves a defence against such forces, admitting as they did in the sphere of action no powers external to the individual's karma-causality. Possession, therefore, was doubly irrational: it obliterated the purity of self-control and contradicted the metaphysics of autonomy and responsibility.[90]

It was precisely because these forces threatened the Hindu's "impotent purity" that they invited a visionary mysticism of fearless omnipotence, of unfettered super-agency through the controlled assimilation of their lawless power in occult manipulations of impurity. Thus it is that in Kashmir we find about the path of purity, a vigorous polydaemonistic culture of power. The high Tantric soteriology which obliterated the extrinsicism of Brahmanical purity in the privacy of an ecstatic, all-devouring self-revelation of consciousness came out of the traditions of orders of exorcistic visionaries who, knowing the emanative clan-systems and hierarchies of the powers of impurity, freed and protected the uninitiated from their assaults and at the same time cultivated the practice of controlled possession, seeking permeation by the forms of Bhairava and Kālī which stood at the centre of and controlled as their emanations the clans of these impurity-embodying and impurity-addicted obsessors of the orthodox identity.[91]

Smeared with the ashes of funeral pyres, wearing ornaments of human bone, the initiate would carry in one hand a cranial begging-bowl and in the other a *khaṭvāṅga,* a trident-topped staff on which was fixed beneath the prongs a human skull adorned with a banner of blood-stained cloth. Having thus taken on the appearance of the ferocious deities of his cult,[92] he roamed about seeking to call forth these gods and their retinues in apocalyptic visions and thereby to assimilate their superhuman identities and powers. These invocations took place precisely where the uninitiated were in greatest danger of possession: on mountains, in caves, by rivers, in forests, at the feet of isolated trees, in deserted houses, at crossroads, in the jungle temples of the Mother-Goddesses, but above all in the cremation-grounds, the favourite haunts of Bhairava and Kālī and the focus of their macabre and erotic cult.[93] The initiate moved from the domain of male autonomy and responsibility idealised by the Mīmāmsakas into a visionary world of permeable consciousness dominated by the female and the theriomorphic.[94] Often transvestite in his rites[95] he mapped out a world of ecstatic delirium in which the boundaries between actual women and the hordes of their celestial and protean counterparts, between the outer and the inner, was barely perceptible. Intoxicated with wine, itself the embodiment of these powers,[96] he sought through the incantation of mantras and the offering of mingled menstrual blood and semen,[97] the quintessential impurities, to induce these hordes to reveal themselves. Taming them with an offering of his own blood,[98] he received from them the powers he desired. At the same time he was alert to perceive their incarnation in human women and was provided by the tradition with the criteria by which he might recognize their clan-affinities.[99] For a divinatory rite at the time of his initiation had determined his occult link with one of these clans,[100] in order that by the grace of his clan-sisters, who embodied the clan-goddesses and were his spiritual superiors,[101] he might attain by the most direct route liberating possession by the ferocious cosmic deity who was the controller and emanator of all these forces.

The women of this cult, his vehicle to power and the transmitters through sexual intercourse of esoteric gnosis,[102] were the antithesis of the Brahmanical ideal of the docile dependent. Lawless and promiscuous "deities", feared and revered, they unleashed all the awesome power of impurity, that feminine essence whose recognition and suppression in the daughter, wife and mother was enjoined on the orthodox as essential to the preservation of the social order through caste-purity. Thus that which could not be suppressed in them, the monthly discharge of their inner depravity,[103] contact with which was feared by the orthodox as the destroyer of wisdom, strength and sight,[104] was revered by the devotee of Bhairava and Kālī as the most potent of power-substances, irresistible to the deities he invoked into himself or into his presence.[105]

Power with purity: from super-agent to actor

It was within the scriptural traditions which prescribed this Kāpālika cult of power through impurity that there developed the new idealist vision of internal transcendence in the Kālī-self.[106] In the archaic substratum the adept experienced the presence of the deity and its emanations as something external to his consciousness or as penetrating his consciousness from outside. Now the resulting divinisation was represented as the removal through bliss of cognitive impediments in an implosion which revealed an already latent divine essence, a total surrender of self-contraction which uncovered his identity as Kālī, the unutterable focus of cosmic powers radiating out as the vibrant light of a now enlightened consciousness. The complex schemes of the deity-hierarchies of the circumambient possession cult were partly recoded and partly replaced in new esoteric taxonomies which expressed a vision of the universe (the deity's cosmic form) as a projection of powers within an unlocated, timeless essence of consciousness, an autonomous, egoless power. The act of sexual union which produced the quintessences necessary to invocation, became in this inner idealism the vehicle of illumination itself; for it was in orgasm that the deity revealed itself as the transcendental core of the energies of cognition and action, the unity of light and emptiness.[107]

Though the essential core of this visionary idealism continued to be the teaching of the macabre skull-bearers,[108] this internalisation equipped the tradition to colonise the mental life of the Kashmirian householder.[109] Splitting off from the culture of the cremation-grounds,[110] one stream of this tradition reduced itself to its erotic essentials and emerged as the Kaula secret societies, practising collective orgiastic worship, internally casteless but pretending to caste-conformity in their social interactions.[111]

These secret societies were no fringe phenomenon in the Kashmir of our period. The Vaiṣṇava satirist Kṣemendra saw them as one of the major social evils of his time[112] and it appears that they had deeply penetrated the court and the patrician intelligentsia.[113]

From the turn of the ninth and tenth centuries we see the emergence from one such Kaula sect, the Trika, of a socially ambitious avant-garde which presented the new idealism to a wider public by clothing it in the philosophically reasoned, anti-Buddhist discourse of high Brahmanism.[114] It argued in its Doctrine of Recognition that all should recognize as their true identity a single, unified and autonomous consciousness which projects itself through innate powers of impulse, cognition and action as all things, experiences and persons.[115] In no other terms, it claimed, can we account for the synthetico-analytic spontaneity of our awareness.[116] By equating the deity with this metaphysical ground it equipped the sect within which it arose with a sect-neutral hermeneutical framework for its upgrading and consolidation. For the abstract powers attributed to this commodious absolute could not only be identified as the real meaning of the constituents of the deity-structure which empowered its own cult. They could also reach out to subsume in exegesis those of rival and, in one case, more prestigious traditions.[117]

In its bid to colonise the souls of Śaivas in general, arguably the most numerous religious group in Kashmir, it had to confront the conservative "Śaiva Orthodoxy" (Śaivasiddhānta) then dominant in the valley.[118] Whatever connections that Tantric system may have had with the heterodox culture of the cremation-grounds,[119] they had no doubt been long concealed and forgotten beneath a systematic epistemology, ontology and injunctive orientation which aligned it, in spite of its theism, with the orthodox world-view of the Mīmāṃsakas. Extrinsicist and pluralist[120] it bound its eternal and pervasive agent-selves[121] to a ritualistic and anti-visionary conformity to the social order which assimilated them to their non-Tantric, orthodox contemporaries,[122] deodorising, as it were, their Tantric aspiration to the realisation of an innate omnipotence and omniscience through Śiva's liberating grace.[123] Thus while the devotees of

Bhairava and Kālī believed that initiation obliterated one's former caste, the doctors of the Śaivasiddhānta, eager that the initiate should not be deprived of his qualification through caste to fulfil the Brahmanical duties of the path of purity, adhered to the orthodox view that caste was an intrinsic quality of the body which could be destroyed only by death.[124]

This Veda-congruent, soft Tantric theology stood in the tenth century directly between the ascendant Kaulas and the raw material of popular Śaivism in Kashmir, the cult of Svacchandabhairava. This cult's roots were indeed in the culture of the cremation-grounds, as the deity's name suggests, but its position as the standard Śaivism of the Kashmirian householder had modified its heteropraxy, permitting its coexistence with pan-Indian orthodox dharma and its colonisation by the theological exegesis of the Śaivasiddhānta.[125]

In the Recognition-texts at the beginning of the tenth century the first Kaula systematic metaphysicians had concealed from the public they addressed their special sectarian background and had referred to the prestigious Kashmirian doctors of the Śaivasiddhānta only where they could do so with respect.[126] By the eleventh, however, their order had gathered sufficient strength to displace its once dominant rivals without such self-concealment, propagating a new wave of non-dualist, idealist commentaries on the scriptural literature from which the cult of Svacchandabhairava and its annexes drew their authority. The evidence for the succeeding centuries and the current situation among the Brahmans of Kashmir indicate that this success was permanent.[127]

That the Trika, though a Kaula sect, should have had so great an influence on the majority of the Śaiva community needs explanation. Of course, there must have been a certain plausibility in the claim of these non-dualists that as worshippers of Bhairava and Kālī they rather than the Śaivasiddhāntins were the natural transmitters of the inner soteriology of the public Śaivism.[128] For the Śaivasiddhāntins' liturgical tradition was the worship not of the ferocious gods of the Kashmirians but of the mild Sadāśiva. Yet the enduring success of this reassertion of sectarian continuity after the inroads of the Śaivasiddhānta was due to the power of the Trika's view of the person. For out of the visionary traditions of the quest for super-agency on the fringe of Brahmanically ordered society it had forged a perception of the self as an actor concealed within his lower nature as an agent on the path of purity. The power of the heterodox culture of the cremation grounds had been over-coded to emerge as the power of an uncontaminable essence invisible behind the public appearance of conformity to the orthodox life, freely projecting this lower nature in the expression of its autonomy.[129]

The Kaula's blissful adoration of the outer field of experience as the expansion of the deity immanent in consciousness was universalised in the concept of liberated social conformity, integrating the antagonistic paths of purity and power. Thus one could be "internally a Kaula, externally a Śaiva [a worshipper of Svacchandabhairava in the Kashmirian context] while remaining Vedic in one's social practice."[130] The new Śaiva was to see his self as an actor with his individuality as its stage, and his faculties as an audience of aesthetes initiated into the appreciation of the outer world not as a system of external values exacting the extrinsicist impotence of a contentless consciousness but as the expression of the self's infinite inner autonomy, pervaded by a vibrant beauty.[131]

Having seen the outlines of self-representation in Kashmir in the doctrines of the agent, the non-agent, the superagent and the actor, and their interrelation within the paths of purity and power, we may end by considering the respects in which this picture, though more diverse than that which Mauss offers with his three agency-negating doctrines of renunciation, would still incline him to his conclusion that the Indians had little beyond a promising start to contribute to his sociocentric, evolutionist scheme. He would still look in vain for the notion that individual conscious entities are, ultimately speaking, different from each other in more than a numerical sense. The Mīmāṃsaka self, which opposed Mauss's three doctrines as heresies, though it was a radically autonomous entity, saw as its highest good a totally impersonal cessation of experience as the fruit of unmotivated conformity to duty. Nor was it invested with independent rationality. This faculty, while differentiating the human from the animal, could benefit the Brahman only to the extent that it enabled him to realise his dependence upon revealed injunction, his inability to constitute his own values and determine his own good. As we have seen, the culture of the cremation-grounds recognised the acceptance of the Veda-determined identity through purity as self-limitation through ignorance; but the freedom from it to which it aspired was to be found in depersonalising visions of superhuman power in the delirious zone of exclusion that pressed in upon the ordered world of the social agent. The Kaulas, for their part, identified the world of extrinsicist inhibition with the spontaneous projection of a transcendental self. Their freedom from it was therefore a freedom not of their existence but of a metaphysical, aesthetic essence.[132] Where the authority of the Veda was rejected altogether we find that it was in the name of a radical scepticism which denied man any knowledge but that given by the contact of his senses with their objects,[133] or, in the Buddhist case, of an impersonalism in which the autonomous social agent was replaced by a flux of momentary cognitions whose capacity for moral responsibility was an unfathomable mystery, at least to outsiders tied to the categories of common sense.[134]

These views are as far removed in their emphasis from the values constitutive of the European personhood which Mauss chooses to place at the summit of evolution as the two social systems which contain them are from each other. One unfamiliar with the diversity of cultures might easily be forgiven his amazement that a civilisation could produce such sophisticated analyses of consciousness and personal identity without wishing to derive the forces which determine moral choice from within the social agent; but to define the Indian views only in terms of what they are not and to attribute this lack to the influence of certain schools of thought, as though but for them Indian personhood might have progressed along more European lines, as Mauss's evolutionism implies, is unsociological in the extreme.

Abbreviations in the notes

ĀD	Jayanta Bhaṭṭa, *Āgamaḍambara* (Mithila Inst. Ser.: Ancient Text No.7)
ASB	Asiatic Society of Bengal, Calcutta
Bṛ	Prabhākara, *Bṛhatī* (*Tarkapāda*) (Madras Univ. Sansk. Ser., No.3, Pt.1)
BLO	Bodleian Library, Oxford
BS	Maṇḍana Miśra, *Brahmasiddhi* (Madras Govt. Oriental Ser. No.4)
BY-PM	*Brahmayāmala-Picumata,* NAN MS No.3.370, ŚT 129
ĪPVV	Abhinavagupta, *Īśvarapratyabhijñāvivṛtivimarśinī* (KSTS Nos.60,62,65)
JY 1	*Jayadrathayāmala, Ṣaṭka* 1, NAN MS No.5.4650, ŚT 431
JY 2	idem, *Ṣaṭka* 2, NAN MS No.5.4650, ŚT 432
JY 3	idem, *Ṣaṭka* 3, NAN MS No.5.1975, ŚT 429
JY 4	idem, *Ṣaṭka* 4, NAN MS No.1.1468, ŚT 422

KKKA	Vimalaprabodha, *Kālikulakramārcana*, NAN MS No.5.5188, ŚT 163
KSTS	Kashmir Series of Texts and Studies
LGSMB	Devapāla, *Laugākṣigṛhyasūtramantrabhāṣya* (KSTS Nos.49, 55)
MK	Sadyojyoti, *Mokṣakārikā* (ed. N.Kṛṣṇaśāstrī)
Mn	*Manusmṛti*
MNP	Anon., *Mahānayaprakāśa* (Trivandrum Sansk. Ser. No.130)
MPĀ^1, MPĀV^1	*Mataṅgapārameśvarāgama* (*Vidyāpāda*) with commentary (*-vṛtti*) by Rāmakaṇṭha (ed. N.R. Bhatt)
MPĀ^2, MPĀV^2	idem (*Kriyāpāda, Yogapāda, Caryāpāda*) with commentary (*-vṛtti*) by *Rāmakaṇṭha* (ed. N.R.Bhatt)
MTV	*Mṛgendratantra* with commentary (*-vṛtti*) by Nārāyaṇakaṇṭha (KSTS No.50)
MV	Abhinavagupta, *Mālinīvārttika* (KSTS No.31)
MVUT	*Mālinīvijayottaratantra* (KSTS No.37)
NAN	National Archives of Nepal, Kathmandu
NĀSAP	Takṣakavarta, *Nityādisaṃgrahābhidhānapaddhati*, BLO, MS Stein Or. d.43
NeT, NeTU	*Netratantra* with commentary (*-uddyota*) by Kṣemarāja (KSTS Nos.46, 61)
NĪP, NĪPP	Sadyojyoti, *Nareśvaraparīkṣā* with commentary (*-prakāśa*) by Rāmakaṇṭha (KSTS No.45)
NM	Jayanta Bhaṭṭa, *Nyāyamañjarī* (Kashi Sansk. Ser. No.106)
PMNK, PMNKV	Sadyojyoti, *Paramokṣanirāsakārikā* with commentary (*-vyākhyā*) by Rāmakaṇṭha (ed. N.Kṛṣṇaśāstrī)
PP	Śālikānātha Miśra, *Prakaraṇapañcikā* (Chowkhamba Sansk. Ser. No.17)
PTV	Abhinavagupta, *Parātriṃśikāvivaraṇa* (KSTS No.18)
ŚBh	Śabara, *Mīmāṃsāsūtrabhāṣya* (*Tarkapāda*) (contained in Bṛ)
ŚD	Somānanda, *Śivadṛṣṭi* (KSTS No.54)
ŚT	Śaivatantra
ŚV	Kumārila, *Ślokavārttika* (Chowkhamba Sansk. Ser. No.3)
SvT, SvTU	*Svacchandatantra* with commentary (*-uddyota*) by Kṣemarāja (KSTS Nos. 31, 38, 44, 48, 51, 53, 56)

SYMT	*Siddhayogeśvarīmatatantra,* ASB MS No.5465 (G)
TĀ, TĀV	Abhinavagupta, *Tantrāloka* with commentary (*-viveka*) by Jayaratha (KSTS Nos. 23, 28, 30, 36, 35, 29, 41, 47, 59, 52, 57, 58)
TS	*Tantrasadbhāva,* NAN MS No.5.1985, ŚT 1533
YST	Aparārka, *Yājñavalkyasmṛtiṭīkā* (Ānandāśrama Sansk. Ser. No.46)
YV	*Yogavāsiṣṭha* (ed. Wāsudeva Laxmaṇa Śāstrī Paṇsīkar, Bombay, 1918)

Notes

1. All three doctrines had this in common, that they denied the truth of statements in which one represents oneself as the agent of actions. The Sāṃkhyas maintained that the actions represented in such apparently unobjectionable statements as "I know", "I touch" or "I sacrifice" belong not to the self denoted by the first person pronoun but to an unconscious material principle external to the self, with which the "I" falsely identifies itself (see *Sāṃkhyakārikā* 19–20; 64 with Vācaspatimiśra's commentary; S.A. Srinivasan, *Vācaspatimiśras Tattvakaumudī, . . .* , Hamburg, 1967, p. 170). For the Upanishadic monists, in place of the Sāṃkhyas' plurality of inactive monads, there was a single super-self (*paramātman/Brahma*). The world of qualities and change, which for the Sāṃkhya dualists existed as a reality external to selves (as the substratum of their false projections), was for these monists nothing but the projections themselves, an apparent transformation produced by ignorance of one's unchanging, inactive, transindividual identity. The Buddhists maintained the non-existence of any stable entity at any level of consciousness and saw "self" and *a fortiori* "agent" as fictions which the fluxes of momentary cognitions we call persons superimpose upon themselves (see notes 29 and 30).
2. For the theory of the orthodox consensus and the covertness of these cults' impurities see NM, Pt.1, p.243. Cf. YSṬ, pp.9–19 on the exclusion of the tantras.
3. These two poles, of purity and power, were seen as corresponding to the two domains of revealed literature, the Tantric (the domain of power) and the Vedic (the domain of purity). The former covers a wide range of possession-cum-self-divinisation cults sharing a non-Vedic liturgical system but differentiated by deities, public conduct and gnosis. The primary division among them was between Vaiṣṇavas and Śaivas. The first, the Tantric cultists of the god Viṣṇu-Nārāyaṇa, did not exercise an influence strong enough to justify their being treated separately here. The Śaivas relevant to us are the extreme Tantric (Kāpālika and Kaula) devotees of Bhairava and Kālī (Śiva and his consort in the spheres of death, eroticism and impurity) and the "pure" Tantric worshippers of the mild Sadāśiva form of Śiva. The Vedic literature, on the other hand, defines the duties and salvific gnosis of the orthodox. However, just as there were Tantrics who aspired to orthodox status (for the Śaivas, see text discussion; for the Vaiṣṇavas see the Vedic ritualist's impotent invective against the well-connected Pāñcarātra *arrivistes* of ninth-century Kashmir in Jayanta Bhaṭṭa's *Āgamaḍambara* ["Much Ado about Scripture"], Act 4, pp.75–6), so the religion of those who saw themselves as properly Vedic was deeply impregnated with toned-down versions of Tantric liturgies (see YSṬ, p.14,17–p.19,12 on "safe" Purāṇic worship of the Tantric deities) and in the field of magic and exorcism, it recognised rites whose distinction from the properly Tantric is not easily perceived (see, e.g., *Atharvapariśiṣṭa* [ed. Bolling and von Negelein], XXXI, XXXVI and XL).

4. It must be emphasised that what follows deals almost exclusively with the self-idealisations of the Brahman caste. Such are the limitations of our sources.
5. See MPĀV[2], p.150,18–19 (the view of the "pure" Śaivas against the extremists) and PP, p.31,2–7.
6. The Vedic revelation was variously conceived. The ritualists (Mīmāṃsakas) held that it was eternal and uncreated, the Naiyāyika epistemologists that it was the creation of an omniscient, world-ordaining God (see NM, Pt.1, pp.213–20) and the monistic Grammarians that it was the self-differentiation of an autonomous Word-Absolute (see Bhartṛhari, *Vākyapadīya* 1.5 with the author's *vṛtti*). This last doctrine was incorporated by the Tantrics: see *Jayākhyasaṃhitā* 1.76–79b (Pāñcarātra); Rāmakaṇṭha, *Nādakārikā* 19–21 (Śaivasiddhānta); SvT 8.27–31b; JY 3, fol. 2r1–5; PTV, pp.3–16; MV 1.15–435. For its currency in Kashmirian Vedic exegesis see MTV, p.18,1–12 and LGSMB, vol.1, pp.248–9 and *passim*. Its popularity as an inclusivist, trans-sectarian theory is suggested by Ratnākara, *Haravijaya* 6.53–58; 47.61–92; Maṅkha, *Śrīkaṇṭhacarita* 17.22–23.
7. See Mn 2.6–11 (conformity or loss of caste).
8. See Kṣemendra, *Caturvargasaṃgraha* 1.3. Cf. Mn 4.238–44.
9. See Mn 2.8–100.
10. Though none of their works has reached us, the presence and influence of the Mīmāṃsakas in Kashmir is certain. See ĀḌ which dramatises in a humorous spirit the tensions between them and the Tantrics in the late ninth century. Some names have survived. We know of Harṣadatta in the tenth century (Vāmanadatta, *Dvayasampattivārttika* 23 [ed. R.Gnoli in *Gurumañjarikā: Studi in onore di Giuseppe Tucci,* Naples, 1974, vol.2, pp.451–5]) and of Śrīgarbha, Trailokya, Jinduka, Gunna and Janakarāja in the twelfth century (see Maṅkha, *Śrīkaṇṭhacarita* 25. 48–50; 65–5; 71–2; 87–8; 92–3). Of the two schools, the Kaumārila/Bhāṭṭa and the Prābhākara, the former seems to have exercised the greater authority in Kashmir, if we may judge from the works of Jayanta Bhaṭṭa, Abhinavagupta and Rāmakaṇṭha.
11. See ŚBh, pp.68–90.
12. See ŚBh, p.85,2–3; ŚV, p.318 (v.182); ĪPVV, vol.1, p.151,21–p.154,8; vol.2, p.53,11–16; TĀV, vol.7, *āhnika* 10, p.16,2–4; NĪPP, p.18,19–22; NM,Pt.1, p.15,31–p.16,17.
13. See ŚV, p.650 (v.42c)–p.673 (v.113); MPĀV[1], p.220,12–13.
14. See ŚV, p.558 (v.48); p.622 (v.34).
15. See ŚV, p.120 (vv.242c–243b); TĀ 4.228cd.
16. See ŚV, p.719 (v.115)–p.724 (v.139); NM, Pt.2, p.3,21–p.4,17; p.92,24–5. Cf. Bṛ, p.235,7 and NĪPP, p.17,20–2.
17. See ŚV, p.723 (v.133cd); p.707 (v.74)–p.708 (v.77).
18. See Kṣemarāja, *Spandanirṇaya,* p.18,18–19.
19. See ŚV, p.695 (v.28).
20. See ŚV, p.693 (v.20)–p.696 (v.31).
21. See Kumārila, *Tantravārttika* (ed. Paṇḍit Gaṅgādhara Śāstrī), p.376,13–17; ĪPVV, vol.1, p.136,2–3. Cf. NĪPP, p.92,12–17.
22. See ŚV, p.711 (vv.88–9); PP, p.158,9–18.
23. See ŚBh, p.47,11–p.51,2.
24. See ŚV, p.59 (v.47); p.151 (v.56); pp.91–2 (v.154).
25. See ŚBh, p.20,6–p.32,3.
26. See PP, pp.172–96.
27. See PP, p.37 (v.66).
28. See ŚV, p.217 (vv.1–4).
29. See Dharmakīrti, *Pramāṇavārttika, Pratyakṣapariccheda* 354 (cf. ŚV, p.271 [v.14]–p.272 [v.17]); Jñānaśrīmitra, *Advaitabinduprakaraṇa* (in *Jñānaśrīmitranibandhāvali,* ed. Anantlal Thakur), p.354,1–4; p.354,1–4.

30. See Bṛ, p.234,2–4; NĪPP, p.6,8–p.7,5; ŚD, 6.37; Prajñākaragupta, *Pramāṇavārtikabhāṣyam* (ed. R.Sāṃkṛtyāyana), p.369,15–20 (vv.755–757) (on ŚV, p.227 [v.44]).
31. See ŚV, p.683 (vv.11c–12b).
32. See ŚV, p.708 (v.79b)–p.709 (v.80b).
33. See PP, p.158,9–18.
34. See MTV, p.17,11–p.18,12.
35. See ŚV, p.657 (v.69)–p.662 (v.83).
36. See SD 6.27a^{2}b; MPAV^1 p.43,10.
37. See ŚV, p.659 (v.75); MK 7. The idea that the atheist Mīmāṃsakas substitute karmic law (*niyati*) for the divine cosmic Power (Devī/Śakti), 'worshipping' her, as it were, through this concept, is expressed by the Nepalese King Pratāpamalla in A.D. 1652 in his *Mahāparādhastotra* (v.16). For text see Gautamavajra Vajrācārya, *Hanumān Ḍhokā Rāja Darbār* (Kathmandu, n.d.), Inscription No.20.
38. Cf. BS, p.27,4–12; p.36,13–17.
39. See ŚV, p.671 (vv.108–10); PP, p.156,18–p.157,6; NM, Pt.2, p.89,12–p.90,23; Sureśvara, *Naiṣkarmyasiddhi* 1.9–22.
40. See PP, p.153,8–9 (emending *saṃbhūta-* to *saṃhṛta-*); p.157,12–p.158,18.
41. Rāmakaṇṭha (*c.*A.D.975–1050) distinguished between a Vedānta which sees the world as the real transformation of the Absolute (*Pariṇāma-Vedānta*) and one which considers it an illusion (*Māyāvāda*), an apparent transformation projected by ignorance. He admits that the passage on which he is commenting (PMNK, 21b; cf. 48–51) gives the former as representative of the Vedāntins, but expounds instead the latter, pleading that it was the doctrine followed by the foremost interpreters of the Upanishads (see PMNKV, p.5,6–7). This preeminence of illusionism goes back at least to Somānanda (*c.*A.D.900–950) (see ŚD 6.4–24b, esp.23) and probably to the time of the *Haravijaya* of Ratnākara (*c.*A.D.830) (see 6.40; 44–6; 49). Sadyojyoti whose emphasis on transformationism in the PMNK suggests his relative antiquity cannot, however, be dated beyond the fact that he was known to Somānanda (ŚD, 3.13c).

    When Vedānta is expounded by its opponents in Kashmirian sources of our period it is the doctrine of Maṇḍanamiśra which is generally in mind. See PMNKV, p.4,3–p.5,3; p.57,3–p.62,3; NM, Pt.2, p.77,28–p.78,10; p.94,6–p.96,9; TĀV, vol.3, p.32,4–12. To my knowledge no source betrays familiarity with the doctrines of Śaṅkara.
42. See note 38 and NM, Pt.2, p.91,21–2.
43. See YSṬ, p.1030,10–12; BS, p.22,11–12.
44. See BS, p.6,12; p.7,23–24; NM, Pt.2, p.95,8; PMNKV, p.4,8–9; 13–14.
45. See BS, p.12,7–17; p.35,1–18.
46. See NM, Pt.2, p.78,2–3 and 9; TĀV, vol.3, p.32,9–10.
47. See NM, Pt.2, p.94,7–22; BS-*kārikā* 1.1–3; 2.27.
48. *Gautamadharmasūtra* 1.3.1; *Jābālopaniṣat* 4; *Brahmasūtra* 3.4.1–27; BS, p.36,4–12.
49. See *Brahmasūtra* 3.4.18; ŚV, p.671 (v.110); NM, Pt.2, p.91,17–23.
50. The (Śaiva) Naiyāyikas also upheld renunciation (*saṃnyāsa*) as the necessary context for liberation (see NM, Pt.2, p.82,23–p.91,28), while conceiving the state of the self in release (*mokṣa*) as a featureless individuality devoid not only of action but also of cognition (see NM, Pt.2, p.77,1–28; p.81,1–14) much as did the Prābhākaras (see here note 47), though a splinter-group of the Naiyāyikas following the Kashmirian Bhāsarvajña (*c.*A.D. 900) modified the austerity of this vision by lending the released ens the Vedānta's inactive consciousness and bliss (see Bhāsarvajña, *Nyāyasāra* [ed. V. Subrahmaṇyaśāstrī and S. Subrahmaṇyaśāstri], pp.158–67; ĪPVV, vol.1,p.134,12–23) thus distinguishing the no longer cognitive from the originally unconscious. Within these conceptual strategies the constant is the negation or voiding of agency. This the Naiyāyikas and the Vedāntins shared with the Sāṃkhyas (see note 1). It also coloured

sectarian asceticism, being taken in by the Pramāṇa-Pāśupatas (Lākulas) (see PMNKV, p.6,17–p.7,13).

51. See Kṣemendra, *Cārucaryā* 92 and 95; idem, *Darpadalana* 7.15.
52. See Mn 6.35. The three debts (*ṛṇa*) binding the twice-born (males of the first three castes) are that to the ancient sages (*ṛṣi*) paid by the study of the Veda as a celibate student (*brahmacārin*) after one's initiatory "second birth" from the womb of the Veda, and those to the ancestors (*pitṛ*) and gods (*deva*) paid by offerings and sacrifices when, one's studentship complete, one has married and entered the estate of the householder (*gṛhastha*).
53. See NM, Pt.2, p.85,30–2; TĀV,vol.6, pp.76–77 (on TĀ 9.89c–90b); *Kūrmapurāṅa* (ed. Ramaśaṅkara Bhaṭṭamacārya, Benares, 1968) 7.28; 15.23–9; YSṬ, pp.960, 961, 972, 1027 and 1033.
54. Thus the Paurāṇikas condemned both as heretical. See, e.g., *Padmapurāṇa* (ed. Rao Saheb Vishvanāth Nārāyaṇa), *uttarakhaṇḍa* 268.70cd; 73–6b. This description of the ritualist Mīmāṃsakas as atheist autonomists is Somānanda's (ŚD 6.27a^{2}b).
55. See Kṣemendra, *Daśāvatāracarita* 1.1; SD 6.16–24b; YSṬ, p.973,8–p.975,15; NIPP, p.91,18–21.
56. See *Bhagavadgītā* 4.13.
57. See NĪPP, p.106,5–7; TĀV, vol.3, p.31,5–p.32,4; JY 1, fol.55r9–v4; YSṬ, p.973,19–21. These sources show the close connection in Kashmir between emanationist monism and Vaiṣṇava-Pāñcarātra theism. One group among the latter, the Sāṃkarṣaṇa-Pāñcarātras, eliminated the individual self as distinct from the complex of internal faculties altogether from their taxonomy of the real (*tattvakrama*). For them see NĪPP, p.87,22–p.88,4 and Ratnākara, *Haravijaya* 47.55 (emending crux *saṃkarṣaṇī/sāṃkarṣaṇī* to *sāṃkarṣaṇe*).
58. See YSṬ, p.961,17–19, Cf. TĀ 15.147–59.
59. See TĀV, vol.6, p.76,7–p.77,7 (on TĀ 9.89c–90b). Cf. *Bhagavadgītā* 5.8.
60. See LGSMB, vol.1, p.59,19–p.60,5. For his Vaiṣṇava leanings see vol.1, p.60,20; vol.2, p.44,6—8; p.46,12–13; p.51,11–12.
61. See YSṬ, p.18,21–4: for the orthodox even the sight of a Śaiva was contaminant. See NM, Pt.1, p.239,15–p.248,21 and ĀḌ, p.96 (v.100)–p.97 (v.103) for the more politic view of the Naiyāyikas which excluded only those Tantrics whose practices involved impurities and sexual licence. Though the extreme Tantrics excluded the orthodox in their turn (e.g., *Kubjikāmata,* ASB MS No. 4733 [G], fol.49r6 ["The Kaula must avoid Buddhists and Mīmāṃsakas"]; TĀ 15.570 [from *Mādhavakulatantra*] prohibiting commensality, etc.; TĀV, vol. 11, *āhnika* 29, p.52,15–16 enjoining avoidance of all subject to concepts of purity) these terms, orthodox and heterodox, are not relative. For the Tantric's sense of power was inseparable from his sense of transgression (see, e.g., TĀ 37.10–12b).
62. See TĀV, vol.3, p.164,8–9; vol.7, *āhnika* 12, p.104,6–8; p.107,1–2 (from *Niśisaṃcāratantra*); TĀ 13.198c; PTV, p.235,8; p.236,15.
63. See Kṣemendra, *Caturvargasaṃgraha* 1.8c.
64. See TĀ 12.20c.
65. See TĀ 4.213–77, esp. 244c–245b; TĀ 12.20c–21b.
66. See TĀV, vol.3, p.164,7.
67. See TĀ 12.24cd; TĀV, vol.7, *āhnika* 12, p.104,1–3.
68. See MV 1.15–24b
69. As that which sustains the orthodox identity it assumes the form of the eight "demonic possessors" (*graha*), so called because they conceal the true self (autonomous, unitary consciousness) beneath a phantasmagoric pseudo-identity, contaminating and impoverishing it with categories unrelated to its essence: obsession with caste (*jātigraha*), Vedic learning (*vidyā-*), the social standing of one's family (*kula-*), with orthodox con-

duct (*ācāra-*), with one's body (*deha-*), one's country (*deśa-*), with conventional virtues (*guṇa-*), and material prosperity (*artha-*) (see TĀ 15.595c–601b [from *Kulagahvaratantra* and *Niśisaṃcāratantra*]). As that which holds the Brahman back from the path of power it is fear of loss of identity (*ātmaśaṅkā*), of participation in non-Vedic rites (*divyakarmaśaṅkā*), of impure Tantric incantations (*mantraśaṅkā*), fear of contact with the forbidden substances that are offered and consumed in Tantric worship (*dravyaśaṅkā*), fear of contamination by untouchables in caste-promiscuous sexual rites (*jātiśaṅkā*), fear of entering the cremation grounds and the other impure sites in which the cult of power is celebrated (*sthānaśaṅkā*), fear of assault or possession by the forces that inhabit these sites and are handled in the Tantric liturgies (*bhūtaśaṅkā*, *śarīraśaṅkā*) and finally, fear of an alien taxonomy of reality (*tattvaśaṅkā*) (see TĀV, vol.8, p.126,20–p.127,3 [qu. *Niśisamcāratantra*] and JY 3, fol.230r5).

70. See TĀ 15.593b (from *Rātrikulatantra*).
71. See TĀ 3.260c–264; 4.253; 12.19cd; 13.198; 15.109ab; 17.22ab; 29.10; 29.15b; 37.11c–12b; 37.13ab; PTV, p.231,6–p.236,15.
72. For orgasm as the scene of this enlightenment see MNP 9.35–7; *Ciñcinīmatasārasamuccaya,* NAN MS. No. 1.767, fol.21r1; fol.21r6–10; JY 4, foll.203v2–206r6 and *passim;* KKKA, fol.23r4–5.
73. For these vows (*samaya*) see TĀ 15.521c–609b.
74. See TĀ 4.221c–247; TĀV, vol.11, *āhnika* 29, p.7,10–11 (qu. *Ucchuṣmabhairavatantra*).
75. See TĀV, vol.3, p.164,17–p.165,1.
76. For this "rise of the cycle of cognition" (*saṃviccakrodaya*) as the inner nature of the worship of the twelve Kālīs (Sṛṣṭikālī to Mahābhairavacaṇḍograghorakālī) which, as the "phase of the Unnameable", was the climax of the Krama liturgy of the Kālī-cultists of Uḍḍiyāna (Swat [see *Kumārapālacaritasaṃgraha,* p.54 (*Kumārapālaprabodhaprabandha*)]) and its neighbour Kashmir, see TĀ 4.121c–181b and commentary.
77. See *Śivasūtra* 1.6 (*śakticakrasaṃdhāne viśvasaṃhāraḥ*).
78. See TĀV, vol.7, *āhnika* 12, p.106,6 (qu. *Gamaśāstra*); ibid.,8 (qu. *Sarvavīratantra*); TĀ 4.21c–22b with 6.56a and 57a. Conversely Abhinavagupta describes his Absolute as the radical fusion of powers, consciousness's implosion into its innate bliss, in which "no trace remains of that contraction through inhibition which is the outsurge of externality" (MV 1.21ab).
79. See TĀ 4.147.
80. See MVUT 3.31; Kṣemarāja, *Śivasūtravimarśinī* on 1.4 and 3.19; idem, *Spandasaṃdoha,* p.20,1–p.21,3; PTV, p.39,9–p.44,5. All these express the theme of enslavement by the powers of externalisation, these same powers being seen as the bestowers of liberation when recognized as internal to consciousness as its modes. Cf. Kallaṭa, *Spandakārikā,* 3.13–19.
81. See TĀ 4.252–53: the extrinsicism of the Veda is the "truth" (*jñāna*) of the enslaved (*pāśava*); TĀ 37.8c–11b and commentary: though through their doctrines of the self the orthodox catch a glimpse of reality, they do not develop it. For their principal purpose is the preservation of their world of objective values (*sargarakṣaṇa*); ĪPVV, vol.3, p.379,10–p.380,11. For the theory that correlates doctrines and the levels of self-representation which constitute the world see MV,1.14–435; Kṣemarāja, *Pratyabhijñāhṛdaya* (KSTS), p.16,12–p.20,12; TĀV, vol.1, p.64,8–p.72,13; SvT 11.68–74 and commentary.
82. See TĀV, vol.3, p.165,9–13 (qu. *Kramastotra* on Yamakālī [stage 4], 'destroyer of the tyrannical Death [Yama] which impedes the internalisation of the world').
83. See TĀ 1.107–16.
84. See TS, foll.75r1–84v1 (*paṭala* 15 and 16); SYMT, foll.45r3–47v2; 58v5–62v4 (*paṭala* 22 and 26); JY 3 (*Yoginīsaṃcāraprakaraṇa*), foll.171r–172v; BY-PM, foll.243v–246v (*paṭala* 53); foll.2894–291r (*paṭala* 70).

85. See NeT, *paṭala* 19 and 20.
86. See NeT, 19.43; *Īśānaśivagurudevapaddhati, pūrvārdha, paṭala* 42.4–5b.
87. See ibid., 5b–7; NeT 19.34c–44.
88. See NeT 19.46d.
89. Cf. TĀV, vol.11, *āhnika* 29, p.13,17–18; p.19,19–20; NeT 20.1–40 (Yoginīs, Śākinīs and other female obsessors suck life from their victims into themselves as an offering to their regent Mahābhairava enthroned in their hearts. This extraction [*ākarṣaṇa*] is "imitated" by the worshippers of Bhairava and Kālī: see JY 3, fol.184v5–8; BY-PM, fol.10v2–4. These extracted "nectars" are the fuel of Kapālakuṇḍalā's magical flight in Bhavabhūti's play *Mālatīmādhava,* Act 5, v.2). The method of extraction mentioned there [*nāḍyudaya*] is described in minute detail in JY 3 above.)
90. See PMNKV, p.12,8–9; p.19,15–16: on these grounds the "pure" Śaivas attack the doctrine that liberation is possession (*āveśa/samāveśa*) by Śiva's powers. For the identification of this doctrine as that of the Kāpālikas see Śivāgrayogīndrajñānaśivācārya, *Śaivaparibhāṣā,* p.156,22–4.
91. Exorcism and the control of spirits pervade the scriptural texts which host the higher doctrines. This was their background. This is graphically illustrated by the fact that the Śaivas of Kashmir, while assigning a canon of texts whose principal concern was witchdoctoring and exorcism to a sect-tradition (the "Western" [*paścimasrotas*]) outside the mainstream, attributed to this "lower" canon a group of texts belonging to that form of Kālī-worship (Mata/Krama) which was the main source of the ecstatic idealism with which we began and which entered the esoteric core of Abhinavagupta's syncretistic Trika system (see TĀ 1.207; 3.70a–c; 3.250c–53b; 4.123c–80b; 5.20–36 and *passim*) to which we shall come. See NĀSAP, foll.13r4–15v4 (qu. *Śrīkaṇṭhī, srotobhedapaṭala*). For invocation and empowerment by possession see BY-PM, foll. 103r3–v4; JY 3, fol.201v3–6 (in *ghorakāpālavrata*).
92. For the accoutrements of one who adopted the *mahāvrata/kāpālikavrata* see BY-PM, foll.307v5–312r4; JY 1, fol.139r1–5; JY 3, fol.201v3–6; JY 3, fol.232r1–v2; SvT 9.18 and comm.; TS, fol.75r11–12; Bhāskara, *Śivasūtravārttika* on 3.26.
93. Cf. *Īśānaśivagurudevapaddhati, pūrvārdha, paṭala* 42.4–5b with TS, fol.75r9–10 (equals *Kubjikāmata,* ASB MS. No.4733 [G], foll.117v9–118r1); TĀ 5. 102c–104b (from *Vīrāvalihṛdaya*); JY 2, fol.9v1; fol.33v9; JY 3, fol.94r4–5; BY-PM, fol.67v4; JY 1, fol.104r6–7.
94. While Bhairava maintains his human aspect in all his forms, many of the Kālīs of the exorcistic-cum-idealistic traditions (Mata/Krama) were to be visualised as having animal-heads or as in a state of kaleidoscopic flux in which the animal and the human are confounded. Such are the three Mata Goddesses of JY 3 (Trailokyaḍāmarā, Matacakreśvarī and Ghoraghoratarā [alias Matalakṣmi]), the Krama-based ten-headed Guhyakālī and many of her emanations (the Pañcavāhadevīs, the Antaḥ[/Mantra]siddhās, the Melāpakasiddhās and the Śāmbhavasiddhās). For the iconography of the Krama deities see KKKA. Instability of physical form is an essential characteristic of the female adept-cum-spirit. See SvTU, vol.2, p.28,11–14; JY 3, foll.226v8–27r1; fol.234r2–3; SYMT, fol.24r1–4; TS, fol.80r3.
95. See JY 1, fol.70v5; fol.127v1; fol.128r7; fol.135r8; fol.154v3; fol.200v7; JY 2, fol.49r6; JY 3, fol.201v1; *Kālīkulapañcaśataka,* NAN MS. No. 1.252, fol.49v4 (equals 5.54c).
96. See TĀ 29.11–13; 37.42; JY 4, foll.235r7–36r1; Jayadratha, *Haracaritacintāmaṇi* 31.85 (emending *madhyabhairavatāṃ* to *madyabhairavatāṃ* [cf. Īśvara Kaula, *Kaśmīraśabdāmṛtam,* p.4,2]).
97. See TĀV, vol.11, *āhnika* 29, p.18,18–21 (*kuṇḍagolaka.* See TĀV, vol.1, p.12,9–14); p.92,1–p.93,7 (3rd qu. equals JY 3, foll.76v8–77r2 [cult of Matacakreśvarī]); TS, fol.80r5.
98. See SYMT, fol.24r4–6; JY 3, fol.173r4–6 and *passim.*
99. See refs. in note 84.

100. See TĀ 29.190; BY-PM, fol.37r.
101. See TĀV, vol.11, *āhnika* 29, p.87,10–11.
102. See TĀ 29.122c–23b; JY 3, fol.234r4–6.
103. See Mn 5.108.
104. See Mn 4.40–1.
105. See JY 4, fol.132r4–6; TĀV, vol.2, p.216,10–p.217,8.
106. The cult of the skull-bearing (*Mahāvratin* / *Kāpālika*) devotees of Bhairava and Kālī represented in such texts as the BY-PM, the JY and the TS ("yoginītantras" [see SYMT, fol.69v1–5] or tantras of the Vidyāpīṭha [see JY 1, fol.169r8–169v1; fol.174r6–v4]) was also the substratum of the Heruka-cult of the Buddhist Anuttarayogatantras. In addition to those of practice and terminology there are textual continuities. For example, *Sampuṭodbhavamahātantra,* NAN MS. No. 1.113, fol.22r2–7 and foll.34v10–35r3 with JY 3, fol.209r5–v2 (definitions of seven yoginī-types) and fol.208r6–8 (glossary of monosyllables belonging to the sect's secret language [*chommāḥ*]) respectively. The Cakrasaṃvara-texts' central system of 24 pīṭhas (see, e.g., *Saṃvarodayatantra, Selected Chapters* [ed. S.Tsuda], 7.3–15) is seen to have a Śaiva prototype at TS, fol.78v9–13. The anomalous Gṛhadevatā of the Buddhist list after Saurāṣṭra can be diagnosed as the result of contamination from a parallel list seen in the Śaiva source which specifies a class of deities for each pīṭha. Gṛhadevatās (house-deities) are assigned there to Saurāṣṭra.
107. See refs. in note 72; JY 4, foll.92v6–93r7 (esp. 93r5–6) (*Rāviṇīcakrodaya*) with which cf. PTV, p.231,6–p.232,4; JY 4, foll.145r7–46r7 (*Melāpakālīvidhi*); foll.150r7–51r7 (*Nityākālīvidhi*); foll.203v2–206r6 (*Ādyayāgavidhi*); TĀ 29.104c–127b. For the unity of light and emptiness see JY 4, fol.58r2–3; Cakrapāṇi, *Bhāvopahāra* 41. Cf. Advayavajra, *Advayavajrasaṃgraha,* p. 49,16.
108. For skull-bearing Krama masters see Arṇasiṃha (*c.*A.D.1050–1100), *Mahānayaprakāśa,* NAN MS. No. 5.358 ("*Kālīkulapañcaśataka*"), vv.156,157 and 164; Cakrabhānu (*c.*A.D.925–975), *Śrīpīṭhadvādaśikā,* ibid., v.12b (cf. Kalhaṇa, *Rājataraṅginī* 6.108–12); Cakrapāni, *Bhāvopahāra* 46–7. The Kashmirian Harihara (between Kallaṭa [*c.*A.D.900–950] and A.D.1216 [oldest MS]) saw no incongruity in explaining *Mālatīmādhava,* Act 5, v.2, in which a female Kāpālika vaunts her powers, with the Krama doctrine of the goddesses of the five flows (*pañcavāhadevī: Vyomavāmeśvarī* etc.) (*Mālatīmādhavaprakaraṇaṭīkā,* ASB MS. No. 4805 [G], fol.45v3–5).
109. The mainstream was a tradition of ascetics (*vīra, naiṣṭhika*). Householder devotees were permitted versions of its rites to be performed without mortuary accoutrements or "terrible" (*ghora*) offerings (human flesh, blood, excrement etc.). See, e.g., JY 1, fol.104r5–7 (*Kālasaṃkarṣaṇīyāga*); JY 2, fol.9v1–3 (*Vāmeśvarīyāga*); SvTU, vol.1, p.7,6–8; p.10,6–7; p.12,2–5; SvT 2.147–53; TĀ 15.66–8 (from *Nirmaryādaśāstra*).
110. See TĀV, vol.3, p.288,9–p.299,3; TĀ 15.591c–592b (from *Ānandaśāstra*); *Kulapañcāśikā,* NAN MS No. 1076, 3.53 and 59 (former qu. by Kṣemarāja, *Śivasūtravimarśinī* on 3.26). The distinction between Kula and Kaula traditions mentioned *passim* but not clarified (see TĀ 13.301; 320–21b; MNP 1.30; etc) is best taken to refer to the clan-structured tradition of the cremation-grounds seen in BY-PM, JY, TS, SYMT, etc. (with its Kāpālika *kaulikā vidhayaḥ*) on the one hand and on the other its reformation and domestication through the banning of mortuary and all sect-identifying signs (*vyaktaliṅgatā*), generally associated with Macchanda /Matsyendra. See also JY 4, foll.70r6–73r1 (*Unmanodayakulāvatāra*).
111. See TĀV, vol.3, p.27,11–13; YSṬ, p.10,12–13; Kṣemendra *Deśopadeśa* 8.11–13.
112. See Kṣemendra, *Daśāvatāracarita* 10.25–27; idem, *Deśopadeśa* 8.2–51; idem, *Narmamālā* 2.100–3.86.
113. See Ratnākara, *Haravijaya* 47.28; 47.96–9; Kalhaṇa, *Rājataraṅginī* 6.10–12; 6.108–12; 7.276–83; 7.523; Maṅkha, *Śrīkaṇṭhacarita* 5.40; TĀV, vol.12, p.428,12–p.435,2.

114. For the Kaula practice of Somānanda (c.A.D.900–950) and his pupil Utpaladeva, the initiators of this Recognition (*Pratyabhijñā*) doctrine, see TĀV, vol.3, p.194,8–10 (Krama) and Somānanda's authorship of a commentary on the *Parātriṃśikā* (see PTV, p.16,9–13, etc.).
115. See ŚD 1.2.
116. See Utpaladeva, *Īśvarapratyabhijñākārikā* I.22–45.
117. I refer to the Krama. See note 91.
118. See Kṣemarāja, *Śivasūtravimarśinī* (KSTS 4), p.2,7–8; SvTU, vol.1, p.15,5–11.
119. These connections subsisted in the practices of the seeker of powers (*sādhaka/bubhukṣu*) as opposed to those of the seeker of release (*mumukṣu*). See MPĀ[2], *caryāpada, paṭala* 9 (*Rudravrata*). Cf. ibid., *kriyāpāda, paṭala* 11,vv.41–53 (*Asidhāravrata* [sexual]). They are very apparent in the Śaivasiddhāntin but extra-canonical *Niśvāsatattvasaṃhitā*, NAN MS. No. 1.227, fol.49r1–4 (*Śmaśānavrata, Gaṇavrata, Citravrata* [transvestite], *Asidhāravrata* [sexual] etc.).
120. See NĪP 1.2–75 (esp. 3ab; 16–17; 32ab; 56; 58–9).
121. See NĪPP, p.13,5–p.17,2; NĪP 1.18–21; NĪPP, p.92,6–p.95,14.
122. See MK 145–6 and commentary.
123. See NĪP, 1.60; 1.65; MK vv.44c–45b.
124. See MPĀV[2], p.150,6–p.151,5; YSṬ, p.14,18–28; SvTU, vol.2, p.27,8–p.29,19.
125. See SvTU, vol.6, *paṭala* 15, p.146,11–16 and NeTU, vol.2, p.343,21–2 (tradition of Siddhāntin commentaries on these texts) SvTU, vol.1, *paṭala* 2, p.8,17–p.9,6 and p.75,5–11 (ordinary worshippers of Svacchandabhairava who perform the Vedic dawn-rite before the Tantric and offer the God scented water instead of wine, "since their minds are still conditioned by their pre-initiatory caste"). That this cult was the basic form of Śaivism in Kashmir is indicated by the existence of both dualistic and non-dualistic commentaries on the *Svacchandatantra* and by the various manuals of Śaiva initiation and daily worship in use there in medieval and modern times such as the NĀSAP, Manodadatta's *Kalādīkṣāvidhi* (India Office Library, MS Sansk. 3835a; etc.) and the current *Karmakāṇḍa* (publ. Keshavabhatta Jotishi, Bombay, 1936). Even the *Somaśambhupaddhati* for all its Śaivasiddhāntin orthodoxy drew on the Svacchanda-cult (ed. H.Brunner-Lachaux, Pt.2, p.203 [v.5]). For Somaśambhu's having been a Kashmirian, born at Padmapura into the Rājānaka-vaṃśa, see the panegyrics of Śitikaṇṭha (late fifteenth century) and Ānanda (second half of seventeenth century) in "Commentary on the Naiṣadhacarita called Tattvavivṛti by Rājānaka Ānanda", BLO, MS Stein Or. e17, p.2(vv.11–12) and p.9(v.2).
126. See ŚD, 3.13c–15b.
127. Anti-Kaula resistance is seen at MPĀV[1], p.1,13; p.41,3–4; PMNKV, p.15,11; Śrīkaṇṭha, *Ratnatraya*, v.14a; Rāmakaṇṭha, *Sārdhatriśatikālottarāgamavṛtti* (ed. N.R.Bhatt), p.65,1–10.
128. The Kālasaṃkarṣaṇī form of Kālī whose esoteric cult is the subject of the Kashmirian JY's 24,000 stanzas and is in the core of the syncretistic Trika expounded in TĀ could also claim continuity with public Śaivism. See Kṣemendra, *Bhāratamañjarī*, p.824 ([*Harivaṃśa*-section] v.1323) (where the author has substituted a Durgā-hymn of his own [cf. *Harivaṃśa* (ed. P.L. Vaidya), Appendix 35]) and *Karmakāṇḍa* (see note 125), vol.4, p.286,8–p.287,11 which gives the Mahākālasaṃkarṣaṇī-invoking Vyomeśvarī-mantra to be uttered only in the cremation-ground, into the ear of the corpse at the moment before it is burnt. For elements of Kashmirian mythology of Kālasaṃkarṣaṇī connected with Śivarātri see Jayadratha, *Haracaritacintāmaṇi* 31.33c–97b (from *Anantabhāskara* and *Dūtiḍāmara*); NĀSAP, foll.145v6–149r7 (qu. *Dūtiḍāmara*); *Sarvāvatāra, Sureśvarīmāhātmya*, BLO, MS Stein Or. d. 48(i), fol. 2r 12r[6]–; *Bhṛṅgīśasaṃhitā, Vitastāmātmya, Haranāgavarṇana*, BLO, MS Stein Or. d.55(ii), fol.4r[12]–; Nityasvatantra, *Śivarātrirahasya*, BLO, MS Stein Or. e.24(i). Cf. *Tridaśaḍāmaratantra*

(*paṭala* 81 and 82) in NAN MS No. 3.30 ("*Tridaśaḍāmarāpratyaṅgirāviṣayakanānātantra*"), foll.1v3–3r2; YV, p.807 (18.1)–p.810 (19.11) and cf. 18.20–1 with TĀV, vol.11, *āhnika* 29, p.36,15–16; JY4, fol.92r1–2; NeT 10.17c–34; 11.12–18. The dominance in Śaiva circles of the Bhairava-Kālī dimension is also reflected in the YV (Kashmir, *c.*11th century A.D.). See, e.g., p.1244(81.1)–p.1258 (85.28).

129. See MV 1.15–21; 413–16.

130. See TĀV, vol.3, p.27,10–13; p.277,9–p.278,6.

131. See Bhāskara, *Śivasūtravārttika* and Kṣemarāja, *Śivasūtravimarśinī* on 3.9–11.

132. See MV 1.313–15: freedom from karma-determination on the plane of transcendental aesthesis. This injunction to aestheticise experience contains the view that the relish of the beautiful in nature and in art mirrors the state of release and can be a means thereto. See TĀ 3.209c–210; 229; 237c–241b; 4.120c–121b; PTV, p.45,4–p.52,7 (aesthetic experience and orgasm. Cf. JY 4, fol.151r3–6 [Nityākālī / Kāmakalā; experienced by yogin through orgasm or music]); TĀ 37.45 (natural beauty of Kashmir); ĪPVV, vol.2, p.177,18–p.179,13 (esp.p.179,9–11 [hierarchy of joy, from the gratification of appetite, through aesthetic rapture to the latter's fulfilment in the blissful expansion of enlightenment]).

133. The doctrine of the Cārvākas. For their epistemology see ĀḌ, pp.56–71.

134. See ŚV, p.689 (v.1)–p.703 (v.57); NĪPP, p.13,19–p.14,18; NM, Pt.2, p.36,17–p.39,13; p.44,5–9. For the various theories with which the Buddhist schools attempted to get round the contradiction between atomistic impersonality and moral agency see Vasubandhu, *Karmasiddhiprakaraṇa* (transl. E.Lamotte from the Tibetan and Chinese versions in *Mélanges chinois et bouddhiques,* vol.4 [1935–36]), pp.151–205). The central mystery continued into Śaivized Buddhism where the divine syzygy (Śiva–Śakti / Bhairava–Kālī) was read as the blissful unity (*mahāsukha*) of insight into voidness and the sentiment of compassion for all beings. See, e.g., *Hevajratantra* (ed. D.Snellgrove) I.i,7ab; *Saṃvarodaya,* Kaiser Library, Kathmandu, MS No.749b, fol.61r2 (equals 33.17–18); Advayavajra, *Advayavajrasaṃgraha,* p. 49 (*Yuganaddhaprakāśa* v.8ab).

10

Of masks and men

Martin Hollis

'There's no art to find the mind's construction to the face', King Duncan reflects sadly in Act I of *Macbeth* on hearing that the traitorous Thane of Cawdor has died confessing his treasons. As if to emphasise the point he confers the title on the loyal Macbeth and sets his own murder in train. We understand the trouble in reading faces very well and it is not just a practical one. The mind's construction is not only a matter of motives. It involves the concepts and categories with which we shape our experience, order our aims, find meaning in events and understand ourselves. That makes the reading of our neighbours' faces hard enough – indeed it makes it hard to read our own. But it can make the reading of distant faces seem almost impossible. Other cultures at other places and other times are guided by minds opaque to us, defying us to understand as they do. The mind's construction is built around an understanding of self and that is elusive partly because it changes with time and place, partly because we do not grasp it properly even amongst ourselves.

That suggests two lines of address, the historical and the analytic. Historically we can say at least something about changing conceptions of what it is to be a person. For instance Homeric culture scarcely conceived the self outside social roles and, it has been said, had no single generic word for each and every human being. Protestant Christianity, on the other hand, thought of everyone as a soul and divorced the soul from social and even from bodily life. Those two cultures lie on a path which leads to our own day and, in telling the historical tale, we shall be able to see what we have learnt (or at least be less parochial about our own account). By contrast, the analytic approach picks on the conceptual puzzle in self-knowledge. The nature of man is a single, timeless enigma which has troubled all thinkers in all places. It troubled the Pueblo Indians, the Greek tragedians, the ancient Chinese sages and the fathers of social science and it continues to trouble us. The living and the dead all contribute to the same debate. The dead, annoyingly, cannot attend in person but they supply evidence by artifact and in writing, which living interpreters kindly shell out of its archaic language and historical period. Thus rejuvenated, all who have ever tackled the topic become candidates for this year's prize in mental philosophy.

The two approaches are not in collision but there is a tension between them, which every student of the social sciences will recognise. It is palpable in Mauss's magnificent study and I shall start by picking it out. (That will involve a few lines of summary but I excuse myself on the grounds that, with so rich and ambiguous a text, it is as well to be clear how I mean to take it.) Then, being a philosopher by trade, I shall choose some analytical loose ends and ask what is to be done with them. The answer will, however, touch on his historical account too, since not even a philosopher can suppose the mind's construction purely timeless.

Mauss ranges from the Pueblo to the Romans, from mediaeval Christianity to the individualism of today, showing the different forms which the idea of self has taken. To this extent his lecture is a chronicle, stretching from the first use of ceremonial masks in symbolic dances to the private sense of our own uniqueness, which each of us now has. But it is offered as an 'example of the work of the French school of sociology' and is part of a social history of the categories of the human mind, and of a project of explaining them one by one. This gives it a Durkheimian concern with social structures and externally generated norms. Yet the note struck is not a glum social determinism. There is also a moral concern to improve our self-understanding, just as there is in Durkheim too. The concept of a person, Mauss says in the opening paragraph, 'originated and slowly developed over many centuries and through numerous vicissitudes, so that even today it is still imprecise, delicate, fragile, one requiring further elaboration'. Thus a tension among history, sociology and philosophy is built deep into the whole enquiry. It is a symptomatic and fertile tension, as I hope to show.

Mauss states his principle for investigating categories of the mind thus: 'we describe particular forms of them in certain civilisations and by means of this comparison try to discover in what consists their unstable nature and their reasons for being as they are'. His chronicle starts with the

Pueblos and the clan. 'On the one hand the clan is conceived of as being made up of a *certain number of persons,* in reality of "characters" (*personnages*). On the other hand, the role of all of them is really to act out, each insofar as it concerns him, the prefigured totality of the life of the clan' (Mauss's italics). In other words, we start with something which we can hardly recognise as a concept of a person at all. Among the Pueblo it is membership of a clan, together with sets of roles within the clan, which constitutes persons. It is the life of the clan which constitutes agency; and personhood is symbolised by the ceremonial masks which an actor wears in sacred dramas. Yet roles, masks, titles and property also set family apart from clan and a man thinks of himself as surviving death and reappearing on Earth as one of his descendents. By the same token he must think of himself as his own ancestor. So there is, to our eyes, a second concept of person already there; but also one we can scarcely recognise. This phase of human history is summed up by remarking that 'a whole, immense group of societies has arrived at the notion of "rôle", (*personnage)* of the role played by the individual in sacred dramas, just as he plays a role in family life'.

The Latin *persona* takes a step further. It sets off as 'a mask, a tragic mask, a ritual mask and the ancestral mask' but soon becomes 'a fundamental fact of law'. The route is from masks to privileges of those with a right to the masks, to *patres* who represent their ancestors, to anyone with ancestors, a cognomen and family property. Hence we arrive at a notion of a person as a possessor of rights, a group from which only slaves are excluded. At the same time the Stoics, aided by later Greek ideas about a person as a kind of private *prosopon,* have contributed a notion of the person as a moral fact, which comes to inject a concept of moral conscience into the juridical concept of a right.

But there was no 'firm metaphysical foundation' until the Christians supplied one. 'Our own notion of the human person is still basically the Christian one'. The Council of Nicaea marks a milestone with its '*Unitas in tres personas, una persona in duas naturas*' (unity in three persons, one person in two natures). Mauss finds in this pronouncement on the dual nature of Christ the metaphysics of substance and mode, body and soul, consciousness and action. That may be a daring leap but at any rate a person presently becomes a 'rational substance, indivisible and individual'. Cassiodorus is cited in proof but he failed to make of it 'what it is today, a consciousness and a category'. That was the achievement of long years of labour by the philosophers. Mauss's essay ends *au grand galop* with Descartes, Kant and Fichte. The category of self emerges, to replace the mere concept of self which went before, and each person now has his own self or ego, in keeping with the various Declarations of Rights.

I shall want to say more presently about the category of self as a philosophical achievement and as a psychological innovation. But that is enough about Mauss's historical chronicle, which he sums up thus: 'From a simple masquerade to the mask, from a "rôle" (*personnage*) to a "person" (*personne*) to a name, to an individual, from the latter to a being possessing metaphysical and moral value, from a moral consciousness to a sacred being, from the latter to a fundamental form of thought and action – the course is accomplished'. Nor is the journey ended. Our modern category of self is 'formulated only for us, among us' and may evolve in its turn as we learn 'to perfect our thought and to express it better'.

Apart from its own evident fascination, this saga poses large problems of method. As promised, I pose one which brings out the tension among history, sociology and philosophy. It lies broadly in the way to conceptualise self and role. More precisely, it lies in Mauss's apparent suggestion that the story leads from a start in pure role without self to a finish in pure self without role. This is not, I hasten to add, a fair digest of the central theme, as will be stressed in a moment. But certainly the current notion of a person as an individual ego is not the Pueblos' notion, nor the Greeks', not the Romans', nor the mediaevals'. It is undeniably true that something 'originated and slowly developed over many centuries', the something being, roughly, a sharp distinction of self from role. At the same time, however, something else has remained unchanged. Mauss notes firmly that all languages in all societies have had ways for a speaker to refer to himself and that 'the "self" (*Moi*) is everywhere present'. For, he continues, 'there has never existed a human being who has not been aware, not only of his body but also of his individuality, both spiritual and physical'. In every culture, then, whatever its place in the chronicle, there has been a constant element, a sense of self, present as much in the American Indian masks as in Hamlet's soliloquy, Descartes's *Meditations* or the existentialist's *je suis mes actes*. It seems to me that Mauss is right on both counts. Yet the risk of sheer incoherence is alarming.

Mauss himself skirts the danger. He draws a line between, on the one hand, linguistic anthropology and psychology, where the sense of self is universal but largely a matter of grammar and self-reference; and, on the other hand, law and morality, where a concept of self has been evolving. The distinction of disciplines here does not convince me and I shall not dwell on it. But I am struck by his division between the universal *sense* of self, the evolving *concept* of self and, as we reach Kant, the recent *category* of self. This trio will be of interest later, when more has emerged about the changing self and the unchanging self. It will do so more easily, I fancy, if we start at the other end with the notion of *role*.

Even if the notion arises with masks worn in sacred dramas, it is not so simply divorced from that of self as the image of the mask suggests in our secular age. Today, it has, I suppose, two main uses. One is in analysing social institutions and practices, where it can be formally defined as the dynamic aspect of a social position. The other is in analysing more intimate reaches of social life, where it borrows from the theatre, making a dramaturgical analogy with *dramatis personae* or characters in a play. Both uses, it seems to me, still involve the oldest perplexity about the self.

Institutionally, roles set structure in motion. For example, British society has positions for priests, grocers, mothers and prime ministers, recognised by law and public opinion, prepared for by education and practice, and filled in authorised ways. Each has normative expectations or duties attached, which are sparked by social interaction. It is possible to regard these dynamics as automatic and to try to explain social change as an automatic response to an overall conflict in roles. But nothing in the idea of structural roles requires it and I do not myself find it plausible to make actors the creatures of social structure. For instance, there is a fairly well-specified role of local councillor but it is not thereby a predetermined one. What is well specified is a set of imperatives and, to go with them, a set of legitimating languages which govern the proper interplay with sundry role-partners. Thus, as city father, a councillor is required to advance the good of the community with due regard for economy, justice, humanity and local prosperity; and all citizens at large may demand these virtues of him. As party representative, his supporters charge him with carrying out their manifesto and keeping the party faith. As committee man, he interacts with his civil servants in a language of rational solutions to technical problems. In each of these aspects (and there are several others) his role has specific ends and negotiable means, so that he is both enabled and constrained in striving for consistency. He has a duty to innovate in interpreting a loose brief and by, so to speak, inventing the orders which he is obliged to obey. There is hence some distinction between man and office built into the role itself and I believe myself that this is true of institutional roles in general. So, even on the premises of a structural role theory, it soon becomes plain that the incumbents of a seemingly impersonal system are in fact less marionettes than stewards.

Conversely it would be false to think that the dramaturgical notion of role yields a clear picture of actors as individuals. The relation of actors to the characters they play does not yield an easy distinction of men from masks. We may be inclined to view actors as donning and doffing masks like hats but that is not the only way to conceptualise theatre. Acting can also be regarded less as representation than as expression. This may not seem plausible for village hall theatricals but it rings truer for professional acting and is almost irresistible for the special case, which the dramaturgical analogy is supposed to illuminate, that of the human agent playing himself in the drama of his own life. Here the self cannot be the mask alone, as the point of the analogy is to deny that we are merely beings-for-others; nor can it be the man alone, without destroying the analogy; so it must be some fusion of man and mask, which therefore reinstates the initial perplexity. Meanwhile plays have scripts, plots and conventions, which constrain and enable the players in their interpretation of character, just as norms enable and constrain the incumbent of a social position. There is no one-sided truth about theatre either.

With self and role so entwined, it cannot be right to think of self emerging as butterfly from a caterpillar of role and chrysalis of persona. Consider, for instance, the tragedies which Ancient Greek dramatists wove from older legends and sacred mimes. They would clearly belong in date to the caterpillar period, and, witness the carved masks which prevented facial expression and let one actor play many parts, there are no modern 'individuals' in them. Conflicts are always role-conflicts. Yet the puzzle of self and role is fully there. For example, the characters in Sophocles' *Antigone* are trapped in their societal roles. Antigone must decide whether to bury her brother Polynices, who lies dead outside the walls of Thebes after his luckless invasion. Family duty commands burial but she is also subject to the king's edict forbidding burial for a traitor. The king is Kreon and his edict embodies hallowed custom; but he is also her uncle, head of her house, and bound by family duty. Antigone decides to follow what she takes to be the higher law and buries her brother; Kreon does what he takes to be his greater duty and has her walled up alive. This is a tragedy without individualism or private moralities. Yet it is not a 'tragedy' as newspapers now use the term to report blows of fate, like the flattening of a mother-to-be by a runaway steam roller. Antigone and Kreon *choose* the path which dooms them. They choose as persons who *are* their masks, not as individuals who play their parts. There is an anguished fusion of self and role, which reduces neither to the other. I find this fusion very hard to grasp, I confess, but not because it belongs to an antique world which we have lost. The trappings are antique but the puzzle is wholly modern.

If Greek tragedy could work modern marvels with a fifth-century notion of a person, what exactly has changed since? When Antigone uses the first person singular, she displays more than a grammatical *sense* of self; she has at least a *concept* of self; but, Mauss would say no doubt, she lacks a *category* of self. Since, I agree, something has changed, let us see whether the difference might lie between the concept and the category. The suggestion is that Greek thought is not individualistic enough for self to be a category. It is only with legal ideas about rights, Christian ideas about the soul, and Cartesian ideas about the ego that our modern, categorial self is born. It is then licked into shape by Kant and bequeathed as the individualism, which Durkheim held to be the intellectual spirit of our times. The suggestion is interesting enough but, I find, hard to make out. How, historically, does the concept of self turn into the category?

Mauss does not explain and I dare say that he is counting on the version of Kant given credence by Durkheim. I have nothing to add to what Steven Collins says about that in his excellent essay, except to note that the question still stands. It is also of some help to register Durkheim's approving view of Kant's moral philosophy, as recorded, for instance, in 'Individualism and the Intellectuals': 'According to Kant, I am only certain of acting well if the motives that influence me relate, not to the particular circumstances in which I am placed, but to my quality as a man *in abstracto*'.[1] But the abstraction suggested will need to be an epistemological one, if we are to speak of categories; and so I prefer a different route to Kant, one which lies along the seventeenth century 'way of ideas'.

Descartes opened this chapter in philosophy by grounding our knowledge of the world in the 'I' of the cogito (and in the being of a God who is no deceiver). The *ego* was a monadic spirit communing directly with God and, be it noted, owing nothing to social location. It was a *res cogitans,* a mind meditating reflexively on what was present to it and thus coming to know a metaphysical reality. Thanks to Descartes and then to Locke, it came to seem beyond dispute that all rested with the mind's contents and an enduring self aware of them. These mental contents acquired the generic name of ideas and, as analysed by Locke and Berkeley in particular, presently became the momentary, private, atomic perceptual phenomena now familiar to every English-speaking first-year philosophy student. Such fleeting fragments of experience could not, it seemed plain, constitute or guarantee the solid, persisting world of physical objects and the way of ideas set a threatening problem.

A tempting solution was to make the mind itself the ground of continuity. But that thought fell foul of Hume's sceptical empiricism. His *Treatise of Human Nature* set out to base all other sciences on what could be established by the science of Man, which rested in turn on the impressions and ideas directly given to the mind. As he confessed gracefully in his closing appendix, however, there was a radical snag. The world's furniture, at least in the doctrine of the vulgar, consisted of lasting existences, whose states over time were connected by real bonds. The mind, on the other hand, was aware only of a series of impressions and ideas. How then did we know of lasting objects and real connections? Hume admitted himself stumped. 'In short there are two principles which I cannot render consistent, nor is it in my power to renounce either of them, viz. *that all our distinct perceptions are distinct existences* and *that the mind never perceives any real connection among distinct existences*' (Appendix, his italics). A lasting self might have done the trick by making the real connexion lie in the fact that a continuous series of data could be presented to the same observer. But Hume, turning his sceptic's eye inward, could find no lasting self. 'When I turn my reflection on *myself,* I can never perceive this *self* without some one or more perceptions; nor can I ever perceive anything but the perceptions. It is the composition of these, therefore, which forms the self'. His inner bundle was quite unfitted to cement distinct existences into enduring things.

A way out of this scandalous impasse was offered by Kant. The continuity and identity of the mind could indeed be used to underwrite the world of things causally related in Newtonian space, provided that it could be established transcendentally. The proposal was grandly termed the 'Transcendental Unity of Apperception'. It relied on a far-reaching novelty, transcendental argument, which let epistemology take over work assigned by Descartes to God. 'Self' does not in fact feature on Kant's list of the categories but it would be claimed to merit categorial status for its work in unifying our judgements. The 'I' stands outside experience but is present in all our orderings of experience. Thus Mauss calls it 'the precondition of consciousness and science', arguing thence to individualism as the form of modern social thought.

There seems to be a confusion here, however, between the two forms of individualism, which Durkheim had picked out. On the one hand there is 'the individualism of Kant and Rousseau, that of the *spiritualistes,* that

. . . [of] . . . the Declaration of the Rights of Man'.[2] This had Durkheim's blessing and he looked to it as 'henceforth the only system of beliefs which can ensure the unity of the country'. On the other hand there was the 'egoistic cult of self' wished on us by 'the narrow utilitarianism and utilitarian egoism of Spencer and the economists'. If we were speaking of the moral form of modern social thought, I would be inclined to suggest that the honours were equally divided between them (excluding other contenders). But 'the precondition of consciousness and science' sounds more like a scientific form of modern social thought. In that case we should, I think, look to the epistemological origins of egoism.

At any rate, despite Kant (and Fichte), English empiricists soldiered on with the mixture of enlightenment and despair bequeathed by Hume. They did not adopt a categorial self or deal in transcendental arguments. The Principle of the Association of Ideas continued to ground mental philosophy and scientific inference. Hopes were pinned on an empirical psychology to complete Hume's science of Man. These endeavours also drew on another kind of atomism, expressed by Hobbes and especially important for social and political thinking. The unit of analysis here was man, conceived as a self-interested, rational, essentially presocial animal. Rationality lay in the shrewd calculation of individual advantage, with conflicts of interest reconciled in principle through a notional social contract. Within this individualist framework, varieties in institutions were accounted for by variations in desires and in distributions of power, given the basic disadvantages of a state of nature. Themes from Hobbes and Hume came uneasily together in Utilitarianism, which offered both a moral science of economics and a scientific ethics of welfare. Utilitarianism is a complex and unstable total theory but it lent itself to popularisation. It summed up a view of human beings as Rational Economic Men, which is, I think, the form of Individualism with the greater claim to have influenced modern social theory.

I do not suggest that individualism is a single or precise thesis. Broadly an individualist is, I suppose, anyone who gives analytical priority to single agents (or their states). The priority may be ontological, epistemological or metaphysical; it may be ethical, political or social. A systematic trawl for individualists nets a very mixed cran of fish, as Steven Lukes notes in his rich essay on the topic.[3] But my business now is with social theory and here I take the typical modern individualism to be the one which we owe to nineteenth-century liberals and utilitarians. As a thesis about actual human behaviour it is a basic blend of economics and psychology, well caught in F. Y. Edgeworth's dictum that 'the first principle of economics is that every agent is actuated by self-interest'.[4] When we look for its origins, we find Hobbes and Hume, rather than Kant.

Hobbes and Hume differ over the concept of a person. Hume, as just noted, can find nothing but a bundle of perceptions from which to compose the self. Social theorists descended from him treat an agent as a set of ordered preferences, which action aims to satisfy. Those of Hobbesian persuasion add a presocial atom, whose preferences they are. Hobbes's atoms had a primary urge to self-preservation and are moved by a restless desire for power after power which ceaseth only in death. That is to build a conflict of interests into the foundations of social life and it generates the Hobbesian problem of order. No such conflict follows from Hume's account however – indeed he held that we have a natural sympathy for our fellows among our dispositions. Individualist social theory is heir to both and that makes it hard to decide quite what concept of a person is involved in it. But these differences matter less for present purposes than the central point upon which they agree. For they agree in making the identity of a person independent of roles and social positions.

On any such account the social system of positions and roles belongs among the externalities or parameters within which individuals decide and manoeuvre. Norms and rules provide standardised reasons for action by rational agents seeking to maximise satisfaction. Some norms will, no doubt, have been internalised, thus becoming a direct source of motives for action, since obedience then brings its own reward. Others remain external and supply only legitimating reasons, in the sense of public justifications for doing what the agent wants to do from other and private motives. But, even when internalised, roles remain secondary, since the currency of the model is the psychological coin of inner satisfaction and not obedience per se. In other words role-distance is built deep into the analysis of social action and role-playing is always instrumental, even when it is gratifying in itself rather than merely convenient. This is explicit in Hobbes, where the individualist distinction of self from role is patent. It is implicit in Hume, where sentiment and not duty moves the individual.

The upshot is to make social action hard, indeed impossible, to understand. Consider, for instance, Erving Goffman with his picture of actors as individuals, living on the seamy underside of society and working the system for their own ends. Their attitude to rules, norms and roles is (largely) instrumental and their real motives (usually) are the pursuit of perceived private advantage. The key to understanding what an actor is up to in Goffman's scene is therefore to spot the man behind the mask; and the theoretical crux is whether there can be such a man. Goffman is oddly silent about the self. There are occasional remarks – 'A self is a repertoire of behaviour appropriate to a different set of contingencies'[5]; by 'personal identity' I mean the organic continuity imputed to each individual, this established through distinguishing marks such as name and appearance[6]; 'the self is the code that makes sense out of almost all the individual's activities and provides a basis for organising them'.[7] But, as far as I know, he never explains what organises the repertoire, supplies continuity of motive or establishes the code. The Hobbesian answer would be that it is the actor himself, which is to make him an utterly mysterious we-know-not-what. The Humean answer would be that there is nothing beyond the repertoire or bundle of coded preferences, which is to lose the actor altogether. I am not sure which nasty horn of this dilemma Goffman would choose.

The dilemma can be generalised. Individualism relies on a 'self' in each actor, which gives shape to his real motives and, in combination with others, accounts for the dynamics of a social system. Yet this self is threatened in two directions. If it reduces to a Humean bundle of preferences, which are then traced to socialisation and hence to the system itself, it vanishes into the system which it was meant to explain. If it is a Hobbesian core, so private and so much at a distance from its public, legitimating masks that the real man is impenetrable, it vanishes from scientific enquiry. The puzzle is how to avoid this two-way vanishing trick. What sort of self do we need?

In hope of an answer, I revert to Greek tragedy, with its acute role-conflicts. When an actor is trapped in conflicting roles, the self is exposed. Examples are not so very common in everyday life, because of inbuilt orderings. For instance a mother, who must steal to feed her starving children, is not thoroughly caught between roles of mother and law-abiding citizen, because her role as mother has a socially recognised priority. She is not being forced to choose between two roles which equally define her being. Greek tragedy, however, specialises in this ultimate kind of choice. Antigone's roles of sister and subject lay equal demands on her. Agamemnon has no appeal to socially recognised priorities in deciding whether to sacrifice his daughter to gain a fair wind for his fleet. Each must resolve not merely what to do but who to be. In trying to grasp this fusion of identity and role, we can hope to understand more about the category of self.

It is tempting to suppose that the ethical fix occurs only because Greek tragedy lacks an ego. The typical modern presumption is that there is a self distinct from both roles, who must choose between them. This presumption, however, far from easing the dilemma, makes it impossible. Consider Sartre's ascription of Bad Faith to anyone who performs the duties of an office just because he holds the office. That suggests a contrast between a person who shuffles off his responsibilities onto his roles and a person who makes choices which are authentically his own. But that is not how Sartre tackles moral dilemmas. For instance, his account of the problem facing a young man, who must decide after the fall of France in 1940 whether to stay with his mother or to join the French forces abroad, certainly insists that there is no hiding behind moral authorities. But the moral authorities are not just those of church or society. They are also those of independent conscience and inner feeling. So it is left utterly unclear what possible test of authenticity remains. There is no self *en soi* and *pour soi* to stand apart from all roles. 'In life a man commits himself, draws his own portrait, and there is nothing but that portrait.'[8] If this were what the category of self comes to, we would not have advanced beyond the Greeks at all. Telling Antigone to choose authentically, to be true to herself or to draw her own portrait would amount to saying that it matter not one whit what she does. Hence, it seems, there has to be a self to be true to, an inner being to sit for the portrait.

But snags persist, when we ask further about this inner being. So far we have tried two versions, neither appealing. In the Hobbesian she is to look to her self-preservation and in the Humean to the order of her preferences. Both try to convict her of a terrible confusion about the claims of duty and both make the confusion worse. The generic source is that both require a rational actor always to have a *further* reason for doing what office gives only a role-governed reason to do. This further reason is typically that conforming will be for her good. Here 'good', like 'utility', is to be defined neutrally so as not to prejudge the relation between prudence and morality. In short, and with a similar *caveat* about neutrality, she is to weigh the claims of role and any other considerations in the scales of expected utility. Can we straighten her out accordingly?

The answer is surely No. But the grounds of it are less clear. It certainly would not do to suggest that she try weighing duty against utility, since the utility of burying her brother is not decidable independently of the role she adopts. For Antigone-as-sister it weighs heavy; for Antigone-as-subject it weighs less. But I posed the dilemma as one where utility held the scales. The trouble is that the metaphor cannot be cashed in, unless we can answer the question 'utility for whom'? That makes it plain, I think, that the self will need to be more than a schedule of preferences, since preferences now must be attached to something. If we attach them to Antigone in her different roles, we are back with the previous snag that they vary systematically with the role. So it might look a better idea to attach them to an atomic self. But, granted that her tragic choice is one which will define this blank self, nothing is achieved thereby. This ultimate self would not be applying a measure but creating one and that would leave us still stuck with my complaint about Sartre. Considerations of utility thus fail to be neutral and the addition of a pure self does nothing to help. If Antigone is to have any sort of assessable choice, we must work with what Sophocles provides. There is no missing piece.

Pure self seems to me an illusion; but a plausible illusion when conjured up against limiting cases at the other extreme. Durkheim says at the end of the *Rules,* 'Individual human natures are merely the indeterminate material which the social factor moulds and stransforms'. The obvious retort is to postulate a pure self independent of the social factor. But there is no call for one, granted that even a structural role-theory need not make role-playing automatic. So a self robust enough not to be absorbed into the system need not be so pure that it vanishes into darkest privacy. This is the moral I want to draw from the conceptual frame of Greek tragedy. *Antigone* offers us implicitly a 'category' of self to secure a precarious space between social factor and inner world.

Now we can turn to Kant, rather than to Hobbes and Hume. There is a social analogue of the task which Kant gives the self in securing a world of persisting, causally related objects amid a mass of experienced phenomena. Analogously the system of social positions and role-playing actors is not given in experience. Each of us knows of it by understanding the interactions which we are caught up in. To understand, we must bring concepts to bear, with the mind, as Kant says of understanding the physical world, acting not as a pupil but as a judge. The social analogue of reflective consciousness is intelligent agency. We identify the positions and roles of the social world by acting intelligently within them. Intelligence depends on continuity of the self, by analogy with the unity of the self required to weave phenomena into physical objects. For meaningful social phenomena, the apperception is that of a social agent.

Antigone's actions are *hers* not because of the sameness of the private will of the pure self behind them but because they are done by the same social actor. What actor is she? *Who* buried Polynices? The answer demanded by the tragedy is that Kreon's royal niece did it, being the same person as Polynices' sister. It adds nothing to this answer to invoke a pure self as a gloss on what is meant by 'same person'. That Antigone is the same social actor is both necessary and sufficient.

We ascribe to actors both a personal and a social identity. The difference seems at first great. Offhand my personal identity is unique and immutable – what makes me myself is peculiar to me and, without it, I would cease to exist – whereas my social identity is a general description, which others could exemplify. It seems that I could not have been born 2,000 years ago, as that would have been someone else, but I could have been an engine driver and still be me. This is, however, only a trick of the example, which works because 2,000 years is a long time from now and an engine driver a short distance from a philosopher. Presumably I would have been the same person if conceived ten minutes earlier but not if brought up in contemporary New Guinea. Self is the unifying agency among my social actions and it can survive only mild dislocation in both time and social space. Just as a personal identity is not to be confused with personality, so social identity is not to be confused with social placement; for both there is a uniqueness.[9]

That much is consistent with the notion of a person in Greek tragedy, which therefore seems to me to have a category of self implicit in it. What then is modern? It is, I think, the idea that we construct our own social identity. Without Roman law and mediaeval Christianity, I doubt if the idea would have come to make sense. It needs notions of individual persona and private spiritual substance. With them behind us, we can picture a social actor as an individual who paints his own social portrait, for whom there is nothing social but the portrait. Yet the idea still verges on the unintelligible. It comes easily to us, I suggest, only because we do not suppose that people construct all of their own personal identity. A *substantia individua rationalis,* to use the mediaeval Christian term, acts as anchor for our idea of personality as a variable, open to self-programming through aversive therapy, biorhythms, colonic irrigation, dianetics, encounter groups and on through the alphabet to yoga and zen. Something similar but more social is also needed to anchor our choice of roles and of interpretations for the roles which we choose. This gives more scope for the construction of self than there is in Greek tragedy but a great deal less than individualism would have us believe.

That is as far as I can take the topic, if there is to be a final comment on the tension between historical and analytic approaches. I shall make it *à propos* of J. S. La Fontaine's absorbing essay in this volume, in which she argues that 'social representations of society itself, and the nature of authority within society, give a characteristic form to related notions of the person'. She points to an undeniable variety of such social representations and to some societies, like the Gahuku-Gama, where there is no concept of a 'person' at all. The analytical approach is thus convicted, if not of simple ignorance, then of parochialism. 'What has been overlooked in discussion of the Western notions is that they exist in the context of a particular concept of society as a whole: the idea of the nation state'. Without trying to doubt her anthropologist's eye and skill, I shall suggest that the true reckoning is more ambiguous.

A historicist view certainly fares well, if it is built on a root distinction between the terms 'individual', referring to 'the moral human being, the object of observation', and 'person', referring to 'concepts such as that of Tallensi which lend the object social significance'. That conveniently assigns individuals to nature and persons to society. But nothing persuades me that this contrast between the natural and the social can do the work required of it. La Fontaine grants that the idea of office implies a distinction between the powers of an office and their exercise by individuals. The sense of 'individual' here is, I submit, clearly social as much as natural. Also, if even an institutional role theory must allow the role-player a creative latitude, then no clear point is scored by the inability of the Gahuku-Gama to grasp the Western idea of friendship as a relation between two unique individuals. Conversely the Western idea of friendship is surely not of a relation between two unique *objects of observation* but of one between two *persons* who, prompted no doubt by liking, have chosen to temper their social relations with friendly regard on stage and off. Here 'off stage' is not the name of a purely natural arena, witness the personal rights and duties which friendship brings. It may well be true that some cultures allow more choice of relationships (as well as choice within relationships) than others. But this is not to say that some choices occur – or can be coherently conceived as occurring – outside all relationships. The core idea seems to me to be that of personal agency and it cannot be expunged in certain cultures by drawing the line between social and natural so as to make it optional.

There is a risk here of confusing the question of what a person is with that of what various people take it to be. I have been arguing that, on the one hand, roles enable as well as constrain and that, on the other, pure self is an illusion. This is addressed to the question of what a person is. Since not everyone will agree, it is clearly possible, in one sense at least and as a matter of fact, to conceive of persons in other ways and anthropology is duly instructive on this score. But that is not to make the concept wholly variable. It forces at most a distinction between core and penumbra and a well-chosen core can be ambiguously policed forever by pointing out the hermeneutic options involved in mapping terms in one language onto those of another. There is no such thing as anthropology without presuppositions and the findings of anthropology cannot be direct support for the truth of what they presuppose. Although it is rash to confuse the two questions, it is equally a mistake to suppose them independent. For instance there are several concepts of a person to be found even among the authors of this volume. La Fontaine's own, presumably, is not identical with mine and, even within the context of the idea of the nation-state, current philosophy can supply many others. When tracking down the self, an anthropologist is bound to be a philosopher too. The hunt is affected by the hunter's idea of the truth.

Analytically, I have suggested that social forms can never shape human beings completely, because social forms owe their own shape to the fact that human beings are social agents with ideas about social forms. I have denied, however, that persons are natural first and social afterwards. That still leaves plenty of elbow room and the moral I draw from Mauss is finally philosophical. It is that human beings have slowly been learning to express what has all along underlain their universal sense of self. The Pueblo expressed it by regarding himself both as a clansman absorbed into his clan and as identical with his own ancestor, the ancient Greek by recognising choice as an aspect of institutional role, the Roman by making a cognomen a source of personal rights, the mediaeval Christian by ascribing duties to the soul. We ourselves are inclined to make the self more private but, even so, we hold on to an idea of identity as what is expressed in relations with others. Each view contains an unresolved tension and our own is no exception. Not all steps are forward. So I do not think it perverse to treat the dead as candidates for this year's prize in mental philosophy. I wish only that it was plainer to me how the prize should be awarded.

Notes

I would like to thank Steven Lukes for his helpful comments on the previous draft and Steven Collins, whose splendid essay in this volume I have read with great pleasure and profit. I have also learnt much from discussing the topic with Richard Gordon.

1. 'Individualism and the Intellectuals', which can be found translated by S. and J. Lukes and with a preface by S. Lukes in *Political Studies* vol.XVII, 1969, pp.14–30.
2. See 'Individualism and the Intellectuals', *loc.cit.*, pp. 20 *ff.* for the remarks from Durkheim quoted in this paragraph.
3. 'Methodological Individualism Reconsidered', *British Journal of Sociology,* XIX, 1968. See also Lukes, *Individualism,* Blackwell, 1973.

4. *Mathematical Psychics: An Essay on the Application of Mathematics to the Moral Sciences,* London, Kegan Paul, 1881, p.16.
5. *The Presentation of Self in Everyday Life,* New York, Doubleday, 1959.
6. *Relations in Public,* Penguin, 1971, Ch.5, p.189.
7. *Ibid.,* Appendix, p.366.
8. *Existentialism and Humanism,* London, Methuen & Co., 1973, p.42. The discussion of the young man's dilemma is on pp.35 *f.*
9. For further discussion see my *Models of Man,* Cambridge University Press, 1977, Ch.5.

11

An alternative social history of the self

Michael Carrithers

I

In his essay Mauss argues that the history of the notion of person can be told as a single narrative, beginning with the role (*personnage*) played in a putative primeval society and ending with the modern self who is also the citizen of an as yet imperfectly realized social democratic state.

Much of the persuasiveness of this dazzling piece lies in the strategy of argument. Mauss maintains at the outset that he will consider in this narrative history only social and legal history. He will not refer to what he admits is a universal fact, "that there has never existed a human being who has not been aware not only of his body, but also of his individuality, both spiritual and physical". He will even "leave aside everything which relates to the 'self' (*moi*), the conscious personality as such". This seems at first an innocent expression of scholarly caution, especially since Mauss is addressing an audience of social anthropologists, not of psychologists or philosophers who might consider the conscious personality as their preserve. Mauss seems in these opening moves to commit himself to discuss only legal, social, or political matters, not the psychic or the philosophical.

But gradually, by slow degrees and on first reading imperceptibly, Mauss re-introduces the self, *le moi,* into the narrative as he edges nearer the modern West. It first re-appears, heavily bracketed by inverted commas, when his story reaches India. Then it turns up again disguised as Christian notions of the soul, which are gradually transmuted into modern psychological ideas. Finally it is placed in apposition to the person – "*la personne, le moi*" – as if for the modern West they are the same thing.

Indeed Mauss asserts that now "the person = self, [and] the self = consciousness". This person-cum-self is "natural, clearly determined in the depths of his consciousness". So at least for the modern West Mauss does in fact speak of the psychic and the philosophical, of the conscious personality, of the sense of mental and physical individuality.

This argument – or rather narrative, for that is in fact what it is – has the effect of a magical trick, for what had seemed to disappear completely at first reappears, and in fact turns out to be the object of the whole act. What we naïvely take to be a psychic, or inner, or spiritual, or at least a natural matter, our notion of our self, is revealed by Mauss to be something else altogether, a product of social history and a matter wholly explicable through sociological exegesis. Mauss had seemed to set the self aside only to retrieve and explain it triumphantly at the end. To trespass upon the preserves of psychology and philosophy was one of the fondest pursuits of the *Année Sociologique,* but perhaps nowhere in the works of that school was it done with such amiable cunning as here.

There is, I think, a great deal of lasting value in Mauss's recounting of history from his viewpoint, but there is also a good deal which is now difficult to accept. What I want to suggest here is that Mauss rendered as a single story what is in fact a complex plot, made up of at least two different and distinguishable subject matters, one of which, the story of the self or *moi,* Mauss systematically distorted or ignored.

Precisely because they are words so important to us, "person" and "self" are vexing and confusing, so I will introduce two terms of art to replace them. In what follows *personne* will mean the subject of the narrative which Mauss tells most convincingly, that of the social and legal history of the conception of the individual in respect of society as a whole. The *personne,* that is, is a *conception of the individual human being as a member of a (1) significant and (2) ordered collectivity.* That at any rate is what Mauss seems to mean when he speaks of the person or role in the putative primitive society, and similarly when he speaks of the person as a citizen in a modern state such as France. To say that this collectivity is *significant* is to say that the power it wields over the individual human being subject to it is not trivial, but vitally affects the formation and exercise of the individual's aims. To say that this collectivity is *ordered* is to say that it has a specific form which bears a clear relationship to the conception of the *personne* that goes with it. In the ideal primitive society, for example, the order is that of kinship or clan membership, and the *personne* found in that society is one determined by kinship or clan membership. The *personne* in democratic France, on the other hand, is a citizen, and the conception of citizenship is determined by the ordered form of the whole, namely democracy and its attendant institutions. That the *personne* has a social and legal history is no surprise, for social and legal history are precisely what make any particular example of the *personne* itself and nothing else.

What is not necessary for the term *personne* as I use it is the assumption that the collectivity to which it relates is simply given and unproblematical, or that the relationship between an individual human being and the collectivity which bestows a form of the *personne* is straightforward. An individual human being may be subjected to an alien notion of the *personne,* as are black South Africans. Or an individual might find himself part of different collectivities, for example, a German of the early nineteenth century might have found himself to be a citizen of a small principality, a member of the Catholic Church, and a member of some notionally powerful German nation. The political community to which one belongs may not be one's moral or religious community. (It is just the Durkheimian assumption that societies are bounded and harmoniously organized wholes without internal conflict or contradiction that vitiates much of the *Année*'s work.)

The other term of art is *moi,* defined as a *conception of (1) the physical and mental individuality of human beings within (2) a natural or spiritual cosmos, and (3) interacting with each other as moral agents.* The Christian notion of the soul, which includes the soul's relation to the body, to the overarching spiritual universe, and to other souls, is just such a conception, as is the Freudian notion of the psychophysical complex in relation to the biological world and the family. These ideas of the *moi* have, no doubt, a social history, in that the circumstances of society in which a certain *moi* conception comes into being influence the form which the *moi* conception might take. For example, the *psyche,* the "soul" of which Socrates spoke, was quite different from related concepts in the heroic Homeric Greece of some centuries before, and the difference seems roughly compatible with profound changes in the social order. Indeed just because conceptions of the *moi* include a view of morality, of how psychophysical individuals ought to interact face to face, some decisive influence from circumambient social forms of life is inevitable.

But a view of how individual human beings should interact face to face is not necessarily the same as a view of how they should act in respect of a significant collectivity. An individual who was both a Christian and a German citizen in Nazi Germany would potentially have found his *moi* conceptions, his ideas of himself and what he owed other selves, and his notion of his *personne,* his obligations within the German state, deeply at odds. Nor do theories of the *moi* have only a social history. They also have an intellectual history which is irreducible to social history. It would be impossible to show, for example, that Socrates' idea of the *psyche* is merely a reflection of Athenian society when he lived. So any narrative of the development of different versions of the *moi* must include a relatively autonomous intellectual component. Also, since the physical and mental individuality of human beings is partly subject to the natural world, such an intellectual history might well include empirical observations of, for example, a medical sort.

In what follows I will be concerned to disentangle a narrative history of the *moi* from that of the *personne.* On the one hand this involves showing why and how Mauss blended them into one and gave precedence to the *personne.* On the other it involves showing that views of the *moi* have the same relatively wide distribution and relative autonomy that views of the *personne* enjoy.

To make this last point I will use Mauss's own strategy. He showed, for example, how the use of masks on the Northwest Coast of America is for his purposes similar to the use of masks in ancient Rome. I will argue analogously that a conception of the *moi* current in nineteenth- and twentieth-century Germany is essentially similar to views of the *moi* held in India in the fifth century B.C. Indeed I will be able to go further and show that the ancient Indian views could be, and have been, faithfully and easily translated into a modern European idiom. The ease and fidelity of this translation certify that *moi* views share among them some profound features which attest to a more than accidental resemblance between widely separated manifestations.

Once this is clear it will be possible to turn to Mauss's own ideas of psychophysical individuality in their relation to the collectivity to show its weaknesses in detail. And finally I will convey some notion of how *moi* theories relate to *personne* theories, using the ancient Indian material.

It is important to bear in mind that the two narratives, of the *moi* and the *personne,* concern ideas or notions. The mortal Socrates' own presumed self is not in question, but his idea of the *moi* is. The detailed legal, social, and political persons of Cicero and his Roman contemporaries are not at issue, but their notion of the *personne* is. It will be implicit in the argument, however, that these ideas are not detached from life, but are embodied not only in texts but also in the actions and practices of those who hold them.

It would be possible to trace something suggestive of the *moi,* or the *personne,* in any society. But here I am concerned only with the most clear-cut cases of both.

II

Mauss wished to explain both the *moi* and the *personne* by reference to what might fairly be set in the upper case as Society. The foundations of this idea are old and complex, but it certainly reflects two important lines of thought in eighteenth- and especially nineteenth-century France. One is the visionary elevation of the collectivity and collective purposes over the individual and individual purposes. The positive side of this appeared in what have been called the "social religions" of France[1], the investing of religious fervour in the collectivity; while the negative side is reflected in the coinage of the word "individualism" as a pejorative designation of socially destructive self-interest.[2] So moral value is laid on the collective, not on the individual.

The second visionary strain is that of the cult of science,[3] under which social science took its place. Here, especially in the teachings of Comte, the view is represented that the collective is what is real, what is really to be studied, what really explains matters in the human world.[4] So cognitive value is laid upon the collective, not the individual.

Durkheim, Mauss's teacher, combined these visionary views with clarity and decisiveness, and took them one step further. For he wished to argue not only that the collectivity and its forms explain the forms of human life, and that it should do so, but also that the collectivity can be used to explain the forms of intellectual life. Thus he wrote of the categories, those basic parameters of thought which for him include space and time, the whole and the parts, as well as the *personne,* that they possess "a special sort of moral necessity which is to the intellectual life what moral obligation is to the will".[5] So an argument that a certain matter, let us say the intellectual equipment of a Zuñi Indian, can be explained by reference to the forms of Zuñi society is buttressed by the attitude that individuals should, in this way, be subject to the imperatives of the collectivity. And an argument that such an individual's attitudes ought to be subjected to collectivist values is buttressed by the reflection that they are already formed by the influence of the collectivity. Everywhere one turns in human affairs one finds the design and the purpose of the collectivity at work.

Durkheim added to this view another visionary conviction, that of the inevitable progress of mankind, and therewith produced some striking arguments which, though their premises have faded away, are still very much with us. One such argument, which lies in the immediate background to Mauss's essay on the person, was presented in 1898 to defend the Dreyfusard cause of individual liberty against the authoritarian anti-Dreyfusards. One might have thought that Durkheim's attitude to the collectivity would lead him to side with the authoritarians, but for very good reasons he stood on the liberal side, the side of the inalienable rights of the individual. One hidden premise of his case is an uncompromisingly collectivist one: religion began as nothing but society worshipping itself. This of course is Durkheim's reading of putative primitive religion, but the form of the explanation is extended to all cases. A second assumption is that modern society is moving toward a desirable recognition of all human beings' nature as human individuals, a consummation brought about by the complexity of modern society: what binds men together among centrifugal social forces is the one thing they indisputably share, their nature as human individuals. Therefore we are moving toward a new kind of sacredness, the sacredness of the human individual, "a religion of which man is, at the same time, believer and God".[6] This logic is carried by the convenient coincidence that the word "man" (*l'homme*) can refer both to an individual example or to the collectivity. If one separates the senses, the dictum loses its persuasiveness.

Nevertheless this argument was a rehearsal for Mauss's arguments forty years later, and the convictions which pin together Mauss's narrative are precisely the ones which lead Durkheim to his deceptive conclusion. On the surface one witnesses that the individual is lent decisive value, but underneath the real value and the real determining power lies with the collectivity; so all *mois* are *personnes*.

One sees how Mauss was able to read the last few centuries of Western thought as he did. Licensed by Durkheim's reading of religion as a secular affair of the collectivity, he could treat Fichte, Kant, Leibniz, and the Protestant thinkers as having contributed, quite despite their own best efforts, to the development of the *personne*. Mauss even uses one of Durkheim's favourite tactics, that of declaring what he finds distasteful to be socially pathological or aberrant. Thus Mauss finds that Spinoza has the "soundest" view of ethics and that the *fin de siecle "culte du moi"* is an "aberration". There is a good deal of Durkheim's visionary opinion and visionary methods even in Mauss's gentler presentation.

That an opinion is visionary and badly argued does not make it wrong. But there are a number of assumptions here which are now very difficult to share. The faith in evolutionary progress in both Durkheim and Mauss is now singularly unconvincing. Nor does it seem at all likely, in view of the sheer breadth of Western thought in the last few centuries, that Mauss's reading of it should be especially privileged. There have been others which cast quite a different light upon Western conceptions of the *moi* and the *personne*.

III

Another reading of Western history was Anton Gueth's, of whom I have written at length elsewhere.[7] Gueth was a well-educated German Catholic, a slightly younger contemporary of Mauss. His reading and the influences upon him could not, however, have been more different, nor could his conclusions, for he decided in 1905 to go to the East to become a Buddhist monk. He was thereafter known as Nyanatiloka, and the bulk of his published work consists of superb translations and exegesis of Theravāda Buddhist texts. Gueth did however leave us a quite clear idea of the sources of his inspiration in the West, and those sources deal almost exclusively, not with the *personne* as part of a collectivity, but with various views of the *moi,* the psychophysical individual in respect of a spiritual natural order. Indeed Gueth's own reading was roughly chronological, so that he began with Christian views of the *moi* and moved on toward more secular views and toward scientific views which were current at the end of the nineteenth century. In seeing how Gueth's own thought changed toward the characteristic *moi* views of Mauss's and our own times, we see a more general movement in thought. It may seem peculiar that Gueth followed this by becoming a Buddhist. But in fact the Buddhism which he discovered was by no means the mystic, hazy, otherworldly affair which perhaps hovers in the minds of many in the West. It was far closer to those secular and scientific views which were Gueth's springboard to the East.

Gueth was familiar with Greek ideas of the *moi,* but he really began with Christian ideas as they were expressed in Thomas à Kempis's *Imitatio Christi.* This text contains everything that I have characterized as a complete conception of the *moi.* The emphasis lies upon the psychophysical individual, and in particular upon how the individual Christian might make his own body and mind or soul conform to that exemplary body and soul, Christ's. Hence a good deal of the text is concerned with how to understand and how to discipline oneself inwardly. It is assumed that reality and responsibility lie here, and not with some collectivity, whether church or state. Arrayed around this central concern, then, are the other usual *moi* concerns. A good deal of the self-understanding and self-discipline is to be directed (implicitly) toward achieving a good moral relationship with other individuals. And the spiritual development of the individual takes place in the Christian spiritual universe with the Trinity, and especially Christ, at the head.

There are properties associated with the *Imitatio Christi* which are difficult to assimilate to Mauss's scheme. True, the idea of the inward spiritual individual lent weight to the estimate of value placed on what, in Mauss's account, was ultimately to be the citizen of a democratic state. But on the other hand such an inward emphasis seems to fit historically, not with Mauss's and Durkheim's conception of the collectivity, but with small-scale, face-to-face societies, monasteries or prayer groups. The *devotio moderna* movement, of which the *Imitatio Christi* was an expression, formed itself into small communities of laymen and religious, and in that respect was a not-too-distant forerunner of later small-scale Protestant movements: not Calvin's commonwealth, but small churches and small groups of the elect. This stream of Protestantism leads on, not to thought about citizenship in the state, but to what was later called civil disobedience, to an emphasis on the individual and his conscience in the face of the collectivity.

Gueth was also deeply influenced by later *moi* theories, those of the late eighteenth century in Germany. One kind of *moi* theory was represented in, and partly created by, Goethe. Though this theory evidently has roots in the Christian version, it has already begun to move away from it. It is, wrote Erich Trunz, "a picture of man finding within himself the way to the Absolute. . . . The more a man listens to his deepest self, the more surely he finds himself directed to the God above us, finds himself associated in his dependence with the earth beneath us and allied morally with his fellows. Reverence for oneself is reverence for the God in us and the mystery of life".[8] Here we find the same single-minded emphasis upon the self and its inner workings, and the connection of one self with other selves, but the Christian spiritual order is giving way to a pagan and increasingly, a natural order.

As the natural order came more into the foreground the question of the relationship of the mind and body, of the composition of the *moi*, gained importance. At this time, the end of the eighteenth and beginning of the nineteenth century, empirical observation began to creep into *moi* theories. In particular, philosophers and physicians began to treat as serious and important problems the effect of physical disorders on the mind, and of psychic distress upon the body.[9]

Drawing evidence from a number of witnesses – Goethe and Herder,

Schleiermacher and Cabanis, Lavater and Wilhelm von Humboldt – one might compose the following picture of the *moi* at the beginning of the nineteenth century: it is deep, and therefore mysterious; but it is investigable, and to an extent malleable; it is the microscope through which the cosmos is seen; it is the living core around which society is built, principally through face-to-face relations; and it is embodied, and therefore bound to the vast organic world. The centre of this thought lies squarely in cosmopolitan bourgeois Germany, with its small states and consequent vision of the world as a greater place than that encompassed by any political entity, any one significant collectivity. Certainly these thinkers would not have been inclined to believe that morality is imposed from above, by the collectivity, as Durkheim and Mauss assumed. (But *their* experience, of course, was of one of the most entrenched nation-states, France.) Nor would the German thinkers have been inclined to identify the legal person or the citizen, the *personne,* with the self, the *moi.*

On this evidence we can speak of *moi* theories emphasizing one area of philosophical interest and value, that of the psychophysical individual, but as being attended by two consequent concerns, the form of the overarching cosmos in which the *moi* exists, and the relationship of the *moi* as moral agent to others like itself. As we follow Gueth's reading to sources later in the nineteenth century and to those figures who influenced him most directly, we can see how these areas of concern slowly took on different shapes.

One profound influence on Gueth was Ernst, Freiherr von Feuchtersleben, a medical writer and popular moralist. He wrote the *Medical Psychology* of 1845,[10] a series of lectures given at Vienna where he was dean of the faculty of medicine, and the popular work, *Dietetics of the Soul,* published in 1838.[11] Feuchtersleben now languishes in obscurity, but his medical book was the first of its kind, "an altogether new departure in psychiatric writing with its orderly and digested collection of facts and theories historical and contemporary, grouped within a balanced overall view of the aims, principles, and scope of the subject".[12] His work of popular moralizing was tremendously popular and was reprinted continually throughout the nineteenth century.

As a moralist he represented, I suppose, that nineteenth-century "religion of healthymindedness" described by William James. In the *Dietetics of the Soul,* Feuchtersleben begins from an already conventional *moi* theory, quoting Herder: "each individual bears within him in his bodily form and mental capacity that symmetry which he is ultimately to attain through self-development".[13] Here we see achievement and morality growing organically out of the inner self through that quintessentially German process, *Selbstbildung,* self-cultivation or self-development. This now leads on to what is becoming a creed, that "the happiness or misery of the individual depends on the deeply marked impressions or conceptions of his own mind".[14] And this in turn is necessarily (if somewhat vaguely) connected to morality: "self-government is the great and eternal law which life, duty, and mental dietetics enjoin upon man. . . . "[15] But while a morality growing from within is enjoined, society as such is a "net of falsehood",[16] distracting us from these pursuits.

More interesting, however, are Feuchtersleben's medical philosophical views as propounded in his *Medical Psychology.* Man, he asserts, is the union of the natural world and the spiritual, and it is clear from the context that he means by "natural" something very like that world of material, force, and pattern, obeying its own rules and investigable by scientific methods, which we envision today. By "spiritual" he means something as yet mysterious but evidenced in its corporeal effects. He maintains a resolute scepticism in the face of German metaphysics. He is unable and unwilling to offer any further view of the mind–body relationship, but he does look optimistically to animal magnetism, phrenology, and physiognomy for some eventual evidence, however fragmentary, on the matter.

Perhaps most revealing is one remark that Feuchtersleben passes about the mind and body, that "all attempts to deduce them from one principle (except the Deity) have failed".[17] From the *Dietetics* it is clear that the parenthetical remark is not really much felt by Feuchtersleben, and is probably there to protect him from Catholic sentiment in imperial Vienna. But without the Christian cosmological content the spiritual and/or natural world in which the *moi* exists is puzzling, as is the composition of the psychophysical individual itself. Out of this puzzle were to grow various naturalistic solutions which bear directly upon Gueth's later career and upon the thought of many of his contemporaries.

Another great influence upon Gueth was Schopenhauer. Schopenhauer certainly emphasized the psychophysical individual as the chief area of philosophical concern, a site of interest and difficulty both morally and intellectually. Much of his argument is drawn from writers who would now be recognised as the forerunners of psychology, neurology, and psychiatry. In one extended figure he likens consciousness to a plant. The root is the will, the force behind the organic and inorganic worlds. The corona, the part of the plant above ground, is the intellect. The rhizome, where they meet, "would be the I, which as their common extreme point, belongs to both".[18] The morality of this I, this *moi,* is a morality of asceticism and compassion embodied in the selflessness of the saint, and in that sense, like other *moi*-related moralities, it is not conceived as being imposed by the collectivity.

Indeed Schopenhauer expressed the precedence of the individual over the collectivity in an especially striking way.

> In regard to knowledge of the true nature of mankind, I must concede a greater value to biographies, and particularly to autobiographies, than to history proper. . . . In history proper, it is not so much men that act as nations and armies, and the individuals who do appear seem to be so far off, surrounded by such pomp and circumstance, clothed in the stiff robes of state, or in heavy and inflexible armour, that it is really very difficult to discern human movement through it all. On the other hand, the truly depicted life of the individual in a narrow sphere shows the conduct of men in all its nuances and forms. . . . It is quite immaterial whether the objects on which the historical action hinges are, relatively speaking, farmhouses or kingdoms. For all these things are without significance in themselves. . . .[19]

It would be difficult to find a view more opposed to Durkheim's collectivism.

Finally, Gueth read the works of Edward von Hartmann, a philosopher of the later nineteenth century who added scientific and Darwinian views and vocabulary to Schopenhauer's metaphysics. For our purposes he added little to the currents already at work except a more naturalistic vision, the subjection of the *moi* to causal explanation drawn from, or at least inspired by, scientific explanation.

With von Hartmann we reach the world of Gueth himself, and of his contemporaries. One of his contemporaries was Sigmund Freud: not, that is, the legendary Freud, the solitary genius of psychoanalytic myth, but the revised Freud who has been shown to have exemplified his age and to have founded his teachings in those of his predecessors.[20] Freud's achievement must now be seen as having lain in his discovery – however credible that may now be in its details – of a single structure, a single causal description, of the individual mind in the individual body, answering as it were the puzzlement of Feuchtersleben in the previous century. This explanation was patterned on biology, for all that it has been represented as a new creation.[21] And of course von Hartmann and Schopenhauer, no less than the medical psychologists and biologists, are known to have exerted a decisive influence on Freud.

That Freud's version of the *moi* met with acceptance is explained partly by Bruner as the

> readiness of the Western world to accept a naturalistic explanation of organic phenomena and, concurrently, to be readier for such explanations in the mental sphere. There had been at least four centuries of uninterrupted scientific progress, recently capped by a theory of evolution that brought man into continuity with the rest of the animal kingdom.[22]

The other component of Freud's plausibility is of course the conviction that it is within the psychophysical individual that the search for important truths should be undertaken.

Another such contemporary writer who combined a concern with the *moi* and naturalistic explanation was William James, the philosopher and psychologist. In this company the Buddhist Gueth may seem incongruous, but in fact his version of Buddhism spoke directly to the same preoccupations which moved Freud and James. Buddhism is certainly a *moi* theory, focussing on the psychophysical individual and relating it to both a morality and a cosmic order. (I hasten to add that Buddhists do not believe this *moi* to be eternal or anything of the sort. It is not a soul, nor is it some Self with an upper-case *S*.) And Buddhism calls itself a *hetuphalavāda,* a teaching of causes and effects, conceived in a naturalistic way.

In his first publication after he became the monk Nyanatiloka, Gueth describes this naturalistic view of the psychophysical individual, embodied in the principle of dependent co-origination (*paṭicca samuppāda*), which goes something like this: the mechanism of both our attention and our habitual action leads to suffering. Though suffering is created by a complex interaction of various factors, at base it is founded on a deep propensity to craving, which leads us here and there mentally and physically, without our finding any lasting satisfaction. The habit of craving, moreover, is such that it reproduces itself, creating further mental states of craving. And not only that – craving also works within an overarching cosmic scheme of transmigration, death and rebirth, to create a further psychophysical individual after the death of the present one, so in that sense craving is seen to be the explanation not only of the nature and form of the mind but also, historically, of the body. This last of course seems to us least scientific, but the sort of explanation made of it is, in the fineness of its detail, still quite naturalistic.

This is how Nyanatiloka – as he must now be called – saw it:

> The (law of dependent co-origination) is the teaching of the strict conformity to law of everything that happens, whether in the realm of the physical or the psychical. It shows how the totality of phenomena, physical and mental, the entire phenomenal world, that depends wholly on the six

> senses, together with all suffering . . . is not the mere play of blind chance, but instead has an arising and an existence that are *conditioned*, that are dependent on pre-existing conditions. . . .[23]

The naturalistic vocabulary of this Nyanatiloka may owe to von Hartmann. But the point is that "the entire phenomenal world" here is that of the psychophysical individual, quite in keeping with Nyanatiloka's intellectual forebears and with the discourse on the *moi* which had come into being by the turn of the century. Aside from the exotic touch of the six senses, which include the mind as a sense, this could be a characterization of some relatively modern psychology or version of psychoanalysis.

So Nyanatiloka's version of Buddhism is, from one point of view, part of a recent chapter in the Western history of the *moi*. Though on the surface there are tremendous differences between such thinkers as Freud, James, and Nyanatiloka, beneath the surface they share what might be called a structure of plausibility, a similar set of preoccupations and similar views of what answers those preoccupations.

From another point of view, however, Nyanatiloka's is a careful and meticulously orthodox rendering into a European language and a European idiom of Buddhist thought. It is the idiom used by the most orthodox missionaries from Sri Lanka or Burma today. And in that respect his translation points not only to the Europe of the twentieth century, but to present-day Asia and indeed to the India of the fifth century B.C. when the Buddha propounded his views. This underlying structure of plausibility is by no means a parochial European obsession, but a far more widely distributed way of seeing. Mauss traced his *personne* through all continents and all ages. The same might be done for conceptions of the *moi*.

IV

Mauss himself had more to say about the psychophysical individual, however, than he revealed in the essay on the person, and he summarised his views by assigning some tasks to psychology and others to sociology. To psychology he assigned the explanation of two kinds of facts. First, it would explain purely psychoneurological phenomena. And second, it would show in detail how the collectivity exerted its force directly on the physiological individual through collective representations and through collectively determined habitual behaviour. He had, in other words, already prejudged a great deal.

In this matter of the direct effect of the collectivity upon the body of the individual there are certainly traces of that late nineteenth-century idea of the group mind, which, however, Mauss does not mention. For him the paradigm case seems to be rhythm, in which a group submerges the individual in itself. Addressing an audience of psychologists he spoke of rhythm's "obsessive character", of "the way it pursues those it has impressed".[24] He considered rhythm "the direct union of the sociological and the physiological".[25] And he went on to assert of both rhythm and collective symbols that "the general psychological fact appears so very distinctly because it is social; it is common to all those participating, and because it is common it is stripped of all its individual variants. In social facts you have a kind of natural laboratory experiment, abolishing the harmonics and, so to speak, leaving only the pure sound".[26] Mauss was even willing to speak of sociology as "collective psychology".[27] This was, however, no concession to psychology. For he still insisted that chief moral and explanatory value be awarded to the wholly englobing collectivity. The individual in his idiosyncracy is accidental to the real phenomenon, "the pure sound", the statistical individual as an instance, a refraction, of the collective.

Mauss is not entirely one-sided in this judgement, however. He also wrote that ". . . whatever the suggestive power of the collectivity, it always leaves the individual a sanctuary, his consciousness. . . ".[28] But even this is tempered by the remark that "it seems that between the social and the corporeal the layer of individual consciousness is very thin. . . ".[29] The overwhelming impression left by the bulk of his writings is that in human affairs a collectively transmitted and collectively received impulse, whether a symbol or a drumbeat, is directly transformed into the action of the individual.

But if we really take this to mean that collective representations or collective values are translated directly into action, such an idea is open to many objections. Insofar as collective representations do involve values – fraternal solidarity, say, or social justice – their translation into action by individuals is anything but straightforward. There is a great deal about human beings as mental and physical individuals – their fear of mortality, their conflicting desires, their simultaneous adherence to contradictory values – which resists or prevents such translation. Indeed, as Louis Dumont has pointed out on several occasions, what constitutes values as values, to be sought after and emulated, is the very fact that they are not automatically observed. Indeed, as Martin Hollis has argued in this volume, individuals as social actors must be considered to be separate from their social roles – their place in the collectivity – for otherwise it would be impossible to explain a good deal of human behaviour in circumstances of conflicting values. On these grounds it is impossible to wholly divorce our thought about the individual in social life from considerations of the "conscious personality" or the "spiritual and physical individuality", which Mauss at first set out to do in his essay on the person.

Mauss himself was aware of this. He wrote, as concerns "the civilized man of the higher castes of our civilizations and of a small number of other, earlier ones, oriental ones or backward ones", the following: "his intelligence, the will that follows from it, the postponement he imposes on the expression of his emotions, the way he dominates the latter, his critical faculty . . . prevent him from ever abandoning all his consciousness to the violent impulses of the moment".[30] This civilised man, in fact, acts "thanks to his education, to his concepts, to his deliberate choices". Part of the grounds on which such people act, to be sure, can be considered to be legal, and to that extent are part of the history of the *personne*. But this does not exhaust the systematic and culturally received systems for deliberate action. For there are also moral systems, views of the *moi* – Stoicism, Christianity, Buddhism – which are by no means legal, which recommend deliberate action, and which are not simply to be thought of in terms of collective representations weighing directly on the individual.

These *moi*-oriented moral systems are substantially different from the sort of collectively organised and collectively impressed representations which Mauss derives from his ideal type of the primitive society. For they have begun, not from an image of man in the primeval ritual dance, but from images of human beings alone: communing with Nature for the German Romantics, acting according to his own intrinsic human nature for the Stoics, meditating in the forest for Theravāda Buddhists, struggling in one's room in prayer for Protestant Christians. These certainly have their own social history. They have certainly produced Dionysian cults of subjection to the collective as well as the Apollonian moral constraint they overtly prescribe. They by no means lead us to reject the collectively conceived legal and political history of the *personne* which Mauss desiderates. But they do have their own development, their own logic, and their own relative autonomy. Insofar as they expressly set out some reflective and argued view of human mental and physical individuality, of how the individual should act, these systems cannot be considered apart from that individuality, as Mauss attempted to do. We must add the *moi* of these moral systems to Mauss's *personne* to render a picture more fully representative of our notions of the human being, and more truly faithful to the complexity of human experience.

V

How do the history of *personne* theories and the history of *moi* theories relate to each other? It is only by answering this question that we can gain a decisive understanding of why and how the two kinds of theory differ.

We must first be clear that neither of the two histories can now be thought of as a grand procession through history, after the fashion of Mauss's essay. We must think more of distinct episodes moving toward no very clear conclusion. One generalisation that might nevertheless be made is this: as concerns both *moi* and *personne* theories, there are those found in complex societies which simply could not be characteristic of a simple society. In the case of *moi* theories, for example, it seems inconceivable that the sort of abstracted and systematised views of Buddhism or Stoicism would be found among the Dinka, about whom Godfrey Lienhardt has written in this volume. There is at least one very good reason for this: the Dinka just do not have the full-time specialists who might devote themselves, generation after generation, to posing and answering increasingly subtle questions about such matters. Another general pattern seems to be that, once a relatively abstract version of the *moi* is devised, it is not easily lost. Like those other inventions, money and writing, such conceptions have great longevity. But beyond this general grain in the the episodes, a movement from simple societies to complex ones – and I have considered only cases from the latter so far – it is difficult to discern any very credible pattern.

There are two ways in which *moi* and *personne* views relate to each other. First, they influence each other. Mauss, for example, was able to argue that Stoic and Christian views of the *moi* influenced conceptions of the *personne*. We could in turn point out that legal notions of the Roman *persona* or the citizen contributed to the moral and psychological conception of the *moi* in Latin Stoicism and Latin Christianity. One could furthermore judge, in each episode, the relative weight of the *moi* and the *personne*. We might judge, for example, that however much Stoicism gave to the history of the *personne*, its main emphasis was on the *moi*.

And second, the two episodic histories relate to each other comparatively. For example, once we have accepted that the Classical world made great steps toward creating and defining the *personne*, and that India did the same for the *moi*, we must go on to give some account of why and how these two episodes differ from each other. That is perhaps the grandest sort of question to which we could hope to give a more or less cogent answer. And it is to that question I will address myself. How did ancient India and the Classical world differ, that they made such different and in some ways opposed contributions to the stock of human self-conceptions?

Mauss can give us a start here. For, as he points out, the development of the Roman version of the *personne,* the *persona,* was accomplished not only through changes in legal thought but also through socio-political experience, the development of the Roman Republic. The Roman *persona* was such, a matter of functions, honours, duties, and rights, precisely by virtue of being a citizen of a concretely conceived political group, a collectivity. As Mauss writes: "I believe that the revolt of the plebs, the right to full citizenship that . . . was gained by all the plebean members of the 'gentes', was decisive. All freemen of Rome were Roman citizens, all had a civil *'persona'*." If Mauss is correct in this judgement then he has put his finger on a specific moment at which some part of some human beings' self-consciousness changed decisively.

But of course this was not an isolated phenomenon of Roman history, for much of the Classical world had this sort of experience. The Greeks, too had their city-states, their citizens, and their constitutional changes which fostered consciousness of human beings as members of significant collectivities. In this respect Aristotle's dictum that man is a creature of the city-state quite accurately depicts a pervasive collective experience and collective representation in Antiquity. Indeed, if Stoicism and Christianity began as opposition views, espousing a vision of humanity which dwelt chiefly upon the individual in relation to an asocial natural or spiritual order, they were very soon infected with this official view. The late Stoic, Cicero, for example, notes that man's nature is to form civic associations; and Augustine portrays the Christian as a citizen of the City of God. In this perspective Durkheim and Mauss but represent an ancient and honourable tradition in Western civilisation.

But if we turn to India it is clear that this is by no means an inevitable development. True, there were oligarchic republics of a sort in ancient India, and perhaps had they survived they would have given rise to some view resembling Mauss's *personne.* But they did not. They disappeared from the Indian scene at about the time of the Buddha, when monarchical states engulfed them. The republics gave practically nothing to Indian thought about the political constitution, and Indian thought about such matters always assumed – which fairly represented the reality – that the political order was monarchical.

Moreover the Brahman theoreticians who elaborated the dominant theory of monarchy also held, and maintained throughout Indian history, the centre stage of social thought as well. (The Buddhists only contributed the idea that kings were subject to ethical considerations.) That social thought had no place for some sort of human *personne* as the bearer of moral rights and obligations as part of an ordered collectivity. Rather, the Brahmans propounded the view that human beings are divided into estates (*varṇa*), social categories the members of which are radically different from each other in their physical purity, their moral capabilities, and their social functions. This was the theoretical gloss on the Indian caste system. On the one hand, the individual was endowed with rights and obligations, not through his membership in the body politic, the state, but by virtue of birth among, and kinship with, a category of people who held those rights and obligations. It was kinship, not citizenship, membership of a social category, not of a state, that conferred status and function. And on the other hand, the state, in the person of the king, owed that individual nothing but the preservation of his already established traditional rights and status. Indeed the individual's status and function were referred not to the state, but past it, to the Brahmanical conception of the cosmic order. No emotion could be more alien to the ancient Indian world than patriotism, no concept more alien than that of the Western *personne*.

Nor can one imagine Indian kings countenancing much thought about such matters. But creative Indian thought about individual nature was free to move toward consideration of the *moi*. Any history of the early stages of this development must be at least as speculative as Mauss's history of the Roman *persona*, but in the interest of brevity I think it may be regarded as passing through four stages.

In the first stage we can dimly discern the sources of the Indian *moi* in the ancient pre-Buddhist Vedic sacrificial religion. This was the religion of a dominant group whose ethos was that of nomadic warriors, which in fact they had been at a yet earlier period. It seems consistent with such an ethos that the central religious rite, the sacrifice, was aimed at achieving the individual purposes of the sacrificer. It was for his own wealth, his own power, his own long life that he sacrificed, and only secondarily for any collective purpose, such as general fertility. Quite naturally a good deal of emphasis was laid on the physical and mental individuality of the sacrificer. His *moi*, or perhaps better his proto-*moi*, was conceived either in the image of the man with his limbs, identified in ritual with the cosmic man, the body of the universe; or as vital breath, identified in ritual with the sacrificial fire and with the sun or the wind. Here already the reference was made directly between the individual and the natural-spiritual order, without a place for an intervening category of society, as we have seen in other theories of the *moi*. Furthermore, the sacrifice was made more effective by the sacrificer knowing that his own breath was the sacrificial fire, or his own limbs the cosmic man.

In the second stage, still centuries before the Buddha, there seem to have evolved a body of devotees who concerned themselves more and more with this knowledge, and with ascetic techniques, techniques of *self*-mortification, which accompanied it.[31] Their gradual formation as a distinct group also involved an increasing concern with otherworldly purposes, with aims not so crassly material as those of the sacrificial religion itself. They were concerned with the construction through ritual knowledge of an immortal self, in the world beyond or after death. This involved moreover subtler and increasingly elaborate thought about the nature of what was now becoming an autonomous spiritual world. Indeed, the formation of a group of devotees and the elaboration of an esoteric knowledge must have gone hand in hand: for the knowledge was so far still authenticated by its being in the hands of a chosen few, while the chosen few were distinguished partly by their initiation into the knowledge. Indian society was growing more complex.

The really decisive step came in the third stage, perhaps not very long before the Buddha, when these amateurs became full-time renouncers who left the world of family and kinship, of production and reproduction, of caste, to concern themselves solely with their own Selves. Here three vital steps were taken. First, the esoteric knowledge began to take on a systematic appearance, with its own internal coherence and a new capability of being formulated as propositions to be affirmed or denied. We might best think of this as the development of a theory with its own theoretical entities and logic, lying behind the appearances of the human world much as scientific theories point to entities and a logic behind the appearances of the physical world. These were theories of moral causation, objectively conceived laws which decreed that the moral quality of personal acts in this life affect the nature of one's rebirth in the next life.

Second, the chief theoretical entity of this new thought was the Self, the *moi* proper, now abstracted from ritual thought and ritual identifications and given a potentially universal sense, as being found not only in human beings as such but, in some theories, in other living beings as well. And third, this knowledge was now no longer merely that of received esoteric truths. It had become an introspective knowledge that apprehended the Self through an internal intellective faculty.

At this stage all these developments were certainly not fully worked out. But in the fourth stage, which includes the Buddha, this thought about the Self, about objective introspection, and about moral causation gave rise to one of the most creative periods of thought in human history, comparable to the development of Greek thought through Socrates, Plato, and Aristotle. It was a period of debate, of the cultivation of abstract argument and logical criteria for argument. It was assumed, above all by Buddhism, that human beings necessarily have the faculties to find these arguments true or false as regards themselves. Propositions about the nature of the Self and of moral causation were increasingly couched in what Basil Bernstein has called an "elaborated code", a language capable of existing apart from the speaker and his immediate context, capable of speaking beyond local social divisions and to posterity. Here there appeared theories of the *moi* which were universal in the sense that they referred abstractly to human nature as such, and did so in a language that enabled them to be transported across frontiers. If abstraction and portability are the criteria of maturity in this Indian episode of the *moi,* then Buddhism was the most mature of these theories. It was eventually disseminated throughout Asia and to the West.

A good deal of this maturity of Buddhism can be found in the rigour with which it pursued its cause-and-effect argument concerning the *moi.* For it was Buddhism which proposed the theory of dependent co-origination, a thorough and thoroughly abstract conception of the individual mind and body. This cause-and-effect view underpins the characteristic Buddhist teaching of *anattā,* non-self, which directly contradicted other views, current at the time, of the indissoluble and eternal nature of the Self. In the Buddhist view the human *moi* can be shown to be causally composed to form what appears to be a unitary unchanging self, but which is in reality an evanescent and perpetually changing complex. Mauss objected that this in effect dissolved the *moi.* But, to the contrary, it certified the *moi* as the central concern of human existence, an area subject to systematic thought and systematic self-discipline. If Roman law constituted one decisive step in abstract thought about humans as persons in a collectivity, Buddhism constituted a decisive step in human thought about humans in relation to their mental and physical individuality.

One can sympathize with Mauss, for the doctrine of non-self certainly seems a shaky support for ethics or morality, for a view of the individual in relation to others. But in fact the Buddhist view is one which is at heart moral as well as universalistic. True, the analysis of the *moi* is aimed at one's own purposes. One is to regard the constituents of one's individuality and individual experience from the viewpoint of what is skilful (*kusala*), cleaving to those states of consciousness and those acts which conduce to one's own peace and well-being, and avoiding those which are unskilful. There is nothing moral in this. But this description of states of mind and acts – skilful and unskilful – is in Buddhism always fundamentally linked to another description of states of mind and acts: whether they are good or evil (*puñña* or *pāpa*). In fact the word "skilful" in Buddhism always embraces both meanings, morally good and psychologically wholesome. What is well, skilfully, done for oneself is the same as what is good, well done for others.

The reasoning behind this is that, first, all beings wish well for themselves. Second, the form of that well-wishing is that they desire peace, security, freedom from harm or anxiety. Therefore, third, by acting to secure others' peace and well-being, the others will respond in like manner. What is good for me is good for you as well, and vice-versa; we all share the same precarious plight, between birth and death, subject to forces beyond our control. The Buddhist analysis of the *moi* is one which is profoundly moral and social, but the society which it envisages is that of all living beings interacting face to face, each action of one individual affecting the welfare of another individual as well as his own.

It is not difficult to connect this version of moral causation with the social experience of the ancient Indians. The India of the Buddha was witnessing the rapid expansion of monarchical states, and many other forms of rapid social change as well. So hitherto significant ordered collectivities, and the individuals within them, were no longer able to construe or to guide their own fate. Part of the rapid social change as well was the growth of cities and of a cosmopolitan culture with an increasingly complex division of labour. The Brahmanical doctrine of estates did attempt to embrace this change, but it was bound to the conception that all individuals possessed rights and duties by virtue of belonging to an hereditary functional category, and that the rights and duties of individuals toward one another were prescribed by their respective categories. But these theoretical categories could by no means comprehend the complexity of social relations then growing up. There was therefore room for theories, such as the Buddha's, which provided a criterion by which all individuals, regardless of their category or caste, could interact according to their universal sentient nature. It is typical of Buddhism that it accepted as given the existence of both kings and the social categories of the Brahmanical doctrine, while insisting that the behaviour of individuals, whether king or not, whatever their category, be subject to the universal moral criteria of good and evil. Buddhism was the very type of a mature *moi* theory, an opposition view which dwelt upon human mental and physical individuality in respect of the morally conceived social interaction of such individuals within a natural-spiritual order.

VI

To call Buddhism an opposition view is to draw attention to the fact that it existed in a rich and varied environment of conflicting viewpoints. Though it is now impossible to reconstruct the Buddha's world at all accurately, one can trace in ancient India a long-standing and deeply-felt opposition between Brahmanical theorists of society and theorists of the *moi* such as the Buddha. Similarly, the Germany of Schopenhauer supported Hegel as well, whose emphasis lay wholly upon the *personne.* In that case we do know that they contended directly with one another. These sorts of complex society make available such rich and disparate experiences to their members that both *moi* and *personne* theories can flourish in them. Indeed the very robustness of a *moi* theory such as the Buddha's or the *personne* theory of a Hegel, presupposes a spirited opposition on the other side.

But neither side in such a debate can embrace the whole truth about human behaviour. Certainly a collectivist sociology such as Mauss's cannot, for it can never fully comprehend the place and representation of the psychophysical individual in social and cultural life, or in history.

The notion of the *personne* opens one window on human nature, while the notion of the *moi* opens another, and the two views are not easily reconciled. Charles Taylor, in his chapter, suggests that we consider each individual at birth to be inducted into a great conversation. But the problem is that each individual is inducted into several great conversations, at least in the complex societies, and these conversations have different matter and different rules for what constitutes an interlocutor. In some the interlocutor is a mind or soul, in others a citizen. For so long as one can take a different view as a mind or soul than as a citizen – so long, for example, as one can object conscientiously to the political order – these conversations will remain separate.

Notes

1. D.G. Charlton, *Secular Religions in France, 1815–1870,* Oxford University Press, 1973, especially pp. 65–95.
2. Steven Lukes, *Individualism,* Basil Blackwell, Oxford, 1973.
3. Charlton, *op. cit.,* pp. 38–64.
4. *Ibid.*

5. E. Durkheim, *The Elementary Forms of Religious Life,* Allen and Unwin, London, 1915 (first French edition, 1912), p. 18.
6. E. Durkheim, "L'Individualisme et les Intellectuels", *Revue Bleu,* 4e Série, no. 10, 1898, pp. 7–13. Translated in S. Lukes, "Durkheim's 'Individualism and the Intellectuals'," *Political Studies,* Vol. XVII, No. 1, 1969, pp. 14–30. The reference is to this translation.
7. Michael Carrithers, *The Forest Monks of Sri Lanka, an Anthropological and Historical Study,* Oxford University Press, Delhi, 1983.
8. Quoted in Bruford, *The German Tradition of Self-Cultivation,* Cambridge University Press, 1975, p. 110.
9. See L.L. Whyte, *The Unconscious Before Freud,* Tavistock, London, 1963; and Henri Ellenberger, *The Discovery of the Unconscious,* Basic Books, New York, 1970.
10. Ernst, Freiherr von Feuchtersleben, *The Principles of Medical Psychology,* The Sydenham Society, London, 1847 (Vienna, 1845).
11. Ernst, Freiherr von Feuchtersleben, *The Dietetics of the Soul,* London, 1852 (Vienna, 1838).
12. Richard Hunter and Ida McAlpine, *Three Hundred Years of Psychiatry,* Oxford University Press, 1963, p. 951.
13. Feuchtersleben, *Dietetics,* p. 15.
14. *Ibid.,* p. 16.
15. *Ibid.,* p. 154.
16. *Ibid.,* p. 139.
17. Feuchtersleben, *Medical Psychology,* p. 15.
18. A. Schopenhauer, *The World as Will and Representation,* trans. E.F.J. Payne, Dover Books, New York, 1969, Vol. II, p. 203.
19. *Ibid.,* Vol. I, p. 247.
20. Iago Galdston goes so far as to write: "Had Freud never lived and never labored . . . psychiatric knowledge, psychiatric theory, and psychiatric practice would in all vital essentials not have been any different from what they are currently." In the context this is in aid of showing how orthodox Freud really was. From "Freud and Romantic Medicine", in Cioffi, ed., *Freud: Modern Judgments,* Macmillan, London, 1973, p. 120.
21. See the excellent book by Frank Sulloway, *Freud, Biologist of the Mind,* Burnett Books, New York, 1979.
22. J. Bruner, "Freud and the Image of Man", in Cioffi, ed., *op. cit.*
23. Nyanatiloka Thera, *The Word of the Buddha,* privately published, London, 1914, pp. 65–6.
24. M. Mauss, *Sociology and Psychology,* trans. Ben Brewster, Routledge & Kegan Paul, London, 1979, p. 22.
25. *Ibid.,* p. 22.
26. *Ibid.,* p. 23.
27. *Ibid.,* p. 9.
28. *Ibid.,* p. 10.
29. *Ibid.,* p. 10.
30. *Ibid.,* p. 28.
31. For evidence on this see H.W. Bodewitz, *Jaiminīya Brāhmaṇa I,* 1–65, E.J. Brill, Leiden, 1973; and the same author's *The Daily Evening and Morning Offering According to the Brahmaṇas,* E.J. Brill, Leiden, 1976. Otherwise the movement from earlier to later is to be read in the contrast between the purely sacrificial and the truly renunciant sections of the *Upaniṣads,* the *Chāndogya* and the *Bṛhadāraṇyaka.*

12

The person

Charles Taylor

I

What do we mean by a person? Certainly an agent, with purposes, desires, aversions, and so forth. But obviously more than this because many animals can be considered agents in this sense, but we don't consider them persons.

So generally philosophers consider that to be a person in the full sense you have to be an agent with a sense of yourself as an agent, a being which can thus make plans for your life, one who also holds values in virtue of which different such plans seem better or worse, and who is capable of choosing between them.

On our normal unreflecting view, all these powers are those of an individual. It is the individual who can form life plans, who already has a sense of himself as an agent, whose values are normally the determining ones, and who chooses. Many things, of course, can go wrong: we all need a long period of development and tutelage by others in order to become fully adult persons. And many things can go wrong on the way: some fail altogether; and perhaps most of us fail to some degree to become fully adult persons in this sense. But this is what we normally grow towards.

But we are aware at the same time that other times and places didn't share our conception of the individual, or of the person. We know that this is an historical creation. Some writers have claimed that men of earlier epochs didn't have the same notion of the unity of the subject (Bruno Snell, for example); others argue that they differ in that the subject is not fully distinct from the cosmos surrounding him (again Snell, also Foucault). These construals have sometimes analogies to conditions we consider pathologies today. But we can't understand these earlier conceptions simply as illness.

What we need ideally is a theory of the subject which can allow us to understand these various views; how different views can be dominant at different times, and how ours could become dominant, and perhaps irreversibly so, with the development of modern civilisation. In the best outcome, we should also be able to understand why our modern conception tends to make other views incomprehensible to us, or at least very opaque.

1

We should first try to clarify what is involved in this package of capacities typical of a person: making life plans, holding values, choosing. We may think that the crucial factor underlying them is consciousness: consciousness of self, of a time-scale beyond the present, of alternate possibilities. And there is obviously something in this. But we will fall too easily into one of the blind spots of the modern understanding of the subject if we are too quickly satisifed with this answer. For one thing the phenomenon of consciousness itself is not all that unproblematic.

I want to say something first about agency. What is it to be an agent? We might start off by saying, a being who encompasses purposes, who can be said to go after, and sometimes attain goals. But what does this involve? Just having behaviour which meets a certain pattern in a regular way doesn't amount to fulfilling the purpose of realising this pattern. Old Faithful spouts water every *n* minutes, but this doesn't make it an agent with the corresponding purpose.

Agency obviously has something to do with what underlies the pattern, what brings about, the causal background. But here two theories part company. According to one, we can speak of purpose when the end sought plays some role in explaining the action. And this is the case, for instance, when the entity concerned is guided by some element of feedback connected with the end concerned. Thus a self-guided missile is designed so that its path is controlled by its direction and distance from a target of a certain description. One way of stating the way in which the information fed back controls the path of the missile is to identify what the target is. In this sense the end sought figures in the explanation.

This view marks no difference of principle between the animate and the inanimate. The difference between human and missile would be seen, first as one of complexity, and secondly, as residing in consciousness: we are aware of ourselves and missiles presumably aren't. But between missiles and lower animals to whom we don't attribute consciousness, there is no difference of principle.

The alternative view, which I want to defend, does make a distinction of principle between animal and artefact. This distinction can best be brought out by noting the way in which we attribute action terms to the two kinds of things.

First of all, we should see that we use the same terms very often to describe an action in one case, and a non-action in aother. Old Faithful spouts water every *n* minutes; but so may George be turning on his hose at regular intervals in order to water his flowers. The planets sweep out equal areas in equal times, and so may some human agent; and so on. We recognize clearly that the use of these terms in the inanimate cases doesn't involve actions.

One way of marking this distinction is to note that in the inanimate case, there is no way of saying that this is what they're really doing. Every event can bear a great number of descriptions: Old Faithful is also wetting some particular area of forest, displacing molecules, releasing some underground pressure, stabilizing the water table, amusing tourists, increasing Wyoming's revenues, etc. We recognise that there is nothing in the process itself which privileges one of these descriptions over any other. It is our interest, the way the phenomenon strikes us, which determines the description to be applied.

But in the case of genuine action, descriptions are not all on the same footing. There is a hierarchy of privilege. As I type, I am also displacing air, raising the noise level in the house, wearing out typewriter ribbons, increasing the custom of our local typing supplies shop, and so on. But what I'm *doing* is writing a paper on the person. This is not to say that the other descriptions don't apply to my action; but that we recognise hierarchy of privilege. These descriptions enjoy very different status in the kingdom of action. Some only make it accompanied by a qualification like 'unwittingly', 'inadvertently', 'unintentionally'. 'Displacing air' above has such a lowly status. Others may be attributed without qualifiers (e.g., 'raising the noise level') but are recognised as being subordinate to a range of higher ones ('writing a paper on *X*', 'explaining my views on *X*') which describe my action properly and informatively. These give the ends to which it was directed.

We can establish this hierarchy of privilege, because we see my action in the context of purposes. We see it as directed to certain goals. Now in the case of artefacts, there seems to be something analogous. We are ready to hierarchise descriptions applying to them as well. The computer also hums, heats up the room, and so on, but what it is really doing is calculating the payroll; the thermostat also clicks, brings about alternative expansion and contraction of the column of mercury, decreases our dependence on Middle-East oil. But what it's really doing is keeping the temperature of the house at 20° C.

Hence we may be tempted to class artefacts with us over against geysers and planets. But this is to miss the crucial difference: that this hierarchisation is purely derivative in the case of artefacts. The purposes which form the context against which we rank their action descriptions are our own; that is, those which are implicit in the design of the artefacts or their regular use. There is no way of answering a question about the artefact's purpose except by reference to design/use. Concerning a human agent regulating the heat in his house by raising and lowering the flow of fuel, we can ask whether he is also trying to reduce his country's dependence on oil from the Gulf. We are asking whether this ought to figure among the most privileged descriptions; and this is to ask whether he is also acting out of this patriotic purpose, or just to reduce his bills, or be comfortable. The corresponding question about an artefact either makes no sense, or it can only be answered by reference to the policy context of its design/use. Say the government imposed thermostats in homes previously regulated manually, in order to free the country from economic blackmail, then someone who said 'these things are freeing us from the sheikhs' might be taken as offering a privileged description.

In the human case, the purposes are intrinsic, in that of the artefact derivative. So the second view is one that sees an agent as a subject of intrinsic purpose. It is not sufficient just that the end figure in the explanation: the action must be directed in this intrinsic sense.

It will be helpful to introduce a term of art here. When we attribute intrinsic purpose to an agent, we can say that we are saying that something – here the end sought – has a certain significance for him. Real agents can thus be described with this term, as beings for whom things can have significance; and this is what differentiates them from artefacts. 'Significance' is acting as a term of art for me, because of course, we could also apply it to artefacts. For example, we could speak of the significance for my car of sand in the gasoline, or of a big rock which was teetering on the bluff above it.

But naturally here, the same point holds as above. The significances in this case would be derived. The rock is a danger to my car, it threatens to crush it. That is its significance. But this is only a danger to the car qua artefact; qua collection of metal and glass bits it merely bodes rearrangement. It is only in the light of the derivative purpose intrinsic to its design that the rock threatens disaster.

I recognise this derivative use, but I want to apply 'significance' only to intrinsic significance. So it will be a mark of agents. I want to use it as a highly general term as well, so that we can say not only agents' purposes, but also their desires, aspirations, feelings, aversions, emotions represent different ways in which things have significance for them.

I could use fewer syllables, and say an agent is a being to whom things matter. 'Mattering' would then be my key term. But I want a term I can use as a count noun; and you can speak of 'significances' (barely), but not of 'matterings'.

Now I have distinguished these two different views of agency, one of which makes central the significance feature, because it makes a difference when we go on to work out a theory of the person.

A person, as we saw above, we conceive of as a special kind of agent, an agent-plus, who can also make life-plans, hold values, choose. The two views of agency make us see this 'plus' in different terms. For the first view, which ignores the significance feature, the crucial difference is consciousness, a power to form inner representations. This means that I can represent to myself different life plans, hence consider different options, and envisage the different possibilities as more or less valuable.

But if we are aware of the significance feature, what is striking about being a person is not simply consciousness in this sense. Rather we should say that consciousness goes along with a transformation of the significances we live by; and this leads to a view of man as a self-interpreting animal.

Perhaps this last point can be relatively easily brought out by reflecting on common experience. We often have it happen that our becoming more aware of what we feel alters what we feel. We overcome some confused feeling of guilt for instance, and are now clearer on what it was that was troubling us. We see that the grounds for guilt were inadequate, and we now *feel* differently about it. Even if we go on feeling guilty in some sense, the feeling is different just because we now understand it as something irrational. Or again, when we sort out different feelings we have for the same person, two different ways in which she was important to us, our experience of them may be different. One may atrophy relatively easily while the other remains, for instance.

What emerges from this is that how things are with us, in this case what we feel and are inclined to do, is not something separable from our understanding of it. How we understand it and are aware of it is constitutive of how we feel. We can't interpret this consciousness on the model of a representation, where this means representation of some independent reality. For there is nothing here which our awareness of our feelings could represent in this sense. There is no core of feeling *an sich,* separable from how we understand it.

The view which takes account of this I have called the view of man as self-interpreting animal because the understandings we have of ourselves are not arbitrary construals. To say that what we feel is partly constituted by our understanding is not to say that thinking makes it so. Our understandings reflect what seems to us to be the truth about what we feel. This may indeed be wrong. We have all sorts of motives to conceal the truth from ourselves on many occasions. And we are at least dimly aware of this, and hence often uncertain about our true feelings.

Thus to say that our understanding is constitutive of what we feel is not to deny that there is a right and a wrong, or at least a more and a less adequate here. What it does mean is that there can be false, or inauthentic, or confused, or self-deluded *feelings.* The inter-penetration of feeling and understanding means that we sometimes need quasi-epistemic terms, like the above, to give an adequate description of how we feel (although in some cases, we may only be able to apply them retrospectively).

That is the force of the term 'interpretation'. The understanding we have of ourselves is not some arbitrarily applied descriptive term, but an attempt to interpret how things are with us, something which is rarely entirely clear, and needs to be made clearer. The attempt to understand can be seen as analogous to that to interpret enigmatic texts; hence the root metaphor of hermeneutical views of man and science.

This view of man as a self-interpreting animal obviously fits with the notion of an agent as a being with the significance feature. That things are significant for a creature does not require, obviously, that that creature be conscious; at least not in the strong sense that we attribute consciousness to humans. Animals are beings with the significance feature, and numbers of things matter to us that we haven't focussed or formulated.

But that something is significant to *A* requires that in some way *A* be sensitive to this. Becoming conscious of the significance of some *X* to us alters our mode of sensitivity to *X*. And since our sensitivity to *X* is part of its having significance for us, we can see how consciousness can transform significance.

By contrast, the other view which sees consciousness as purely representative cannot explain how awareness can be constitutive of how we feel. The very notion of representation requires that of an independent object. We can see how this kind of consciousness would alter how we operate, because we can now envisage certain possibilities, as, for example, about the distant future, and we can ascribe evaluations. We can thus direct our activity in a much more effective way, and towards more complex and far-reaching ends. This is certainly part of what we require of a person, because we do consider that a crucial characteristic is being able to choose in the light of different life-plans. But it concentrates purely on the executive side of this requirement. We can see easily how representative consciousness is necessary for *planning* one's life to any end. But what isn't clear is how moving from unconscious agency to personhood affects the ends we seek themselves; or in our jargon, transforms the significances things have for us.

But I think something like this is involved in being a person. And we can only get at this by seeing persons as self-interpreting beings. Hence I have wanted to insist on a view of agency as involving the significance feature. Let me therefore continue and see where this leads.

2

The general conception of a person has a certain reflexive element. A person is an agent who has an understanding of self as an agent, and can make plans for his/her own life; this, as against a dog for instance, to whom this kind of reflexivity can't be attributed. But this shouldn't be seen simply as consisting in superior powers of representation: that dogs can only be aware of the objects that surround them immediately, while persons can also have themselves for object, as well as future states of self and world. This way of sorting things out would make the crucial difference turn on the objects that our awareness can be of, what we can represent in inner space as it were.

But this doesn't seem to be the crucial difference. Rather what seems important about a person's conception of self is that it incorporates a range of significances which have no analogue with non-person agents. For it is not just that we are aware of ourselves as agents that distinguishes us from dogs, say, It is more that we have a sense of certain standards which apply to us as self-aware agents.

Let us take shame as an example, because it will serve to make a number of the points I want to argue for. A human being who can feel shame differs from a dog (or if we want to get anthropomorphic about dogs, substitute wolf) not just in that he has an awareness of significances that have the dog does not, these remaining the same; rather shame involves a significance of a radically different kind.

I am ashamed when I am shown up as contemptible or unworthy before others. (We can derivatively be ashamed in our own eyes, at least we of this highly individualistic, interiorizing civilisation can be; but this is always secondary; the primary locus of shame is before others, in public space.) This means not only that I must be self-aware in order to be conscious of what is shameful about me. It is also that what is shameful can only be explained in terms of an awareness of the person: for the shame of my situation is partly constituted by my appearing unworthy in public space. Moreover, the unworthiness is one which essentially attaches to a self-aware being. A dog (or wolf) just couldn't be unworthy in this sense. A being can only be shamefully unworthy who is capable of a sense of shame, that is, who is sensitive to the standards which hold of a self-aware subject, and which demand that he show concern for his dignity and his good name, in short, for his standing among men.

In other words, shame as a significance for a person, unshared by non-personal agents, shows the difference between the two not just to reside in the person's greater awareness, or self-awareness. It is not as though the person were aware of something which could have just as well been there before with the animal. Rather, the significance the person is aware of is something new, something that could only be a significance for a person, for it concerns standards which only apply to a being who is self-aware, and moreover who shares this awareness of his personhood with others.

We can see this best if we contrast it with other significances which do hold quite unproblematically of animals, although beyond their ken. The chicken in the barnyard which I feed is in real danger for her life. She is being fattened for dinner one day. Her lack of reasoning faculty and time perspective forbid her ever knowing this until it's too late, but the danger is there nonetheless.

By contrast, the self-awareness involved with shame is not just a matter of some independent significance which is now in our ken; it is rather a significance bound up with our being self-aware beings, that is, persons. The same goes for pride (closely linked to shame), for dignity; for guilt – arising here from the sense of a breach of moral standards, which only hold of me qua responsible, self-aware agent; for the sense of worthiness and for that whole host of emotions which are qualified by a reflective sense of their importance in our lives – for example, my love for *A* which I sense as the one really good thing in my life, my feelings of estrangement from *R* which is based on my shame at having treated him shabbily, and so on.

In other words, we have to understand the step from sub-personal agent to person not just as an increase in consciousness in the sense of the power to form representations of self and world, but much more as the onset of a range of significances which are essentially those of self-aware agents. Our self-consciousness doesn't offer us a representation of these significances; rather it is partly constitutive of them, for they concern standards holding of persons qua persons, and which can only be understood within the life of a person.

This last point should be expanded a little. One could think of a standard which would apply to self-aware agents even within the compass of a thoroughly representative theory of consciousness. Thus if we think of consciousness as representation, we could think of a self-aware being, one who had representations of his own representations, as well as of his own activities. It would be a being who could monitor himself. And we could easily form an idea of a standard which would apply to this being qua self-aware, which is that he form correct representations, that he monitor himself well. This would undoubtedly reflect itself in his performance, his ability to guide action, etc. This kind of excellence could also be found among self-monitoring machines (although applied in a derivative sense, to be sure).

But this is not a standard of the kind I have been invoking above, in discussing shame and the other characteristically human emotions. For it doesn't involve an original significance which attaches only to persons. It invokes the standard involved in representation, which applies equally to beings who register only their surroundings and have no self-awareness, and extends this to self-awareness. But with shame, we have a significance which only makes sense in relation to persons, to agents who are aware of themselves. These are standards which apply to persons, and which arise essentially out of what it is to be a person. They cannot be constructed out of standards that apply to sub-personal agents.

There is in fact a reciprocal relation between personhood and the characteristically human significances; they are essentially connected both ways. We couldn't attribute these significances to any being that couldn't be aware of himself as an agent, and hence was a person at least in this sense, but at the same time we wouldn't recognise as a person a being who was constitutionally incapable (and not just in fact pathologically incapacitated) of experiencing shame, guilt, a sense of dignity, or other emotion).

Thus the step from sub-personal agent to person involves not just self-awareness, but a range of significances which could only be those of a self-aware being, and which help to define the kind of self-aware agent that we call a person.

Because these significances are essentially bound up with self-awareness we can see more clearly why the corresponding feelings are shaped by our understanding of them.

3

The general notion of a person includes not only self-awareness but holding values. And this too is very differently conceived by the two traditions. For the representative view, persons apply values to the facts and possibilities of which they are aware. These values can be seen as chosen, or as arising from psychological causes, or as both. But in any case, to evaluate is to confer value on what is originally neutral domain.

But the significance view sees it very differently. Establishing the significance of *X* is not establishing a neutral fact about it. Moreover the particular significances which I called characteristically human involve strong evaluation. By strong evaluation, I mean the recognition of goods which are seen to be intrinsically worthy, that is, goods or ends which are not valued insofar as they are objects of choice or desire, but are rather seen as ends we should seek. They are ends such that our not choosing them reflects on us rather than undermining their status as ends.

The values which underly such emotions as shame, guilt, or our sense of dignity are plainly of this kind. The shameless man is not someone to whom the whole range of judgements concerning the shameful no longer applies, but on the contrary one who is judged even more harshly. Again, the man who feels no guilt at some terrible action is even more to be condemned (or perhaps pitied). Shamelessness is shameful, because one is even farther away from the standard involved if one has no sense of what is demanded.

By contrast, if I cease to like strawberry ice cream, this is the end of the road for this flavour of ice cream as an object of value for me. There is no further purchase for an ought statement enjoining me to go on liking it and choosing it. Or perhaps there might be, and this is revelatory. If we take a less trivial example, I might be condemned or looked down on for my taste in cars, in interior decoration, for my sense of humour. But this will be because taste is seen as an important part of what makes a human life worthwhile; it will be the object of admiration, contempt; something of which one should be ashamed or proud.

These human significances involve strong evaluation. But they cannot be construed as evaluations we apply to a neutral realm of facts. On the contrary, as we saw above, they are the objects of interpretations, which can be judged as adequate or inadequate, distorting or true, superficial or profound. My finding something shameful is not a matter of my deciding to apply, or even finding I cannot but apply some value predicate to a neutral domain. This is not what the issue looks like at all when I want to ask whether I should feel ashamed at such and such a situation.

I don't ask whether I really feel like applying the evaluation; I ask rather whether this is really shameful. Moreover, I conduct this enquiry through a series of other terms: 'unworthy', 'cowardly', 'petty', 'incompetent', and so on, which are themselves 'evaluative', but which equally well cannot be construed as applied to a neutral domain of facts. For each of them will have criteria which have the same basic logic.

These significances which involve strong evaluation are the object of assessments, where we try to get clear what is really shameful, what one should really be guilty about, in what consists real dignity, what is truly admirable, what contemptible, and so on.

The two views of what is involved in being a person thus diverge quite markedly. For one perspective, which takes no account of significance, consciousness is seen as forming representations. These are of the world or the self, and take as their content either neutral fact, or at best things in the significance they have for us as sub-personal agents, as living or sentient beings. The characteristically human significances are then understood as valuations which we put on facts and possibilities so represented. Guided by these valuations, we choose. And so we have the capacities definitive of a person: self-awareness, values, choice; and from all these the ability to make life-plans.

What gets lost from view here is the nature of the peculiarly human significances. Why are these specially hard to see? What makes us shy away from them? The answer is partly rooted in the epistemological tradition which has been so important in shaping our understanding of modern science. At the very beginning of the scientific revolution, in the seventeenth century, the attempt was made to overcome the purely anthropocentric, and to understand the world in terms which were not relative to our subjectivity. Properties can be said to be anthropocentric or relative, if they are properties that things can only have insofar as they are objects in the experience of subjects, or human subjects. The classical examples of seventeenth-century discussion were the secondary properties. Colour, for instance, was a property of things only insofar as they are experienced by sighted creatures. In a universe without sighted creatures, there would still be light reflected off surfaces at different wave lengths, but there wouldn't be what we know as colour.

It is clear that significances are anthropocentric properties of things in this sense. There is thus a built-in mistrust of them in our scientific tradition. But why does this mistrust affect particularly the peculiarly human significances? Why does it tolerate more easily the sub-personal ones, those which apply to living beings as such or sentient beings as such?

There are two, I think, connected answers. The first is that the human ones involve strong evaluation. A science which uses the language of the human significances is one which is involved in evaluating different ways of living. It is part of the debate about what the real nature of these significances are, which rages in our society and will probably never cease. But science in our dominant tradition sees itself as value free, as capable of inter-subjective validation and agreement regardless of value differences. Thus one *must* be able to finesse the language of the human significances.

Of course, it is part of the data of a human science that people *feel* this way about things, for they feel guilty, ashamed, see their dignity as consisting in *X* or *Y*. But this must be capable of redescription in order to fit into a science. In describing what subjects *A* finds shameful, one cannot simply take over his strongly evaluative vocabulary. We have to identify criteria for the shameful or the unworthy or whatever in some neutral language. (Of course, interpretivists immediately want to challenge whether this is possible, whether one does not either miss what is essential to this society's discriminations, or doesn't rather make them intelligible just because one can read the significances so well through the 'neutral' descriptions – or thinks one can, for nothing is easier than unconscious ethnocentricity here. But I leave all this aside; I'm just trying to explain the rival position.) And so we get the view of things which redescribes significances in terms of neutral descriptions and evaluations.

The second reason why the human significances are particularly mistrusted is that we can believe a priori that those having to do with life and sentience can be more easily reduced in terms of a physical or physiological language. As a living being things can have the significance for me of being good for health, say, or mortally dangerous; as a sentient being, they can threaten pain or offer pleasure. There is a widespread belief in our scientific culture that necessary and sufficient conditions can be given for these in, say, physiological terms. We can be precise in what such-and-such a substance is good/bad for health; why such an event would be lethal; why the application of this treatment is painful, and so on. No doubt much of this is well founded (though whether it is across the board is another matter that we don't need to examine here).

In this, vital and sentient significances differ from the human ones. It is just evident that it is hopeless to try to offer necessary and sufficient conditions in physical/physiological terms for a situation's being shameful, or guilt-provoking, or an insult to dignity, or for an action's being admirable, and so on. It is clear that the shameful, for instance, doesn't correspond to any natural kind on the physical level, or range of natural kinds; whereas toothache may well do so.

By contrast, vital and sentient significances aren't the locus of strong evaluations. Few motives are stronger or more immediate than the desire to preserve life and to avoid pain. But these ends are not such that of themselves they are seen as commanding our allegiance, so that someone who was ready to give up his life or undergo pain would be ipso facto condemnable. On the contrary – for these self-sacrificing actions to be condemnable, we need a context provided by human significances. We feel disapproval, even contempt for the professional martyr, who is looking for suffering out of a desire for self-dramatisation or to assuage misplaced guilt. But in order to express what is contemptible here, we have to invoke the human significances.

Of course, the reducibility of vital and sentient significances wouldn't mean that we had made clear in physiological terms what *matters* here. We would just have offered criteria, necessary and sufficient conditions for a significance holding. But imagine the following thought experiment: a sapient race comes from Alpha Centauri. They are large gaseous clouds somehow endowed with sapience. They are not living organisms in our sense but they understand, and care about things in their own (to us incomprehensible) way. They might come to understand that some process, for example, electric shock, had some significance for us, they would perhaps understand that this significance was negative, provided they saw us as sapient, and thus took our avoidance of it as purposeful. They might be able to understand the physiological conditions of this being unpleasant, that is to say, something we want to avoid, so they could identify thresholds. But just what the experience of pain was would forever be beyond them.

There is something irredeemably opaque about any range of significances for those who don't share them. We have something of this experience as well within the human significances and these vary from culture to culture, as I want to discuss more below. People from another society can be quite opaque to us; only in our case, there is an in-principle remedy. We are capable, at least theoretically, of learning another language and becoming inducted into another way of life; and then we can understand.

In any case, the reducibility of the vital and sentient has been the basis for one of the pervasive trends in the history of social science, the attraction of materialism. The Marxist case is the clearest, the most 'upfront'. A theory is thought to be 'materialist' because it deals with motivations at its bottom level of explanation, which belong to the vital range of significance. At base, what moves men is getting what they need to live. The rest, various conceptions of honour, morality, blessedness, and so on, is to be understood derivatively, and frequently as a confused or mystified way of coming to grips with the primary issue.

In a sense, the very notion of this kind of materialism is confused. It is not because the significance is allegedly subject to physical reduction that the *theory* is necessarily materialist. A genuinely materialist theory would be one like behaviourism, say, or certain contemporary theses in cognitive psychology, which propose to explain human behaviour as events happening in a physical system. But we are still far from doing this, if we characterise what men do in terms of action, purpose, aims, aspirations; even if these purposes are purely vital and hence the consummations allow of our giving necessary and sufficient conditions in physical terms. Suppose I am an abstract painter. I am now trying to create an elliptical shape on my canvas. Just because a mathematical formula can be given for the shape I want to create, it doesn't follow that my action can be understood in mathematical terms. This kind of materialism is probably deeply confused for the same reason, but one can see how any theory that finds the basic motivations in vital significances can come across to itself as tough-minded, truly scientific, and 'materialist'.

This, of course, does not apply to all Marxisms. There are other strands, which don't attempt reduction. But, on the other hand, it does apply to a great deal of non-Marxist social science. Sociobiology is an example; as are a great number of functional theories. The instinct here seems to be to ground explanation in the vital, since this is both free from evaluative dispute, and susceptible of grounding in physical criteria.

Naturally, this whole attempt to finesse the characteristically human significances is seen as an illusion from the standpoint of the other perspective, for these are central to human motivation, central even to how our vital needs are conceived, as they are conceived differently from culture to culture. This brings us to the place of language in this, which I now want to explore.

4

The human significances are closely tied up with language; only a language animal could have them. To see this, we might take two emotions, which are close to each other, but which are contrasting: anger and indignation. Anger we can attribute to (some) animals, at least in some sense, but not indignation – at least if we leave aside our anthropomorphic indulgence for our pets. The difference is that we can only ascribe indignation to a being with something like the thought: this person has done an injustice. One is only indignant at a wrongdoer; one can be angry at anyone who is provoking, even innocently, even though he is in the right and one is in the wrong (especially so).

But what are the conditions for some agent's having a thought like that? That he can make discriminations right/wrong, as against just hurting or not hurting; or advantageous/disadvantageous. But this requires that the agent have some notion of standards that hold of a given domain, here human action; and by this I mean be aware of these standards, recognise that they are standards.

Of course, many living things can be said to 'apply standards' in some loose sense; the cat turns up its nose at sub-standard fish, only goes for the best. There are some standards, in the sense of criteria of acceptability, which will help explain its behaviour. There are standards here *an sich,* but not *für sich.* The cat doesn't recognize that it is applying standards, has not focussed on the standards as standards.

But that is what an agent must be doing to be considered a moral subject. There is no such thing as morality completely *an sich.* Imagine a non-linguistic animal which always behaved according to what we identify as morality. It was unimaginably benevolent. We still wouldn't call it a moral subject if it had no sense that this action was meeting some standard, was something that it ought to do, had in this sense a higher significance, was not simply on all fours with any other inclination. This is of course the insight that Kant works up into his duty/inclination distinction. But one doesn't need to take it where Kant does, into a sharp dichotomy. Nothing rules out the spontaneously good person, one who is benevolent out of love of human beings. Only for him there must be some sense that acts of charity have an additional, a higher significance than other things he is inclined to do, such as eat ice cream, or feel the breeze on his hair.

But to be open to this significance, to recognize that these acts meet some standard, we have to have language. It is only in language, or some other symbolic activity, that we can be aware of standards qua standards. It is in language, at least in this broad sense (that of Cassirer's "symbolic forms"), that standards can be disclosed, can become objects of our awareness, as against just being explanatory notions accounting for our behaviour.

Something similar goes for the other human significances mentioned above. A being can only feel shame who is aware of the demands laid on him by his being a subject, thus who has some sense of standards; the same goes for a sense of dignity, of fulfilment, of integrity, of pride, and so on.

These significances are inherently linguistic. We already saw that they are bound up with self-awareness; now we see that they are also intrinsically connected with language. And the connection is three-way, for self-awareness itself is bound up with language – or at least, the kind of self-awareness central to being a person. Let's look closer at what it is about language which allows it to play this role of disclosing the human significances.

To see this let's examine what is involved in formulating something, putting something into words which we didn't know how to say before. What does formulation bring off? Well, first of all, that we can focus on the thing in question. When I still don't know how to describe how I feel or how something looks, for example, objects concerned lack definite contours; I don't know quite what to focus on. Finding an adequate articulation for what I want to say about these matters brings them into focus.

To focus on something is to identify its features, to grasp its contours. Language gives us, that is, formulation gives us an articulated grasp of what we're focussing on. We can lay out and trace the contour. We describe people as 'articulate' who are capable of expressing themselves, and hence formulating things, and hence acquiring an articulated grasp on things.

Language, in short, enables us to be aware of what we discourse about in a way which has no analogue for non-linguistic animals. Being able to say it is being able to make it the focus in a way which is peculiar to language. And this kind of focus allows us to have an articulated view of, and hence be articulate about the matter in question. It is this articulate focussing which makes it possible for linguistic beings to be aware of standards qua standards, and thus to be capable of the feelings and perceptions which depend on this. A non-linguistic creature can act in such a way that we can understand it as guided by a standard; its behaviour is shaped by a standard. But only a linguistic being can recognise a standard. The standard needs to be focussed in language.

There is a second dimension to language which is very relevant here.

Let's look at another side of formulation. We are strangers travelling on a train together through some southern country. It is terribly hot, the atmosphere is stifling. I turn to you and say 'Whew, it's hot'. This doesn't tell you anything you didn't know; neither that it is hot, nor that I find it so. Both these facts were plain to you before. Nor were they beyond your power to formulate; you probably already had formulated them. What the expression has done here is to create a rapport between us, the kind of thing which comes about when we do what we call striking up a conversation. Previously I knew that you were hot, and you knew that I was hot, and I knew that you must know that I knew that . . . up to about any level you care to chase it. But now it is out there as a fact between *us* that it's stifling in here. Language creates what one might call a public space, or a common vantage point from which we survey the world together.

This is therefore another crucial feature about formulation in language: it creates the peculiarly human kind of rapport, of being together, that we are in conversation together. To express something, to formulate it can be not only to get it in articulate focus, but also to place it in public space, and thus to bring us together qua participants in a common act of focussing.

Of course, given this human capacity to found public space, we can and do ring all sorts of changes on it. There is the whole variety of conversations, from the deepest and most intimate to the most stand-offish and formalised. Think of a heart-to-heart talk with a lover or old friend versus casual chatter at a cocktail party. But even in the latter case, what is set up is a certain coming together in a common act of focus. The matter talked about is no longer just for me or for you, but for *us*. This doesn't prevent us from putting severe limits on how much will be in the common realm. In the cocktail party context, by tacit but common consent what will be focussed on are only rather external matters, not what concerns us most deeply. The togetherness is superficial.

In another dimension, we can distinguish various kinds of public space, all the way from small conversations (here including both the heart-to-heart and the cocktail party chat) on one hand, and formal public space established in institutions on the other; discussions in Parliament, or on the media, or in convocation. These various kinds of institutional or pan-societal public spaces are, of course, very important parts of the dispensation of human life. You can't understand how human society works at all, I should like to maintain, unless you have some notion of public space.

The usual use of this term 'public space' is to refer to the institutional, societal manifestations. I am extending it to conversations, and everything in between, because I want to stress that the same human power of bringing us together in a common focus through speech is at work in these other contexts; and that the public space of our political discussions, what we refer to for instance when we say that such and such a fact is 'in the public domain', constitutes a special case – albeit a crucial one – of this general capacity.

Picking up on this side of language shows even more decisively how essential it is for some human significances. The whole business of shame is inseparable from public space. Shame is essentially at my appearance as unworthy in public space. It is essential that beings who feel shame not only be social animals, but have created something like public space.

It might be thought that the public space of shame has nothing to do with language; that it can be physically defined. If I am ashamed of how I look I don't want to appear in public. But 'in public' here seems to mean simply 'anywhere where I can be seen by people', which seems to be a physical rather than linguistically defined location. But this forgets that the public space is not only created by open space without obstacles to vision, but also by the common standards which we hold together. This is what makes the open space a potential locus of shame. This is all the clearer where one is not ashamed of the thing concerned before one's intimates, but only before strangers. In the intimate public space, this feature (perhaps how I look) has been neutralized, or given another meaning. And open space is often very finely discriminated in regard to shame; what you reveal on television, what in Parliament, what in a smaller group, even among strangers; all these may have a different significance. This apart from the fact that many of the things we are ashamed of are only revealed in speech. And even for things which are not (such as how I look), it is all the more mortifying if they are formulated publicly. This is the most intense shame space of all, to be pointed out as contemptible before everyone, which is why self-respecting warriors fight for a word of contempt. The slighting remark of my interlocutor, said in public, creates a space of shame for me, in which I am an object of ridicule and contempt, unless I can wipe this aside by my challenge.

5

Language makes things clear in two ways: it brings them into articulate focus, and it brings them out into public space. We have managed to disconnect these to some extent in a civilisation which has brought solitary formulation to a high art. But they in their origins are not separate and never can be entirely. Our solitary formulations depend on the language which we could only learn in conversation. And indeed, one has only to reflect how much certain ranges of our vocabulary continue to depend on our formulating things together, in one or other kind of public space (remembering that this also applies to intimate conversations in my usage).

Thus our grasp on our emotions, on what is deep and what is superficial, what is fundamental commitment, and what is passing fancy, what is profound love and what is mere dalliance, can depend crucially on our conversations with others. By which I mean that we can often doubt our own grasp of these terms, that is, our own discriminations made with them, where we can come to no understanding with others on these discriminations. This is not just a matter of using other people as checks on ourselves, tests of our understanding; it is also that we can need other people, the conversation and understanding with them, even to come clear on what it is we feel. The matter can come to clear formulation when the agency focussing is *us* (for some favoured interlocutor or group) and not simply *me*.

We call people influenceable when they are undiscriminating as to who stands in this relation to them, and above all, when they themselves do not contribute to this mutual understanding very strongly, but are mostly passengers. But the opposite of the influenceable lightweight may not be the total monad; rather it is a being whose conversations are profound, with selected interlocutors, and equally shaped by himself. The ideal of understanding oneself all alone strangely ignores the way in which understanding requires language, and language is bound to conversation.

The clarity language brings through articulation is linked with the clarity through presentation in public space. Language discloses, to use Heidegger's term, in these two related ways. The connection is close, because at the beginning it is an identity. We learn language in conversation, and hence the original acquisition of articulacy is something *we* do, rather than *I* do. Later we learn to do it to some extent on our own. But we do so in a language which is ours, and hence in principle our formulations should always be capable of being common formulations. That is why they are all in principle addressed to others, and open to criticism by others. And for certain key matters, the human significances among them, the connection between the attainment of clarity and continuing conversation is never relaxed very far.

II

1

All this leads to a very different view of the person. We can leap back to the beginning where the person was seen to be an agent-plus. The 'plus' consisted in self-awareness, valuation, choice. But these could be thought to be powers of the individual. And this is how the representative view tends to take them. These are powers the individual has of representative consciousness, imposing values, and choosing.

But I have tried to draw a very different portrait. Being a person is being self-aware, but this is inseparable from being open to different significances, the specifically human ones, which can't be reduced to the vital and the sentient. These involve our being open to strong evaluations, which have to be treated as assessments, rather than as conferrals of preference. And they are bound up with language, disclosed in language. This finally makes clear why our human feelings and emotions are constituted by our understanding of them. They are shaped by the language in which they are disclosed. This is reflected both in the fact the different cultures have both different emotive languages and a different gamut of emotions; and also in the fact that we are always struggling to find the right way of thinking/talking about ourselves.

But language as the locus of disclosure is not an activity of the individual primarily, but of the language community. Being a person cannot be understood simply as exercising a set of capacities I have as an individual, on all fours with my capacity to breathe, walk, and the like. On the contrary, I only acquire this capacity in conversation, to use this as a term of art for human linguistic interchange in general; I acquire it in a certain form within this conversation, that of my culture; and I only maintain it through continued interchange. We could put it this way: I become a person and remain one only as an interlocutor.

This doesn't mean simply that the representativist view is wrong. I want to judge it so philosophically, but it ought to be interesting to us for another reason. It follows from the view I developed here that men are self-interpreting animals, as I said above. They are persons in part because they understand themselves as persons, that is, are open to the characteristically human significances, and are open to them through language and the interpretations enshrined in their language. There are different ways of being a person, and these are linked with different understandings of what it is to be a person. This doesn't mean that all are of equal value. Some may be based on illusion and distortion. But it still is the case that they inform a certain manner of being, however wrong.

Thus it is not just sufficient to denounce a wrong view, we also have to understand it as a self-interpretation; understand the way of being a person which it helps sustain. And of course, it may turn out that this way is not all bad, and can be improved by removing the false self-understanding, that is, something importantly continuous with it will emerge.

What is interesting from this point of view in the representativist view is that it is an attempt to interiorize personhood, to read these powers as possessions of the individual. A proper theory of the person should help us to understand what is afoot in this centuries-long cultural shift which is basic to our civilisation. I think there are three points which may help in this, and which emerge from the above account. The first is the notion of public space. Language discloses, but in public space. But this is not necessarily seen as linked with human language. The public space of disclosure can be identified with some region of the cosmos, some physical or mythical region, for instance. It can be some sacred space; or it can be the space of social intercourse but seen as independent of the actual conversation of men. By space of disclosure, I mean the locus where things emerge at thier fullest, clearest, most salient; where the archetypes emerge, perhaps if the reigning view allows of archetypes. For Plato, this space was that of the ideas. But if we turn not to philosophers, but to earlier societies, there may be a host of answers to this. It may be some sacred space, some mythical region, as mentioned above. Or it may be that there are many, and not a single such space.

The first important set of changes connected with the development of the modern subject/person involves the unification of these spaces – without which the modern conception of a unified personality may not be possible – and then interiorization. Finally, the space of disclosure is considered to be *inside*, in the 'mind'. We may want to judge this in the end as fanciful a view as the ones which preceded it, but this doesn't dispense us from understanding the process of self-transformation which was partly constituted in this shift.

The second important set of changes concerns the place of articulation. A view which places the space of disclosure outside of us, in real or mythical or metaphysical space, obviously puts human articulacy in the shade, gives it no important role. The articulation is seen as already there, in the structure of things. The world itself is to be understood in terms of meanings, and meaning-connections.

A parallel movement to interiorization undermines this perception of cosmic meanings. It stresses the important role of human language in setting the classification of things in the world. I am thinking here of the nominalist tradition, and its important place in the development of modern thought. But this nominalist outlook tends to be blind to the nature of linguistic expression, its power of disclosure, and particularly its social dimension.

Thirdly, it may be useful to follow the different readings of our status as interlocutor. The fact that we are human only in conversation may be recognised in earlier societies in relation to extrahuman, or non-living interlocutors; that we can maintain ourselves only in interchange with spirits, or ancestors. Or there may be more than one level of life which corresponds to interchange with different interlocutors. This sense of dependency has been abolished as well by the movement of interiorisation, which suppressed altogether the sense that we are persons only as interlocutors; and gave us a view of the subject as capable of purely inner, monological thought; of this monological thought as preceding any conversation.

These are three dimensions in which we might follow the development of the modern notion of a person. And together they might point beyond to a post-interiorised understanding, in which we could preserve the modern understanding of freedom, responsibility, individual originality, while reinstating the insights about significance and conversation which have been lost. There is, of course, a broad movement of modern culture which attempts something like this, but this is too big a subject to go into here.

2

Perhaps I could try to connect the above rambling reflections with Mauss's programme.

The first point to be made briefly is about the genesis of the '*moi*'. Mauss seems to hold that there is always a kind of sense of self: 'it is evident . . . that there has never existed a human being who has not been aware, not only of his body but also of his individuality, both spiritual and physical'. But what Mauss wants to study is the development of the *notion* of the self. I'd like to substitute something else for this distinction. Human beings always have a sense of their individuality. At the limit, when the wild boar charges in my direction, I know that it is *this* life which is in danger. But being a person is more than being an agent. It is also to be capable of strong evaluation, to be open to the peculiarly human significances. These arise only in language, and are shaped by the different interpretations offered of them in language. But it is not only the significances themselves which can admit of different interpretations – pride, honour, dignity, purity, and so on. There also can be different interpretations of what it is to be open to them, that is, to accede to a fully human life, as against that of a lower form of agent.

In our day, we tend to think of these as capacities anchored biologically in members of our species; they only need normal conditions of nurture for the standard senses of morality, shame, honour, personal worth to mature in them. They emerge at the ontogenetically appropriate moment in everyone's inner experience, feelings, reactions. But we can speculate that some earlier societies may have had a radically different understanding, a radically externalist one. Acceding to the status of full human subject (to use our language), for example, becoming a subject of personal honour, that is, a candidate for honour or dishonour, for satisfaction or wounding of honour, is only possible within what I have called a certain space of disclosure. This space may be defined socially, that is, by who can participate, although the definition may also be cosmic, in the sense that the participants are seen as having affinities with certain regions, animals, and so forth, and almost surely it will also be defined ritually: the space has to be brought on or renewed by some acts of heightened significance which re-affirm it.

This is the theoretical direction I'd like to go in to explore the ethnographical material of the kind Mauss cites in the first part of his lecture. I'd want to see this kind of way of life as grounded on an interpretation which sees the status of agent-plus as residing not in us but in a region outside us to which we must accede. What is relevant is not the capacity to have some inner sense of the human significances – this is a typically 'internalist' way of understanding it – but rather access to some force or to some region which lies outside of us.

Naturally these interpretations are sensitive, in a way we have partly lost, to the way in which we accede to the status of human subjects through being taken up as interlocutors in an exchange that pre-exists us. Indeed, that this is one of the fundamental structures of human life is what provides the basis for such an interpretation. And this may help explain the importance of personae and names in some of the societies examined. Being given a name is being inducted into a linguistic exchange, being designated as an interlocutor. One of the root ideas behind some of these early interpretations may be that one comes to full status as agent-plus by being inducted as interlocutor into some great conversation, which is alone the locus of agents-plus. To have the name, or perhaps the mask, is to be the interlocutor. Indeed, the individuality of the historical individual may be secondary, and his identity may fade into that of the continuing interlocutor, a role taken up by succeeding generations. All this would seem less bizarre to us if we understood better the way language is linked to conversation, and both to the disclosure of human significance.

Starting from this angle, we can perhaps understand the development of *'le moi'* as an interiorisation. But not in one fell swoop. Perhaps one crucial stage along the way involves a re-interpretation of the space of disclosure, making it progressively less confined and parochial, either to some special social groups, or to some region, or to some special rituals. At the end of this line of development we might see a philosophy like that of Plato: being properly human still means being in contact with some privileged space of disclosure; but this is no longer tied to any social group, is utterly unlinked with ritual – rather we have access to it through reason and contemplation; and in a sense, all men are in some way linked to it, in that all in a sense love it although the many fail to understand, fail that is of proper and full access.

The kind of self-interpretation of which this philosophy represents a highly articulate version utterly banishes earlier views of specialised spaces of disclosure, so that they even cease to be fully comprehensible. In a sense, we might argue that early polis life involved such a notion of a specialised public space, that in which citizens were recognised as competitors and interlocutors. Plato's philosophy was very hostile to this agonistic way of life. The *Republic* abolishes this kind of space. But it was starting from the basis of this kind of interpretation that the modern movement towards interiorisation properly speaking took place. This involved in some stages a total suppression of any recognition of a space of disclosure, and its replacement in one very influential family of interpretations by a purely inner space, in the 'mind'. What makes man an agent-plus arises purely within the mind. Indeed, it is having a mind and self-consciousness which makes us a person. We are back to the roots of the view of the person which stresses consciousness and representation which I argued against earlier.

This view is tremendously influential in modern society and culture. It may be transposed in more materialist and biological form, but it still emerges in the view that our being persons resides in the fact that there develops within each of us in the normal course of growth the appropriate senses. And that is the view we tend to be trapped in today, so that the outlooks of earlier societies are close to incomprehensible to us. It is true that hints of less internalist views are still around, or have been reintroduced. We can see this in certain modern philosophies, or in another way in modern nationalism. But the dominant view is internalist.

How faithful have I been to Mauss? I think there is some kind of rough correspondence. The distinction sense/notion, I'd like to express in terms of the notion of interpretation; and like him I'd like to outline very schematically three great phases in the development of the modern interpretation of the self: the first in which personality is an interlocutor's role that exists in some special space which we have to accede to; the second in which humanity still consists in being in relation to some space, or interlocutor to divinity, but it is now de-localised – ancient Stoicism, early Christianity represent paradigm cases of this; the third involves the interiorisation of personhood: it starts with the definition *substantia rationalis individua* and ends up generating the modern notion of the individual as monad.

Like Mauss, too, I'd like to be able to argue that there is something very valuable which has emerged from this development, that something has been gained in our self-interpretations. But I also think that something has been lost in the interiorisation, particularly an understanding of the significance of being an interlocutor. Is this one of the sources of '*le culte du moi*' which Mauss condemns as an 'aberration'? In any case, it certainly shows that something needs to be done to develop this interpretation, 'to express it better'.

Conclusion

Steven Lukes

A magnificent answer – but what was the question? That is how a reflective reader might reasonably respond to Mauss's provocative and perplexing essay. If the other essays in this volume succeed in helping to answer *that* question, they will have gone a long way. They do, by implication, show that Mauss's question was not one but several questions, and that some of these questions are intimately related. They also offer some intriguing answers, some agreeing with Mauss, others disagreeing. In this concluding essay, I shall try to distinguish these questions and identify some of the answers, agreements and disagreements.

The first and most obvious fact about the object, or subject matter, of the essay, and this volume, is its inherently theoretical character. It is not possible to specify it in a theory-free manner, and theoretical agreement or consensus in this area is not readily to be expected. Accordingly, every attempt to state *what* is being discussed embodies a distinctive view *about* it, and language only compounds the problem, since every way of making such a statement uses terms which standardly suggest one such view rather than another. Hence the revealing complexity of Mauss's very title: are we dealing with a 'category' or a 'notion', and, if either, in what sense? Are the 'person' and the 'self' equivalent or distinct? If the latter, with which are we concerned and how are they related? (And are these equivalent to '*personne*' and '*moi*'?) We found this problem in choosing a title for the volume as a whole, and, again revealingly, could find no satisfactory, non-question-begging single, overall title.

I shall try to identify some alternative answers to the question of what is at issue. What are Mauss and our other contributors inquiring into, and what methods are appropriate to their inquries? What, in short, is this book about?

A transcendental illusion

It is often said that the Durkheimians were seeking to give sociological answers to Kantian questions. Yet, on Kant's view, which is not Mauss's, the self, or thinking subject (*das Ich*), is *not* a category, but 'the vehicle of all concepts' and itself transcendental but not knowable. What is illusory here is any claim that one might 'know what he is in himself'.[1] As Steven Collins writes in this volume,

> I can know with absolute certainty *that* I am; I can know myself, know what I am, to a greater or lesser degree, in terms of the empirically apparent person or self that I appear to myself to be; but I cannot know anything about *what* I am, in terms of my real self.

As Kant wrote, beyond the self as it appears in experience, a man

> must suppose there to be something else which is its ground – namely his ego as this may be constituted in itself; and thus as regards mere perception and the capacity for receiving sensations he must count himself as belonging to the *sensible* world, but as regards whatever there may be in him of pure activity (whatever comes into consciousness, not through affection of the sense, but immediately) he must count himself as belonging to the *intellectual* world, of which, however, he knows nothing further.[2]

In short, 'the self proper, as it exists in itself', the 'transcendental subject', is to us, and necessarily, 'an unknown being'.[3] It is, on the other hand, presupposed by all experience, and by Kant's ethics. Plainly, it was not, in itself, a fit subject of inquiry at all, least of all of empirical inquiry. In any case, Kant's subject matter was 'reason itself and pure thinking' and 'to obtain complete knowledge of these, there is no need to go far afield, since I come upon them in my own self'.[4] But of the nature of that self I can know nothing.

A fundamental category

Abandon Kant's metaphysics, with its distinction between the sensible and intellectual worlds, and a second answer, or rather range of answers, comes into view. We are now dealing with a 'category of the mind', and this was in part both Durkheim's and Mauss's (neo-Kantian) view. This is that the 'category of the person' is 'one of a certain number of essential notions which dominate all our intellectual life', 'like the framework of the understanding', which 'are distinguished from all other knowledge by their universality and necessity' and 'independent of every particular subject . . . constitute the common ground where all minds meet'.[5] As Mauss put it, 'the idea of a "person", the idea of "self" ' was 'one of the categories of the human mind – one of the ideas we believe to be innate' (falsely) and whose 'social origins and successive forms', in the Durkheimian manner, he traces.

Now, we should try to make precise exactly what, on this view, is being claimed. It is that there is a 'universal and necessary' framework of thinking which is like an 'anatomical structure' that takes different 'forms' in 'various times and in various places', taking on 'flesh and blood, substance and form in modern times' when it has become 'clear and precise'. In other words, a certain structure of thinking concerning the person or self is held to be fundamental, universal and necessary, but to take different forms in different contexts. It is fundamental in the sense that it is basic to the rest of human thinking; universal in that it is to be found in all human cultures, in varying forms, however distorted or impoverished; and necessary in being inescapable for beings like us living in what is recognisably a society. What, then, is this structure? How is it to be characterised, independently of its varying substantial forms? There is a range of answers to this question, from narrow to wide.

The narrowest answer, which is cited by Mauss, is simply the use of the personal reflexive pronoun. In this form, the person is, arguably, fundamental, universal and necessary, but it is not Mauss's concern. Nor is what he calls the 'sense of self', man's awareness 'not only of his body, but also of his individuality, both spiritual and physical', which Mauss explicitly sees as fundamental, universal and necessary.

A modern formulation of this narrow sense is to be found in P. F. Strawson's *Individuals,* according to which the concept of a person (understood as 'the concept of a type of entity such that *both* predicates ascribing states of consciousness *and* predicates ascribing corporeal characteristics, a physical situation &c. are equally applicable to an individual entity of that type')[6] is one of those 'categories and concepts which, in their most fundamental character, change not at all'. It is part of that 'massive central core of human thinking which has no history', not a product of 'the most refined thinking' but one of 'the commonplaces of the least refined thinking' and yet part of 'the indispensable core of the conceptual equipment of the most sophisticated human beings'.[7] Moreover, persons are among 'the basic or fundamental particulars' and 'concepts of other types of particular must be seen as secondary in relation to the concepts of these'.[8] But this answer to the question is not yet sufficiently wide.

What preoccupies Mauss, and the contributors to this volume, is, rather, 'the notion or concept that different men in different ages have formed' of the person in the narrow sense – more particularly 'according to their systems of law, religion, customs, social structures and morality'. What is this wider 'notion or concept' or structure of thinking concerning the person that is held to be fundamental, universal and necessary?

Is it, perhaps, a *structure of sentiments,* including moral sentiments – a 'general framework of attitudes' that 'we are given with the fact of human society'?[9] This is a thought elsewhere suggested by Strawson: that there is a 'natural human commitment to ordinary inter-personal attitudes' that is 'part of the general framework of human life'. These comprise non-detached 'reactive attitudes', such as gratitude, resentment, forgiveness, love and hurt feelings; the more impersonal or 'vicarious' reactive attitudes we associate with morality, such as indignation and disapproval; and 'self-reactive attitudes associated with demands on oneself for others', such as feeling obliged and feeling compunction, guilt, remorse, responsibility, and 'the more complicated phenomenon of shame'. Strawson concedes that 'no doubt my own descriptions of human attitudes have reflected local and temporary features of our own culture' but claims that 'an awareness of a variety of forms should not prevent us from acknowledging that in the absence of *any* forms of these attitudes it is doubtful that we should have anything that *we* could find intelligible as a system of human relationships, as human society'.[10]

This is certainly one way of expanding the category of the person – and certainly it bears directly on the themes of Taylor's essay in this volume. Moreover, it raises acute questions in turn, suggested by Strawson's concession: are (all or some of) these inter-personal attitudes, thus characterised, really fundamental, universal and necessary, and must they be *presupposed* before any intelligible human relationships can be *discovered?* To this question I shall return. But, in any case, Mauss, and most of our contributors, expand the category of the person in another direction, seeing it rather as a *structure of beliefs.*

For them, the 'anatomical structure' that has 'taken on' a 'succession of forms' is, I suggest, a set of very general beliefs that can perhaps be seen as involved in the attitudes indicated and as underlying the varying forms of 'law, religion, customs, social structure and mentality'. These beliefs can best be seen, perhaps, as a series of answers to some or all of such very general questions as: What distinguishes human persons from other conscious agents? How are we to understand the relation of the individual to society? How does the self relate to the roles it plays, and to its ends, or purposes? In what does the unity of an individual's life consist? In other words, certain answers, or elements of answers to such basic questions are taken to be inescapable – and thus to be fundamental, universal and necessary (to beings like us). Various accounts of what such answers might be are to be found in this volume. All, interestingly, employ what we might call a strategy of 'deep interpretation'.[11] They discern an underlying structure of belief beneath the varying cultural forms; and they interpret these forms as expressing or representing that structure, more or less adequately. Indeed, they allow (and this is partly what makes such interpretation appear 'deep') that some forms misrepresent and distort the underlying structure (for explicable reasons) and can be interpreted *as* such misrepresentations and distortions.

The Durkheimian account, which Mauss both exemplifies and modifies, has certain distinctive features. The person, on this account, was *homo duplex,* split, as Pascal said, between angel and beast, between mind and body, between 'the intellectual and moral life' and 'sensations and the sensual appetites'. For Durkheim, this traditional theme of both philosophy and religion expressed a real 'constitutional duality' within the individual: that individual had 'a double existence . . . the one purely individual and rooted in our organisms, the other social and nothing but an extension of society'. In every age, Durkheim wrote, 'man has been intensely aware of this duality', and

> a belief that is as universal and permanent as this cannot be purely illusory. There must be something in man that gives rise to this feeling that his nature is dual, a feeling that men in all known civilisations have experienced. Psychological analysis has, in fact, confirmed the existence of this duality: it finds it at the very heart of our inner life.[12]

There was moreover a true antagonism between these two aspects of the individual's existence, a permanent tension between the demands of social life and those of his individual, organic nature, a tension which only increased with the advance of civilisation (a thought Durkheim shared with Freud). In short, Durkheim interpreted the beliefs, and more particularly the religious beliefs, of all cultures (including his own) as in part ways of interpreting, in more or less coded form, this permanent duality of society and individual and the tension between them. (Consider, in this volume, for example, Sanderson's orthodox Brahman, who achieved 'depersonalisation within the scrupulous execution of his obligatory rites through the renunciation of all personalising motivation'; and Elvin's account of the philosophical crisis in China in the second half of the fourth century B.C., one aspect of which was the opposition between human nature and the demands of society.)

Mauss too focusses upon both the duality and the growth of the tension, and representations of it. Among the Pueblo, the person is seen as 'absorbed in his clan', yet already detached from it in ceremonial; among the Romans, 'persons' are both ritually linked to society and their ancestors and the bearers of rights, and, with the Stoics, come to acquire 'a sense of being conscious, independent, autonomous, free and responsible' (a consciousness which then entered the law); with Christianity and modern secular philosophy, 'the revolution in mentalities is accomplished' so that we are both social beings and bearers of 'metaphysical and moral value', indeed sacred beings. Furthermore, Mauss refined and extended Durkheim's conception of 'society' (seeing for example the North American Indians' social system as 'a vast exchange of rights, goods and services, property, dances, ceremonies, privileges and ranks', thus allowing for more complex relations between 'society' and the 'individual'. In particular, he notices the notion of 'role' – the 'role played by the individual in sacred dramas, just as he plays a role in family life' – observing that this 'formula is found in very primitive societies and subsists in societies to the present day'.

It is this rich idea, of the entwining of self and role, the fusion of man and mask, that is taken up by Hollis who is concerned with 'the way to conceptualise self and role' and 'what has remained unchanging in this'. (One might look to George Herbert Mead for further, highly developed reflections on this theme. His 'social theory of the self' seeks to explain how it can be, in all societies and cultures, that 'all selves are constituted by or in terms of the social process, and are individual reflections of it' while 'every individual self has its own peculiar individuality, its own unique pattern').[13] Hollis proposes the 'core idea' of 'personal agency' which 'cannot be expunged in certain cultures' (as La Fontaine claims with respect to the Gahuku-Gama, as described by Read). This idea invokes roles that constrain and enable, and intelligent social actors who must interpret their import. Thus Antigone exemplifies this idea in her 'anguished fusion of self and role'; and what distinguishes the modern view is the idea that we construct all of our social identity. But Hollis's central conclusion is that

> human beings have slowly learned to express what has all along underlain their universal sense of self. The Pueblo expressed it by regarding himself both as a clansman absorbed into his clan and as identical with his own ancestor, the ancient Greek by recognising choice as an aspect of institu-

> tional role, the Roman by making the cognomen a source of personal rights, the medieval Christian by ascribing duties to the soul.

Hollis suggests that certain modern conceptions of the self, specifically those stemming from empiricism – from Hobbes, Hume and Bentham – distort and conceal the true view, that is, however, universally sensed if not universally clearly understood.

Taylor likewise argues against a distorting account of what *he* takes to be the inescapably true view. He criticises the 'representativist' view of the person (to which self-awareness, valuation and choice are central) as 'based on illusion and distortion' and on a misleading 'attempt to interiorise personhood'. He proposes, instead, a view that shows persons to be self-interpreting agents 'open to the peculiarly human significances' which arise only within language and are disclosed within public space between interlocutors. He can be read as suggesting that this understanding, or 'anatomical structure' of beliefs, can be seen as taking different forms in different cultures – yielding different ways of identifying public space (cosmic, mythical, social) and different readings of people's status as interlocutors. And he proposes an alternative story to that of Mauss – an overall process of de-localisation and unification, with Plato, the Stoics and early Christianity (Dumont's essay is pertinent here, tracing the 'unification of the field and the conversion of the individual to this world') and the eventual interiorisation of personhood which 'suppressed altogether the sense that we are persons only as interlocutors' and 'ends up generating the modern notion of the individual as monad', a movement that involves a significant loss of understanding.

These three accounts of what Mauss's 'deep structure' might be are all attempts to grapple with what can be said about the most general features of society and about what beliefs about the nature of its subjects they impose and require us to presuppose in investigating and interpreting its particular forms. The claim that the 'person' is a fundamental category thus has two aspects. First, it is to say that a certain structure of thinking about persons arises out of completely general features of social existence (what Collins calls 'human predicaments') and is in this sense unavoidable to minimally rational beings in all cultures, though they may be differently expressed and understood, and with greater or less clarity or depth, and may even be explicitly denied within certain theoretical traditions or in certain segments of people's lives. It is in this sense, as Meyer Fortes has put it, that 'the notion of the person in the Maussian sense is intrinsic in the very nature of the structure of human society and human social behaviour everywhere'[14] (an observation which neatly captures the sense in which the category is both necessary and universal). Second, it can be seen as a hermeneutic injunction: to read and interpret the explicit and implicit ideas of different cultures as versions, or perversions, of some such core notion or deep structure.

A range of explicit theories

This leads me to the next two answers to the question: what is the object of our inquiries? The first is that we are dealing with articulated theories and intellectual structures, involving systematisation and abstraction, developed by full-time specialists. This is also, in part, Mauss's view, at least when he deals with Stoicism, Christianity and modern Western conceptions. On this view, we are concerned with what intellectuals, philosophers, interpreters of texts, priests and religious specialists have had to say about the person or self, cooking, as Sanderson puts it, metaphysical systems out of the raw material of what is implicit in ordinary social life. We are concerned, in short, with bodies of theory that have a certain coherence and internal development over time. Of course, it may be held, as it was by Mauss and the Durkheimians, that such theories express the collective representations of a given society. (Thus, for example, Durkheim could write of the France of his time as divided between the 'individualism of Kant and Rousseau, of the *spiritualistes,* that . . . of the Declaration of the Rights of Man' and the 'narrow utilitarianism and utilitarian egoism of Spencer and the economists'.)[15] On this view, then, we are dealing with explicit and elaborated theoretical systems and traditions.

Such is the subject-matter of a number of our essays: notably, those by Dumont, Elvin, Sanderson and Carrithers. Thus Dumont treats of 'configurations of ideas and values' (as he does in his *Homo Hierarchicus*) through the study and interpretation of canonical texts. Interested in 'universes of thought', he examines, in this case, Origen, Gelasius and Calvin, among others, in developing his thesis that the universe of 'modern individualism' originated in another that was of 'the traditional holistic type' and that a transformation in the conception of the individual from 'outworldly' to 'inworldly' was central to that development. In early Christianity, there prevailed a world view of 'the same sociological type that we found in India', in which 'the individual had to recognise in the world an antagonistic factor'; with Calvin, we have 'the unification of the field and the conversion of the individual to this world'.

Elvin, too, is largely concerned with traditions of thought, with 'schools', and with 'conceptions of the self' to be found in the poets and philosophers of Chinese antiquity, the Daoist philosophers, the Chinese theoreticians of statecraft and in the writings of neo-Confucian philosophers. He displays some of the richness and variety of Chinese ideas relating to the person or self, in particular as it in turn relates to the cosmos, to nature and to the social whole, through the medium of extensive quotation from sophisticated texts. But, as he notes, these elaborated theoretical notions are at some remove from the everyday view of the self, which the ancient Chinese share with us, 'in the non-devotional and non-philosophical parts of our lives', as 'a relatively coherent, enduring and self-contained entity that makes decisions, carries responsibilities, is possessed by feelings, and, in general, can be said to have a fate, a fortune and a history'.

Even more remote from such an everyday view (though rooted in it) is the 'sophisticated discourse of religious systems' and the 'visionary and magical cults seeking superhuman power' investigated by Sanderson through the medium of texts, from the philosophical and theological to the prescriptive and expository, in medieval Kashmir. His extended interpretation presents a range of 'sophisticated analyses of consciousness and personal identity' which are radically divergent from the Western tradition. They do not derive the forces determining moral choice from within the social agent, but present rather an extraordinary range of variations on the themes of transpersonal power and personal purity, extending from a kind of Brahmanic 'solipsistic conformism', depersonalising the individual of all autonomous motivations, to the Tantric visions of the dissolution of all individuality through the cults of impurity.

Finally, Carrithers, distinguishing between *moi* and *personne* theories, comments that these are both 'found in complex societies' and require 'full-time specialists who . . . devote themselves, generation after generation, to posing and answering increasingly subtle questions about such matters'. His suggestion is that his distinction marks distinct, if interrelated, theoretical traditions, with 'their own development, their own logic, and their own relative autonomy'. The *personne* tradition is part of the social and legal history of the conception of the individual in respect of society as a whole, focussing on the person as the locus of relations of kinship, clan membership, citizenship, and so on. The *moi* tradition is concerned, rather, with the individual's relation to the natural and spiritual cosmos and his face-to-face relations with other moral agents and includes such doctrines as the Christian notion of the soul, Freudian theory and Buddhism. Roman law was, as Mauss saw, a decisive development of *personne* theorising ('abstract thought about humans or persons in a collectivity'); Buddhism likewise 'constituted a decisive step in human thought about humans in relation to their mental and physical individuality' which invokes both a universalistic psychological theory and a moral view.

Buddhism was an archetypal *moi* theory (distorted and neglected in Mauss's account), dwelling upon 'human mental and physical individuality in respect of the morally conceived social interaction of individuals within a material and spiritual order'. It represents a kind of extreme point in the range of explicit theories of the person, as it holds that the idea of the self is 'an imaginary, false belief which has no corresponding reality, and it produces harmful thoughts of "me" and "mine", selfish desire, craving, attachment, hatred, ill-will, conceit, pride, egotism, and other defilements, impurities and problems'.[16] Buddhism is a cosmic view, a teaching of causes and effects, conceived in a naturalistic way, together with an explanation of the origins of the 'imaginary, false belief' and of its harmful effects. On the other hand, at the level of everyday, implicit, common-sense belief, there is plainly no undermining (though ideally there may be a transforming) of the everyday 'sense of self', the pursuit of self-interest and the mutual understanding and interaction between persons as normally conceived.

A range of implicit theories

Which leads me to the next answer to our question: namely, that we are dealing with the interpretation of behaviour, practices, institutions and everyday beliefs in order to unearth underlying, and often unacknowledged, assumptions. This was certainly in part Mauss's approach, especially in the earlier part of his essay. As Allen remarks, since it is 'embedded in beliefs and institutions of various kinds, the concept of the person is not the sort of entity that is immediately accessible'. As Mauss himself wrote, 'beneath the information of the best of the natives, Oceanian or American, the ethnographer must recover the deep phenomena, the ones which are almost unconscious, since they exist only in the collective tradition'.[17]

A clear statement of this position is to be found in Meyer Fortes's study of the concept of the person among the Tallensi:

> I shall try to give an account of the Tallensi notion of the person (in the Maussian sense) and of some of its correlates and implications, as the actors see it. I shall try to show how the ideas, the beliefs, the linguistic usages, the dogmas and so forth – in short what the ethnographer repre-

> sents as a conceptual scheme – are accessible to discovery primarily by reason of their realisation in the customary or institutionalised activities of people.

Among the Tallensi there were no 'elites of priests, doctors, men of wisdom and learning, who have a specialised (in some respects, esoteric) knowledge' of the subject in question. It was only

> by observing and conversing with the common man, so to speak, that one could see how the ideas and beliefs relating to such abstract notions as that of the person were channelled through his daily activities. They were more commonly exhibited in action and utterance than being formulated in explicit terms.[18]

We are, in short, dealing here with what have been called 'indigenous psychologies' – common-sense beliefs concerning oppositions such as self/non-self, mind/body, inner/outer, conscious/unconscious, will/destiny or fate, hot/cold, reason/emotion, up/down, public/private, unitary self/fragmented self, subjective/objective. Rather than structures of abstract thought, we are dealing with functioning realities operating within society 'which play a key part in helping to fix the bounds of that very human nature, of which they are supposed to be a model'.[19]

This answer to the question of what we are investigating is to be found in the essays here by Lienhardt, La Fontaine and, to some extent, Momigliano. Thus Lienhardt, in presenting Dinka ideas of the person, cites folktales, humour and drama, songs, proverbs, daily conversation, the implications of Dinka idioms, etc. In this way he deploys his argument against 'too much one-sided stress on the collectivist orientation of African ideas of the person' and for the importance to Dinka, 'no matter how much store may be set by role and status, of individual, private, intellectual and emotional activities: the private self', of an 'inner, mysterious, *individual* activity', and the integration of 'moral and physical attributes of persons together within the physical matrix of the human body'. Indifferent to metaphysical speculation, Dinka achieved a distinctive integration of thought and feeling in metaphor and bodily imagery.

La Fontaine, whose essay draws on that of Fortes cited above and uses his approach, likewise refers to ethnographic material, but she seeks to draw general conclusions from comparisons between four non-Western societies and their contrast with the individualist West. Relating their indigenous psychologies to their social and political contexts, she seeks to show how their variant social forms are to be seen as shaped by the principles which underlie the major social institutions and determine the nature of authority or succession to office. So for the Tallensi, personhood is the fulfilment of social roles, the culmination of a moral career, whereas the Taita allow for greater influence of an actor on his role. In the modern West, it is defined by the legal principles of the nation-state. Among the strangely desocialised Gahuku-Gama, because, it seems, the distinction between the individual and his social role is not drawn, La Fontaine concludes there is no general category of personhood – a conclusion Hollis gravely doubts.

Finally, Momigliano also engages in a kind of unearthing of implicit assumptions – though he does so by interpreting the writings of intellectuals and 'specialists' – historians, biographers and autobiographers. Disputing the stereotypical view that the Greeks lacked a concept of the personality and of the inner life, Momigliano argues that classical historiography built up 'images of individuals from given evidence'; later Greek and Roman biography 'wrestled with the problem of how to use external evidence to build up a character – or, if you prefer, a person'; and 'Greek and Roman historians, and especially biographers, talked about individuals in a manner which is not distant from our own', while early autobiographies may have helped towards the recognition of a person with a definite character, purpose and achievement'. Plutarch's heroes and Diogenes' philosophers 'look like persons to us', which leads us to the fifth view of our subject matter. How *do* 'we' see 'persons'?

A modern Western achievement

This view sees the object of our discussion as both culturally specific and a historical product – 'our' concept of the person (which, however, is widely and falsely thought to be 'innate', 'natural' and unchanging). This view was certainly, in part, Mauss's view. His evolutionary story culminates in the 'anatomical structure' taking on flesh and blood and becoming 'clear and precise'; it becomes identified with 'self-knowledge and the psychological consciousness' and 'a fundamental form of thought and action'. It is 'formulated only for us, among us' and invokes the 'sacred character of the human "person".' In arguing thus, Mauss was a true Durkheimian, seeing the modern liberal West (and above all republican France) as based upon the modern secular religion of individualism – a brave view to advance in 1938.

Among our contributors, Allen defends Mauss's grand 'evolutionary perspective', while Carrithers is sceptical of a 'grand procession through history', suggesting, of both *moi* and *personne* theories, that we must think more of 'distinct episodes moving toward no very clear conclusion'.

In substance, Dumont is probably closest to Mauss's evolutionary story and his conception of 'the modern individual',[20] and Sanderson farthest from it, expressing considerable scepticism that this lies 'at the summit of evolution'. And, as we have seen, both Taylor and Hollis see certain prevalent conceptions of the person, abroad in philosophy and the human sciences, as severely deficient and distortive.[21]

What is clear is that one may reasonably question not only Mauss's evolutionism and his claim that there *is* an overall story: on these points, Carrithers's arguments and suggestions are very fertile and should generate yet further distinctions and further stories. We must also place Mauss's vision of modernity and its conception of the person or self alongside other, less sanguine views. I shall, in conclusion, refer to just two. Both raise large questions about the culmination of Mauss's story in a modern world in which the person becomes a sacred being, the possessor of metaphysical and moral value and of moral consciousness – the bearer of rights and responsibilities, the source of autonomous motivation and rational decision, valuing privacy and capable of self-development. According to the first, this constellation of ideas is a construction that is part of a larger story that includes the massive growth of surveillance, discipline and control. According to the second, it represents an ideal that is, under modern conditions, increasingly impossible to attain, as both the social identity and the inner unity of the person are dissolved.

For Michel Foucault, the modern conception of the individual is an artificially constructed unity, naturally associated with the language of morality and law, with notions of sovereignty, rights, rationality, responsibility, sanity and sexuality. In his genealogies of epistemes, medicalisation, madness, punishment and sexuality, Foucault deconstructs the modern subject by investigating the institutions and norms that have formed it, which include apparatuses of discipline and control, of confinement, treatment, rehabilitation and therapy. The autonomous, rational and normal self is sustained by how society deals with unreason, madness, delinquency and perversity – through an 'on-going subjugation, at the level of those continuous and uninterrupted processes which subject our bodies, govern our gestures, dictate our behaviours, etc.'. In this way, subjection is 'a constitution of subjects'. The 'individual is not to be thought of as a sort of elementary nucleus, a primitive atom', but rather it is

> one of the prime effects of power that certain bodies, certain gestures, certain discourses, certain desires, come to be identified and constituted as individuals. . . . The individual which power has constituted is at the same time its vehicle.

In Foucault's vision,

> Modern society . . . from the nineteenth century up to our own day, has been characterised, on the one hand, by a legislation, a discourse, an organisation based on public right, whose principle of articulation is the social body and the delegative status of each citizen; and, on the other hand, by a closely linked grid of disciplinary coercions whose purpose is in fact to assure the cohesion of this same social body.[22]

Consider, finally, the vision of Robert Musil, which carries Max Weber's theme of rationalisation to a refined extreme. It portrays a social world whose implicit conceptions and explicit theories become ever more impersonal and in which the individual no longer has a clearly defined and intelligible historically given social identity and is no longer a unifying centre of experience and a locus of personal responsibility. As Musil's hero, Ulrich, reflects:

> In earlier times one could be an individual with a better conscience than one can today. People used to be like the stalks of corn in the field. They were probably more violently flung to and fro by God, hail, fire, pestilence and war than they are today, but it was collectively, in terms of towns, of countrysides, the field as a whole; and whatever was left to the individual stalk in the way of personal movement was something that could be answered for and was clearly defined. Today, on the other hand, responsibility's point of gravity lies not in the individual but in the relations between things. Has one not noticed that experiences have made themselves independent of man? They have gone on to the stage, into books, into the reports of scientific institutions and expeditions, into communities based on religious or other conviction, which develop certain kinds of experience at the cost of all the others as in a social experiment; and insofar as experiences are not merely to be found in work, they are simply in the air. Who today can still say that his anger is really his own anger, with so many people butting in and knowing so much more about it than he does? There has arisen a world of qualities without a man to them, of experiences without anyone to experience them, and it almost looks as though under ideal conditions man would no longer experience anything at all privately and the comforting weight of personal responsibility would dissolve into a system of formulae for potential meanings. It is probably that the dissolution of the anthropocentric attitude (an attitude that, after so long seeing man as the centre of the universe, has been dissolving for some centuries now) has finally begun to affect the personality itself; for the belief that the most important thing about experience is the experiencing of it, and about deeds the doing of them, is beginning to strike most people as naive. Doubtless there are still people who experience things quite personally, saying 'we were at So-and-So's yesterday' or 'we'll do this or that today' and enjoying it without its needing to have any further content or significance. They like everything that their fingers touch, and are persons as purely private as is

> possible. The world becomes a private world as soon as it comes into contact with them, and shines like a rainbow. Perhaps they are very happy; but this kind of people usually appears absurd to the others, although it is as yet by no means established why.[23]

These, then, are the questions that Mauss's essay addresses: identifying a fundamental category, exhibiting a range of explicit and implicit theories, and telling a story that culminates in the modern conception of the person. But this in turn raises a further question: namely, are these questions independent of one another, or are they, as Mauss appears to have thought, all parts of a single overall question? Can they be explored in isolation from one another? More particularly, can explicit theories of the person be interpreted in isolation from implicit conceptions? Must the intepretation of either presuppose there to be a fundamental category of the person? And can it avoid the making of some connection with 'our' conception or conceptions?

Obviously, the distinction between implicit and explicit theories is, in part, a matter of degree. Ways of thinking may be more or less articulated and reflected upon, theories may be more or less elaborated and systematic. But there is also a difference in kind here. Robin Horton has drawn a distinction between 'two distinct yet intimately complementary levels of thought and discourse': namely, 'primary theory' and 'secondary theory'. 'Primary theory', which 'does not differ very much from community to community or from culture to culture', gives 'the world a foreground filled with middle-sized . . . enduring, solid objects,' related spatially and causally, and distinguishing between human beings and other objects, and between self and others. 'Secondary theory', by contrast, shows 'startling differences in kind as between community and community, culture and culture'. It makes reference to 'hidden' entities and processes (such as gods and spirits in traditional African thought and currents, particles and waves in modern Western thought) by which it purports to explain the given world of primary theory, whose surface manifestations and limited causal vision it purports to transcend.[24]

The distinction between primary and secondary theory does not, of course, correspond to that between implicit and explicit theory: the spiritualistic world view of traditional African communities is, for Horton, a paradigm example of secondary theory. Nevertheless, it seems plausible to suggest that, in conceptualising the person, where secondary theory becomes explicit, the often esoteric preserve of religious or philosophical specialists, the scope for cultural variation greatly expands, as the constraints set by practical livng contract. It is noticeable, in this volume, that a number of contributors stress the parallels between everyday conceptions of the person and our own. The more exotic plants flourish in the hot-house of high theory.

Just as secondary theory is rooted in and dependent upon primary theory, in various ways, so, we may suppose, is explicit theorising about the person rooted in and dependent upon implicit conceptions. It builds upon these, sometimes reacts against them and seeks in turn to transform them. Sanderson's examination of the Tantric cults in the context of Brahmanic conceptions (which, although given explicit theoretical formulation, are also implicit in the whole of Indian orthodox social behaviour) is a vivid example of these connections. Certainly, studying the interrelations between implicit and explicit theories of the person in a given culture is likely to be highly illuminating about both; and it is hard to see how the study of either could be satisfactorily undertaken without engaging in it.

Does such a study require the presupposition of a fundamental category of the person? The present volume does not, it seems to me, enable us to answer this question with confidence. It seems undeniable that the category in the narrow sense defined above *is* a presupposition of all inquiry, a part of primary theory which, as Horton puts it, 'provides the cross-cultural voyager with his cross-cultural bridgehead'.[25] But what about the expanded version? Is any given set of Strawson's interpersonal attitudes or any specified set of general beliefs *about* persons a necessary presupposition of social inquiry? It is obvious enough that a number of Strawson's attitudes – love, guilt, responsibility, shame – are given, to say the least, remarkably different emphases in different cultures. According to Adkins, for example, the 'concept of moral responsibility' among the Greeks from Homer to Aristotle 'undeniably held a minor position'[26]; nor is it clear that all cultures exhibit what we would recognise as 'shame' or 'love' (though we may in turn doubt whether these are unitary concepts, rather than homonyms for a variety of loosely related attitudes). It would be rash, to say the least, to assume that just these attitudes must exist in all cultures, or that unless we presuppose that they do, we can discover nothing further about them. And, as for the suggested fundamental structure of belief, it seems hard to suppose that either the dualism suggested by Durkheim or the notion of self and role stressed by Hollis are inescapable in the sense indicated. Perhaps the most we can say is that, in applying the so-called 'Principle of Humanity' (which counsels the minimising of unintelligibility) in the interpretation and translation of beliefs, we must, as Grandy suggests, have 'some model of the agent that we use to assist us in making a prediction': success will 'depend heavily on the similarity of his belief-and-desire network to our own. . . . If a translation tells us that another person's desires and beliefs are connected in a way that is too bizarre for us to make sense of, then the translation is useless for our purposes'.[27] We need, in short, *some* shared beliefs about and attitudes towards one another for interpretation and translation to get off the ground. But whether any determinate set can be specified is not clear. Perhaps the bridgehead is best thought of as floating.

Finally, no such study could avoid reference to 'the idea of "person", the idea of "self",' in its present 'still imprecise, delicate and fragile form', as 'each one of us finds it' – 'natural, clearly determined in the depths of his consciousness, completely furnished with the fundaments of the morality which flows from it' as Mauss stated. For, in the first place, and most trivially, the bridgehead links 'us' to 'them'. And second, therefore, we are in need of an 'interpretative term' which serves, in translation and the reporting of indirect speech, 'both to render through stipulation an indigenous category and to suggest how that category might be understood'. Intepretation always involves a compromise – 'between adequacy to the things represented and effectiveness in the formation and formulation of ideas'.[28] Obviously enough, such effectiveness will involve the making of connections – even if only by contrast – with our own conceptions. So, quite unsurprisingly, all our contributors do precisely this.

But third, and more deeply, there is a further reason why reference to our modern notions of the 'person' or 'self' is inescapably part of any inquiry into other such notions. For, as both Taylor and Hollis make clear, there is an individualist mode of thought, distinctive of modern Western cultures, which, though we may criticise it in part or in whole, we cannot escape. It indelibly marks every interpretation we give of other modes of thought and every attempt we make to revise our own.

Central to this mode of thought is a distinctive picture of the individual in relation to his roles and to his aims or purposes. To the former he exhibits role distance: confronting all possible roles, he may in principle adopt, perform or abandon any at will (though not all, and probably not even many, at once). Over the latter he exercises choice: as sovereign chooser, he *decides* between actions, conceptions of the good, plans of life, indeed what sort of a person to be. The will, choice, decision, evaluation and calculation are central to this picture; and the individual to whom these features are essential thinks and acts as an autonomous, self-directing, independent agent who relates to others as no less autonomous agents. Other *men,* that is: for the individual, in this picture, is exclusively (or virtually so) male. For, as Mary Midgley has well said, the 'whole idea of a free, independent, enquiring, choosing individual, an idea central to European thought, has always been essentially the idea of a male . . . taking for granted the love and service of non-autonomous females (and indeed often of the less enlightened males as well)'.[29] It is a picture that has many well-known variants, from Hobbes through Bentham and the Utilitarians to modern existentialism. Some of these take extreme, caricatural forms: for Nietzsche the individual does not merely choose between values but creates them, while for many liberals and neoclassical economists he becomes no more than a calculating machine interacting with others in the marketplace on the basis of revealed preferences.

This picture contrasts with that in which the individual is largely identified with and by his roles (though these may conflict) and who relates to his ends or purposes less by choice than through knowledge and discovery. This second picture is one in which self-discovery, mutual understanding, authority, tradition and the virtues are central. Conceptions of the good are not seen as subject to individual choice, let alone invention, but rather as internal to practices within which individuals are involved by reason of their roles and social positions. Reason, innovation, criticism, argument can all be a part of this picture, but are differently understood within it, as operating within an accepted social framework. And, most important, that framework is seen as constitutive of the identity of the persons within it: *who* I am is answered both for me and for others by the history I inherit, the social positions I occupy, and the 'moral career' on which I am embarked. A number of our contributors offer striking variants of this familiar picture (while insisting that it too should not be caricatured). Fortes describes with particular force its Tallensi variant: through their totemistic observances, ordinary people are 'constantly reminded and made aware of who and what they are as persons, of the sources of these attributes in their descent group membership and other kinship connections, of their dependence on their ancestors, of the rights and duties, both secular and ritual, that bind them'. Adherence to such obligations

> is the basis of each individual's knowledge of who he is and where he belongs as a person identified by kinship, descent and status. It is the principal medium for appropriating to himself – for internalising we might say – the capacity for exercising the rights and duties, the roles and all the proper patterns of behaviour that pertain to his status as a person. It is the medium, also, by which he at the same time exhibits himself as a person to

> others. When young children and madmen are said to be devoid of sense, this refers primarily to their not being expected to have the understanding to conform to these prescriptions. It is a concession to their marginal personhood.[30]

My point is simply this: that once the first picture has been imprinted upon the cultural tradition, we are thenceforth irrevocably transformed and can no longer live by the second. We may choose to attack 'the notion of a self barren of essential aims and attachments' underlying modern liberalism[31] or reject liberal individualism and seek for a revival of Aristotelianism, in which politics ceases to be a civil war carried on by other means, and promises a 'shared vision of and understanding of goods' in which the virtues have a central place.[32] We may, with Taylor and Hollis, reject individualistic ways of conceiving the person that are typical of the first picture. But these are the ways by which we are culturally formed and they inevitably colour our every attempt to interpret the worlds of others or to seek to change our own.

Notes

1. I. Kant, *Critique of Pure Reason* (translated by N. Kemp Smith). London, Macmillan, 1963, A 341–2/B 399–400.
2. *Foundations of the Metaphysics of Morals* (translated by H. Paton as *The Moral Law*). Hutchinson, London, 1948, p. 112.
3. Kant, *Critique of Pure Reason,* A 492/B 520.
4. *Ibid.*, Preface to First Edition, A xiv.
5. E. Durkheim, *The Elementary Forms of the Religious Life.* London, Allen & Unwin, 1915, pp. 9, 13 (amended translation, S.L.).
6. P. F. Strawson, *Individuals. An Essay in Descriptive Metaphysics.* London, Methuen, 1959, p. 104.
7. *Ibid.*, p. 10.
8. *Ibid.*, p. 11.
9. P. F. Strawson, *Freedom and Resentment and Other Essays.* London, Methuen, 1974, p. 23.
10. *Ibid.*, pp. 13, 15, 24.
11. See A. C. Danto, 'Deep Interpretation', *Journal of Philosophy,* vol. 78, no. 10, 1981, pp. 691–706.
12. E. Durkheim, 'The Dualism of Human Nature and its Social Conditions', in K.H. Wolff (ed.), *Emile Durkheim 1858–1917. A Collection of Essays with Translations and a Bibliography.* Columbus, Ohio State University Press, 1960, pp. 326, 337, 326.
13. *The Social Psychology of George Herbert Mead* (edited with an introduction by Anselm Strauss). Chicago University Press (Phoenix edition), 1965, pp. 247–8.
14. M. Fortes, 'On the Concept of the Person among the Tallensi' in *La Notion de personne en Afrique noire.* Editions de C.N.R.S., Paris, 1973, p. 288.
15. E. Durkheim, 'Individualism and the Intellectuals', *Political Studies* 17, 1969, pp. 20–1.
16. W. Rāhula, cited in S. Collins, *Selfless Persons. Imagery and Thought in Theravāda Buddhism.* Cambridge University Press, 1982, p. 4.

17. M. Mauss, 'Méthode d'ethnographe, méthode sociologique', in M. Mauss, *Oeuvres*, presented by V. Karady, Paris, 1969, vol. III, p. 369.
18. Fortes, *op. cit.*, p. 284.
19. See P. Heelas and A. Lock (eds.), *Indigenous Psychologies. The Anthropology of the Self.* London, Academic Press, 1981, p. 13, citing D. Bohm.
20. See L. Dumont, 'The Modern Conception of the Individual', in *Contributions to Indian Sociology*, no. VIII, October 1965.
21. Compare C. Taylor, 'Atomism', in A. Kontos (ed.), *Powers, Possessions and Freedom.* University of Toronto Press, 1979; and M. Hollis, *Models of Man.* Cambridge University Press, 1977.
22. M. Foucault, *Power/Knowledge. Selected Interviews and Other Writings.* Edited by C. Gordon. Brighton, Harvester, 1980, pp. 97, 98, 106.
23. R. Musil, *The Man without Qualities.* Translated by E. Wilkins and E. Kaiser. London, Secker and Warburg, 1979, vol. 1, pp. 174–5.
24. R. Horton, 'Tradition and Modernity Revisited' in M. Hollis and S. Lukes (ed.), *Rationality and Relativism.* Oxford, Blackwell, 1982, esp. pp. 227–38.
25. *Ibid.*, p. 228.
26. A. W. H. Adkins, *Merit and Responsibility. A Study in Greek Values.* Oxford, Clarendon, 1960, p. 1.
27. R. Grandy, 'Reference, Meaning and Belief', *Journal of Philosophy,* vol. 70, 1973, p. 443.
28. D. Sperber, *Le Savoir des anthropologues.* Paris, Hermann (Collection Savoir), 1982, pp. 33, 20,
29. M. Midgley, 'Sex and Personal Identity. The Western Individualistic Tradition', *Encounter,* vol. 63, no. 1, June, 1984, p. 51.
30. Fortes, *op. cit.*, pp. 313–4.
31. See M. J. Sandel, *Liberalism and the Limits of Justice.* Cambridge University Press, 1982.
32. See A. Macintyre, *After Virtue.* London, Duckworth, 1981, esp. ch. 15.

Bibliography

The following is a selection of recent writings on the subject. Details of other works referred to in the papers of this volume are to be found in the notes.

Ayer, A.J. 1963. *The Concept of a Person and other Essays*. London: Macmillan.

Beattie, J. 1980. 'Representations of the Self in Traditional Africa'. Review of Dieterlen (ed.), 1973. *Africa*, vol. 50(3).

Berenson, F.M. 1981. *Understanding Persons*. Brighton: Harvester Press.

Collins, S. 1982. *Selfless Persons: Imagery and Thought in Theravāda Buddhism*. Cambridge University Press.

Dieterlen, M. (ed.). 1973. *La Notion de Personne en Afrique Noire*. Paris: Editions du Centre National de la Recherche Scientifique.

Geertz, C. 1973. 'Person, Time and Conduct in Bali', in *The Interpretation of Cultures*. New York: Basic Books.

1983. 'From the Native's Point of View: on the nature of anthropological understanding'. In *Local Knowledge: Further Essays in Interpretative Sociology*. New York: Basic Books.

Harré, R. 1983. *Personal Being*. Oxford: Blackwell.

Hollis, M. 1977. *Models of Man*. Cambridge University Press.

Kasulis, T.P. 1981. *Zen Action, Zen Person*. Honolulu: University of Hawaii Press.

Leenhardt, M. 1979. *Do Kamo: Person and Myth in the Melanesian World*. Translated by B.M. Gulati. University of Chicago Press.

Lienhardt, R.G. 1961. *Divinity and Experience*. London: Oxford University Press.

Meyerson, I. (ed.) 1973. *Problèmes de la Personne*. Colloques du Centre de Recherches de Psychologie Comparative, XIII. Paris: Mouton.

Mischel, T. (ed.) 1974. *Understanding Other Persons*. Oxford: Blackwell.

1977. *The Self*. Oxford: Blackwell.

Monist. 1979. 'The Concept of a Person in Ethical Theory,' vol. 62, no. 3. (July).

Östör A., Fruzzetti L., and Barnett, S. 1982. *Concepts of Person: Kinship, Caste and Marriage in India*. Cambridge, Mass.: Harvard University Press.

Parfit, D. 1984. *Reasons and Persons*. London: Oxford University Press.
Perry, J. (ed.) 1975. *Personal Identity*. University of California Press.
Popper, K.R. and Eccles, J.C. *The Self and Its Brain*. Berlin: Springer International.
Rorty, A.O. (ed.) 1975. *The Identities of Persons*. University of California Press.
Rosaldo, M.Z. 1980. *Knowledge and Passion: Ilongot Notions of Self and Social Life*. Cambridge University Press.
Ruddock, R. 1972. *Six Approaches to the Person*. London: Routledge & Kegan Paul.
Shoemaker, S. 1963. *Self-knowledge and Self-identity*. Ithaca: Cornell University Press.
Strawson, P.F. 1959. *Individuals*. London: Methuen.
Wiggins, D. 1980. *Sameness and Substance*. Oxford: Blackwell.
Williams, B.A.O. 1973. *Problems of the Self*. Cambridge University Press.

Index